Advisor-Consultants

Vincent J. Altamuro
Assistant Principal,
Thomas Jefferson School
Queens, New York

Sandra Pryor Clarkson
Associate Professor
of Mathematical Sciences
Hunter College of CUNY
New York, New York

Jeanette Gann
Mathematics and Science
Coordinator, High Point
Public Schools
High Point, North Carolina

Zelda Gold
Mathematics Advisor,
Los Angeles Unified
School District
Los Angeles, California

Dorothy Keane
Professor of Education
California State University,
Los Angeles
Los Angeles, California

Joel Levin
Teacher, Chicago Public Schools
Chicago, Illinois

Gail Lowe
Principal, Conejo Valley
Unified School District
Thousand Oaks, California

Kozo Nishifue
Administrator of Mathematics,
Oakland Unified School District
Oakland, California

James A. Peters, Jr.
Elementary Mathematics
Resource Teacher,
Samuel Powel School
Philadelphia, Pennsylvania

Andria P. Troutman
Professor, University
of South Florida
Tampa, Florida

LAIDLAW
Mathematics

LAIDLAW BROTHERS • PUBLISHERS

RIVER FOREST, ILLINOIS
Sacramento, California • Chamblee, Georgia • Dallas, Texas

Acknowledgments

Developed by Kirchoff/Wohlberg, Inc.,
in cooperation with Laidlaw Brothers, Publishers

Editorial Director   Mary Jane Martin

Laidlaw Editorial Staff

Editorial Manager   David B. Spangler

Editor/Consultant   Barbara J. Huffman

Editors   Robert C. Mudd, Judith A. Witt

Educator/Reviewers
   Deborah Abbott, Carole Bauer, Lynn Cohn, Cynthia Frederick,
   Patricia A. Schwartz, Helene Silverman, Larry A. Tagle,
   Josephine Wraith

TABLE OF CONTENTS

CHAPTER 4 MULTIPLICATION BY TENS

CHAPTER 5 GEOMETRY

CHAPTER 6 PLACE VALUE

CHAPTER 7 ADDITION AND SUBTRACTION OF WHOLE NUMBERS

CHAPTER 8 ADDITION AND SUBTRACTION OF LARGER NUMBERS

CHAPTER 9 FRACTIONS AND PROBABILITY

CHAPTER 10   ADDITION AND SUBTRACTION OF DECIMALS

CHAPTER 11   METRIC MEASUREMENT

CHAPTER 12   METRIC MEASUREMENT

CHAPTER 13   MULTIPLICATION BY A 1-DIGIT NUMBER

CHAPTER 14   DIVISION BY A 1-DIGIT NUMBER

CHAPTER 15   GEOMETRY

CHAPTER 16   GEOMETRY

CHAPTER 17   DECIMALS

CHAPTER 18   DECIMALS AND MONEY

CHAPTER 19   ADDITION AND SUBTRACTION OF DECIMALS

CHAPTER 20   MULTIPLICATION BY A 1-DIGIT NUMBER

CHAPTER 21   DIVISION BY A 1-DIGIT NUMBER

CHAPTER 22 GRAPHS

CHAPTER 23 FRACTIONS

CHAPTER 24 FRACTIONS AND MIXED NUMBERS

CHAPTER 25   MULTIPLICATION BY A 2-DIGIT NUMBER

CHAPTER 26   DIVISION BY A 2-DIGIT NUMBER

CHAPTER 27   DIVISION BY A 2-DIGIT NUMBER

CHAPTER 28   CUSTOMARY MEASUREMENT

CHAPTER 29   CUSTOMARY MEASUREMENT

CHAPTER 30   GEOMETRY AND LOGIC

CHAPTER 31 ALGEBRA

CHAPTER 32 USING LARGER NUMBERS

Understand how math relates to interesting jobs.

Using Mathematics
Introduction to the Book

These workers are doing jobs they like and have been trained for. Their work is different, but there is one thing they all share. They all have math skills. They learned some of these math skills when they were your age. They did not know then how important these skills would be to them. Now they use these math skills every day on their jobs.

A recipe can be written to serve six people, but a chef could be serving sixty! Increase the recipe, and the time and temperature must be increased, too. Ingredients must be measured and serving sizes planned. Chefs must even know how long it will take people to eat a meal.

Cattle ranchers have to determine the amount of feed available for their herds. They must check market prices when they buy and sell livestock. Prices change daily so it is important for ranchers to know the best times to buy and sell.

Farmers take their produce to markets nearby. They must figure out transportation time and costs. They must also plan to take just enough produce to sell.

Calories are units of energy that the body uses as fuel. Nutritionists find out the amount and kind of food people need to stay healthy. Different body types use different amounts of energy. Nutritionists help plan an eating and exercising plan that will keep people well.

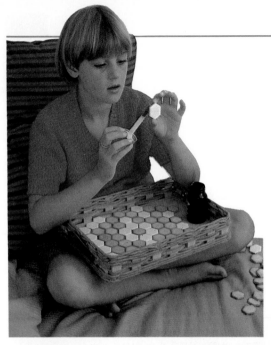

Identify the seven math strands used in this book.

Mathematics is a science that you use all the time. Shopping in stores, playing a card game, checking a calendar, or setting a clock, all involve math skills.

Mathematics is adding, subtracting, multiplying, dividing, and much, much more. In a way math is somewhat like cloth. The whole cloth is made of many strands of thread that are woven together. Mathematics is made of thinking strands that are also woven together.

In this book you will be using seven of these math strands. Read the math strand descriptions and look at the pictures of the children. Which strands are the children using? Many strands can combine to solve a problem.

1. You use NUMBER SKILLS when you add, subtract, multiply or divide.

2. You use MEASUREMENT when you tell time, deal with money, or find length and weight.

3. You use GEOMETRY when you work with shapes, lines, and angles.

4. You use PATTERNS AND FUNCTIONS when you find a pattern in shapes or numbers.

5. You use STATISTICS AND PROBABILITY when you make graphs and tables or when you know your chance for success.

6. You use LOGIC when you plan your next move or make a reasonable guess.

7. You use ALGEBRA when you write a number sentence.

NUMBER SKILLS

Getting Started

You are using number skills each time you add, subtract, multiply, or divide. Number skills are used with whole numbers, fractions, decimals, and other kinds of numbers you will be studying.

The following exercises will help you review some of the number skills you have already used.

Write as a number and then in words.

1.

2.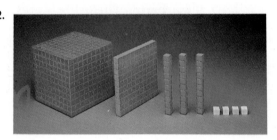

Add, subtract, multiply, or divide.

3. 34
   +25

4. $7.45
   +3.16

5. $18.24
   + 4.39

6. 76
   −42

7. $8.97
   − 5.94

8. 8.4
   −4.8

9. 6 × 9

10. 8 × 7

11. 8 × 40

12. 6)‾42

13. 9)‾81

14. 8)‾76

15. 8.2 + 5.3

16. 9.6 − 4.7

17. $\frac{2}{5} + \frac{4}{5}$

18. $\frac{9}{8} - \frac{3}{8}$

Count how much money. Write the amount.

19. 5 dimes
    6 nickels
    9 pennies

20. 1 quarter
    8 dimes
    4 nickels

21. 3 quarters
    6 dimes
    7 pennies

22. 1 half dollar
    2 quarters
    4 dimes

Rewrite from the least to the greatest.

23. 8,062   945   7,990   8,103   957

24. 4.3   6.2   8.9   5.0   4.7

25. Andrew bought three cassette tapes for a total of $9.00. How much did each tape cost?

26. Kim spent $6.00 on a box kite. She gave the salesperson $10.00. What was Kim's change?

FOCUS | Review NUMBER skills.

MEASUREMENT

Getting Started

Whenever you use money, tell time, or find the length, weight, or area of something, you are using measurement.

These exercises will help you review some of the measurement skills you have already studied. First look at pages 456 and 457 of the Data Bank to review measurement facts. Then complete all the exercises.

27. Find the perimeter.

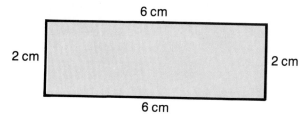

6 cm

2 cm · 2 cm

6 cm

28. Find the area.

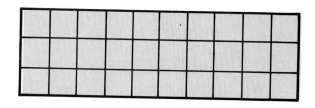

29. Find the volume.

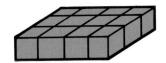

30. Does each hold more than a liter? Write *yes* or *no.*
  a. barrel   b. soup bowl
  c. paper cup   d. fish tank
  e. spoon   f. bathtub

Write the correct time.

31.

32.

33.

34.

Write the kinds of money you would give a salesperson for each of the following amounts. Use the smallest number of coins and bills you can.

35. $0.78   **36.** $1.04   **37.** $1.62   **38.** $2.57

39. $0.94   **40.** $5.18   **41.** $6.27   **42.** $8.46

Review MEASUREMENT.

GEOMETRY
Getting Started

You are using geometry whenever you work with shapes, lines, and angles.

Doing these exercises will help you remember some of the geometry skills you have already studied. Look at page 454 in the Data Bank to go over geometry facts.

Name each figure.

1.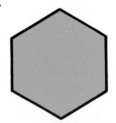

2.

3.

4.

5. Which one of the above figures has right angles?

6. Which triangle below is congruent to triangle A?

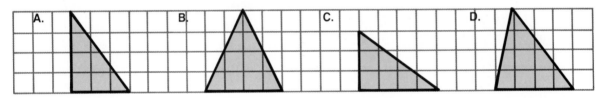

7. In which name does every letter have a line of symmetry?

   a. PEGGY   b. ADAM   c. GARY   d. BRIAN

Count the number of sides and angles. Then write the name of each polygon. Choose from *triangle*, *square*, *pentagon*, or *hexagon*.

8.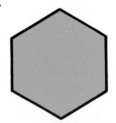

9.

10.

11.

FOCUS   Review GEOMETRY.

8

PATTERNS AND FUNCTIONS
Getting Started

If you use a rule to form or follow a pattern, you are using patterns and functions. Complete the exercises.

Guess the rule. Then write the next two numbers in the pattern.

12. 2, 4, 6, 8, 10, 12, ____, ____

13. 100, 200, 300, 400, 500, ____, ____

14. 4, 8, 12, 16, 20, ____, ____

15. 9, 18, 27, 36, 45, ____, ____

16. 3, 6, 12, 24, 48, ____, ____

17. 100, 95, 90, 85, 80, ____, ____

18. 2.8, 2.9, 3.0, 3.1, ____, ____

19. 200, 400, 800, 1,600, ____, ____

Look at the part of the calendar. Remember there are 31 days in March. Use a pattern to answer the questions.

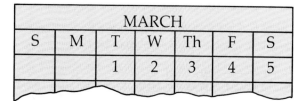

MARCH						
S	M	T	W	Th	F	S
			1	2	3	4	5

20. Gino has Tennis Club meetings every Wednesday. What are the dates for the month of March?

21. Bettina baby-sits on Friday afternoons. On what dates will she be sitting in March?

22. E.J. is going fishing with his grandfather on the first and third Saturdays in March. What are the dates?

23. Beth works after school on Tuesdays and Thursdays. How many days will Beth work during the month of March? What are the dates?

Copy the pattern. Draw and color the next two shapes.

24.

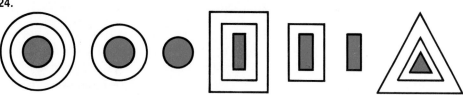

Review PATTERNS AND FUNCTIONS.

9

STATISTICS AND PROBABILITY
Getting Started

You are using statistics and probability when you make a graph to record how many times a spinner stops on the color yellow, the color blue, or any other color on the spinner.

Exercises 1–4 deal with statistics. Exercises 5–12 use probability.

Complete the exercises.

Look at the bar graph and answer the questions.

1. Which team won the most games?

2. Which team won the fewest?

3. Which two teams are tied?

4. Which two teams have the best chance of playing in the finals?

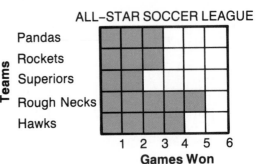

You want to join a soccer team. Luckily, there are still a few openings left on some of the teams.

TEAM OPENINGS
Pandas 3   Rough Necks 2   Rockets 4   Superiors 1

Write the probability of picking the following teams from a hat if you draw only one team name.

5. Pandas

6. Rockets

7. Rough Necks

8. Superiors

9. Rockets or Superiors

10. not the Rockets

11. Which team do you have the greatest probability of choosing?

12. Which team do you have the least probability of choosing?

FOCUS | Review STATISTICS AND PROBABILITY.

LOGIC
Getting Started

If you use careful reasoning before making a guess or figuring something out, you are using logic.

Complete the exercises.

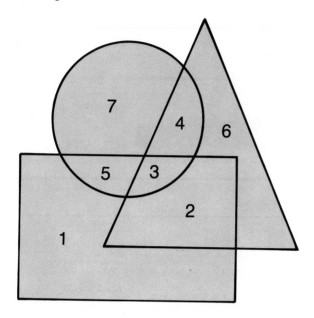

Find the sum of:

13. the numbers in the triangle.

14. the numbers in the circle but not the triangle.

15. the numbers in the circle and the triangle. (Use each number only once.)

16. the numbers in the rectangle and circle but not the triangle.

17. the numbers in the circle, the triangle, and the rectangle in all.

ALGEBRA
Getting Started

Each time you write or solve a number sentence, you are using algebra skills. Remember that > means **greater than** and < means **less than.**

Complete. Write >, <, or =.

18. 226 ● 230

19. $\frac{1}{4}$ ● $\frac{1}{2}$

20. 1,029 ● 1,101

21. 348 ● 341

22. 4,002 ● 3,999

23. $\frac{2}{4}$ ● $\frac{1}{2}$

Copy and complete.

24. 5 + ■ = 9

25. ■ − 6 = 7

26. 4 + ■ = 12

27. 12 − ■ = 5

28. 6 + ■ = 15

29. 14 − ■ = 8

Review LOGIC and ALGEBRA.

Understanding the Way This Book Works

In this book you will always know what kind of lesson you are doing and why you are doing it. The titles above the lines give you an idea of what you will be learning. Titles below the lines tell more exactly what the lesson is about. The FOCUS at the bottom of the page tells the aim of the lesson.

Each chapter begins with a two-page FORMULATING PROBLEMS lesson. Here you will be forming problems from data and other information.

Next comes a two-page lesson which is set up like this:

1. First, you are shown a model of a new skill and how to work it.
2. Next comes GUIDED PRACTICE. This gives help in practicing your new skill.
3. Then you PRACTICE the skill on your own.
4. MIXED PRACTICE comes next. This helps you keep your skills sharp.
5. A CHALLENGE problem offers another way to use your new skill.

The next two pages give you time to practice or extend the skill.

1. First you review or extend the skill.
2. Then you PRACTICE it again.
3. More MIXED PRACTICE comes next.

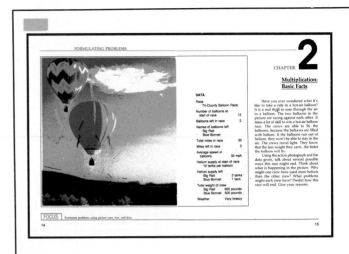

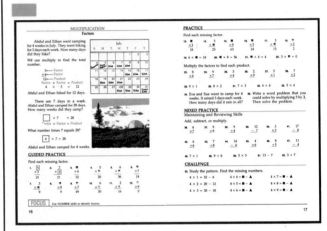

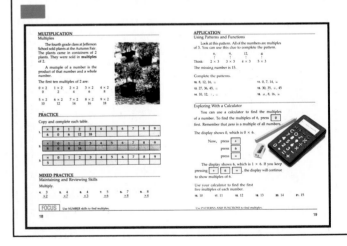

FOCUS | Understand the organization of this book.

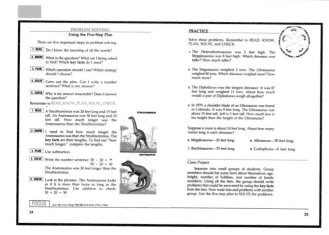

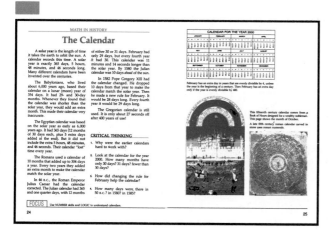

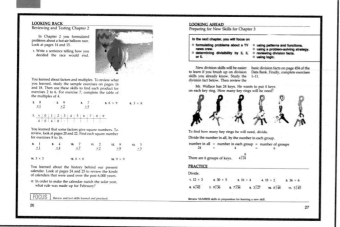

4. Then you apply the new skill and use it with another math strand.

There are some special PROBLEM SOLVING lessons in your book. They follow the first new skill lesson in some chapters. These lessons show you a 5-step plan for solving problems. Having a good plan for solving problems is a big help.

In MATH IN THE CONTENT AREAS you will learn how math is used in history, art, and other subjects. MATH IN TECHNOLOGY teaches you about computers and calculators.

LOOKING BACK comes near the end of every chapter. Here, you will review and be tested on your new skills. By doing this, you will know which skills to keep working on and which skills you have mastered.

LOOKING AHEAD is the very last page of the chapter. Here, you will preview the new skills coming up in the next chapter. You will be shown which old skills you will need in order to do well with the new work. By doing a few exercises, you will be able to decide how much skill sharpening you want to do ahead of time. Knowing you are ready for the next step makes learning math easier.

FOCUS | Formulate problems using picture cues, text, and data.

2

Multiplication: Basic Facts

DATA

Race
    Tri-County Balloon Race

Number of balloons at
    start of race   15

Balloons left in race   2

Names of balloons left
    Big Red
    Blue Bonnet

Total miles in race   30

Miles left in race   5

Average speed of
    balloons   30 mph

Helium supply at start of race
    10 tanks per balloon

Helium supply left
    Big Red   3 tanks
    Blue Bonnet   1 tank

Total weight of crew
    Big Red   600 pounds
    Blue Bonnet   500 pounds

Weather   Very breezy

Have you ever wondered what it's like to take a ride in a hot-air balloon? It is a real thrill to soar through the air in a balloon. The two balloons in the picture are racing against each other. It takes a lot of skill to win a hot-air balloon race. The crews are able to fly the balloons, because the balloons are filled with helium. If the balloons run out of helium, they won't be able to stay in the air. The crews travel light. They know that the less weight they carry, the faster the balloon will fly.

Using the action photograph and the data given, talk about several possible ways this race might end. Think about what is happening in the picture. Why might one crew have used more helium than the other crew? What problems might each crew have? Predict how this race will end. Give your reasons.

Factors

Abdul and Ethan went camping for 4 weeks in July. They went hiking for 3 days each week. How many days did they hike?

We can multiply to find the total number.

$$3 \longleftarrow \text{Factor}$$
$$\underline{\times 4} \longleftarrow \text{Factor}$$
$$12 \longleftarrow \text{Product}$$

Factor × Factor = Product
$$4 \times 3 = 12$$

Abdul and Ethan hiked for 12 days.

July						
S	M	T	W	T	F	S
				1	2	3
4 Fireworks	5 Camp Begins!	6 Hike	7 Hike	8 Hike	9	10
11	12	13	14	15 Hike	16 Hike	17 Hike
18	19 Hike	20 Hike	21 Hike	22	23	24
25	26	27	28 Hike	29 Hike	30 Hike	31 Camp Ends

There are 7 days in a week. Abdul and Ethan camped for 28 days. How many weeks did they camp?

$$\boxed{} \times 7 = 28$$

Factor × Factor = Product

What number times 7 equals 28?

$$\boxed{4} \times 7 = 28$$

Abdul and Ethan camped for 4 weeks.

GUIDED PRACTICE

Find each missing factor.

1. $\boxed{5}$
    $\underline{\times 3}$
    15

2. 7
    $\underline{\times \boxed{3}}$
    21

3. ■
    $\underline{\times 4}$
    32

4. 5
    $\underline{\times ■}$
    20

5. 6
    $\underline{\times ■}$
    36

6. ■
    $\underline{\times 7}$
    14

7. 3
    $\underline{\times ■}$
    9

8. ■
    $\underline{\times 9}$
    9

9. ■
    $\underline{\times 7}$
    49

10. 6
    $\underline{\times ■}$
    30

11. 2
    $\underline{\times ■}$
    16

12. ■
    $\underline{\times 9}$
    0

FOCUS | Use NUMBER skills to identify factors.

PRACTICE

Find each missing factor.

13.
$$\begin{array}{r} \blacksquare \\ \times 3 \\ \hline 18 \end{array}$$
14.
$$\begin{array}{r} 5 \\ \times \blacksquare \\ \hline 25 \end{array}$$
15.
$$\begin{array}{r} \blacksquare \\ \times 9 \\ \hline 63 \end{array}$$
16.
$$\begin{array}{r} \blacksquare \\ \times 3 \\ \hline 24 \end{array}$$
17.
$$\begin{array}{r} 3 \\ \times \blacksquare \\ \hline 15 \end{array}$$
18.
$$\begin{array}{r} \blacksquare \\ \times 2 \\ \hline 2 \end{array}$$

19. $6 \times \blacksquare = 18$ **20.** $\blacksquare \times 8 = 56$ **21.** $\blacksquare \times 4 = 4$ **22.** $3 \times \blacksquare = 0$

Multiply the factors to find each product.

23.
$$\begin{array}{r} 8 \\ \times 6 \\ \hline \end{array}$$
24.
$$\begin{array}{r} 9 \\ \times 7 \\ \hline \end{array}$$
25.
$$\begin{array}{r} 3 \\ \times 4 \\ \hline \end{array}$$
26.
$$\begin{array}{r} 2 \\ \times 9 \\ \hline \end{array}$$
27.
$$\begin{array}{r} 5 \\ \times 1 \\ \hline \end{array}$$
28.
$$\begin{array}{r} 7 \\ \times 2 \\ \hline \end{array}$$

29. 9×1 **30.** 8×2 **31.** 7×3 **32.** 4×4 **33.** 5×4

34. Eva and Sue went to camp for 4 weeks. It rained 3 days each week. How many days did it rain in all?

35. Write a word problem that you could solve by multiplying 5 by 3. Then solve the problem.

MIXED PRACTICE
Maintaining and Reviewing Skills

Add, subtract, or multiply.

36.
$$\begin{array}{r} 6 \\ \times 7 \\ \hline \end{array}$$
37.
$$\begin{array}{r} 9 \\ \times 9 \\ \hline \end{array}$$
38.
$$\begin{array}{r} 9 \\ + 4 \\ \hline \end{array}$$
39.
$$\begin{array}{r} 12 \\ - 7 \\ \hline \end{array}$$
40.
$$\begin{array}{r} 3 \\ \times 3 \\ \hline \end{array}$$
41.
$$\begin{array}{r} 17 \\ - 8 \\ \hline \end{array}$$

42.
$$\begin{array}{r} 6 \\ + 6 \\ \hline \end{array}$$
43.
$$\begin{array}{r} 7 \\ + 8 \\ \hline \end{array}$$
44.
$$\begin{array}{r} 14 \\ - 6 \\ \hline \end{array}$$
45.
$$\begin{array}{r} 4 \\ \times 6 \\ \hline \end{array}$$
46.
$$\begin{array}{r} 8 \\ + 5 \\ \hline \end{array}$$
47.
$$\begin{array}{r} 11 \\ - 4 \\ \hline \end{array}$$

48. 7×1 **49.** $9 + 6$ **50.** 5×5 **51.** $13 - 7$ **52.** $3 + 7$

CHALLENGE

53. Study the pattern. Find the missing numbers.

$4 \times 1 = 10 - 6$ $4 \times 4 = \blacksquare - \blacktriangle$ $4 \times 7 = \blacksquare - \blacktriangle$

$4 \times 2 = 20 - 12$ $4 \times 5 = \blacksquare - \blacktriangle$ $4 \times 8 = \blacksquare - \blacktriangle$

$4 \times 3 = 30 - 18$ $4 \times 6 = \blacksquare - \blacktriangle$ $4 \times 9 = \blacksquare - \blacktriangle$

MULTIPLICATION
Multiples

The fourth grade class at Jefferson School sold plants at the Autumn Fair. The plants came in containers of 2 plants each. So the plants were sold in **multiples** of 2.

A multiple of a number is the product of that number and a whole number.

The first ten multiples of 2 are:

0×2	1×2	2×2	3×2	4×2
0	2	4	6	8

5×2	6×2	7×2	8×2	9×2
10	12	14	16	18

PRACTICE

Copy and complete each table.

1.

×	0	1	2	3	4	5	6	7	8	9
6	0	6	12	18						

2.

×	0	1	2	3	4	5	6	7	8	9
8	0	8	16							

3.

×	0	1	2	3	4	5	6	7	8	9
5										

MIXED PRACTICE
Maintaining and Reviewing Skills

Multiply.

4. $\begin{array}{r} 3 \\ \times 2 \\ \hline \end{array}$
    5. $\begin{array}{r} 4 \\ \times 7 \\ \hline \end{array}$
    6. $\begin{array}{r} 4 \\ \times 3 \\ \hline \end{array}$
    7. $\begin{array}{r} 5 \\ \times 6 \\ \hline \end{array}$
    8. $\begin{array}{r} 7 \\ \times 8 \\ \hline \end{array}$
    9. $\begin{array}{r} 8 \\ \times 4 \\ \hline \end{array}$

FOCUS   Use NUMBER skills to find multiples.

APPLICATION

Using Patterns and Functions

Look at this pattern. All of the numbers are multiples of 3. You can use this clue to complete the pattern.

	6,	9,	12,	■
	↑	↑	↑	↑
Think:	2 × 3	3 × 3	4 × 3	5 × 3

The missing number is 15.

Complete the patterns.

10. 8, 12, 16, ■

11. 0, 7, 14, ■

12. 27, 36, 45, ■

13. 30, 35, ■, 45

14. 10, 12, ■, ■

15. ■, 8, 16, ■

Exploring With a Calculator

You can use a calculator to find the multiples of a number. To find the multiples of 6, press [0] first. Remember that zero is a multiple of all numbers.

The display shows 0, which is 0 × 6.

Now, press [+]

press [6]

press [=]

The display shows 6, which is 1 × 6. If you keep pressing [+] [6] [=], the display will continue to show multiples of 6.

Use your calculator to find the first five multiples of each number.

16. 10   **17.** 11   **18.** 12   **19.** 13   **20.** 14   **21.** 15

Use PATTERNS AND FUNCTIONS to find multiples.

Square Numbers

The numbers 1 and 4 are called **square numbers.**
They form a square pattern.

$1 \times 1 = 1$ $2 \times 2 = 4$

What is the third square number?

$3 \times 3 = 9$

The third square number is 9.

GUIDED PRACTICE

Find the fourth and fifth square numbers.

1.

2.

$4 \times 4 = $ ■ $5 \times 5 = $ ■

FOCUS   Use NUMBER skills to name square numbers.

PRACTICE

Find the square numbers.

3.

$6 \times 6 = $

4.

$7 \times 7 = $

5.

$8 \times 8 = $

6.

$9 \times 9 = $

7. A shape has a length of 6 and a width of 7. Is the shape a square?

8. A shape has a length of 8 and a width of 7. Is the shape a square?

MIXED PRACTICE

Maintaining and Reviewing Skills

Add, subtract, or multiply.

9. $\begin{array}{r} 3 \\ \times 3 \\ \hline \end{array}$ **10.** $\begin{array}{r} 5 \\ \times 5 \\ \hline \end{array}$ **11.** $\begin{array}{r} 4 \\ +7 \\ \hline \end{array}$ **12.** $\begin{array}{r} 17 \\ -\ 8 \\ \hline \end{array}$ **13.** $\begin{array}{r} 5 \\ \times 6 \\ \hline \end{array}$ **14.** $\begin{array}{r} 8 \\ +5 \\ \hline \end{array}$

15. $\begin{array}{r} 7 \\ +7 \\ \hline \end{array}$ **16.** $\begin{array}{r} 16 \\ -\ 9 \\ \hline \end{array}$ **17.** $\begin{array}{r} 13 \\ -\ 4 \\ \hline \end{array}$ **18.** $\begin{array}{r} 6 \\ \times 7 \\ \hline \end{array}$ **19.** $\begin{array}{r} 8 \\ \times 5 \\ \hline \end{array}$ **20.** $\begin{array}{r} 11 \\ -\ 7 \\ \hline \end{array}$

MULTIPLICATION
Square Numbers

Look at this table.

Factor	×	Factor	=	Product
4		6		24
3		3		9
7		5		35
9		9		81

The columns show that a factor times a factor equals a product.

$$4 \times 6 = 24$$
$$3 \times 3 = 9$$
$$7 \times 5 = 35$$
$$9 \times 9 = 81$$

When both factors are the same, the product is a square number.

PRACTICE

Find each product. Write *yes* if it is a square number.

1.	2.	3.	4.	5.	6.
7 ×3 ■	5 ×5 ■	9 ×2 ■	8 ×6 ■	4 ×4 ■	6 ×6 ■

7. $2 \times 2 =$ ■   8. $8 \times 1 =$ ■   9. $7 \times 7 =$ ■   10. $8 \times 4 =$ ■   11. $8 \times 8 =$ ■

12. $1 \times 9 =$ ■   13. $1 \times 1 =$ ■   14. $5 \times 7 =$ ■   15. $9 \times 6 =$ ■   16. $3 \times 4 =$ ■

MIXED PRACTICE
Maintaining and Reviewing Skills

Add, subtract, or multiply.

17.	18.	19.	20.	21.	22.
6 ×4	7 ×7	13 − 8	4 +4	8 +6	10 − 5

23. 7×8 24. $15 - 6$ 25. $14 - 8$ 26. $8 + 9$ 27. $9 - 7$

FOCUS   Use NUMBER skills to find products and square numbers.

APPLICATION

Using Patterns and Functions

28. Copy this multiplication table on centimeter paper.

×	0	1	2	3	4	5	6	7	8	9
0	0	0	0	0	0	0	0	0	0	0
1	0	1	2	3	4	5	6	7	8	9
2	0	2	4	6	8	10	12	14	16	18
3	0	3	6	9	12	15	18	21	24	27
4	0	4	8	12	16	20	24	28	32	36
5	0	5	10	15	20	25	30	35	40	45
6	0	6	12	18	24	30	36	42	48	54
7	0	7	14	21	28	35	42	49	56	63
8	0	8	16	24	32	40	48	56	64	72
9	0	9	18	27	36	45	54	63	72	81

The boxes for the product of 0 × 0 and 1 × 1 are colored in. Color them in on your table. Color in the boxes that show all the other square numbers. Write a sentence to describe the pattern that you see.

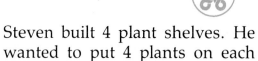

Solving Problems

29. Karen bought 6 bags of tulip bulbs. There were 6 tulip bulbs in each bag. How many tulip bulbs did Karen buy altogether?

30. Steven built 4 plant shelves. He wanted to put 4 plants on each shelf. How many plants did Steven need to get?

31. Linda had 9 ounces of soil. She put the same amount of soil into each of 3 pots. How much soil did she put into each pot?

32. Margaret had 25 tomato seeds. She planted 5 seeds in each row. How many rows of tomato seeds did Margaret plant?

Use PATTERNS AND FUNCTIONS to find square numbers.
Use NUMBER skills to solve problems.

The Calendar

A **solar year** is the length of time it takes the earth to orbit the sun. A calendar records this time. A solar year is exactly 365 days, 5 hours, 48 minutes, and 46 seconds long. Many different calendars have been invented over the centuries.

The Babylonians, who lived about 6,000 years ago, based their calendar on a lunar (moon) year of 354 days. It had 29- and 30-day months. Whenever they found that the calendar was shorter than the solar year, they would add an extra month. This made their calendar very inaccurate.

The Egyptian calendar was based on the solar year as early as 6,000 years ago. It had 365 days (12 months of 30 days each, plus 5 extra days added at the end). But it did not include the extra 5 hours, 48 minutes, and 46 seconds. Their calendar "lost" time every year.

The Romans used a calendar of 10 months that added up to 304 days a year. Every two years they added an extra month to make the calendar match the solar year.

In 46 B.C., the Roman Emperor Julius Caesar had the calendar corrected. The Julian calendar had 365 and one-quarter days, with 12 months of either 30 or 31 days. February had only 29 days, but every fourth year it had 30. This calendar was 11 minutes and 14 seconds longer than the solar year. By 1580 the Julian calendar was 10 days *ahead* of the sun.

In 1582 Pope Gregory XIII had the calendar changed. He dropped 10 days from that year to make the calendar match the solar year. Then he made a new rule for February. It would be 28 days long. Every fourth year it would be 29 days long.

The Gregorian calendar is still used. It is only about 27 seconds off after 400 years of use!

CRITICAL THINKING

1. Why were the earlier calendars hard to work with?

2. Look at the calendar for the year 2000. How many months have only 30 days? 31 days? fewer than 30 days?

3. How did changing the rule for February help the calendar?

4. How many days were there in 50 B.C.? in 1580?

FOCUS | Use NUMBER skills and LOGIC to understand calendars.

CALENDAR FOR THE YEAR 2000

JANUARY

S	M	T	W	T	F	S
						1
2	3	4	5	6	7	8
9	10	11	12	13	14	15
16	17	18	19	20	21	22
23	24	25	26	27	28	29
30	31					

FEBRUARY

S	M	T	W	T	F	S
		1	2	3	4	5
6	7	8	9	10	11	12
13	14	15	16	17	18	19
20	21	22	23	24	25	26
27	28	29				

MARCH

S	M	T	W	T	F	S
			1	2	3	4
5	6	7	8	9	10	11
12	13	14	15	16	17	18
19	20	21	22	23	24	25
26	27	28	29	30	31	

APRIL

S	M	T	W	T	F	S
						1
2	3	4	5	6	7	8
9	10	11	12	13	14	15
16	17	18	19	20	21	22
23	24	25	26	27	28	29
30	31					

MAY

S	M	T	W	T	F	S
	1	2	3	4	5	6
7	8	9	10	11	12	13
14	15	16	17	18	19	20
21	22	23	24	25	26	27
28	29	30	31			

JUNE

S	M	T	W	T	F	S
				1	2	3
4	5	6	7	8	9	10
11	12	13	14	15	16	17
18	19	20	21	22	23	24
25	26	27	28	29	30	

JULY

S	M	T	W	T	F	S
						1
2	3	4	5	6	7	8
9	10	11	12	13	14	15
16	17	18	19	20	21	22
23	24	25	26	27	28	29
30	31					

AUGUST

S	M	T	W	T	F	S
		1	2	3	4	5
6	7	8	9	10	11	12
13	14	15	16	17	18	19
20	21	22	23	24	25	26
27	28	29	30	31		

SEPTEMBER

S	M	T	W	T	F	S
					1	2
3	4	5	6	7	8	9
10	11	12	13	14	15	16
17	18	19	20	21	22	23
24	25	26	27	28	29	30

OCTOBER

S	M	T	W	T	F	S
1	2	3	4	5	6	7
8	9	10	11	12	13	14
15	16	17	18	19	20	21
22	23	24	25	26	27	28
29	30	31				

NOVEMBER

S	M	T	W	T	F	S
			1	2	3	4
5	6	7	8	9	10	11
12	13	14	15	16	17	18
19	20	21	22	23	24	25
26	27	28	29	30		

DECEMBER

S	M	T	W	T	F	S
					1	2
3	4	5	6	7	8	9
10	11	12	13	14	15	16
17	18	19	20	21	22	23
24	25	26	27	28	29	30
31						

February has an extra day in years that are evenly divisible by 4, unless the year is the beginning of a century. Then February has an extra day only if the year is evenly divisible by 400.

This fifteenth century calendar comes from a Book of Hours designed for a wealthy nobleman. This page shows the month of October.

A late fifth century roman calendar carved in stone uses roman numerals.

LOOKING BACK
Reviewing and Testing Chapter 2

In Chapter 2 you formulated problems about a hot-air balloon race. Look at pages 14 and 15.

1. Write a sentence telling how you decided the race would end.

You learned about factors and multiples. To review what you learned, study the sample exercises on pages 16 and 18. Then use these skills to find each product for exercises 2 to 6. For exercise 7, complete the table of the multiples of 4.

2. $\begin{array}{r} 8 \\ \times 1 \\ \hline \end{array}$
3. $\begin{array}{r} 9 \\ \times 2 \\ \hline \end{array}$
4. $\begin{array}{r} 7 \\ \times 5 \\ \hline \end{array}$
5. 6×9
6. 3×8

7.

×	0	1	2	3	4	5	6	7	8	9
4	0	4	8	■	■	■	■	■	■	■

You learned that some factors give square numbers. To review, look at pages 20 and 22. Find each square number for exercises 8 to 16.

8. $\begin{array}{r} 1 \\ \times 1 \\ \hline \end{array}$
9. $\begin{array}{r} 4 \\ \times 4 \\ \hline \end{array}$
10. $\begin{array}{r} 7 \\ \times 7 \\ \hline \end{array}$
11. $\begin{array}{r} 2 \\ \times 2 \\ \hline \end{array}$
12. $\begin{array}{r} 8 \\ \times 8 \\ \hline \end{array}$
13. $\begin{array}{r} 5 \\ \times 5 \\ \hline \end{array}$

14. 3×3
15. 6×6
16. 9×9

You learned about the history behind our present calendar. Look at pages 24 and 25 to review the kinds of calendars that were used over the past 6,000 years.

17. In order to make the calendar match the solar year, what rule was made up for February?

FOCUS | Review and test skills learned and practiced.

LOOKING AHEAD
Preparing for New Skills for Chapter 3

In the next chapter, you will focus on

- formulating problems about a TV news crew.
- determining divisibility by 2, 3, or 5.
- using patterns and functions.
- using a problem-solving strategy.
- reviewing division facts.
- using logic.

New division skills will be easier to learn if you brush up on division skills you already know. Study the division fact below. Then review the basic division facts on page 454 of the Data Bank. Finally, complete exercises 1–11.

Mr. Wallace has 24 keys. He wants to put 4 keys on each key ring. How many key rings will he need?

To find how many key rings he will need, divide.

Divide the number in all by the number in each group.

number in all	number in each group	number of groups
24 ÷	4 =	6

He will need 6 key rings. $4\overline{)24}$ with 6 above

PRACTICE

Divide.

1. $12 \div 3$ **2.** $30 \div 5$ **3.** $16 \div 4$ **4.** $18 \div 2$ **5.** $36 \div 6$

6. $6\overline{)42}$ **7.** $9\overline{)36}$ **8.** $7\overline{)56}$ **9.** $3\overline{)27}$ **10.** $8\overline{)48}$ **11.** $5\overline{)45}$

Review NUMBER skills in preparation for learning a new skill.

FOCUS | Formulate problems using picture cues, text, and data.

CHAPTER 3

Division: Basic Facts

DATA

Job	TV news crew
Deadline	5:30 P.M.

News crew
Reporter	Fred
Cameraperson	Sue
Soundperson	Phil

Schedule of news events
2:00 P.M.	Mayor's speech
3:00 P.M.	Pie-eating contest
4:45 P.M.	Track meet

Time now	4:45 P.M.

Travel time back to TV station	30 minutes

Videotape supply	10 minutes of tape left

Extra equipment
  2 lights
  300-foot power cable
  1 microphone

Working on a TV news show is fun and challenging. Each day, crews go out and report interesting news events. One day the crew might cover a sports event. Other days the crew might cover an election or a big traffic jam.

The crew records the action on videotape. A news crew works quickly because they have to get the videotape back to the station in time for the evening news broadcast. A deadline is set up to make sure they are back on time. The crew can miss the deadline only if they have a very good reason.

Look at the data. Did the crew bring enough videotape to last the day? Will they make it back before the deadline? Think of some other news events the crew might report. What are some problems the crew might have? Predict how the day will turn out. Give your reasons.

Divisibility Rule for 3

Mr. Flynn works at a toy company. He has 81 coloring books to put into plastic bags. If Mr. Flynn puts 3 coloring books in each bag, will there be any books left over?

Use the **divisibility rule for 3** to find out if there will be any books left over. According to the rule, a number **is divisible by 3** if the sum of its digits can be divided by 3 with a remainder of zero.

Can 81 books be divided into groups of 3 with no books left over?

Add the digits: $8 + 1 = 9$

Divide the sum by 3: $3\overline{)9}$ with quotient 3

The remainder is 0, so 81 is divisible by 3. No books will be left over.

Mr. Flynn has 52 crayons to put into plastic bags. If he puts 3 crayons in each bag, will there be any crayons left over?

Add the digits: $5 + 2 = 7.$ Divide the sum by 3: $3\overline{)7}$ with quotient 2 R1

The remainder is 1, so 52 is not divisible by 3. There will be 1 crayon left over.

GUIDED PRACTICE

Are the numbers divisible by 3? Write *yes* or *no*.

1. 21
   $2 + 1 = 3$
   $3\overline{)3}$ with quotient 1
   yes

2. 16
   $1 + 6 = 7$
   $3\overline{)7}$ with quotient 2 R1
   no

3. 57
   $5 + 7$

4. 12

5. 35

FOCUS   Use NUMBER skills to determine if numbers are divisible by 3.

PRACTICE

Is the number divisible by 3? Write *yes* or *no*.

6. 22   7. 11   8. 24   9. 34   10. 46

11. 54   12. 63   13. 72   14. 88   15. 91

16. 13   17. 25   18. 27   19. 37   20. 43

21. 52   22. 56   23. 61   24. 74   25. 83

26. 90   27. 14   28. 17   29. 18   30. 16

31. 67   32. 75   33. 65   34. 55   35. 29

MIXED PRACTICE

Maintaining and Reviewing Skills

Is the number divisible by 3? Write *yes* or *no*.

36. 64   37. 39   38. 58   39. 43   40. 33

Add, subtract, or multiply.

41. $18 - 9$ 42. 6×4 43. $8 + 7$ 44. $14 - 6$ 45. 5×7

46. $7 + 5$ 47. 8×6 48. $15 - 7$ 49. $16 - 9$ 50. 9×5

51. $12 - 6$ 52. $8 + 5$ 53. 5×8 54. $6 + 6$ 55. 3×7

CHALLENGE

56. Find the pattern.

Write the numbers from 1 to 30.

Ring the numbers that are divisible by 3.

Divide each ringed number by 6. If the remainder is 0, the number is divisible by 6. Draw a line under the numbers that are divisible by 6. What pattern do you see?

DIVISION
Divisibility Rules for 2 and 5

A number is divisible by 2 if the digit in the ones place is an even number. These numbers are divisible by 2.

10	26	346
The ones digit is an even number.	The ones digit is an even number.	The ones digit is an even number.

A number is divisible by 5 if the digit in the ones place is 5 or 0. These numbers are divisible by 5.

20	35	255
The ones digit is 0.	The ones digit is 5.	The ones digit is 5.

PRACTICE

Are these numbers divisible by 2? Write *yes* or *no.*

1. 10   2. 13   3. 27   4. 35   5. 22   6. 40

7. 16   8. 45   9. 660   10. 78   11. 942   12. 573

Are these numbers divisible by 5? Write *yes* or *no.*

13. 25   14. 45   15. 65   16. 66   17. 30   18. 37

19. 80   20. 750   21. 309   22. 408   23. 320   24. 945

MIXED PRACTICE
Maintaining and Reviewing Skills

Are these numbers divisible by 2? Write *yes* or *no.*

25. 71   26. 50   27. 136   28. 243   29. 198   30. 640

Are these numbers divisible by 3? Write *yes* or *no.*

31. 49   32. 66   33. 51   34. 146   35. 360   36. 126

Are these numbers divisible by 5? Write *yes* or *no.*

37. 40   38. 134   39. 125   40. 520   41. 258   42. 375

FOCUS   Use NUMBER skills to determine if numbers are divisible by 2 or 5.

APPLICATION

Using Patterns and Functions

A multiplication table can be used to find division facts.

Use the multiplication table to find the quotient for $21 \div 7$.

STEP 1

Find the number you are dividing by in the left column. In this division fact you are dividing by 7.

STEP 2

Move your finger along the row beginning with 7 until you come to the number you are dividing. In this division fact you are dividing the number 21.

×	1	2	3	4	5	6	7	8	9
1	1	2	3	4	5	6	7	8	9
2	2	4	6	8	10	12	14	16	18
3	3	6	9	12	15	18	21	24	27
4	4	8	12	16	20	24	28	32	36
5	5	10	15	20	25	30	35	40	45
6	6	12	18	24	30	36	42	48	54
7	7	14	21	28	35	42	49	56	63
8	8	16	24	32	40	48	56	64	72
9	9	18	27	36	45	54	63	72	81

STEP 3

Move your finger up to the top row to find the quotient. The quotient is 3.

Use the multiplication table to find the answers to these division facts.

43. $3\overline{)18}$ **44.** $7\overline{)49}$ **45.** $2\overline{)14}$ **46.** $1\overline{)6}$ **47.** $6\overline{)48}$ **48.** $4\overline{)24}$

49. $5\overline{)40}$ **50.** $8\overline{)56}$ **51.** $9\overline{)54}$ **52.** $9\overline{)27}$ **53.** $7\overline{)49}$ **54.** $4\overline{)32}$

55. $3\overline{)15}$ **56.** $5\overline{)25}$ **57.** $6\overline{)42}$ **58.** $9\overline{)72}$ **59.** $7\overline{)35}$ **60.** $6\overline{)54}$

Using Mental Arithmetic

Use these groups of numbers to make two multiplication number sentences and two division number sentences.

61. 7, 5, 35 $7 \times 5 = 35$ $5 \times 7 = 35$ $35 \div 5 = 7$ $35 \div 7 = 5$

62. 6, 7, 42

63. 7, 9, 63

Use PATTERNS AND FUNCTIONS and MENTAL ARITHMETIC
to relate multiplication and division facts.

Using the Five-Step Plan

There are five important steps in problem solving.

| 1. READ | Do I know the meaning of all the words?

| 2. KNOW | What is the question? What am I being asked to find? Which **key facts** do I need?

| 3. PLAN | Which operation should I use? Which strategy should I choose?

| 4. SOLVE | Carry out the plan. Can I write a number sentence? What is my answer?

| 5. CHECK | Why is my answer reasonable? Does it answer the question?

Remember to READ, KNOW, PLAN, SOLVE, CHECK.

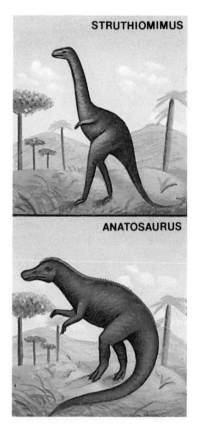

STRUTHIOMIMUS

ANATOSAURUS

| 1. READ | A Struthiomimus was 20 feet long and 15 feet tall. An Anatosaurus was 50 feet long and 10 feet tall. How much longer was the Anatosaurus than the Struthiomimus?

| 2. KNOW | I need to find how much longer the Anatosaurus was than the Struthiomimus. The **key facts** are their lengths. To find out "how much longer," compare the lengths.

| 3. PLAN | Use subtraction.

| 4. SOLVE | Write the number sentence: $50 - 20 = \blacksquare$
$50 - 20 = 30$
The Anatosaurus was 30 feet longer than the Struthiomimus.

| 5. CHECK | Look at the pictures. The Anatosaurus looks as if it is much longer than the Struthiomimus. Use addition to check: $30 + 20 = 50$

| FOCUS | Use the Five-Step PROBLEM-SOLVING Plan.

PRACTICE

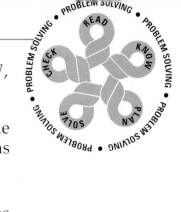

Solve these problems. Remember to READ, KNOW, PLAN, SOLVE, and CHECK.

1. The Heterodontosaurus was 2 feet high. The Megalosaurus was 8 feet high. Which dinosaur was taller? How much taller?

2. The Stegosaurus weighed 2 tons. The Ultrasaurus weighed 80 tons. Which dinosaur weighed more? How much more?

3. The Diplodocus was the longest dinosaur. It was 87 feet long and weighed 11 tons. About how much would a pair of Diplodocus weigh altogether?

4. In 1979, a shoulder blade of an Ultrasaurus was found in Colorado. It was 9 feet long. The Ultrasaurus was about 55 feet tall. Jeff is 5 feet tall. How much less is his height than the height of the Ultrasaurus?

Suppose a room is about 10 feet long. About how many rooms long is each dinosaur?

5. Megalosaurus—20 feet long

6. Allosaurus—30 feet long

7. Brachiosaurus—70 feet long

8. Coelophysis—8 feet long

Class Project

Separate into small groups of students. Group members should list some facts about themselves: age, height, number of hobbies, and number of family members. Using all the lists, the group should write problems that could be answered by using the **key facts** from the lists. Now trade lists and problems with another group. Use the five-step plan to SOLVE the problems.

Dividing With Basic Facts

Jessy wants to buy 12 pairs of socks. There are 3 pairs of socks in each package. How many packages of socks will Jessy need to buy?

To find how many 3s there are in 12, divide.

The division fact can be written two ways.

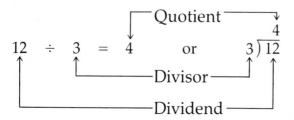

$$12 \div 3 = 4 \quad \text{or} \quad 3\overline{)12}$$

The **quotient** is the answer.

The **divisor** is the number of groups or the number in each group.

The **dividend** is the number in all.

Jessy needs to buy 4 packages of socks.

Mary Ann wants to buy 9 handkerchiefs. They come in packages of 3 handkerchiefs each. How many packages of handkerchiefs will Mary Ann have to buy?

To find how many 3s there are in 9, divide.

$$9 \div 3 = 3 \quad \text{or} \quad 3\overline{)9}$$

Mary Ann will have to buy 3 packages of handkerchiefs.

GUIDED PRACTICE

Find the quotients. Write each division fact another way.

1. $24 \div 4 = 6 \quad 4\overline{)24}$ 2. $5\overline{)45} \quad 45 \div 5$ 3. $15 \div 3$

4. $7\overline{)63}$ 5. $6\overline{)42}$ 6. $54 \div 6$ 7. $32 \div 4$ 8. $3\overline{)27}$

| FOCUS | Use NUMBER skills to review division facts. |

PRACTICE

Find the quotients.

9. $14 \div 2$ **10.** $27 \div 3$ **11.** $36 \div 4$ **12.** $25 \div 5$ **13.** $28 \div 7$

14. $6\overline{)54}$ **15.** $9\overline{)81}$ **16.** $7\overline{)49}$ **17.** $4\overline{)16}$ **18.** $3\overline{)18}$ **19.** $8\overline{)56}$

Find the quotients. Write each division fact another way.

20. $2\overline{)18}$ **21.** $4\overline{)12}$ **22.** $36 \div 6$ **23.** $45 \div 9$ **24.** $5\overline{)20}$

25. $24 \div 4$ **26.** $3\overline{)9}$ **27.** $64 \div 8$ **28.** $42 \div 7$ **29.** $9\overline{)45}$

Copy each division fact. Label each number as quotient, divisor, or dividend.

30. $18 \div 6 = 3$ **31.** $20 \div 4 = 5$ **32.** $6\overline{)42}^{\,7}$ **33.** $8\overline{)40}^{\,5}$ **34.** $9\overline{)72}^{\,8}$

Solve. Write each division fact two ways.

35. Betty wants to buy 24 hair ribbons. The ribbons come 6 to a package. How many packages will Betty have to buy?

36. George wants to buy 12 T-shirts. The shirts come 2 to a package. How many packages will George have to buy?

MIXED PRACTICE
Maintaining and Reviewing Skills

Multiply or divide.

37. $36 \div 6$ **38.** $48 \div 8$ **39.** 4×5 **40.** $45 \div 9$ **41.** 8×7

42. 9×3 **43.** $64 \div 8$ **44.** $42 \div 7$ **45.** 5×6 **46.** 7×4

47. 9×9 **48.** $72 \div 8$ **49.** 3×6 **50.** 5×9 **51.** $16 \div 4$

CHALLENGE

52. There are 24 pairs of shoes in one box and 21 pairs of shoes in another box. If 5 pairs of shoes fit on a shelf, how many shelves will be needed for all the shoes?

EXTRA PRACTICE—page 444

DIVISION
Dividing With Basic Facts

Tony planted 36 pepper plants in his garden. He put 9 plants in each row. How many rows of pepper plants did Tony plant?

Write a division fact to show how many groups of 9 there are in 36.

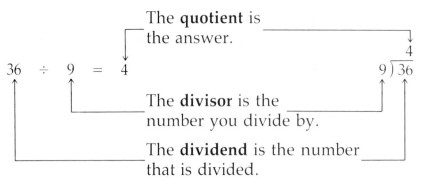

The **quotient** is the answer.

$$36 \div 9 = 4 \qquad 9\overline{)36}$$

The **divisor** is the number you divide by.

The **dividend** is the number that is divided.

Tony planted 4 rows of pepper plants.

PRACTICE

Find the quotients.

1. $25 \div 5$
2. $12 \div 6$
3. $7\overline{)42}$
4. $8\overline{)16}$
5. $6\overline{)30}$

6. $9\overline{)72}$
7. $36 \div 4$
8. $56 \div 8$
9. $8\overline{)64}$
10. $5\overline{)40}$

Find the quotients. Write each division fact another way.

11. $42 \div 6$
12. $3\overline{)18}$
13. $4\overline{)24}$
14. $40 \div 8$
15. $28 \div 7$

16. $3\overline{)15}$
17. $36 \div 6$
18. $16 \div 4$
19. $6\overline{)18}$
20. $54 \div 9$

MIXED PRACTICE
Maintaining and Reviewing Skills

Multiply or divide.

21. $36 \div 6$
22. $18 \div 3$
23. 4×4
24. 3×7
25. $36 \div 4$

26. 5×3
27. 8×4
28. $24 \div 6$
29. 3×4
30. 8×9

FOCUS | Use NUMBER skills to review division facts.

APPLICATION

Using Logic

Is this division sentence true or false?

$27 \div 3 > 8$
Think: $27 \div 3 = 9$ $9 > 8$
Therefore: $27 \div 3 > 8$ The division sentence is true.

Is this division sentence true or false?

$32 \div 4 < 7$
Think: $32 \div 4 = 8$ $8 > 7$
Therefore: $32 \div 4 > 7$ The division sentence is false.

Write *true* or *false*.

31. $25 \div 5 = 5$ **32.** $36 \div 4 = 8$ **33.** $12 \div 6 > 3$

34. $56 \div 8 > 5$ **35.** $27 \div 9 < 5$ **36.** $42 \div 6 < 5$

37. $72 \div 8 > 8$ **38.** $45 \div 9 > 6$ **39.** $18 \div 3 < 7$

Exploring With a Calculator

A calculator can be used for repeated division. Use a calculator to solve this division sentence.

$$100 \div 2 \div 5 \div 5 \div 2 = \blacksquare$$

40. Turn on the calculator. Then press $\boxed{1}$ $\boxed{0}$ $\boxed{0}$. The number 100 should appear on the screen.

41. Press $\boxed{\div}$ $\boxed{2}$ and $\boxed{=}$. The number 50 should appear on the screen.

42. Press $\boxed{\div}$ $\boxed{5}$ and $\boxed{=}$. The number 10 should appear on the screen.

43. Press $\boxed{\div}$ $\boxed{5}$ and $\boxed{=}$ again. The number 2 should appear on the screen.

44. Finally, press $\boxed{\div}$ $\boxed{2}$ and $\boxed{=}$. The number 1 should appear on the screen.

45. Starting with 100, keep dividing on the calculator until you reach 1. Write division sentences for each set of division operations you do.

Use LOGIC and a CALCULATOR to solve problems.

LOOKING BACK
Reviewing and Testing Chapter 3

In Chapter 3 you formulated problems about a television news crew. Look at pages 28 and 29.

1. Write a sentence telling how you predicted how the crew's day might end.

You learned about the divisibility rules for 2, 3, and 5. To review what you learned, study the sample exercises on pages 30 and 32. Then use these skills to tell whether the first number is divisible by the second for exercises 2–9. Write *yes* or *no*.

2. 21 by 3?   3. 51 by 3?   4. 26 by 3?   5. 54 by 2?

6. 77 by 2?   7. 98 by 2?   8. 68 by 5?   9. 95 by 5?

You learned how to use the Five-Step PROBLEM SOLVING Plan. To review, look at pages 34 and 35. Solve these problems. Remember to READ, KNOW, PLAN, SOLVE, and CHECK.

10. Sarah found 17 clams.
    Robert found 9 clams.
    Who found more clams?
    How many more?

11. Larry caught 13 fish.
    Beth caught 9 fish.
    Who caught fewer fish?
    How many fewer?

You learned about dividing with basic facts. To review, look at page 36. Find each quotient for exercises 12–26.

12. $3\overline{)15}$ 13. $5\overline{)25}$ 14. $30 \div 6$ 15. $81 \div 9$ 16. $2\overline{)16}$

17. $16 \div 4$ 18. $8\overline{)24}$ 19. $7\overline{)56}$ 20. $4\overline{)36}$ 21. $18 \div 3$

22. $7\overline{)49}$ 23. $27 \div 9$ 24. $6\overline{)12}$ 25. $5\overline{)40}$ 26. $48 \div 8$

FOCUS | Review and test skills learned and practiced.

LOOKING AHEAD
Preparing for New Skills for Chapter 4

In the next chapter, you will focus on

- **formulating problems about a cattle roundup.**
- **multiplying tens.**
- **using Roman numerals.**
- **identifying letters used as placeholders.**
- **using patterns and functions.**
- **how math is used in technology.**

New multiplication skills will be easier to learn if you brush up on multiplication skills you already know. Study the multiplication fact below. Then review the basic multiplication facts on page 454 of the Data Bank. Finally, complete exercises 1–19.

There are 3 stacks of tape cassettes on the counter. There are 6 cassettes in each stack. How many cassettes are there in all?

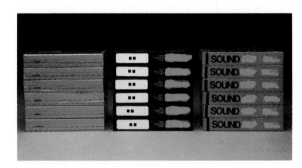

To find how many in all, multiply.

number of groups		number in each group		number in all
3	×	6	=	18

$$\begin{array}{r} 6 \\ \times 3 \\ \hline 18 \end{array}$$

There are 18 cassettes in all.

PRACTICE

Multiply.

1. 4 × 6   **2.** 3 × 7   **3.** 2 × 6   **4.** 8 × 3   **5.** 6 × 5

6. $\begin{array}{r}5\\ \times 3\\ \hline\end{array}$ **7.** $\begin{array}{r}8\\ \times 6\\ \hline\end{array}$ **8.** $\begin{array}{r}6\\ \times 7\\ \hline\end{array}$ **9.** $\begin{array}{r}9\\ \times 8\\ \hline\end{array}$ **10.** $\begin{array}{r}7\\ \times 4\\ \hline\end{array}$ **11.** $\begin{array}{r}4\\ \times 8\\ \hline\end{array}$ **12.** $\begin{array}{r}2\\ \times 9\\ \hline\end{array}$

13. $\begin{array}{r}3\\ \times 3\\ \hline\end{array}$ **14.** $\begin{array}{r}8\\ \times 7\\ \hline\end{array}$ **15.** $\begin{array}{r}6\\ \times 6\\ \hline\end{array}$ **16.** $\begin{array}{r}9\\ \times 7\\ \hline\end{array}$ **17.** $\begin{array}{r}5\\ \times 8\\ \hline\end{array}$ **18.** $\begin{array}{r}8\\ \times 8\\ \hline\end{array}$ **19.** $\begin{array}{r}3\\ \times 9\\ \hline\end{array}$

Review NUMBER skills in preparation for learning a new skill.

4

Multiplication by Tens

DATA

Job	Cattle roundup
Ranch	Flying L Ranch
Size of ranch	2,000 acres
First snowfall due	November 12
Today's date	November 9
Cowhands	Big Ed
	Sam
	Suzie
Cattle missing	300
Cattle rounded up so far	450
Average number of cattle rounded up per day	100
Last year's average per day	80

Working on a cattle ranch is a rugged, challenging way of life. Each fall, the cowhands round up the cattle which are scattered all over the ranch. The cowhands then move the cattle south where the winter weather is not as cold.

The cowhands take pride in their work. Each day they try hard to round up as many cattle as they can. The cowhands must work fast. They know that the first snowfall will come soon. Once the snow comes, it is too difficult to round up any more cattle.

Look at the picture and the data. Think of what it must be like to be a cowhand. How many days are left before the first snowfall? Will the cowhands be able to round up all the cattle before the snow comes? Are they working faster this year than they did last year? Think of some problems a cowhand might have. Predict how the roundup will end. Give your reasons.

Multiplying Tens

Each shelf holds 10 books. There are 6 shelves. How many books are there in all?

To find how many in all, multiply: 6×10.

$$6 \times 10 = 60 \qquad \begin{array}{r} 10 \\ \times\ 6 \\ \hline 60 \end{array}$$

There are 60 books in all.

Counting by tens and multiplying by tens are a lot alike.

$$\begin{array}{ccccccccc} 10 & 10 & 10 & 10 & 10 & 10 & 10 & 10 & 10 \\ \times\ 1 & \times\ 2 & \times\ 3 & \times\ 4 & \times\ 5 & \times\ 6 & \times\ 7 & \times\ 8 & \times\ 9 \\ \hline 10 & 20 & 30 & 40 & 50 & 60 & 70 & 80 & 90 \end{array}$$

Multiplying multiples of ten and multiplying ones are a lot alike.

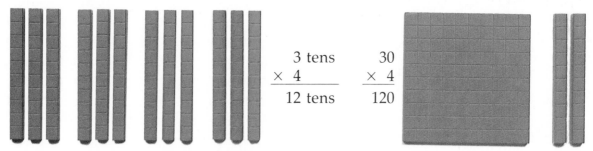

$$\begin{array}{r} 3 \text{ tens} \\ \times\ 4 \\ \hline 12 \text{ tens} \end{array} \qquad \begin{array}{r} 30 \\ \times\ 4 \\ \hline 120 \end{array}$$

Sometimes when three factors are being multiplied, it helps to look for multiples of ten.

$2 \times 3 \times 10$ equals $(2 \times 3) \times 10$ equals $6 \times 10 = 60$
$2 \times 3 \times 10$ equals $2 \times (3 \times 10)$ equals $2 \times 30 = 60$

GUIDED PRACTICE

Multiply.

1. $10 \times 5 = 5\blacksquare$ **2.** $10 \times 4 \times 2 = \blacksquare 0$ **3.** 10×7 **4.** $2 \times 4 \times 10$

5. $\begin{array}{r} 10 \\ \times\ 3 \end{array}$ **6.** $\begin{array}{r} 10 \\ \times\ 6 \end{array}$ **7.** $\begin{array}{r} 20 \\ \times\ 2 \end{array}$ **8.** $\begin{array}{r} 50 \\ \times\ 9 \end{array}$ **9.** $\begin{array}{r} 30 \\ \times\ 7 \end{array}$ **10.** $\begin{array}{r} 90 \\ \times\ 4 \end{array}$

| FOCUS | Use NUMBER skills to multiply tens. |

PRACTICE

11. Count by tens to 90.

10, 20, ■, ■, ■, ■, ■, ■, ■

Multiply.

12. 6×10 13. 2×10 14. 8×10 15. 4×10 16. 3×10

17. $3 \times 3 \times 10$ 18. $2 \times 2 \times 10$ 19. $3 \times 2 \times 10$ 20. $2 \times 4 \times 10$

21. $\begin{array}{r} 10 \\ \times\ 5 \\ \hline \end{array}$ 22. $\begin{array}{r} 10 \\ \times\ 7 \\ \hline \end{array}$ 23. $\begin{array}{r} 10 \\ \times\ 9 \\ \hline \end{array}$ 24. $\begin{array}{r} 10 \\ \times\ 1 \\ \hline \end{array}$ 25. $\begin{array}{r} 40 \\ \times\ 6 \\ \hline \end{array}$ 26. $\begin{array}{r} 30 \\ \times\ 3 \\ \hline \end{array}$

27. $\begin{array}{r} 20 \\ \times\ 3 \\ \hline \end{array}$ 28. $\begin{array}{r} 50 \\ \times\ 8 \\ \hline \end{array}$ 29. $\begin{array}{r} 90 \\ \times\ 2 \\ \hline \end{array}$ 30. $\begin{array}{r} 60 \\ \times\ 7 \\ \hline \end{array}$ 31. $\begin{array}{r} 80 \\ \times\ 4 \\ \hline \end{array}$ 32. $\begin{array}{r} 70 \\ \times\ 6 \\ \hline \end{array}$

33. Barbara tied up 4 bundles of newspapers. There were 40 newspapers in each bundle. How many newspapers did Barbara have in all?

34. Terry made 7 piles of magazines. There were 10 magazines in each pile. How many magazines were there in all?

MIXED PRACTICE

Maintaining and Reviewing Skills

Multiply or divide.

35. $\begin{array}{r} 10 \\ \times\ 6 \\ \hline \end{array}$ 36. $\begin{array}{r} 50 \\ \times\ 3 \\ \hline \end{array}$ 37. $\begin{array}{r} 7 \\ \times 4 \\ \hline \end{array}$ 38. $\begin{array}{r} 3 \\ \times 9 \\ \hline \end{array}$ 39. $\begin{array}{r} 6 \\ \times 7 \\ \hline \end{array}$ 40. $\begin{array}{r} 8 \\ \times 6 \\ \hline \end{array}$

41. $36 \div 4$ 42. 6×5 43. $45 \div 9$ 44. $21 \div 7$ 45. $32 \div 8$

CHALLENGE

46. Mrs. Johnson spent 2 days tying magazines up in bundles. She made 4 bundles each day, and each bundle contained 60 magazines. How many magazines did Mrs. Johnson have in all?

MULTIPLICATION
Multiplying Tens

Tony wants to buy 7 model airplanes. Each model costs $10. How much money does Tony need to buy all 7 models?

To find how much he needs altogether, multiply: 7 × $10.

$$7 \text{ tens} = 70 \qquad 7 \times 10 = 70 \qquad \begin{array}{r} 10 \\ \times\ 7 \\ \hline 70 \end{array}$$

Tony needs $70 to buy the 7 models.

Mrs. Johnson likes to build model ships. Each of her models costs $40. She has made 6 models. How much did the models cost altogether?

$$\begin{array}{r} 4 \text{ tens} \\ \times 6 \\ \hline 24 \text{ tens} \end{array} \longrightarrow \begin{array}{r} 40 \\ \times\ 6 \\ \hline 240 \end{array} \qquad \begin{array}{r} \$40 \\ \times\ 6 \\ \hline \$240 \end{array}$$

The models cost $240 altogether.

PRACTICE

1. 3 × 10   2. 7 × 10   3. 6 × 10   4. 8 × $10   5. 5 × $10

6. $20   7. $60   8. $30   9. $90   10. $40   11. $70
   × 4   × 7   × 3   × 2   × 6   × 5

12. Sue wants to buy 10 small model cars. Each model costs $4. How much will the model cars cost in all?

13. Jack saw models of a space station and a rocket he wanted. They each cost $30. How much money would Jack need to buy the models?

MIXED PRACTICE
Maintaining and Reviewing Skills

Multiply.

14. 3 × 40   15. 2 × $70   16. 7 × 8   17. 4 × 4   18. 6 × 9

FOCUS | Use NUMBER skills to multiply tens.

APPLICATION

Using Roman Numerals

Some clock faces use Roman numerals for numbers. The Roman numerals on clock faces use the following letters.

I = 1
V = 5   VI is 5 + 1 or 6.   IV is 5 − 1 or 4.
X = 10   XI is 10 + 1 or 11.   IX is 10 − 1 or 9.

To write larger numbers, use the letters L and C.

L = 50   LX is 50 + 10 or 60.   XL is 50 − 10 or 40.
C = 100   CX is 100 + 10 or 110.   XC is 100 − 10 or 90.

To write numbers from 1 through 90 combine the letters I, V, X, L, and C.

LXI = 61   LXV = 65   LXX = 70   LXXV = 75

Write the standard number for each Roman numeral.

19. V   **20.** VII   **21.** III   **22.** IV   **23.** X   **24.** XVI

25. L   **26.** LX   **27.** LXX   **28.** XL   **29.** XXX   **30.** LV

31. XC   **32.** XX   **33.** LIII   **34.** LXXII   **35.** LXXX   **36.** LXIV

37. Count by tens from 10 to 100 using Roman numerals.
X, ■, ■, ■, ■, ■, ■, ■, ■, C

Problem Solving: Using the Five-Step Plan

Remember to READ, KNOW, PLAN, SOLVE, and CHECK all problems.

38. There are 40 calories in a cup of raspberries. How many calories are there in 3 cups?

39. There are 70 calories in an orange. How many calories are there in 2 oranges?

40. There are 60 calories in a cup of strawberries. How many calories are there in 6 cups?

41. How many calories are there in a fruit salad made with 3 oranges and 3 cups of strawberries?

Use NUMBER skills to identify and write Roman numerals.
Apply the Five-Step PROBLEM SOLVING Plan.

Using Number Sentences

There are 10 tables in Mrs. Ludlaw's restaurant. Each table can seat 4 people. How many people can Mrs. Ludlaw seat in her restaurant altogether?

Use a letter to show the missing product. Any letter can be used.

$$\text{Factor} \times \text{Factor} = \text{Product}$$
$$10 \times 4 = n$$
$$10 \times 4 = 40$$
$$n = 40$$

Mrs. Ludlaw's restaurant can seat 40 people.

The Fine Food Restaurant has 10 tables. It can seat 60 people in all. If each table seats the same number of people, how many people can sit at each table?

Use a letter to show the missing factor.

$$\begin{array}{ccc} \text{Number of} & \times & \text{People at} & = & \text{People} \\ \text{tables} & & \text{each table} & & \text{in all} \end{array}$$
$$10 \times a = 60$$
$$10 \times 6 = 60$$
$$a = 6$$

Each table can seat 6 people.

GUIDED PRACTICE

Find the missing numbers.

1. $10 \times 5 = n \quad n = 50$ **2.** $10 \times b = 20 \quad b = 2$ **3.** $10 \times 7 = b$

4. $10 \times 4 = l$ **5.** $10 \times 3 = a$ **6.** $20 \times a = 60$ **7.** $40 \times m = 80$

8. $80 \times y = 160$ **9.** $30 \times z = 90$ **10.** $20 \times d = 80$ **11.** $50 \times n = 150$

FOCUS | Use NUMBER skills to identify letters used as placeholders.

48

PRACTICE

Tell whether the letter represents a factor or a product.

12. $10 \times 3 = k$ **13.** $10 \times 2 = a$ **14.** $10 \times b = 60$ **15.** $10 \times c = 20$

16. $20 \times 6 = b$ **17.** $60 \times 5 = l$ **18.** $50 \times b = 150$ **19.** $20 \times n = 120$

Replace each letter with a number.

20. $10 \times n = 70$ **21.** $40 \times 4 = a$ **22.** $30 \times 6 = b$ **23.** $10 \times h = 80$

24. $20 \times 6 = z$ **25.** $70 \times y = 140$ **26.** $60 \times 4 = k$ **27.** $10 \times 5 = b$

Write each sentence using a letter as either a missing factor or product.

28. $10 \times 6 = 60$ **29.** $10 \times 4 = 40$ **30.** $10 \times 3 = 30$

31. $30 \times 4 = 120$ **32.** $80 \times 2 = 160$ **33.** $60 \times 6 = 360$

Write a multiplication sentence using a letter for the missing factor or product. Then solve the problem.

34. The Great Lakes Restaurant has 4 rooms. Each room has 10 tables. How many tables are there in all?

35. The Blue Moon Restaurant has 3 rooms with 60 tables in all. Each room has the same number of tables. How many tables are in each room?

MIXED PRACTICE
Maintaining and Reviewing Skills

Add, subtract, or multiply.

36. 6×70 **37.** 4×10 **38.** $8 + 6$ **39.** $15 - 7$ **40.** $7 + 5$

CHALLENGE

Find the missing numbers.

41. $36 \div y = 6$ **42.** $42 \div a = 6$ **43.** $54 \div 6 = b$

44. $35 \div 5 = n$ **45.** $k \div 3 = 4$ **46.** $49 \div 7 = g$

MULTIPLICATION
Using Number Sentences

There are 6 kinds of trees in the park. There are 4 of each kind. How many trees are there in all?

A multiplication sentence can be written to find how many in all. Any letter can be used to replace a missing number in a multiplication sentence.

$$\text{Factor} \times \text{Factor} = \text{Product}$$
$$6 \times 4 = y$$
$$6 \times 4 = 24$$

$y = 24$ There are 24 trees in all.

There are 12 trees around Mike's house. There are 4 of each kind of tree. How many kinds of trees are there?

Use a letter for the missing factor.

Number of each kind	×	Number of kinds	=	Number in all
4	×	z	=	12
4	×	3	=	12

$z = 3$ There are 3 kinds of trees.

PRACTICE

Find the missing numbers.

1. $5 \times 5 = m$
2. $6 \times 3 = c$
3. $4 \times 7 = a$
4. $6 \times 2 = z$

5. $7 \times 4 = t$
6. $9 \times 3 = a$
7. $3 \times a = 9$
8. $8 \times y = 32$

9. $8 \times y = 24$
10. $7 \times z = 49$
11. $2 \times 7 = z$
12. $5 \times n = 45$

MIXED PRACTICE
Maintaining and Reviewing Skills

Add, subtract, or multiply.

13. 8×6
14. 5×5
15. $7 + 9$
16. $14 - 6$
17. $5 + 8$

FOCUS   Use NUMBER skills to identify letters used as placeholders.

APPLICATION
Using Algebra

Look at the number pattern.

2, 4, 6, 8, 10

Each number is 2 more than the number that comes before it. The rule is add 2.

A number pattern can be written with a letter. The letter stands for the next number in the pattern. If you know the rule for the pattern, you can figure out what number the letter stands for.

3, 6, 9, 12, n 3, 6, a, 12, y

Each number is 3 more than the number that comes before it. The rule is add 3. $n = 15$ $a = 9$ $y = 15$

3, 6, 9, 12, 15   3, 6, 9, 12, 15

What is the rule for each number pattern?

What does each letter stand for?

18. 1, 2, 3, 4, z **19.** 4, 8, 12, 16, n **20.** 6, 5, 4, 3, y

21. 12, 10, m, 6, n **22.** 5, 10, a, 20, b **23.** 2, 5, 8, r, 14, s

24. 10, 20, 30, 40, a **25.** 50, 45, n, 35, 30, p **26.** 1, 6, 11, n

---

Using Mental Arithmetic

Look at the multiplication facts. See how fast you can identify the number that each letter stands for.

27. $4 \times 3 = a$ **28.** $7 \times 3 = b$ **29.** $3 \times 6 = z$ **30.** $8 \times 4 = y$

31. $5 \times n = 25$ **32.** $6 \times y = 18$ **33.** $7 \times m = 42$ **34.** $6 \times r = 54$

35. $8 \times 6 = t$ **36.** $r \times 4 = 24$ **37.** $u \times 3 = 15$ **38.** $6 \times 8 = y$

39. $6 \times 7 = y$ **40.** $8 \times b = 64$ **41.** $4 \times 9 = d$ **42.** $9 \times s = 54$

43. $4 \times c = 16$ **44.** $t \times 9 = 63$ **45.** $6 \times 3 = f$ **46.** $n \times 9 = 81$

Use ALGEBRA and MENTAL ARITHMETIC to identify letters used as placeholders.

The History of Computers

The computer is one of the most advanced and powerful tools people have ever had. But some of the ideas that make computers work are very old.

In 1801, a Frenchman named Joseph-Marie Jacquard built a machine that automatically wove cloth in different patterns. Each pattern was controlled by holes punched in a card.

In the 1830s, an English mathematician designed a calculating machine called an analytical engine. This design is considered the ancestor of the modern computer.

In 1880, an American named Herman Hollerith built another machine controlled by holes punched in cards. It was used to add up data from the United States census.

These three machines all worked without electricity. In 1944, an American mathematician named Howard Aiken built the first digital computer (a computer that works by converting information into numbers). It was made from mechanical and electrical parts. ENIAC (Electronic Numerical Integrator and Calculator) was the first all-electric digital computer. It was built in 1946 at the University of Pennsylvania. ENIAC worked with vacuum tubes. It took up almost an entire building.

In 1948, transistors were invented. Transistors were smaller, less expensive, and more reliable than vacuum tubes. Computers that could do more and that cost less money were built.

In the 1970s, tiny integrated circuit chips made from thousands of transistors were invented. Integrated circuit chips made computers even smaller, more powerful, and cheaper.

The latest advance is the personal computer. Personal computers are small enough to fit on a desk, but they can work thousands of times faster and do much bigger jobs than ENIAC.

CRITICAL THINKING

1. How old an idea is the computer?

2. Are smaller computers better than larger ones? Why?

3. What are some of the differences between ENIAC and a personal computer?

FOCUS | Use LOGIC to understand differences between computers.

The ENIAC computer contained about 18,000 vacuum tubes. A later computer built in the 1950s was called UNIVAC.

Student volunteers work with small computers in a hospital. Many hundreds of these could fit in the space taken by ENIAC.

LOOKING BACK
Reviewing and Testing Chapter 4

In Chapter 4 you formulated problems about a cattle roundup. Look at pages 42 and 43.

1. Write a sentence telling how you decided the roundup would end.

You learned about multiplying tens. To review what you learned, study the sample exercises on pages 44 and 46. Then use these skills to find each product for examples 2–13.

2. 10×3 **3.** 7×10 **4.** $5 \times \$10$ **5.** $3 \times 2 \times 10$

6. $\begin{array}{r} 10 \\ \times\ 2 \\ \hline \end{array}$ **7.** $\begin{array}{r} 10 \\ \times\ 8 \\ \hline \end{array}$ **8.** $\begin{array}{r} 40 \\ \times\ 2 \\ \hline \end{array}$ **9.** $\begin{array}{r} 80 \\ \times\ 3 \\ \hline \end{array}$ **10.** $\begin{array}{r} \$20 \\ \times\ 9 \\ \hline \end{array}$ **11.** $\begin{array}{r} \$70 \\ \times\ 6 \\ \hline \end{array}$

12. Calvin put 30 boxes of pens on each of 3 shelves. How many boxes of pens were there in all?

13. Karen bought 3 sweaters. Each sweater cost $20. How much did the sweaters cost in all?

You learned how to use letters as placeholders in multiplication sentences. To review, look at pages 48 and 50. Find the missing numbers for exercises 14–21.

14. $10 \times 9 = a$ **15.** $90 \times 1 = b$ **16.** $5 \times 3 = p$ **17.** $8 \times 9 = m$

18. $10 \times m = 60$ **19.** $70 \times r = 350$ **20.** $2 \times n = 18$ **21.** $6 \times y = 48$

You learned about the history of computers. To review look at pages 52 and 53.

22. What are some of the differences between vacuum tubes and transistors?

23. Do personal computers work with vacuum tubes, transistors, or integrated circuit chips?

| FOCUS | Review and test skills learned and practiced. |

In the next chapter, you will focus on

- formulating problems about organizing a July 4th festival.
- identifying polygons.
- using logic.
- identifying line segments, lines, rays, and lines of symmetry.
- using measurement.

New geometry skills will be easier to learn if you brush up on geometry skills you already know.

First, study the geometry facts below. Then complete exercises 1–6.

A triangle has 3 sides and 3 angles.

A quadrilateral has 4 sides and 4 angles.

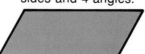

A pentagon has 5 sides and 5 angles.

A hexagon has 6 sides and 6 angles.

An octagon has 8 sides and 8 angles.

PRACTICE

Name each shape.

1.

2.
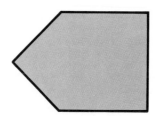

3.
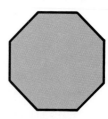

4.

5.

6.

Review GEOMETRY in preparation for learning a new skill.

CHAPTER 5

Geometry

DATA

Event	July 4th Festival
Number of guests	240

Food needed
Pounds of

Potato salad	60
Cole slaw	60
Chicken	120
Fruit salad	40

Beverages needed
Gallons of

Iced tea	30
Juice	40
Paper plates	500
Paper napkins	300
Plastic forks and spoons	500

The 4th of July, Independence Day, is a time for Americans to celebrate. In big cities and small towns across the country, people gather in backyards and in town squares. They often plan events such as parties or festivals. A festival is fun to attend, but it takes a great deal of planning for a festival to succeed!

Businesspeople in the town of Kingston have been planning a festival for several months. Last year, about twice as many people as were expected actually came to the festival. This created some problems that the planners want to avoid this year.

Use the picture and the data to find out what the festival organizers must do to make this special day a success. Decide what problems they might face.

GEOMETRY
Identifying Polygons

A **polygon** is a flat, closed figure with straight sides.

These figures are polygons.

 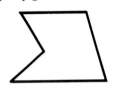 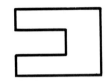 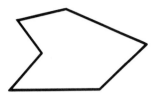

These figures are not polygons.

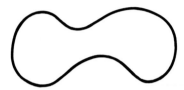 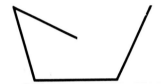 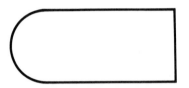

Where two sides of any polygon meet they form a **vertex.** Every polygon has several vertices.

Some polygons have special names.

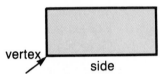

vertex   side

Triangle   Square   Hexagon   Octagon
3 sides   4 sides   6 sides   8 sides
3 vertices   4 vertices   6 vertices   8 vertices

GUIDED PRACTICE

Write *yes* if the figure is a polygon. Write *no* if the figure is not a polygon.

1.    2.    3. 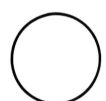   4.

no

FOCUS   Use GEOMETRY to identify polygons.

58

PRACTICE

On a piece of paper, write *yes* if the figure is a polygon.
Write *no* if the figure is not a polygon.

5.

6.

7.

8.

9.

10.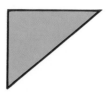

11.

12.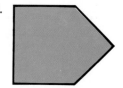

Tell how many sides and vertices each of these polygons
has.

13.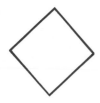

14.

15.

16.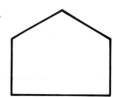

MIXED PRACTICE

Maintaining and Reviewing Skills

Add, subtract, multiply, or divide.

17. 7×6 18. $17 - 9$ 19. $4 + 8$ 20. $36 \div 4$ 21. $14 - 8$

22. $5 + 8$ 23. $21 \div 7$ 24. 5×5 25. 3×8 26. $56 \div 8$

CHALLENGE

27. Draw the figure at the right on a
piece of paper. Next use a ruler to
draw straight lines from vertex to
vertex to form triangles. Then cut
along each line. How many
triangles are there?

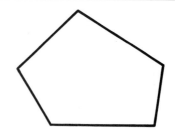

GEOMETRY
Identifying Polygons

Polygons are flat, closed figures with straight sides. The sides of a polygon never cross each other and are never curved. By putting several polygons together, you can make other polygons.

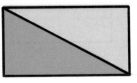 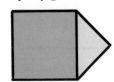 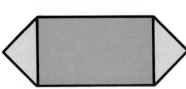 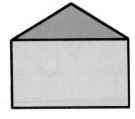

2 triangles   1 square   2 triangles   1 rectangle
                 1 triangle   1 rectangle   1 triangle

PRACTICE

Name the shapes that make up these polygons.

1.
2.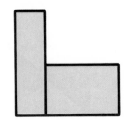
3.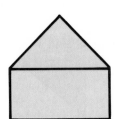
4.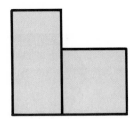

5.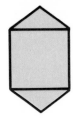
6.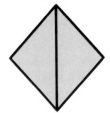
7.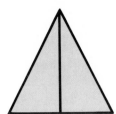
8.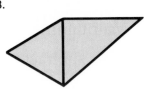

MIXED PRACTICE
Maintaining and Reviewing Skills

Name these polygons.

9.
10.
11.
12.

FOCUS   Use GEOMETRY to identify polygons.

APPLICATION

Using Logic

One way to organize figures is to use a **Venn Diagram.** A Venn Diagram is made from two overlapping circles. One kind of figure goes in the left circle. Another kind of figure goes in the right circle. Figures that combine shapes from the kinds of figures in the left and right circles go in the middle.

Left   Middle   Right

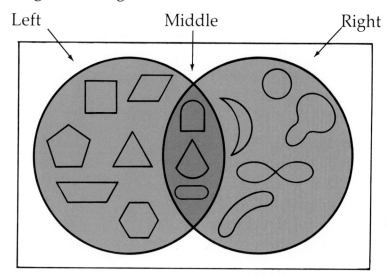

13. What kinds of figures are in the left circle?

14. What kinds of figures are in the right circle?

15. What kinds of figures are in the middle?

16. Where would you put a rectangle?

17. Make a Venn Diagram that shows triangles in one circle, rectangles in the other circle, and figures made from rectangles and triangles in the middle.

Solving Problems

18. Stephanie lives in the country. She has a pool with 6 sides in her backyard. The sides meet to form 6 vertices. What is this special polygon called?

19. Chris has some money in his pocket. He takes out a quarter. He sees that it is a curved figure with no vertices. Can this figure be called a polygon?

Use LOGIC to understand and draw Venn Diagrams.
Use NUMBER skills to solve problems.

Identifying Lines and Line Segments

A **line segment** is always straight and has two **endpoints.**

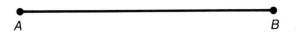

Write: $\overline{AB}$ Read: line segment AB
   or   or
   $\overline{BA}$ line segment BA

Each edge of this rectangle is a line segment. These line segments have names: $\overline{AB}$, $\overline{BD}$, $\overline{CD}$, $\overline{AC}$.

Lines and line segments that go straight across are **horizontal**. Line segments AB and CD are horizontal. Lines and line segments that go straight up and down are **vertical**. Line segments BD and AC are vertical.

A part of a line with one endpoint is called a **ray**. A ray goes on forever in one direction.

A **line** has no endpoints and goes on forever in both directions.

Write: $\overleftrightarrow{CD}$ Read: line CD
   or   or
   $\overleftrightarrow{DC}$ line DC

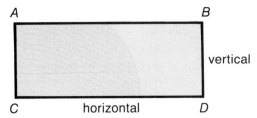

Write: $\overrightarrow{AB}$ Read: ray AB
Name the endpoint first.

GUIDED PRACTICE

Is each a line segment? Write *yes* or *no*.

1.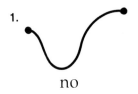
no

2.

3.

4.

Which are vertical lines and which are horizontal lines?

5.
vertical line

6.

7.

8.

FOCUS | Use GEOMETRY to identify lines, line segments, and rays.

PRACTICE

Name each line segment.

9.
   x   y

10.
    R
    S

11.
    M
    N

Name each line.

12.
    B
    A

13.
    P   Q

14.
    E
    F

Name each ray.

15.
    T   U

16.
    G
    H

17.
    K
    J

How many line segments form each polygon?

18.

19.

20.

21.

MIXED PRACTICE

Maintaining and Reviewing Skills

Multiply or divide.

22. 6×4 **23.** $42 \div 7$ **24.** $64 \div 8$ **25.** 3×9 **26.** 6×6

27. $56 \div 8$ **28.** 4×5 **29.** $72 \div 9$ **30.** 8×4 **31.** $40 \div 5$

CHALLENGE

32. Look at the figure at the right. How many vertical line segments are there? How many horizontal line segments are there? How many line segments are there in all?

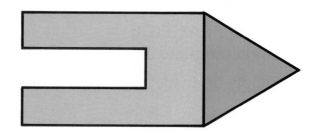

GEOMETRY
Identifying Lines of Symmetry

What happens if this polygon is folded along the dotted vertical line? The two parts match. One part fits exactly over the other part.

A figure is **symmetric** when it can be folded so that both parts match exactly. The line along the fold is called the **line of symmetry.**

What happens if this polygon is folded along the dotted horizontal line? The two parts do not match. The dotted horizontal line is not a line of symmetry.

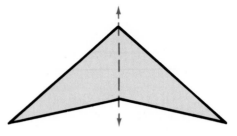

Line of symmetry

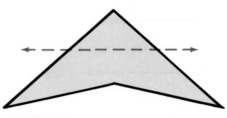

Not a line of symmetry

PRACTICE

Is the green line a line of symmetry? Write *yes* or *no*.

1.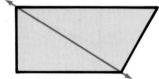

2.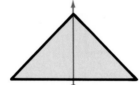

3.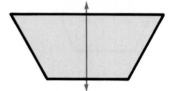

Some figures have more than one line of symmetry. How many lines of symmetry do these polygons have?

4.

5.

6.

MIXED PRACTICE
Maintaining and Reviewing Skills

Multiply or divide.

7. 9×6 **8.** $45 \div 9$ **9.** 3×4 **10.** 7×9 **11.** $36 \div 4$

FOCUS | Use GEOMETRY to identify lines of symmetry.

APPLICATION

Using Measurement

The red line segments in this pattern are horizontal. The blue line segments are vertical. The horizontal line segments are 3 centimeters long. The vertical line segments are 4 centimeters long.

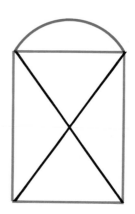

Look at each figure. What color are the vertical line segments? How many centimeters long are they? What color are the horizontal line segments? How many centimeters long are they?

12.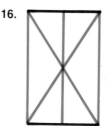

13.

14.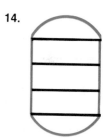

15.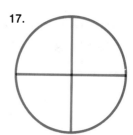

16.

17.

Solving Problems

18. What does a jump rope form when 2 children stretch it straight across as far as it will go? What are the endpoints?

19. A rectangle has 2 horizontal and 2 vertical sides. Each side has 2 endpoints. Are these sides called line segments or rays?

Use GEOMETRY to identify and measure vertical and horizontal line segments.

In Chapter 5 you formulated problems about planning a Fourth of July festival. Look at pages 56 and 57.

1. Write a sentence telling what you suggest the organizers do to make the festival a success.

You learned something new about identifying polygons. To review what you learned, study the sample exercises on pages 58 and 60. Then use these skills to write *yes* or *no* to tell if each figure in exercises 2 to 5 is a polygon. For exercises 6 to 9, name the shapes that go together to make each polygon.

2.

3.

4.

5.

6.

7.

8.

9.

You learned something new about line segments, lines, rays, and lines of symmetry. To review, look at pages 62 and 64. Name each figure for exercises 10 to 13. For exercises 14 to 17, write *yes* or *no* to tell if each green line is a line of symmetry.

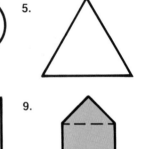

10.   *A*   *B*

11.   *C*   *D*

12.   *F*   *E*

13.   *G*   *H*

14.

15.

16.

17.

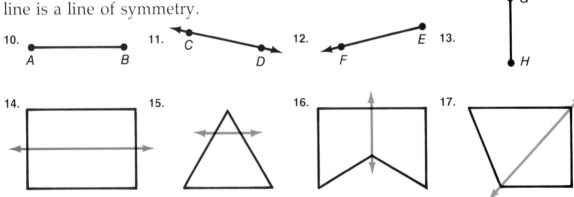

FOCUS | Review and test skills learned and practiced.

LOOKING AHEAD
Preparing for New Skills for Chapter 6

In the next chapter, you will focus on

- formulating problems about a Ping-Pong match.
- recognizing and comparing place values through ten thousands.
- using statistics and probability.

- rounding 5-digit numbers to the nearest ten, hundred, and thousand.
- how math is used in music.

Learning about place value will be easier if you review what you already know. Study the examples below. Then complete exercises 1–10.

How many thousands, hundreds, tens, and ones are in 6,743?

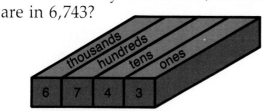

There are 6 thousands in 6,743.
There are 7 hundreds in 6,743.
There are 4 tens in 6,743.
There are 3 ones in 6,743.

Round 1,632 to the nearest hundred.

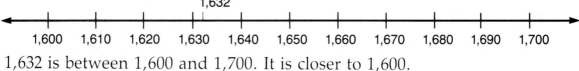

1,632 is between 1,600 and 1,700. It is closer to 1,600.
1,632 rounds down to 1,600. 1,632 is about 1,600.

Numbers that are halfway between (like 1,650) or greater, always round up.

PRACTICE

Answer these questions.

1. How many hundreds are in 2,354? 2. How many tens are in 1,624?

3. How many thousands are in 6,469? 4. How many ones are in 3,216?

Round to the nearest hundred.

5. 7,893   6. 4,213   7. 8,734   8. 3,587   9. 1,263   10. 5,828

Review NUMBER skills in preparation for learning a new skill.

FOCUS Formulate problems using picture cues, text, and data.

6

Place Value

DATA

Game	Ping-Pong
Event	Title match
Players	Mel Santiago
	Luisa Ortiz
Points needed to win a game	21
Points scored so far	
Mel	18
Luisa	11
Games needed for title	3 out of 5
Games won so far	
Mel	2
Luisa	1
Games played earlier in day	
Mel	9
Luisa	15

A small, lightweight ball flies back and forth over a net. Each player is ready to move fast. The game is Ping-Pong. The picture shows you that a player must be alert, or he or she may lose a point.

As you can see from the data, Mel Santiago and Luisa Ortiz are playing each other for a title match. Think about how this match might end. What difficulties might each player face? How would you describe the Ping-Pong match so far? Using the picture and the data, predict who will win the title.

Writing Numbers to 999,999

Erin knows that light travels one hundred eighty-six thousand miles in a second. How can she write this number?

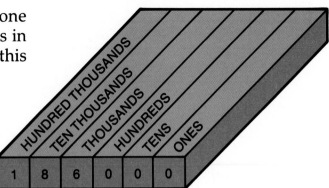

In 186,000

the 1 means	1 hundred thousand	or	100,000 ⎫
the 8 means	8 ten thousands	or	80,000 ⎬ expanded form
the 6 means	6 thousands	or	+ 6,000 ⎭
			186,000 standard form

Use a comma when there are 4 digits or more.

A place value chart can help you read and write numbers in standard and expanded form.

GUIDED PRACTICE

Write the standard numbers.

1. twenty-three thousand, four hundred twenty-six   23,426

2. six hundred thirty thousand, two hundred fifty   63■,2■0

3. forty-five thousand, three hundred sixty-five

4. seven hundred thousand, five hundred seventy-one

5. ninety-two thousand, eight hundred seventy-six

6. three hundred sixty thousand, four hundred twenty

7. 200,000 + 3,000 + 500 + 60 + 8   8. 100,000 + 3,000 + 200 + 40 + 1

FOCUS	Use NUMBER skills to recognize place value.

PRACTICE

Read each number. Tell the place value of the colored digits.

9. 12,465   10. 473,895   11. 20,436   12. 45,601   13. 839,954

14. 43,892   15. 30,048   16. 34,287   17. 80,593   18. 67,309

Write the standard numbers.

19. four hundred thirty-two thousand, four hundred twenty-six

20. seventy thousand, six hundred thirty-three

21. seven hundred eighty-two thousand, five hundred twenty

22. forty-one thousand, two hundred thirteen

23. nine hundred ninety-nine thousand, six hundred eighty-nine

24. 30,000 + 1,000 + 400 + 20 + 5   25. 100,000 + 30,000 + 2,000 + 70 + 6

26. 900,000 + 30,000 + 800 + 30 + 2   27. 40,000 + 5,000 + 100 + 30 + 1

Write the words.

28. 32,461   29. 269,573   30. 527,978   31. 177,290   32. 30,460

MIXED PRACTICE
Maintaining and Reviewing Skills

Write > or <.

33. 19 ● 24   34. 31 ● 27   35. 58 ● 56   36. 73 ● 80

37. 48 ● 49   38. 356 ● 563   39. 721 ● 698   40. 619 ● 640

CHALLENGE

41. How much is 100 more than 23,785?

42. How much is 1,000 more than 62,896?

43. How much is 100,000 more than 36,893?

44. How much is 200,000 more than 12,684?

PLACE VALUE
Comparing 5-Digit Numbers

Which is greater, 23,756 or 23,542?

First look at the ten-thousands place. The digits are the same.
Next look at the thousands place. The digits are the same.
Next look at the hundreds place.
7 hundred is greater than 5 hundred.

     23,756 is greater than 23,542.
        23,756 > 23,542

Which is less, 47,514 or 42,541?

First look at the ten-thousands place. The digits are the same.
Then look at the thousands place.
2 thousand is less than 7 thousand.

     42,541 is less than 47,514.
        42,541 < 47,514

The < or > always points to the smaller number.

PRACTICE

Write < or >.

1. 23,784 ● 23,257
2. 17,634 ● 17,665
3. 40,783 ● 40,789

4. 68,673 ● 58,742
5. 99,632 ● 92,635
6. 12,087 ● 12,487

Put each group of numbers in order from greatest to least.

7. 24,783   26,978   21,563   27,280
8. 12,756   16,386   10,392   13,582

Put each group of numbers in order from least to greatest.

9. 56,835   56,396   56,923   56,525
10. 81,863   81,882   81,734   83,965

MIXED PRACTICE
Maintaining and Reviewing Skills

Put each group of numbers in order from least to greatest.

11. 7,643   7,634   7,392   7,041
12. 463   436   407   639

FOCUS | Use NUMBER skills to recognize place value and compare numbers.

APPLICATION

Using Statistics and Probability

The table below shows how many people several baseball stadiums can seat.

Stadium	City	Seating
National League		
Astrodome	Houston, Texas	45,000
Dodger Stadium	Los Angeles, California	56,000
Wrigley Field	Chicago, Illinois	37,272
American League		
Comiskey Park	Chicago, Illinois	43,695
Fenway Park	Boston, Massachusetts	33,465
Memorial Stadium	Baltimore, Maryland	53,208
Tiger Stadium	Detroit, Michigan	52,806

You can order the National League stadiums by the number of seats they have from least to greatest.

First, order the numbers from least to greatest.

37,272	45,000	56,000
↓	↓	↓
Wrigley Field	Astrodome	Dodger Stadium

Then, you can order the stadiums.

The order of the stadiums by the number of seats from least to greatest is Wrigley Field, the Astrodome, and Dodger Stadium.

13. Rewrite the table listing the American League stadiums in order, by the number of seats, from greatest to least.

Exploring With a Calculator

Use your calculator and the table below to answer Exercises 14 to 16.

14. How many seconds are there in 1 hour?

15. How many hours are there in 1 week?

16. How many months are there in 3 years?

60 seconds = 1 minute
60 minutes = 1 hour
24 hours = 1 day
7 days = 1 week
12 months = 1 year
52 weeks = 1 year

Use STATISTICS AND PROBABILITY to recognize place value and order numbers.
Use a CALCULATOR to find equivalent measures of time.

Rounding

There are 31,646 people living in Bangor, Maine. To the nearest ten, about how many people live in Bangor, Maine?

Round a number to find **about** how many.
Round 31,646 to the nearest ten.

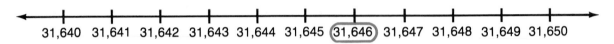

31,646 is between 31,640 and 31,650.
It is closer to 31,650.
31,646 rounds up to 31,650.
31,646 rounded to the nearest ten is 31,650.
31,646 can also be rounded to the nearest hundred.

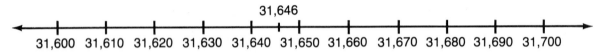

31,646 is between 31,600 and 31,700.
It is closer to 31,600.
31,646 rounds down to 31,600.
31,646 rounded to the nearest hundred is 31,600.

When a number comes halfway between two tens or two hundreds, round up.

28,350 is halfway between 28,300 and 28,400.
28,350 rounded to the nearest hundred is 28,400.

GUIDED PRACTICE

Round to the nearest ten.

1. 21,537   21,540   2. 37,742   3. 52,539   4. 46,523

Round to the nearest hundred.

5. 61,869   61,900   6. 27,542   7. 41,767   8. 34,736

| FOCUS | Use NUMBER skills to round 5-digit numbers to the nearest ten and the nearest hundred. |

PRACTICE

Use the number line to round the numbers down to 23,140 or up to 23,150.

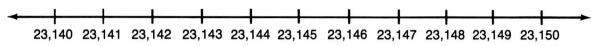

9. 23,146   **10.** 23,142   **11.** 23,145   **12.** 23,147   **13.** 23,141   **14.** 23,144

Use the number line to round the numbers down to 35,700 or up to 35,800.

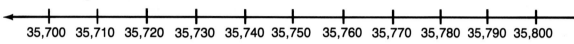

15. 35,798   **16.** 35,750   **17.** 35,710   **18.** 35,746   **19.** 35,787   **20.** 35,723

Round to the nearest ten.

21. 27,624   **22.** 13,519   **23.** 78,454   **24.** 56,175

Round to the nearest hundred.

25. 45,293   **26.** 91,352   **27.** 69,824   **28.** 23,636

29. There are 39,734 people living in Idaho Falls, Idaho. To the nearest ten, about how many people live in Idaho Falls?

30. There are 65,852 people living in Alameda, California. To the nearest hundred, about how many people live in Alameda?

MIXED PRACTICE
Maintaining and Reviewing Skills

Round to the nearest hundred.

31. 56,734   **32.** 4,524   **33.** 315   **34.** 651

Tell the place value of the colored digits.

35. 43,605   **36.** 65,728   **37.** 34,907   **38.** 71,564   **39.** 16,435

CHALLENGE

40. Write a number that rounds down to 45,670 but rounds up to 45,700.

41. Write a number that rounds up to 24,530 but rounds down to 24,500.

PLACE VALUE
Rounding

The passenger ship *Queen Elizabeth II* weighs 67,139 tons. To the nearest thousand, about how much does the *Queen Elizabeth II* weigh?

Round to find about how much.
Round 67,139 to the nearest thousand.

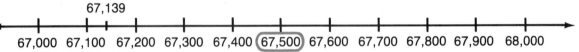

67,139 is between 67,000 and 68,000.
It is closer to 67,000.
67,139 rounds down to 67,000.
Rounded to the nearest thousand, the *Queen Elizabeth II* weighs 67,000 tons.

When a number comes halfway between two thousands it always rounds up. The number 67,500 is halfway between 67,000 and 68,000. It rounds up to 68,000.

PRACTICE

Use the number line to round to the nearest thousand.

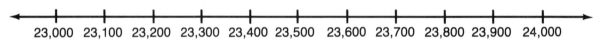

1. 23,674   2. 23,867   3. 23,143   4. 23,368   5. 23,500   6. 23,561

7. The passenger ship *Norway* weighs 70,202 tons. To the nearest thousand, about how much does the *Norway* weigh?

8. The merchant ship *Louisiana* weighs 83,743 tons. To the nearest thousand, about how much does the *Louisiana* weigh?

MIXED PRACTICE
Maintaining and Reviewing Skills

Round each number to the nearest ten, nearest hundred, and nearest thousand.

9. 41,289   10. 15,784   11. 89,354   12. 3,887   13. 8,532   14. 65,243

FOCUS | Use NUMBER skills to round 5-digit numbers to the nearest thousand.

APPLICATION

Using Statistics and Probability

This bar graph shows the populations of several United States cities.

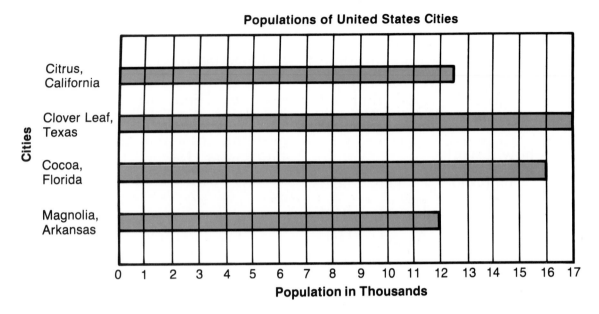

Populations of United States Cities

Look at the numbers along the bottom of the bar graph. They name thousands. The 1 stands for 1,000. The 8 stands for 8,000. The 14 stands for 14,000.

To find the population of Citrus, California, follow these steps:

Step 1: Find the city name in the left column.

Step 2: Move your finger to the end of the bar.

Step 3: Follow the line at the end of the bar to the number at the bottom of the graph.

The population of Citrus, California, is about 12,500.

Use the bar graph to answer these questions.

15. What is the population of Cocoa, Florida?

16. What is the population of Magnolia, Arkansas?

17. Which city has the largest population? How large is it?

18. List the cities in order of their population from smallest to largest.

Use STATISTICS AND PROBABILITY to use information from a bar graph.

Music for Marching

People who write music and those who play it use numbers for every note, beat, measure, and time signature. Each of these elements has a certain number value that all musicians know.

Here is how it works:

If a half note 𝅗𝅥 gets 2 beats

then a quarter note 𝅘𝅥 gets 1 beat

and an eighth note 𝅘𝅥𝅮 gets $\frac{1}{2}$ beat.

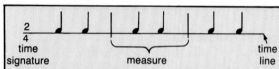

A **time signature** is placed at the beginning of the time line. It looks like a fraction. The top number tells how many beats there are in each measure. The bottom number tells what kind of note gets one beat (in this example, a quarter note).

Music for marching has a strong, steady beat. Each group of two beats is called a **measure**. The bass drum may play only the first beat in each measure—the *stressed*, or more important beat:

"*Left—, Left—, Left—*"
written in half notes:

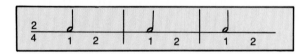

"Yankee Doodle," a popular marching tune, is written below in music notation. The two words, "Yan-kee Doo-dle" fit into one measure. There are four syllables in each measure. Four syllables must fit into two beats, so an eighth note 𝅘𝅥𝅮 is used.

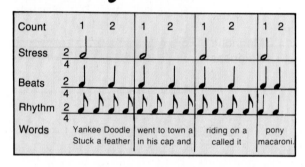

CRITICAL THINKING

1. Name these notes: 𝅗𝅥 𝅘𝅥 𝅘𝅥𝅮 and tell how many beats each gets in $\frac{2}{4}$ time.

2. What is the meaning of the time signature $\frac{2}{4}$?

3. Tap the beats of "Yankee Doodle" while you sing the words. Then clap only the stressed notes while you sing the words.

4. You know how many beats a half note 𝅗𝅥 gets in $\frac{2}{4}$ time. How many does a whole note 𝅝 get?

FOCUS   Use NUMBER skills to understand music for marching.

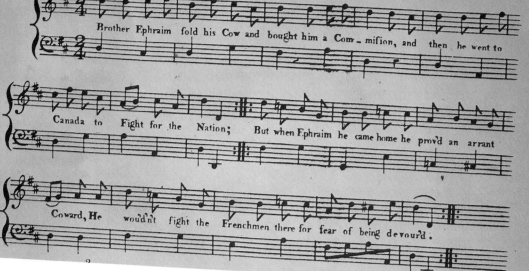

The patriotic spirit of the new country is heard in the song "Yankee Doodle" and shown in this Archibald Willard painting "The Spirit of '76".

Reviewing and Testing Chapter 6

In Chapter 6 you formulated problems about a Ping-Pong title match. Look at pages 68 and 69.

1. Write a sentence telling how you predicted who would win the title.

You learned about naming and comparing larger numbers. To review what you learned, study the sample exercises on pages 70 and 72. Then use these skills to write each standard number for exercises 2 to 5. For exercises 6 to 8, write > or <.

2. two hundred fifty-seven thousand, seventeen

3. eighty-one thousand, six hundred twenty-three

4. 600,000 + 5,000 + 100 + 20 + 7   5. 10,000 + 9,000 + 400 + 10 + 1

6. 72,843 ● 72,743   7. 84,105 ● 48,501   8. 37,071 ● 37,710

You learned about rounding numbers. To review, look at pages 74 and 76. Round each number to the nearest ten, to the nearest hundred, and to the nearest thousand for exercises 9 to 12.

9. 31,627   10. 58,451   11. 13,528   12. 75,365

You learned about music for marching. Look at pages 78 and 79 to review the meanings of note, beat, measure, and time signature.

13. A time signature looks like a fraction. What do the top and bottom numbers tell you?

| FOCUS | Review and test skills learned and practiced. |

LOOKING AHEAD

Preparing for New Skills for Chapter 7

In the next chapter, you will focus on

- formulating problems about an outdoor concert.
- adding 3-digit numbers.
- using patterns and functions.
- using a problem-solving strategy.
- subtracting 3-digit numbers.
- checking subtraction.
- using measurement.

New addition and subtraction skills will be easier if you brush up on addition and subtraction skills you already know. First review Models A and B. Then complete exercises 1–14.

Model A

To find how many in all, add.

Add the ones. Regroup.			Add the tens.	
T	O		T	O
1			1	
3	5	5	3	5
+2	8	+8	+2	8
	3	13	6	3

Model B

To find the difference, subtract.

Regroup.		Subtract the ones.		Subtract the tens.	
T	O	T	O	T	O
4	13	4	13	4	13
5	3	5	3	5	3
−2	6	−2	6	−2	6
			7	2	7

PRACTICE

Add. Use Model A.

1.	2.	3.	4.	5.	6.	7.
43 +28	56 +17	72 +19	47 +28	39 +28	28 +25	65 +26

Subtract. Use Model B.

8.	9.	10.	11.	12.	13.	14.
76 −58	34 −19	93 −65	64 −38	53 −27	31 −13	62 −43

Review NUMBER skills in preparation for learning a new skill.

FOCUS | Formulate problems using picture cues, text, and data.

CHAPTER 7

Addition and Subtraction of Whole Numbers

DATA

Event	Free music concerts
Place	Town of Huntington
How often	Once every 3 weeks

Type of music	Number of people attending last year
Classical	1,500
Jazz	2,500
Rock	1,500
Popular	150

Number of chairs for seating	1,500

A free concert is a time to enjoy music and a place to have fun with friends and family. Some towns and cities present free concerts. The concerts may appeal to fans of opera or of rock music. They may present popular performers or local musicians.

The town of Huntington is going to offer another summer of free concerts. Last year, there were four concerts. The concert organizers are trying to learn from that experience.

Using the picture and the data, decide what lessons the concert organizers can learn about presenting free concerts. What are some of the problems? What decisions can the town of Huntington make to help this summer's free concerts succeed?

Adding 3-Digit Numbers

Mr. Burton has a book store. He sold 245 books in January. He sold 132 books in February. How many books did Mr. Burton sell in all?

To find how many books he sold in all, add: 245 + 132.

Add the ones.

```
 H | T | O
 2 | 4 | 5
+1 | 3 | 2
   |   | 7
```

Add the tens.

```
 H | T | O
 2 | 4 | 5
+1 | 3 | 2
   | 7 | 7
```

Add the hundreds.

```
 H | T | O
 2 | 4 | 5
+1 | 3 | 2
 3 | 7 | 7
```

Mr. Burton sold 377 books in all.

In March Mr. Burton sold 356 books. In April he sold 275 books. How many books did Mr. Burton sell in March and April altogether?

To find how many books he sold altogether, add: 356 + 275.

Add the ones. Regroup.

```
 H | T  | O
    | 1  |
 3 | 5  | 6        6
+2 | 7  | 5      + 5
    |    | 1      1 1
```

Add the tens. Regroup.

```
 H  | T | O
 1  | 1 |
 3  | 5 | 6       1T
+2  | 7 | 5       5T
    | 3 | 1     + 7T
                1 3T
```

Add the hundreds.

```
 1 | 1 |
 H | T | O
 3 | 5 | 6       1 H
+2 | 7 | 5       3 H
 6 | 3 | 1     + 2 H
               6 H
```

Mr. Burton sold 631 books in March and April.

GUIDED PRACTICE

Add. Remember to regroup if necessary.

		1 1		11							
1.	432	2.	547	3.	487	4.	534	5.	473	6.	754
	+153		+825		+256		+ 59		+ 68		+127
	585		1,172		113		593				

7.	567	8.	589	9.	635	10.	536	11.	783	12.	539
	+258		+308		+296		+390		+458		+875

FOCUS | Use NUMBER skills to add 3-digit numbers with and without regrouping.

PRACTICE

Add.

13. 143 $+125$	14. 157 $+116$	15. 264 $+157$	16. 372 $+485$	17. 518 $+194$	18. 859 $+248$

19. 345 $+\ 38$	20. 539 $+\ 27$	21. 435 $+\ 48$	22. 547 $+\ 86$	23. 868 $+\ 95$	24. 958 $+121$

25. 874 $+125$	26. 526 $+257$	27. 547 $+216$	28. 467 $+253$	29. 856 $+829$	30. 468 $+675$

31. 248 + 362 **32.** 716 + 159 **33.** 437 + 367 **34.** 296 + 354

35. 636 + 297 **36.** 342 + 399 **37.** 838 + 192 **38.** 762 + 376

39. Mr. Burton ordered 143 new books in the first half of the year. He ordered 278 new books in the second half of the year. How many new books did Mr. Burton order in all?

40. Mr. Burton had 278 customers in March. He had 345 customers in April. How many customers did Mr. Burton have in all in March and April?

MIXED PRACTICE

Maintaining and Reviewing Skills

Add or subtract.

41. 346 $+235$	42. 604 $+298$	43. 76 -25	44. 54 $+19$	45. 64 -36	46. 47 -38

47. 97 − 28 **48.** 35 + 85 **49.** 83 − 46 **50.** 82 + 19

CHALLENGE

Find the missing digits.

51. 45█ $+135$ 589	52. 482 $+22█$ 706	53. 543 $+34█$ 892	54. 85█ $+134$ 991	55. 62█ $+348$ 976	56. 752 $+14█$ 901

EXTRA PRACTICE—page 445

ADDITION
Adding Three 3-Digit Numbers

Add: 239 + 120 + 175

Add the ones.
Regroup.

H	T	O
	①	
2	3	9
1	2	0
+1	7	5
		4

9
0
+5
①4

Add the tens.
Regroup.

H	T	O
①	1	
2	3	9
1	2	0
+1	7	5
	3	4

1T
3T
2T
+7T
①3T

Add the hundreds.

H	T	O
1	1	
2	3	9
1	2	0
+1	7	5
5	3	4

1 H
2 H
1 H
+1 H
5 H

PRACTICE

Add.

1. 325 132 +321	2. 421 235 +142	3. 523 241 + 28	4. 645 231 + 67	5. 683 136 +103	6. 432 254 +178
7. 635 154 +112	8. 534 329 + 74	9. 423 286 +153	10. 231 211 +209	11. 414 308 +297	12. 560 805 +190

13. Mary picked 134 pears, 254 peaches, and 205 apples. How many pieces of fruit did Mary pick in all?

14. George packed 125 crates of strawberries, 239 crates of raspberries, and 321 crates of blueberries. How many crates did George pack in all?

MIXED PRACTICE
Maintaining and Reviewing Skills

Add or subtract.

15. 416 162 +240	16. 305 476 +164	17. 65 −18	18. 456 +297	19. 31 −26	20. 58 −29

21. 887 + 465   22. 86 − 18   23. 49 + 26   24. 75 − 37   25. 58 + 19

FOCUS   Use NUMBER skills to add three 3-digit numbers.

86

APPLICATION

Using Patterns and Functions

One way to check addition is by casting out 9s.

To cast out 9s from a number, add the digits in the number.

$$347 \longrightarrow 3 + 4 + 7 = 14$$

If the sum is greater than 9, add the digits again.

$$14 \longrightarrow 1 + 4 = 5$$

Continue adding until you reach a single digit.

Here's how to check addition by casting out 9s. Keep casting out 9s until all the numbers are single digits.

$$327 \longrightarrow 3 + 2 + 7 = 12 \longrightarrow 1 + 2 = 3$$
$$256 \longrightarrow 2 + 5 + 6 = 13 \longrightarrow 1 + 3 = 4$$
$$+175 \longrightarrow 1 + 7 + 5 = 13 \longrightarrow 1 + 3 = +4$$
$$758 \longrightarrow 7 + 5 + 8 = 20 \longrightarrow 2 \qquad 11 \longrightarrow 2$$

These two numbers should be the same. If they are not, the answer is wrong.

Add. Check the addition by casting out 9s.

26.	27.	28.	29.	30.
463	327	645	536	645
132	109	198	234	143
+234	+231	+102	+113	+203

Estimating Sums

To **estimate,** round each addend to the nearest hundred. Then add the rounded numbers.

$$89 + 252 + 549 \qquad \text{Estimate}$$
$$\downarrow \qquad \downarrow \qquad \downarrow \qquad \downarrow$$
$$100 + 300 + 500 = 900$$

Estimate. Then find the exact sum.

31. $538 + 206$ 32. $158 + 149$ 33. $117 + 796$ 34. $77 + 486 + 209$

35. $267 + 284$ 36. $505 + 198$ 37. $626 + 319$ 38. $28 + 335 + 555$

Use NUMBER skills to check addition by casting out 9s.
Use NUMBER skills to estimate sums.

The first two steps of the problem-solving plan, READ and KNOW, are important. You must understand a problem before you can solve it. Find the **key facts** in this lesson. Do not solve the problems.

1. READ A Venus day is equal to 120 Earth days. It takes Venus 225 Earth days to revolve around the sun. How many Earth days are there in 7 Venus days?

Ask yourself: Do I know the meaning of each word? Do I understand all the kinds of facts that are given?

2. KNOW Ask yourself: What am I being asked to find? Which **key facts** do I need?

Sometimes, problems have extra information which is interesting but is not needed. It is important to separate the **key facts** from the unnecessary information. Making a table such as the one below will help you.

Facts I Know	What I Need to Find	Key Fact
1 Venus day = 120 Earth days Venus takes 225 Earth days to revolve around sun	number of Earth days in 7 Venus days	1 Venus day = 120 Earth days

Look carefully at the Facts I Know to find the **key fact.**

● Can the number of Earth days it takes Venus to revolve around the sun be used to find the number of Venus days that are equal to Earth days?

● Is the number of Earth days that are equal to 1 Venus day enough information to answer the question?

FOCUS Use the READ and KNOW steps of the Five-Step PROBLEM-SOLVING Plan.

PRACTICE

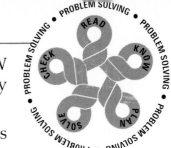

For each problem, think about the READ and KNOW steps. Make a table like the one on page 88 to identify the **key facts**. Do not solve the problems.

1. The planet Jupiter has at least 17 moons. It takes Jupiter 12 years to revolve around the sun. It takes Saturn 29 years. How much longer does it take Saturn than Jupiter to revolve around the sun?

2. Mars travels around the sun at a speed of 15 miles per second. The trip takes 687 days. How many days does it take Mars to complete 2 revolutions around the sun?

3. Mercury travels around the sun at a speed of 30 miles per second. The trip takes 88 days. Earth travels around the sun at a speed of 19 miles per second. Which planet travels faster? How much faster?

4. Pluto has 1 moon and travels around the sun at a speed of 3 miles per second. How far can Pluto travel in 1 minute? (1 minute = 60 seconds)

5. It takes Earth 365 days to revolve around the sun. One day on Jupiter is equal to 10 Earth days. How many Earth days are equal to 7 days on Jupiter?

Class Project

Separate into small groups of students. Write ten questions about your school library. For example, "How many tables are there?" or "How many shelves are there?" Write the questions in a TREASURE HUNT list. Trade lists with another group. Answer the questions without leaving the classroom. Then actually check your answers (with your teacher's approval). How many did your group answer correctly?

Subtracting With Zeros

Subtract: 540 − 271

**Regroup.
Subtract the
ones.**

```
 H | T | O
   | 3 |10
 5 | 4 | 0̸
−2 | 7 | 1
───────────
   |   | 9
```

Regroup 4 tens 0 ones
as 3 tens 10 ones.

**Regroup.
Subtract the
tens.**

```
 H | T | O
   |13 |
 4 | 3 |10
 5̸ | 4̸ | 0̸
−2 | 7 | 1
───────────
   | 6 | 9
```

Regroup 5 hundreds
3 tens as 4
hundreds 13 tens.

**Subtract the
hundreds.**

```
 H | T | O
   |13 |
 4 | 3 |10
 5̸ | 4̸ | 0̸
−2 | 7 | 1
───────────
 2 | 6 | 9
```

Subtract: 705 − 546

**Regroup.
Subtract the ones.**

```
 H | T | O
   | 9 |
 6 |10̸ |15
 7̸ | 0̸ | 5̸
−5 | 4 | 6
───────────
   |   | 9
```

Regroup 7 hundreds
0 tens 5 ones as 6
hundreds 9 tens 15 ones.

Subtract the tens.

```
 H | T | O
   | 9 |
 6 |10̸ |15
 7̸ | 0̸ | 5̸
−5 | 4 | 6
───────────
   | 5 | 9
```

Subtract the hundreds.

```
 H | T | O
   | 9 |
 6 |10̸ |15
 7̸ | 0̸ | 5̸
−5 | 4 | 6
───────────
 1 | 5 | 9
```

GUIDED PRACTICE

Subtract.

1.
```
    3 1 10
    4̸ 2̸ 0̸
  − 1 2 2
  ─────────
    2 9 8
```

2.
```
    6 10
    7 0̸ 6
  − 4 6 2
  ─────────
  �damaged 4 4
```

3.
```
      9
    5 10̸ 14
    6̸ 0̸ 4̸
  − 4 8 9
  ─────────
  ▪ 1 5
```

4.
```
    3 8 0
  − 2 9 6
```

5.
```
    4 0 9
  − 2 3 7
```

6.
```
    7 5 0
  −   2 8
```

7.
```
    3 0 5
  − 1 4 2
```

8.
```
    3 0 3
  −   6 2
```

9.
```
    4 7 0
  − 1 8 4
```

10.
```
    7 0 8
  − 4 2 6
```

11.
```
    9 0 0
  − 6 7 4
```

12.
```
    6 0 2
  − 4 3 9
```

FOCUS | Use NUMBER skills to subtract 3-digit numbers with zeros.

PRACTICE

Subtract.

13. 760 −275	**14.** 520 −275	**15.** 504 −387	**16.** 801 − 92	**17.** 410 −136	**18.** 504 −326
19. 730 −245	**20.** 403 −134	**21.** 307 −125	**22.** 520 −467	**23.** 890 −549	**24.** 601 −496
25. 620 −539	**26.** 370 − 79	**27.** 402 −126	**28.** 701 − 98	**29.** 900 −732	**30.** 380 −197
31. 730 −586	**32.** 401 −326	**33.** 900 −548	**34.** 303 −129	**35.** 605 − 16	**36.** 400 −245

37. 690 − 437   **38.** 206 − 24   **39.** 307 − 138   **40.** 480 − 396

41. 707 − 28   **42.** 510 − 334   **43.** 800 − 15   **44.** 900 − 761

45. This year 809 people watched the Jackson road race. Last year, 528 watched the race. How many more people watched the race this year?

46. Of the 540 people who ran in the race, 417 finished. How many people did not finish the race?

MIXED PRACTICE
Maintaining and Reviewing Skills

Add or subtract.

47. 546 −327	**48.** 804 −675	**49.** 328 +348	**50.** 467 +269	**51.** 75 −68	**52.** 136 +348

CHALLENGE

53. During March, Billy ran in a race with 470 people. During May, he ran in a race with 432 people. During June, Billy ran in a race with 908 people. Did more or fewer people run in the June race than ran in the March and May races combined?

SUBTRACTION

Checking Subtraction With Addition

Carla was asked to do a subtraction exercise and give the answer to the class. Before giving the answer, Carla checked her subtraction with addition.

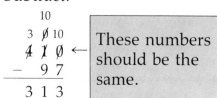

Subtract.

```
        10
    3  ⁄9 10
    4  1 ⁄0  ←
 -     9 7
    3  1 3
```

These numbers should be the same.

Check.

```
    1  1
    3  1 3
 +     9 7
 →  4  1 0
```

PRACTICE

Subtract. Check with addition.

1. 708 − 50	2. 108 − 88	3. 970 − 165	4. 450 − 235	5. 708 − 178	6. 306 − 215
7. 904 − 187	8. 430 − 187	9. 705 − 563	10. 500 − 81	11. 670 − 365	12. 870 − 423
13. 602 − 211	14. 703 − 35	15. 500 − 329	16. 760 − 421	17. 307 − 189	18. 480 − 22

19. 571 − 385 20. 608 − 476 21. 917 − 688 22. 430 − 346

23. 647 − 289 24. 400 − 264 25. 841 − 386 26. 722 − 685

MIXED PRACTICE

Maintaining and Reviewing Skills

Add or subtract. Check each answer.

27. 732 − 564	28. 316 − 175	29. 237 + 496	30. 84 − 26	31. 604 + 296	32. 65 − 36
33. 319 + 394	34. 96 − 58	35. 34 − 25	36. 78 + 78	37. 129 + 677	38. 53 − 27

FOCUS   Use NUMBER skills to check subtraction with addition.

APPLICATION
Using Measurement

Marge wanted to know how much liquid she would have if she added 165 milliliters of water to 240 milliliters of water.

To find how many milliliters in all, add: 240 + 165.

$$\begin{array}{r} 1 \\ 240 \text{ milliliters} \\ +165 \text{ milliliters} \\ \hline 405 \text{ milliliters in all} \end{array}$$

Next, Marge poured out 128 milliliters of the water. How much water did she have left?

To find how many milliliters are left, subtract: 405 − 128.

$$\begin{array}{r} 9 \\ 3\;\cancel{10}\;15 \\ \cancel{4}\;\cancel{0}\;\cancel{5}\text{ milliliters} \\ -1\;2\;8\text{ milliliters} \\ \hline 2\;7\;7\text{ milliliters left} \end{array}$$

39. How much water would you have if you added 123 milliliters of water to 407 milliliters of water?

40. How much would you have left if you poured out 271 milliliters of water?

Using Mental Arithmetic

Round a number to find **about** how many.

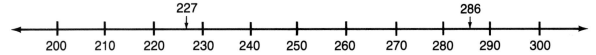

Round 227 to the nearest hundred.

Since 227 is between 200 and 300, and is closer to 200, 227 rounds down to 200. So 227 is about 200

Round 286 to the nearest hundred. Since 286 is between 200 and 300, and is closer to 300, 286 rounds up to 300. So 286 is about 300

When a number is halfway between two hundreds, it always rounds up. Since 250 is halfway between 200 and 300, 250 rounds up to 300.

See how quickly you can round these numbers to the nearest hundred.

41. 345   **42.** 877   **43.** 125   **44.** 652   **45.** 550   **46.** 527

Use MEASUREMENT and NUMBER skills to add and subtract milliliters.
Use MENTAL ARITHMETIC to round numbers to the nearest hundred.

LOOKING BACK
Reviewing and Testing Chapter 7

In Chapter 7 you formulated problems about an outdoor concert. Look at pages 82 and 83.

1. Write a sentence telling which type of concert you would like to attend and why.

You learned about adding 3-digit numbers. To review what you learned, study the sample exercises on pages 84 and 86. Then use these skills to find each sum for exercises 2–11.

2.	517	3.	145	4.	628	5.	497	6.	531
	+281		+807		+ 90		+885		+ 69

7.	425	8.	436	9.	570	10.	908	11.	635
	131		109		219		279		298
	+243		+131		+ 13		+472		+ 57

You learned about the READ and KNOW steps of the Five-Step Problem–Solving Plan. To review, look at pages 88 and 89. For this problem, think about the READ and KNOW steps. Make a table like the one on page 88 to identify the **key facts.**

12. Steven has at least 56 books in his library. He read 54 books last year. Karen read 39 books last year. How many more books did Steven read than Karen last year?

You learned about subtracting 3-digit numbers with zeros. You also learned to check subtraction with addition. To review, look at pages 90 and 92. Find and check each difference for exercises 13–17.

13.	670	14.	803	15.	350	16.	900	17.	700
	−253		−189		− 85		−882		− 97

FOCUS Review and test skills learned and practiced.

Preparing for New Skills for Chapter 8

In the next chapter, you will focus on

- formulating problems about a theater group.
- adding larger numbers.
- using statistics and probability.
- subtracting greater numbers.
- estimating differences.
- using statistics.
- how math is used in science.

New addition and subtraction skills will be easier if you brush up on addition and subtraction skills you already know. First review Models A and B. Then complete the exercises.

Model A

Add the ones.
Regroup.

H	T	O
	1	
3	5	2
+4	5	9
		1

2
+9
1

Add the tens.
Regroup.

H	T	O
1	1	
3	5	2
+4	5	9
	1	1

1T
5T
+5T
1T

Add the hundreds.

H	T	O
1	1	
3	5	2
+4	5	9
8	1	1

1 H
3 H
+4 H
8 H

Model B

Regroup.
Subtract the ones.

H	T	O
	3	16
7	4	6
−5	6	8
		8

Regroup.
Subtract the tens.

H	T	O
	13	
6	3	16
7	4	6
−5	6	8
	7	8

Subtract
the hundreds.

H	T	O
	13	
6	3	16
7	4	6
−5	6	8
1	7	8

Regroup 4 tens 6 ones as 3 tens 16 ones.

Regroup 7 hundreds 3 tens as 6 hundreds 13 tens.

PRACTICE

Add. Use Model A.

Subtract. Use Model B.

1. 543
$+264$

2. 756
$+179$

3. 435
$+368$

4. 647
-268

5. 735
-576

6. 352
-164

Review NUMBER skills in preparation for learning a new skill.

FOCUS Formulate problems using picture cues, text, and data.

8

Addition and Subtraction of Larger Numbers

DATA

Task	Number of Children
Acting	17
Directing	1
Set design	7
Costume design	5
Music	4
Advertising	2
Programs	2
Line prompting	1
Props	6
Research	1
Total	46

Not every play deserves an audience. In fact, some plays are just awful. But the Backyard Players are a whole different story. Their plays are good—really good.

Although the group members are young (between 10 and 16 years old), they take their work seriously. That's one reason why the results are so fine.

The Backyard Players work hard. The theater group is divided into subgroups, each working at a different task. Most of the children will never be seen by an audience. But without their behind-the-scenes efforts, what do you think might happen?

Look at the picture and the data. Why do you think the same children cannot be counted on to do all the tasks? Think carefully. Then predict the kinds of problems a theater group like this one might have.

ADDITION
Adding Larger Numbers

The Johnson family traveled from Seattle, Washington to Los Angeles, California. They traveled 1 833 kilometers going and 1 905 kilometers coming back. How many kilometers did the Johnsons travel altogether?

To find how many kilometers the Johnsons traveled altogether, add 1 833 and 1 905.

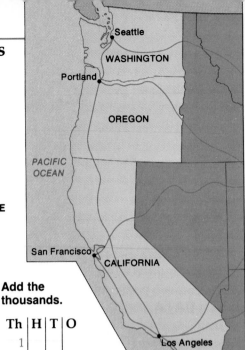

Add the ones and the tens.

Th	H	T	O
1	8	3	3
+1	9	0	5
		3	8

Add the hundreds.

Th	H	T	O
1			
1	8	3	3
+1	9	0	5
	7	3	8

Add the thousands.

Th	H	T	O
1			
1	8	3	3
+1	9	0	5
3	7	3	8

The Johnsons traveled 3 738 kilometers altogether.

Add: 53,426 + 28,398

Add the ones, the tens, and the hundreds.

TTh	Th	H	T	O
		1	1	
5	3	4	2	6
+2	8	3	9	8
		8	2	4

Add the thousands.

TTh	Th	H	T	O
1		1	1	
5	3	4	2	6
+2	8	3	9	8
	1	8	2	4

Add the ten thousands.

TTh	Th	H	T	O
1		1	1	
5	3	4	2	6
+2	8	3	9	8
8	1	8	2	4

53,426 + 28,398 = 81,824

GUIDED PRACTICE

Add.

1.
```
  1
  4,273
 +3,193
  7,466
```

2.
```
  1
  6,593
 +1,867
 ▮,▮▮0
```

3.
```
  14,390
 + 8,244
 ▮2,▮3▮
```

4.
```
  29,466
 +10,296
```

5.
```
  15,690
 +17,503
```

FOCUS	Use NUMBER skills to add large numbers.

98

PRACTICE

Add.

6. 14,215 +16,819	7. 71,426 +19,188	8. 39,436 + 8,025	9. 42,718 +10,496	10. 12,306 +26,714
11. 29,962 +27,119	12. 8,674 +9,427	13. 12,449 +20,396	14. 27,316 + 6,492	15. 36,844 +14,209
16. 65,493 + 9,325	17. 56,432 +14,477	18. 33,606 + 6,918	19. 72,309 +12,491	20. 72,539 +20,622

21. 23,455 + 14,590

22. 25,410 + 41,963

23. 32,392 + 8,908

24. 16,129 + 42,065

25. 36,197 + 5,247

26. 18,394 + 46,390

27. 47,652 + 50,091

28. 64,213 + 9,139

29. 72,438 + 20,277

30. The school library has 16,495 books. They received 3,821 new books. How many books do they have now?

31. A local farm shipped 25,690 tomatoes the first week. During the second week, 16,255 tomatoes were shipped. How many tomatoes were shipped in all?

MIXED PRACTICE
Maintaining and Reviewing Skills

Add or subtract.

32. 41,308 +18,946	33. 645 − 564	34. 7,654 + 797	35. 13,646 + 4,821	36. 941 − 653

CHALLENGE

Use only the digits 8 7 0 6 1 .

37. Write the largest five-digit number you can.

38. Write the smallest five-digit number you can.

39. Find their sum.

EXTRA PRACTICE—page 446

ADDITION

Adding Three Addends

The post office handled 34,239 letters in January, 32,726 letters in February, and 29,014 letters in March. How many letters did the post office handle in the three months?

To find how many letters the post office handled altogether, add: 34,239 + 32,726 + 29,014.

Add the ones, the tens, and the hundreds.

TTh	Th	H	T	O
				1
3	4	2	3	9
3	2	7	2	6
+2	9	0	1	4
		9	7	9

Add the thousands.

TTh	Th	H	T	O
	1			1
3	4	2	3	9
3	2	7	2	6
+2	9	0	1	4
	5	9	7	9

Add the ten thousands.

TTh	Th	H	T	O
1				1
3	4	2	3	9
3	2	7	2	6
+2	9	0	1	4
9	5	9	7	9

The post office handled 95,979 letters altogether.

PRACTICE

	1.	2.	3.	4.	5.
	12,316	7,135	21,411	30,916	6,408
	10,980	1,984	51,692	11,493	96
	+22,119	+6,019	+10,089	+44,321	+ 113

	6.	7.	8.	9.	10.
	54,966	15,975	1,562	10,842	279
	10,423	614	3,901	27,135	13,086
	+12,085	+ 7,199	+6,495	+46,023	+ 9,440

MIXED PRACTICE

Maintaining and Reviewing Skills

Add or subtract.

11. 24,357 + 5,870 + 29,066

12. 17,564 + 22,609 + 46,212

13. 439 − 247

14. 76,381 + 5,647

15. 380 − 56

16. 256 + 429

FOCUS | Use NUMBER skills to add three addends.

APPLICATION

Using Statistics and Probability

23,107   9,690   24,900   19,960

You can order this list of numbers in two ways.

From least to greatest: 9,690   19,960   23,107   24,900

From greatest to least: 24,900   23,107   19,960   9,690

Order each list of numbers from least to greatest.

17. 9,871   12,008   10,962   9,654

18. 14,862   25,015   16,629   23,189

19. 16,339   9,897   9,799   25,431

20. 34,982   36,055   31,821   38,891   32,126

21. 56,624   55,769   59,468   55,290   56,958

Order each list of numbers from greatest to least.

22. 6,758   9,642   9,409   8,471

23. 16,818   13,357   19,442   18,905

24. 29,506   25,264   27,435   29,849

25. 48,055   43,237   44,725   48,196   44,399

26. 72,401   70,934   72,965   72,845   70,148

Exploring With a Calculator

Use a calculator to find the missing numbers.

27. 585; 1,170; 1,755; ▦; ▦

28. 286; 572; 858; ▦; ▦

29. 367; 734; 1,101; ▦; ▦

30. 1,408; 2,816; 4,224; ▦; ▦

31. 10,215; 20,430; 30,645; ▦; ▦

32. 19,506; 39,012; 58,518; ▦; ▦

Use STATISTICS AND PROBABILITY to order numbers.
Use a CALCULATOR to find missing numbers.

Subtracting Larger Numbers

There were 31,764 people at a tennis tournament on Saturday. On Sunday, 18,943 people attended the tournament. How many more people attended the tournament on Saturday than on Sunday?

To find how many more people attended on Saturday than on Sunday, subtract: 31,764 − 18,943.

Subtract the ones and the tens.	Regroup. Subtract the hundreds.	Regroup again. Subtract the thousands and the ten thousands.

TTh	Th	H	T	O
3	1	7	6	4
−1	8	9	4	3
			2	1

TTh	Th	H	T	O
		0¹⁷		
3	1̶	7̶	6	4
−1	8	9	4	3
		8	2	1

TTh	Th	H	T	O
	¹⁰			
2	0̶	¹⁷		
3̶	1̶	7̶	6	4
−1	8	9	4	3
1	2	8	2	1

In all 12,821 more people attended the tournament on Saturday than on Sunday.

Study these exercises.

```
   3 16  2 0̶ 15          4 2 17 5 12          0 13 5 14
   4̶ 6̶, 3̶ 1̶ 3̶          5̶ 3̶, 7̶ 6̶ 2̶          7 1̶, 3̶ 6̶ 4̶
  −3 9, 2 4 8          −    4, 8 4 6          −        9 4 6
   ─────────           ──────────            ──────────────
     7, 0 6 7              4 8, 9 1 6            7 0, 4 1 8
```

GUIDED PRACTICE

Subtract.

```
            0 11                      4 14
1.   3 6, 1 1̶ 1̶      2.   8 0, 6 5̶ 4      3.   1 9, 6 4 8      4.   3 1, 4 0 9
    −2 2, 0 0 9          −2 9, 0 7 7          −1 1, 8 6 3          −1 9, 3 1 2
    ──────────          ──────────          ──────────          ──────────
     1 4, 1 0 2          ▮ ▮, ▮ ▮ 7
```

```
5.   1 6, 5 3 7      6.   3 5, 2 4 7      7.   6 4, 5 4 3      8.   5 2, 0 0 6
    −    9, 6 4 8        −2 6, 1 5 5          −3 7, 0 6 4          −1 8, 4 3 6
```

9. 46,930 − 27,482   10. 29,168 − 16,478   11. 67,058 − 26,471

FOCUS	Use NUMBER skills to subtract larger numbers.

PRACTICE

Subtract.

12. 20,265 −12,407	**13.** 38,849 −26,864	**14.** 12,920 − 8,637	**15.** 23,526 −17,913	**16.** 46,925 − 8,056
17. 31,802 −14,773	**18.** 54,186 − 9,443	**19.** 86,291 −63,216	**20.** 49,130 −48,186	**21.** 29,803 −19,912
22. 70,069 −29,712	**23.** 31,182 −16,088	**24.** 17,936 − 8,043	**25.** 39,716 −27,825	**26.** 60,200 −13,309

27. 22,193 − 18,347   **28.** 52,371 − 27,390   **29.** 38,145 − 29,136

30. 61,910 − 38,106   **31.** 24,496 − 13,237   **32.** 60,183 − 8,296

33. 71,641 − 44,370   **34.** 38,414 − 29,505   **35.** 41,006 − 27,360

36. An egg farm sold 24,609 eggs in March. They sold 26,014 eggs in April. How many more eggs were sold in April than in March?

37. A bakery sold 62,143 loaves of bread in a three-month period. In the same period, 59,086 rolls were sold. How many more loaves of bread were sold than rolls?

MIXED PRACTICE
Maintaining and Reviewing Skills

Add or subtract.

38. 49,328 −17,469	**39.** 36,041 +25,649	**40.** 64,456 + 9,357	**41.** 6,728 −4,306	**42.** 5,721 + 398

CHALLENGE

Find the missing numbers.

43. 4■,18■ − 3,■■6 ■2,203	**44.** ■3,9■0 −4■,■7■ 21,546	**45.** 54,■1■ − ■,648 ■1,3■2	**46.** 6■,298 −■0,■65 43,0■3

EXTRA PRACTICE—page 446

SUBTRACTION
Estimating Differences

Last year 52,386 people visited the Newton Amusement Park. This year 39,763 people visited the park. You can estimate to find out about how many more people visited the park last year than this year.

To estimate, first round each number to the nearest ten thousand and then subtract.

	Estimate	Exact Answer
52,386 $\longrightarrow$	50,000	52,386
$- 39,763 \longrightarrow$	$- 40,000$	$- 39,763$
	10,000	12,623

About 10,000 more people visited the park last year than this year.

PRACTICE

Estimate. Then find the exact difference.

1. 27,937
   $- 16,473$

2. 17,589
   $- 11,647$

3. 34,932
   $- 18,453$

4. 29,302
   $- 8,714$

5. 42,368
   $- 26,942$

6. 49,132
   $- 33,207$

7. 76,477
   $- 58,895$

8. 62,044
   $- 17,971$

9. 51,049
   $- 38,706$

10. 34,816
    $- 13,844$

11. 48,635 − 22,629

12. 21,097 − 9,643

13. 67,219 − 51,146

MIXED PRACTICE
Maintaining and Reviewing Skills

Estimate. Then find the exact answer.

14. 59,432
    $- 52,694$

15. 22,149
    $- 14,028$

16. 29,346
    $+ 12,455$

17. 6,745
    $- 3,129$

18. 7,426
    $+ 2,864$

19. 7,438 − 5,679

20. 4,364 + 4,982

21. 6,741 − 2,364

FOCUS   Use NUMBER skills and ESTIMATION to find differences.

104

APPLICATION

Using Statistics

The table at the right shows the number of people that attended the State Fair during the years 1976 through 1985. Use the information in the table to answer exercises 22–27.

22. During which year did the greatest number of people attend the State Fair?

23. During which years did less than 35,000 people attend the State Fair?

24. How many people attended the State Fair during 1982 and 1983 altogether?

25. How many more people attended the State Fair in 1979 than in 1980?

26. How many less people attended the State Fair in 1985 than in 1984?

27. Estimate how many more people attended the State Fair in 1977 than in 1976?

STATE FAIR ATTENDANCE

Year	Attendance
1976	32,821
1977	41,064
1978	31,666
1979	45,305
1980	32,978
1981	51,364
1982	47,232
1983	50,643
1984	53,069
1985	44,870

Problem Solving: Exploring READ and KNOW

READ the paragraph and the questions. List the **key facts** you must KNOW to answer each question.

A $0.10 1939 *Marvel Comic #1* sold for $18,000 in 1981. A 1938 *Action Comic #1* sold for $16,000.

How many years did it take each comic book to be worth more than $15,000?

28. *Marvel Comic #1*

29. *Action Comic #1*

30. Which comic book sold for more money in 1981? How much more?

31. By how much did the price of *Marvel Comic #1* increase?

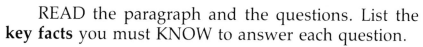

Use STATISTICS to make comparisons of information in a table.
Apply the READ and KNOW steps of the Five-Step PROBLEM SOLVING Plan.

Nutrition

At the Olympics, newscasters often go to the athletes' dining room to find out what they eat before an event. They find certain athletes, like long-distance runners, sitting before huge platters of pancakes, pasta, and bread. Yet these athletes are very thin.

Athletes know that the fuel their bodies run on is the food they eat. It takes so much energy to run a long-distance race that their bodies need large amounts of fuel. Since this fuel is burned up during the race, runners can eat a lot without gaining weight.

Each ounce of food we eat produces a certain amount of energy. Some foods give more energy per ounce than others. **Calories** measure the amount of energy that a food contains.

Runners make a special effort to eat foods that are high in calories because they need a lot of energy for their activity. People who do not exercise as much do not need such high-calorie diets.

The chart lists some foods and their calorie values.

CRITICAL THINKING

1. If you were a long-distance runner trying to eat the food that would provide the most energy, which three foods would you choose?

2. Which foods listed are under 50 calories? What is similar about them? What conclusions can you draw?

3. Choose a filling lunch for yourself that has the least amount of calories. How many calories does it have?

4. When you are adding up calorie values, why is it important to consider how much food the calorie value refers to?

Food	Calories
2 waffles with syrup	640
$\frac{1}{4}$ pound hamburger and bun	550
8 ounces flavored yogurt	230
Lettuce and tomato salad	27
$\frac{1}{4}$ cup drained tuna	100
2 stalks celery	15
Peanut butter and jelly sandwich	550
$\frac{1}{2}$ broiled chicken	270
$\frac{1}{2}$ cup mashed potatoes	100
1 orange	70

FOCUS | Use NUMBER skills to make discoveries about nutrition.

Proper diet and hard work help this gymnast to develop excellent muscle tone.

In Chapter 8 you formulated problems about a young theater group. Look at pages 96 and 97.

1. Write a sentence telling what problems you predicted a theater group like this one might have.

You learned about adding 5-digit numbers. To review what you learned, study the sample exercises on pages 98 and 100. Then use these skills to find each sum for exercises 2 to 9.

2. 4,157
   + 3,809

3. 62,187
   + 28,534

4. 59,021
   + 6,970

5. 10,153
    15,807
   + 23,241

6. 35,800
       299
   + 12,161

7. 17,813 + 4,500

8. 24,324 + 67,906

9. 40,650 + 30,899

You learned about subtracting 5-digit numbers. You also learned more about estimating. To review, look at pages 102 and 104. Estimate each difference for exercises 10 to 17. Then find each exact difference.

10. 8,437
    - 2,782

11. 29,300
    - 13,597

12. 57,821
    - 6,475

13. 63,207
    - 20,588

14. 85,381
    - 66,990

15. 43,923 − 8,574

16. 77,401 − 21,755

17. 83,008 − 54,509

You learned about how calories contribute to good nutrition. Look at pages 106 and 107 to review why calories are important.

18. Which person needs a higher calorie diet, an office worker or an athlete? Why?

FOCUS | Review and test skills learned and practiced.

In the next chapter, you will focus on

- formulating problems about an apple harvest.
- recognizing and writing fractions that are equivalent to one or zero.
- using statistics and probability.
- recognizing and writing equivalent fractions.
- relating fractions and decimals (tenths).
- using geometry.

Learning more about fractions will be easier if you brush up on what you already know about fractions.

First review the examples below. Then complete exercises 1–3.

Look at the circle. It is divided into 3 equal parts. Two of the 3 parts are green. A fraction can be used to tell how many parts are green.

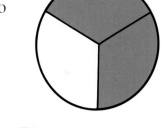

Number of green parts $\longrightarrow$ 2 numerator
Number of equal parts $\longrightarrow$ 3 denominator

Two thirds of the circle is green.

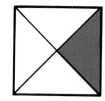

Number of red parts $\longrightarrow$ 1
Number of equal parts $\longrightarrow$ 4
One fourth of the square is red.

Number of blue parts $\longrightarrow$ 1
Number of equal parts $\longrightarrow$ 2
One half of the circle is blue.

PRACTICE

Ring the fraction that tells how much is shaded.

1.

$\frac{2}{4}$ $\frac{1}{3}$ $\frac{3}{5}$

2.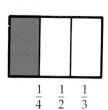

$\frac{1}{4}$ $\frac{1}{2}$ $\frac{1}{3}$

3.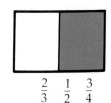

$\frac{2}{3}$ $\frac{1}{2}$ $\frac{3}{4}$

Review NUMBER skills in preparation for learning a new skill.

Write the letter of the correct answer.

Solve.

1. 6×3 A. 18   B. 27   C. 12   D. 32

2. 8×6 E. 45   F. 54   G. 48   H. 42

3. $4 \times \blacksquare = 24$ A. 3   B. 8   C. 5   D. 6

4. $7 \times \blacksquare = 49$ E. 5   F. 7   G. 6   H. 8

Which number is a square number?

5. A. 7   B. 9   C. 3   D. 6

6. E. 36   F. 14   G. 27   H. 22

Which number is divisible by 3?

7. A. 14   B. 12   C. 19   D. 16

8. E. 23   F. 84   G. 28   H. 32

Which number is divisible by 2?

9. A. 12   B. 19   C. 17   D. 75

10. E. 23   F. 35   G. 36   H. 41

Divide.

11. $4\overline{)32}$ A. 6   B. 9   C. 8   D. 4

12. $6\overline{)54}$ E. 7   F. 9   G. 6   H. 8

Multiply.

13. 90×3 A. 270   B. 180   C. 320   D. 150

14. 50×7 E. 450   F. 120   G. 350   H. 650

Solve.

15. There are 20 rose bushes. Each bush has 8 roses on it. How many roses are there?

A. 180   B. 160   C. 120   D. 150

16. Each loaf of bread costs 50¢. How much did 7 loaves of bread cost?

E. $3.50   F. $3.20   G. $2.60   H. $4.50

FOCUS   Review concepts and skills taught in Chapters 2 through 8.

Which figure is a polygon?

17. A.  **B.**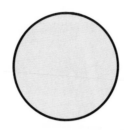

C. **D.**

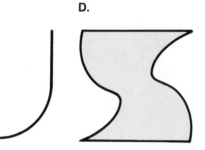

Name this polygon.

18.

E. triangle

F. square

G. octagon

H. hexagon

Which statement is correct?

19. A. $34,143 > 34,265$

B. $45,354 < 44,324$

C. $24,254 < 24,563$

D. $17,534 > 17,879$

Round to the nearest hundred.

| **20.** 45,574 | E. 45,680 | F. 45,600 |
| | G. 45,700 | H. 45,780 |

| **21.** 32,832 | A. 32,830 | B. 32,900 |
| | C. 32,840 | D. 32,800 |

Add or subtract.

| **22.** 564
+278 | E. 842
G. 644 | F. 824
H. 368 |

| **23.** 824
−567 | A. 572
C. 257 | B. 348
D. 265 |

| **24.** 43,567
+18,675 | E. 62,253
G. 62,242 | F. 62,422
H. 62,879 |

| **25.** 37,253
−18,784 | A. 19,436
C. 18,469 | B. 18,479
D. 19,469 |

Solve.

26. Mr. Graham flew 12,436 miles last year. He flew 10,658 miles this year. How many miles did he fly in all?

E. 23,094   F. 23,194
G. 24,090   H. 23,294

27. In July 66,738 people flew on KIT Airlines. In August 17,895 people flew. How many more people flew in July than in August?

A. 48,985   B. 48,589
C. 49,843   D. 48,843

FOCUS   Formulate problems using picture cues, text, and data.

CHAPTER 9

Fractions and Probability

DATA

Pleasant Valley Orchard

First frost is due in 4 days

Sunset   6:45 P.M.

Names of apple pickers
    Mary
    Sally
    Tom

Average number of bushels
   picked per day
    Mary   40
    Sally   35
    Tom   25

Number of trees in
   orchard   100

Number of trees
   not yet picked   30

Number of bushels
   per tree   8

The autumn apple harvest is a busy, exciting time. Apple pickers come to the apple orchard and pick the apples from the trees. The more apples they pick, the more money they will make. They stand on ladders and pluck the apples from the branches. The apples are put into buckets, which are called bushels. The bushels are loaded onto trucks and delivered to supermarkets and fruit stands.

The apple pickers must work fast. Once the first winter frost comes, any apples left on the trees may be ruined.

Look at the picture and the data. Do you think all the apples will be picked in time? It's difficult to work in the dark. Until what time in the evening can the pickers work? What problems might the apple pickers have? Predict how this harvest will end. Give your reasons.

FRACTIONS
Introducing Fractions Equivalent to One and Zero

A **fraction** can be used to tell how much is shaded.
Fractions can be used to name one or zero.

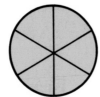 

Number of shaded parts   →6   Number of shaded parts   →0
Total number of equal parts →$\overline{6}$ Total number of equal parts →$\overline{6}$

Six sixths are shaded. $\frac{6}{6} = 1$ Zero sixths are shaded. $\frac{0}{6} = 0$

Other names for 1 whole shaded:

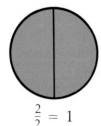   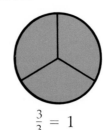   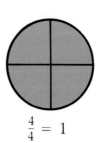

$\frac{2}{2} = 1$ $\frac{3}{3} = 1$ $\frac{4}{4} = 1$

Other names for 0 parts shaded:

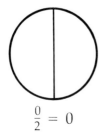      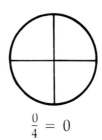

$\frac{0}{2} = 0$ $\frac{0}{3} = 0$ $\frac{0}{4} = 0$

GUIDED PRACTICE

Write a fraction that tells how much is shaded. Then
write 1 or 0.

1. 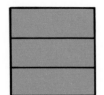 $\frac{3}{3} = 1$ 2. 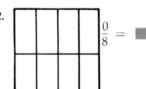 $\frac{0}{8} = \blacksquare$ 3.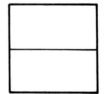

| FOCUS | Use NUMBER skills to recognize and write fractions that are equivalent to one and zero. |

114

PRACTICE

Write a fraction that tells how much is shaded. Then write 1 or 0.

4.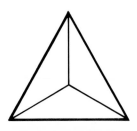

5.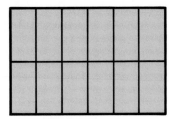

6.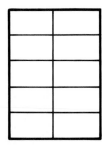

7.

8.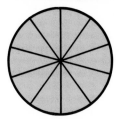

9.

Write 1 or 0.

10. $\frac{0}{5}$ = ■

11. $\frac{0}{12}$ = ■

12. $\frac{7}{7}$ = ■

13. $\frac{0}{4}$ = ■

14. $\frac{15}{15}$ = ■

15. $\frac{8}{8}$ = ■

16. $\frac{2}{2}$ = ■

17. $\frac{0}{9}$ = ■

18. $\frac{20}{20}$ = ■

19. $\frac{5}{5}$ = ■

Copy and complete.

20. $\frac{■}{4}$ = 0

21. $\frac{■}{13}$ = 0

22. $\frac{■}{25}$ = 0

23. $\frac{■}{100}$ = 0

24. $\frac{■}{20}$ = 0

25. $\frac{5}{■}$ = 1

26. $\frac{13}{■}$ = 1

27. $\frac{25}{■}$ = 1

28. $\frac{100}{■}$ = 1

29. $\frac{10}{■}$ = 1

MIXED PRACTICE
Maintaining and Reviewing Skills

Add or subtract.

30. 49,604 + 23,968
31. 72,314 − 50,106
32. 3,949 + 15,715
33. 30,607 − 13,809

CHALLENGE

34. The Montez family bought 2 chicken pies. They ate $\frac{4}{4}$ of a pie on Sunday, $\frac{0}{3}$ of a pie on Monday, and $\frac{3}{3}$ of a pie on Tuesday. How many pies were left?

FRACTIONS

Recognizing Fractions Equivalent to One and Zero

Some fractions can be used to name all of the shaded parts of a region, or the entire region.

Some fractions can be used to show that none of the equal parts of a region are shaded.

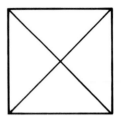

Numerator $\longrightarrow$ $\frac{4}{4}$ are shaded
Denominator $\longrightarrow$

Numerator $\longrightarrow$ $\frac{0}{4}$ are shaded
Denominator $\longrightarrow$

Rule: When a fraction has the same number in both the numerator and the denominator, that fraction is equal to 1.

Rule: When a fraction has a numerator of 0, that fraction is equal to 0.

$$\frac{4}{4} = 1 \qquad \frac{3}{3} = 1 \qquad \frac{6}{6} = 1$$

$$\frac{0}{4} = 0 \qquad \frac{0}{7} = 0 \qquad \frac{0}{10} = 0$$

PRACTICE

Determine if the fraction has the *same numerator and denominator* or if the *numerator is 0*. Then write 1 or 0.

1. $\frac{0}{8}$ 2. $\frac{7}{7}$ 3. $\frac{0}{15}$ 4. $\frac{9}{9}$ 5. $\frac{100}{100}$

Copy and complete.

6. $0 = \frac{\blacksquare}{3} = \frac{\blacksquare}{6} = \frac{\blacksquare}{9} = \frac{\blacksquare}{12}$

7. $0 = \frac{\blacksquare}{10} = \frac{\blacksquare}{20} = \frac{\blacksquare}{30} = \frac{\blacksquare}{40}$

8. $1 = \frac{\blacksquare}{2} = \frac{\blacksquare}{4} = \frac{\blacksquare}{6} = \frac{\blacksquare}{8}$

9. $1 = \frac{12}{\blacksquare} = \frac{24}{\blacksquare} = \frac{36}{\blacksquare} = \frac{48}{\blacksquare}$

MIXED PRACTICE
Maintaining and Reviewing Skills

Copy and complete.

10. $\frac{\blacksquare}{6} = 1$ 11. $\frac{0}{4} = \blacksquare$ 12. $\frac{\blacksquare}{15} = 0$ 13. $\frac{9}{\blacksquare} = 1$ 14. $\frac{0}{17} = \blacksquare$

15. $\frac{13}{13} = \blacksquare$ 16. $\frac{\blacksquare}{75} = 1$ 17. $\frac{\blacksquare}{1} = 0$ 18. $\frac{38}{38} = \blacksquare$ 19. $\frac{\blacksquare}{40} = 0$

FOCUS | Use NUMBER skills to recognize and to write fractions that are equivalent to one and zero.

APPLICATION
Using Statistics and Probability

If you were to spin this spinner, what would be the chance that the arrow would land on

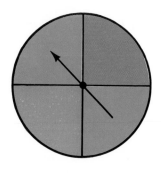

red?   1 chance out of 4 $\longrightarrow \frac{1}{4}$

blue?   1 chance out of 4 $\longrightarrow \frac{1}{4}$

green?   2 chances out of 4 $\longrightarrow \frac{2}{4}$

yellow?   0 chances out of 4 $\longrightarrow \frac{0}{4}$ There is no chance of this.

The chance of something happening can also be called the **probability** of it happening.

For each spinner, write the chance of the arrow landing on each color as a fraction.

20.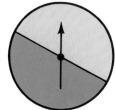

yellow = —

green = —

red = —

21.

blue = —

red = —

yellow = —

22.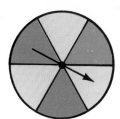

red = —

yellow = —

blue = —

green = —

23.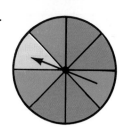

yellow = —

blue = —

green = —

red = —

purple = —

Solving Problems

24. Kathy ran $\frac{2}{2}$ of a mile on Thursday, $\frac{6}{6}$ of a mile on Friday, and $\frac{7}{7}$ of a mile on Saturday. How many miles did she run altogether?

25. A gardener is hired to mow 2 lawns. On his first day, he mows $\frac{8}{8}$ of a lawn. On his second day, he mows $\frac{0}{5}$ of a lawn. How much more does he have to mow?

Use STATISTICS AND PROBABILITY to write the chance (probability) of a single event occurring as a fraction.
Use NUMBER skills to solve problems.

Recognizing Equivalent Fractions

Each whole fraction bar is shaded.

1										→	1
1/2					1/2					→	2/2
1/4		1/4		1/4			1/4			→	4/4
1/6	1/6		1/6	1/6		1/6		1/6		→	6/6
1/8	1/8	1/8	1/8	1/8	1/8	1/8		1/8		→	8/8
1/10	1/10	1/10	1/10	1/10	1/10	1/10	1/10	1/10	1/10	→	10/10

The fractions $\frac{2}{2}$, $\frac{4}{4}$, $\frac{6}{6}$, $\frac{8}{8}$, and $\frac{10}{10}$ are all names for the same number. They are **equivalent fractions.**

$$\frac{2}{2} = \frac{4}{4} = \frac{6}{6} = \frac{8}{8} = \frac{10}{10} = 1$$

One half of each fraction bar is shaded.

1/2					1/2					→	1/2
1/4		1/4		1/4			1/4			→	2/4
1/6	1/6		1/6	1/6		1/6		1/6		→	3/6
1/8	1/8	1/8	1/8	1/8	1/8	1/8		1/8		→	4/8
1/10	1/10	1/10	1/10	1/10	1/10	1/10	1/10	1/10	1/10	→	5/10

The fractions $\frac{1}{2}$, $\frac{2}{4}$, $\frac{3}{6}$, $\frac{4}{8}$, and $\frac{5}{10}$ are all names for the same number. They are equivalent fractions.

$$\frac{1}{2} = \frac{2}{4} = \frac{3}{6} = \frac{4}{8} = \frac{5}{10}$$

FOCUS Use NUMBER skills to recognize and write equivalent fractions.

GUIDED PRACTICE

Use these fraction bars to copy and complete the equivalent fractions.

1.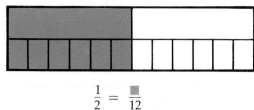

$$\frac{1}{2} = \frac{\blacksquare}{12}$$

2.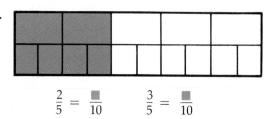

$$\frac{2}{5} = \frac{\blacksquare}{10} \qquad \frac{3}{5} = \frac{\blacksquare}{10}$$

PRACTICE

Use these fraction bars to copy and complete the equivalent fractions.

3.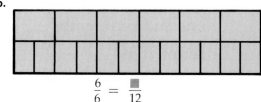

$$\frac{1}{3} = \frac{\blacksquare}{6}$$

4.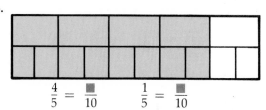

$$\frac{1}{4} = \frac{\blacksquare}{8}$$

5.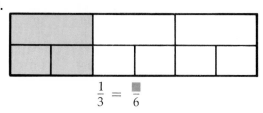

$$\frac{6}{6} = \frac{\blacksquare}{12}$$

6.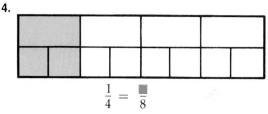

$$\frac{4}{5} = \frac{\blacksquare}{10} \qquad \frac{1}{5} = \frac{\blacksquare}{10}$$

7.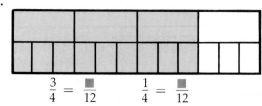

$$\frac{3}{4} = \frac{\blacksquare}{12} \qquad \frac{1}{4} = \frac{\blacksquare}{12}$$

8.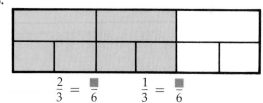

$$\frac{2}{3} = \frac{\blacksquare}{6} \qquad \frac{1}{3} = \frac{\blacksquare}{6}$$

MIXED PRACTICE
Maintaining and Reviewing Skills

Copy and complete.

9. $\frac{0}{2} = \blacksquare$ **10.** $\frac{3}{3} = \blacksquare$ **11.** $\frac{0}{16} = \blacksquare$ **12.** $\frac{5}{5} = \blacksquare$ **13.** $\frac{125}{125} = \blacksquare$

EXTRA PRACTICE—page 446

FRACTIONS
Relating Fractions and Decimals

A point on a number line may have many names.
Fractions in tenths can be written as **decimals.**

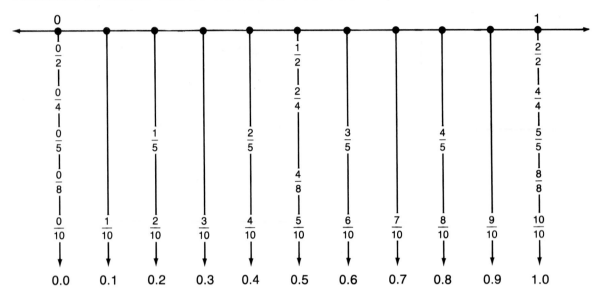

Equivalent fractions	Equivalent decimal	Read as
$\frac{1}{5} = \frac{2}{10}$ =	0.2	two tenths
$\frac{4}{4} = \frac{10}{10}$ =	1.0	one and zero tenths
$\frac{0}{2} = \frac{0}{10}$ =	0.0	zero tenths

PRACTICE

Use the number line to copy and complete the equivalent
fractions and decimals.

1. $\frac{4}{8} = \frac{\blacksquare}{10} = 0.\blacksquare$

2. $\frac{5}{5} = \frac{\blacksquare}{10} = \blacksquare.\blacksquare$

3. $\frac{0}{4} = \frac{\blacksquare}{10} = 0.\blacksquare$

4. $\frac{4}{5} = \frac{\blacksquare}{10} = \blacksquare.\blacksquare$

5. $\frac{1}{2} = \frac{\blacksquare}{10} = \blacksquare.\blacksquare$

6. $\frac{2}{5} = \frac{\blacksquare}{10} = \blacksquare.\blacksquare$

MIXED PRACTICE
Maintaining and Reviewing Skills

Add or subtract.

7. $\begin{array}{r} 46,340 \\ +29,782 \end{array}$

8. $\begin{array}{r} 84,016 \\ -79,384 \end{array}$

9. $\begin{array}{r} 37,417 \\ -\ 8,628 \end{array}$

10. $\begin{array}{r} 71,006 \\ +19,996 \end{array}$

11. $\begin{array}{r} 51,064 \\ -29,649 \end{array}$

FOCUS | Use NUMBER skills to recognize and write equivalent fractions and decimals (tenths) using a number line.

120

APPLICATION
Using Geometry

When a figure is folded so that the parts on each side of the fold match exactly, the figure has **symmetry.**

These figures were folded once. Since the two matching parts are equal parts, each part shows $\frac{1}{2}$.

These figures were folded twice. Since the four matching parts are equal parts, each part shows $\frac{1}{4}$.

Does the figure show symmetry along the fold lines? Write *yes* or *no*.

12.

13.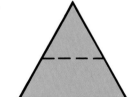

14.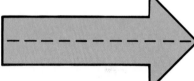

15.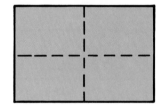

16.

17.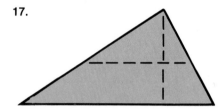

Solving Problems

Think of equivalent fractions and decimals in order to solve these comparison problems.

18. Gary ran $\frac{2}{4}$ of a mile. George ran $\frac{5}{8}$ of a mile. Who ran farther?

19. Sue had $\frac{3}{5}$ of a yard of rope. Martina had $\frac{5}{10}$ of a yard. Who had more?

20. Wally sang for $\frac{1}{2}$ of an hour. Carla sang for 0.6 of an hour. Who sang longer?

21. Josephine spent 0.3 of a day cleaning. Bob spent $\frac{2}{5}$ of a day. Who cleaned longer?

Use GEOMETRY to recognize symmetric figures.
Use NUMBER skills to solve comparison problems involving equivalent fractions and decimals (tenths).

LOOKING BACK
Reviewing and Testing Chapter 9

In Chapter 9, you formulated problems about an apple harvest. Look at pages 112 and 113.

1. Write a sentence telling what you think frost does to the apples.

You learned about fractions that are equivalent to 1 and 0. To review what you learned, study the sample exercises on pages 114 and 116. Then use these skills to copy and complete exercises 2–11.

2. $\frac{\blacksquare}{3} = 0$ 3. $\frac{\blacksquare}{7} = 0$ 4. $\frac{\blacksquare}{12} = 0$ 5. $\frac{\blacksquare}{20} = 0$ 6. $\frac{\blacksquare}{100} = 0$

7. $\frac{6}{\blacksquare} = 1$ 8. $\frac{4}{\blacksquare} = 1$ 9. $\frac{11}{\blacksquare} = 1$ 10. $\frac{30}{\blacksquare} = 1$ 11. $\frac{100}{\blacksquare} = 1$

You learned about equivalent fractions and decimals. To review, look at pages 118 and 120. Use the fraction bars to copy and complete the equivalent fractions for exercises 12 and 13 and the equivalent fractions and decimals for exercises 14 and 15.

12.
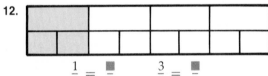
$$\frac{1}{4} = \frac{\blacksquare}{8} \qquad \frac{3}{4} = \frac{\blacksquare}{8}$$

13.
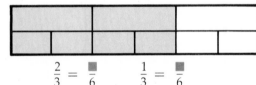
$$\frac{2}{3} = \frac{\blacksquare}{6} \qquad \frac{1}{3} = \frac{\blacksquare}{6}$$

14.
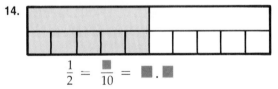
$$\frac{1}{2} = \frac{\blacksquare}{10} = \blacksquare.\blacksquare$$

15.
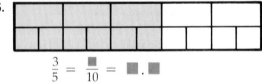
$$\frac{3}{5} = \frac{\blacksquare}{10} = \blacksquare.\blacksquare$$

You learned about solving comparison problems. To review, look at page 121. Solve the problems for exercises 16 and 17.

16. Claire ran $\frac{3}{4}$ of a mile. Sue ran $\frac{7}{8}$ of a mile. Who ran farther?

17. Roy spent $\frac{1}{2}$ hour at the dentist. Carlo spent 0.3 hour. Who spent more time?

FOCUS | Review and test skills learned and practiced.

Preparing for New Skills for Chapter 10

In the next chapter, you will focus on

- formulating problems about a juice stand.
- adding decimals.

- using measurement.
- subtracting decimals.
- how math is used in art.

Learning how to add and subtract tenths as decimals will be easier if you brush up on what you already know about tenths and decimals. First review the examples below. Then complete exercises 1–3.

Look at the rectangle. It is divided into 10 equal parts. Each part equals one tenth of the whole. There are 4 red parts. The red part equals four tenths. Tenths can be written as fractions or decimals.

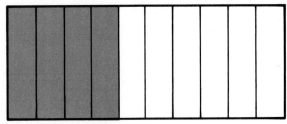

$$\frac{1}{10} = 0.1 \qquad \frac{4}{10} = 0.4$$

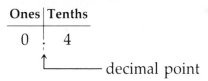

The number line shows how tenths are written as fractions or decimals.

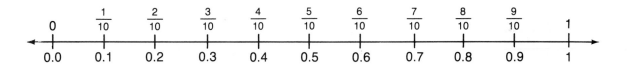

PRACTICE

Write a fraction and a decimal to tell how much is green.

1. 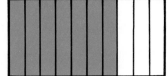   2.   3.

Review NUMBER skills in preparation for learning a new skill.

FOCUS | Formulate problems using picture cues, text, and data.

124

CHAPTER 10

Addition and Subtraction of Decimals

DATA

Alice's Fruit-Juice Stand

Weather   Hot and sunny

Business hours
   1:00 P.M. to 5:00 P.M.

Supplies
   Paper cups   4¢ each
   Fruit juice   15¢ per cup
   Each cup holds 8 ounces

Selling price   25¢ per cup

Number of cups sold
   so far   20

Number of customers
   so far   15

Have you ever thought of starting your own business? You need to work hard and have good ideas in order to get things started. Every business wants to make money. This is called **making a profit.**

Setting up your own fruit-juice stand is one way to learn how a business works. To make a profit, you must keep track of how much you spend on supplies. You have to sell the fruit juice for more than what it cost you.

Look at the picture and the data. What supplies did Alice have to buy? How much profit is she making on each cup sold? What problems might she face? What might she do to improve business? Think of what you would do if you had your own juice stand. Think of some other types of businesses you might like to start. Discuss your answers.

Adding Tenths

Add: 4.7 + 3.2

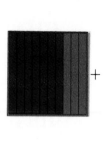

Line up the decimal points.

Ones	Tenths
4	7
+3	2

Add the tenths.

O	Ts
4	7
+3	2
	9

Add the ones. Write the decimal point in the answer.

O	Ts
4	7
+3	2
7	9

Sometimes you need to regroup tenths.
Add: 4.8 + 3.9

Line up the decimal points.

Ones	Tenths
4	8
+3	9

Add the tenths. Regroup.

O	Ts
☐	
4	8
+3	9
	7

    8 tenths
  +9 tenths
  ☐7 tenths

Add the ones. Write the decimal point in the answer.

O	Ts
☐	
4	8
+3	9
8	7

GUIDED PRACTICE

Add. Remember to write the decimal point in the answer.

	1.	2.	3.	4.	5.	6.
	6.3	0.9	5.6	7.2	8.5	9.7
	+2.4	+0.8	+3.5	+5.4	+3.9	+4.6
	8.7	▇.7				

7. 3.8 + 4.1   8. 6.7 + 3.8   9. 4.5 + 4.5   10. 6.5 + 8.7

FOCUS	Use NUMBER skills to add decimals.

PRACTICE

Add.

11. 6.2
    +3.3

12. 7.7
    +2.6

13. 4.8
    +1.8

14. 6.8
    +9.4

15. 3.6
    +4.8

16. 8.2
    +5.3

17. 5.8
    +3.2

18. 16.7
    +21.5

19. 6.3
    +6.1

20. 0.8
    +0.4

21. 7.2
    +5.9

22. 9.4
    +8.9

23. 7.6
    +1.6

24. 12.2
    + 6.9

25. 8.5
    +6.8

26. 5.2
    +16.3

27. 9.1
    +1.9

28. 6.4
    +6.8

29. 4.3
    +7.9

30. 3.6
    +4.8

31. 36.1
    +14.5

32. 5.9
    +3.9

33. 14.4
    + 5.7

34. 9.2
    +1.7

35. 6.8 + 4.5

36. 5.4 + 7.3

37. 8.3 + 1.8

38. 0.4 + 0.9

39. 4.3 + 9.7

40. 5.8 + 6.4

41. 13.6 + 14.8

42. 24.6 + 5.8

43. 7.5 + 3.8

44. 6.2 + 11.6

45. 4.4 + 8.8

46. 6.1 + 3.9

MIXED PRACTICE

Add.

47. 17.2
    + 4.8

48. 5.4
    +6.7

49. 4,629
    +3,764

50. 35,306
    +42,498

51. 57,396
    + 4,694

52. 3,958 + 465

53. 71,410 + 19,306

54. 42,965 + 28,306

CHALLENGE

Add.

55. 4.3
    3.6
    +2.4

56. 6.7
    0.8
    +3.5

57. 2.5
    9.6
    +6.8

58. 3.4
    4.6
    +7.0

59. 8.1
    2.6
    +7.9

60. 5.2
    8.6
    +1.3

ADDITION OF DECIMALS
Adding Tenths

Adding decimals is like adding whole numbers. Sometimes when adding decimals you need to regroup; sometimes you do not.

Without regrouping

```
 T | O | Ts
   |   |
 1 | 4 | 1
 + | 3 | 6
-----------
 1 | 7 | 7
```

With regrouping

```
 T | O | Ts
 1 | 1 |
   | 8 | 6
 +1| 4 | 7
-----------
 2 | 3 | 3
```

Always be sure to line up the decimal points before you add and include the decimal point in your answer.

PRACTICE

Add.

1.   8.6
  +3.2
	2. 4.7
	  +9.8
		3. 13.2
		  + 6.4
			4. 11.6
			  + 1.9
				5. 6.2
				  +3.4
					6. 0.6
					  +0.2

7.   9.4
  +6.9
	8. 46.2
	  +37.8
		9. 3.5
		  +9.7
			10. 5.6
			  +6.3
				11. 10.7
				  + 6.4
					12. 35.8
					  + 9.6

13. 4.3 + 8.2   14. 10.2 + 16.9   15. 5.6 + 3.3   16. 12.6 + 24.7

MIXED PRACTICE
Maintaining and Reviewing Skills

Add.

17.   5.6
  +3.7
	18. 20.4
	  +36.9
		19. 463
		  +389
			20. 642
			  + 97
				21. 435
				 261
				 +187
					22. 604
					 196
					 +195

23. 64 + 126 + 306   24. 728 + 167   25. 296 + 394 + 123

26. 416 + 38 + 295   27. 39 + 86 + 481   28. 369 + 432

FOCUS   Use NUMBER skills to add decimals.

APPLICATION

Using Measurement

This map measures distances between towns in kilometers. Remember that 1 kilometer (km) is equal to 1 000 meters (m).

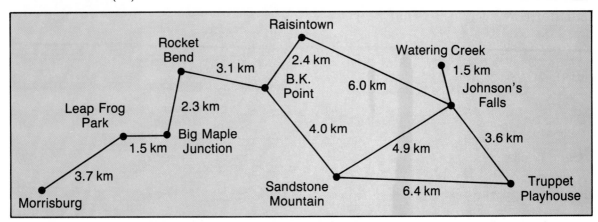

The numbers between each town tell how many kilometers you must travel from one town to the next. For example, to travel from Morrisburg to Leap Frog Park, you would need to travel 3.7 km. If you wanted to travel to Big Maple Junction after that, you would travel 1.5 km further. To find how far it is from Morrisburg to Big Maple Junction, you add.

Morrisburg to Leap Frog Park ⟶   3.7 km
Leap Frog Park to Big Maple Junction ⟶   +1.5 km
Morrisburg to Big Maple Junction ⟶   5.2 km

Solving Problems

Use the map above to help you find the distance between each of the towns listed below.

29. Sandstone Mountain to Truppet Playhouse

30. Sandstone Mountain to Rocket Bend

31. Raisintown to Johnson's Falls

32. B.K. Point to Raisintown

33. Rocket Bend to Leap Frog Park

34. Truppet Playhouse to B.K. Point

35. Watering Creek to Sandstone Mountain

36. Raisintown to Watering Creek

Use MEASUREMENT and NUMBER skills to add decimals.

129

Subtracting Tenths

Ian and Erik are in the long jump competition. Ian jumped 1.5 meters. Erik jumped 1.8 meters. How much farther did Erik jump than Ian?

To find how much farther Erik jumped, subtract: 1.8 − 1.5.

Line up the decimal points.	Subtract the tenths.	Subtract the ones. Write the decimal point in the answer.
Ones | Tenths 1 . 8 −1 . 5	O | Ts 1 . 8 −1 . 5 ‾‾‾3	O | Ts 1 . 8 −1 . 5 0 . 3

Erik jumped 0.3 meter farther than Ian.

Sometimes you need to regroup.
Subtract: 6.4 − 3.7

Line up the decimal points.	Regroup. Subtract the tenths.	Subtract the ones. Write the decimal point in the answer.
Ones | Tenths 6 . 4 −3 . 7	O | Ts 5 | 14 6̸ . 4̸ −3 . 7 ‾‾‾7	O | Ts 5 | 14 6̸ . 4̸ −3 . 7 2 . 7

GUIDED PRACTICE

Subtract. Remember to write the decimal point in the answer.

1. 8.4
   −3.3
   ‾‾‾‾
    5.1

2. ⁶¹¹
    7.1̸
   −3.8
   ‾‾‾‾
    ■.3

3. 16.4
   − 5.7

4. 9.9
   −2.8

5. 6.3
   −5.6

6. 2.2
   −1.6

7. 6.9 − 4.8

8. 3.8 − 1.9

9. 21.6 − 13.8

10. 7.6 − 1.4

PRACTICE

Subtract.

11.	7.8	12.	8.5	13.	6.2	14.	9.7	15.	5.6	16.	6.4
	-4.6		-5.2		-3.5		-6.8		-3.7		-3.4

17.	8.8	18.	4.9	19.	27.5	20.	9.7	21.	13.6	22.	6.1
	-3.9		-2.7		-15.6		-6.8		$-\ 2.1$		-4.5

23.	12.4	24.	6.7	25.	8.6	26.	6.1	27.	21.8	28.	5.4
	$-\ 3.8$		-4.2		-3.7		-3.1		-13.9		-3.7

29.	9.1	30.	10.2	31.	7.3	32.	5.4	33.	13.7	34.	6.3
	-6.3		$-\ 5.1$		-4.4		-4.6		$-\ 2.8$		-5.8

35. $9.5 - 3.7$ **36.** $7.6 - 3.5$ **37.** $19.4 - 5.8$ **38.** $5.2 - 1.3$

39. $6.4 - 2.7$ **40.** $43.6 - 21.9$ **41.** $9.1 - 5.2$ **42.** $8.3 - 6.4$

43. $7.9 - 4.6$ **44.** $9.6 - 2.7$ **45.** $7.7 - 4.9$ **46.** $11.1 - 6.4$

MIXED PRACTICE

Maintaining and Reviewing Skills

Subtract.

47.	5.1	48.	8.4	49.	4,621	50.	64,739	51.	87,304
	-3.2		-3.5		$-2,391$		$-26,842$		$-\ 2,645$

52. $5,936 - 749$ **53.** $40,632 - 27,821$ **54.** $72,329 - 4,764$

CHALLENGE

Find the missing digits.

55.	5 . ■	56.	2 ■ . 4	57.	8 . ■	58.	■ . 8	59.	■ . 6
	$-\ ■ . 6$		$+\ 6 . ■$		$-\ ■ . 8$		$+13 . ■$		$+4 . ■$
	2 . 7		■ 0 . 9		4 . 7		■ 8 . 3		1 4 . 0

SUBTRACTION OF DECIMALS
Subtracting Tenths

When you are subtracting decimals, sometimes you need to write a zero before you subtract.

Subtract: 9 − 6.4

Write 9 as 9.0.	Regroup and subtract.
$\begin{array}{r} 9.0 \\ -6.4 \\ \hline \end{array}$	$\begin{array}{r} \overset{8\ \ 10}{9.\cancel{0}} \\ -6.4 \\ \hline 2.6 \end{array}$

Subtract: 8.4 − 3

Write 3 as 3.0.	Subtract.
$\begin{array}{r} 8.4 \\ -3.0 \\ \hline \end{array}$	$\begin{array}{r} 8.4 \\ -3.0 \\ \hline 5.4 \end{array}$

PRACTICE

Subtract.

1. $\begin{array}{r} 8 \\ -4.7 \\ \hline \end{array}$
2. $\begin{array}{r} 3.5 \\ -2 \\ \hline \end{array}$
3. $\begin{array}{r} 4.6 \\ -3.4 \\ \hline \end{array}$
4. $\begin{array}{r} 15.7 \\ -5.8 \\ \hline \end{array}$
5. $\begin{array}{r} 17 \\ -3.8 \\ \hline \end{array}$
6. $\begin{array}{r} 24.1 \\ -13.9 \\ \hline \end{array}$

7. 8.6 − 4
8. 11.1 − 8
9. 6.4 − 3
10. 14 − 5.9

11. 26 − 13.4
12. 39.6 − 24
13. 9 − 7.6
14. 6.4 − 5

15. 4 − 2.9
16. 8.6 − 5
17. 12 − 10.2
18. 13.6 − 6

MIXED PRACTICE
Maintaining and Reviewing Skills

Subtract.

19. $\begin{array}{r} 6 \\ -3.4 \\ \hline \end{array}$
20. $\begin{array}{r} 9.6 \\ -7 \\ \hline \end{array}$
21. $\begin{array}{r} 365 \\ -196 \\ \hline \end{array}$
22. $\begin{array}{r} 4{,}263 \\ -2{,}456 \\ \hline \end{array}$
23. $\begin{array}{r} 6{,}435 \\ -943 \\ \hline \end{array}$

24. $\begin{array}{r} 85{,}901 \\ -34{,}610 \\ \hline \end{array}$
25. $\begin{array}{r} 73{,}614 \\ -39{,}456 \\ \hline \end{array}$
26. $\begin{array}{r} 47{,}829 \\ -3{,}738 \\ \hline \end{array}$
27. $\begin{array}{r} 39{,}041 \\ -16{,}436 \\ \hline \end{array}$
28. $\begin{array}{r} 96{,}211 \\ -37{,}395 \\ \hline \end{array}$

29. 6.8 − 5
30. 8 − 6.3
31. 5,629 − 849

32. 41,380 − 29,415
33. 7,642 − 5,651
34. 59,820 − 4,679

FOCUS   Use NUMBER skills to subtract decimals.

APPLICATION

Using Measurement

You are going to use a metric ruler and a scale to find the distance from one town to another on this map. The scale you are going to use is 1 cm = 1 km.

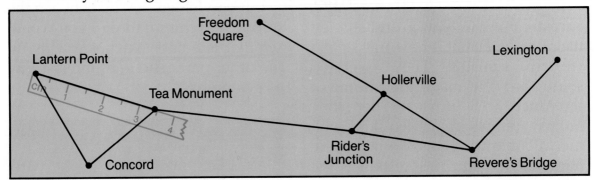

To find the actual distance between Lantern Point and Tea Monument, first measure the distance between the two towns on the map. There are 3.5 cm between the two towns.

To find how many kilometers there are between the two towns, look at the pattern. For every 1 cm of map distance, there is 1 km of actual distance. There are 3.5 km between Lantern Point and Tea Monument.

Measure the map distance between the towns listed below to the nearest 0.5 cm. Then tell the distance between the towns in kilometers using the scale, 1 cm = 1 km.

map distance (cm)	actual distance (km)
1	1
1.5	1.5
2	2
2.5	2.5
3	3
3.5	3.5
4	4
4.5	4.5

35. Lantern Point to Concord

36. Hollerville to Revere's Bridge

37. Tea Monument to Rider's Junction

38. Freedom Square to Hollerville

Solving Problems

Solve these problems using the map above.

39. John traveled from Freedom Square to Hollerville and then went to Revere's Bridge. How far did he travel altogether?

40. Tea Monument is near Concord and Lantern Point. How much farther is it to Lantern Point than it is to Concord?

Use MEASUREMENT to convert map distances to actual distances.
Use NUMBER skills to subtract decimals and solve problems.

Navajo Art

Nearly a thousand years ago, ancestors of the Navajo Indians left their home in what is now Alaska and western Canada. They migrated southward and made their home in the American Southwest. There they hunted animals and traded skins with the Pueblo Indians, who were farmers. In return for skins, the Navajo received Pueblo corn and cotton blankets.

In the sixteenth century, Spanish settlers brought sheep to the Southwest. The Navajo became sheepherders. They roamed with their flocks across what is now Arizona and New Mexico. The Pueblos taught the Navajo women how to weave on looms. Soon they were making beautiful woolen clothing, blankets, and rugs.

Look at the Navajo rugs. Each rug has a repeated pattern. How many dancers do you see in the *Blue Bird Dancers* rug? Are the dancers repeated? Which of these patterns do you see on the rug: the ABBA pattern or the ABAB pattern?

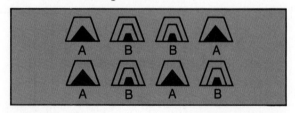

If you folded the rug between the second and third dancers, you would see that one part matches exactly on the other part. The fold line is a **line of symmetry.**

CRITICAL THINKING

1. What is the shape of each rug?

2. List the geometric shapes you see in the *Grand Prize* rug.

3. What does a line of symmetry do? Choose one.
   a. It divides a pattern so that one part matches exactly on the other part.
   b. It shows parts of a design that are different.
   c. It shows how to find the perimeter of a rug.

4. The *Grand Prize* rug has two lines of symmetry. Draw the outline of the rug and show the lines of symmetry.

FOCUS | Use GEOMETRY and PATTERNS to appreciate and analyze the mathematical principles used by Navajo weavers.

Blue Bird Dancers rug

Grand Prize rug

LOOKING BACK
Reviewing and Testing Chapter 10

In Chapter 10 you formulated problems about a juice stand. Look at pages 124 and 125.

1. Write a sentence telling how you would determine how much to charge for a glass of juice.

You learned about adding decimals. To review what you learned, study the sample exercises on pages 126 and 128. Find each sum for exercises 2–11.

2. 2.3
  +4.6

3. 1.8
  +5.4

4. 13.5
  + 6.9

5. 21.7
  +16.3

6. 14.4
  +38.9

7. 1.5 + 6.4

8. 3.2 + 4.9

9. 24.7 + 5.8

10. 56.1 + 8.9

11. The Martinez family drove 10.5 kilometers in the morning and 23.6 kilometers in the afternoon. How far did they drive altogether?

You learned about subtracting decimals. Look at pages 130 and 132. Find each difference for exercises 12–21.

12. 7.6
  −3.4

13. 5.3
  −2.9

14. 16.5
  − 8.4

15. 32.7
  −18.9

16. 25
  −12.6

17. 9.2 − 8.3

18. 23.8 − 4.4

19. 40.1 − 25.6

20. 18 − 13.4

21. Marta ran for 2.3 hours. Alice ran for 1.8 hours. How much longer did Marta run?

You learned about patterns in Navajo art. Look at pages 134 and 135 to review the patterns and what a line of symmetry does.

22. Which line is a line of symmetry?

FOCUS   Review and test skills learned and practiced.

LOOKING AHEAD

Preparing for New Skills for Chapter 11

In the next chapter, you will focus on

- formulating problems about a talent show.
- using metric units to measure length.
- using measurement: area
- using a problem-solving strategy.
- using metric units to measure mass.
- telling time.

Learning more about measuring with metric units will be easier if you brush up on what you already know.

Review the examples. Then complete exercises 1–8.

Centimeters (cm) and **meters** (m) are metric units used to measure length.

Centimeters are used to measure the length of small objects. A paper clip is about 3 cm long.

There are 100 centimeters in a meter. A meter is used to measure the length of longer objects. A baseball bat is about 1 meter long.

Grams (g) and **kilograms** (kg) are metric units used to measure the mass of things.

Grams are used to measure the mass of small things. A leaf has the mass of about 1 gram.

There are 1 000 grams in a kilogram. Kilograms are used to measure the mass of larger things. A pair of shoes has the mass of about 1 kilogram.

PRACTICE

Would you measure in centimeters or meters?

1. an envelope   2. a desk   3. a rug   4. an eraser

Would you measure in grams or kilograms?

5. a chair   6. a person   7. a letter   8. a box of cereal

Review MEASUREMENT in preparation for learning a new skill.

FOCUS   Formulate problems using picture cues, text, and data.

CHAPTER 11

Metric Measurement

DATA

Place	King Grade School
Event	Talent show
Teacher	Mr. Milano
Performers	Class 4-C

Activity	Number wishing to perform this activity
Singing	5
Dancing	5
Doing magic	2
Telling jokes	3
Acting	6
Playing music	8

Time allowed	1 hour

If you can sing, dance, play music, or tell a joke well, you have a talent. People enjoy watching a talented person perform. Sometimes a number of people perform together in a talent show.

The picture shows a performance taking place. The data tells you that 29 pupils are interested in taking part in a class talent show. Using the picture and the data, think about the problems facing the people planning and appearing in a talent show. How can they work together to solve these problems?

Estimating and Measuring Length

The **centimeter (cm)** is a metric unit used to measure length. ⊢——⊣ 1 centimeter

The length of the paper clip is about 5 centimeters.

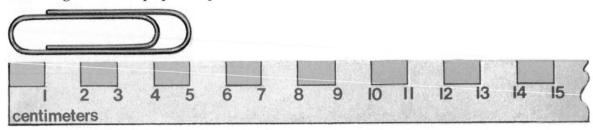

The length of the pencil is about 12 centimeters.

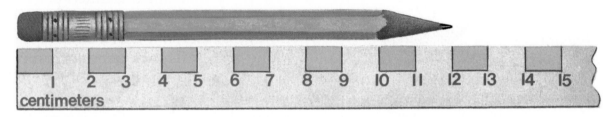

The length of this straw is between 8 and 9 centimeters. It is nearer to 9 centimeters. The length of this straw is 9 centimeters to the nearest centimeter.

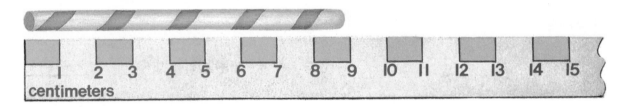

GUIDED PRACTICE

Use a centimeter ruler. Measure the length of each object to the nearest centimeter.

1. 6 cm

2.

FOCUS | Use MEASUREMENT to measure length.

PRACTICE

Use a centimeter ruler. Measure the length of each object
to the nearest centimeter.

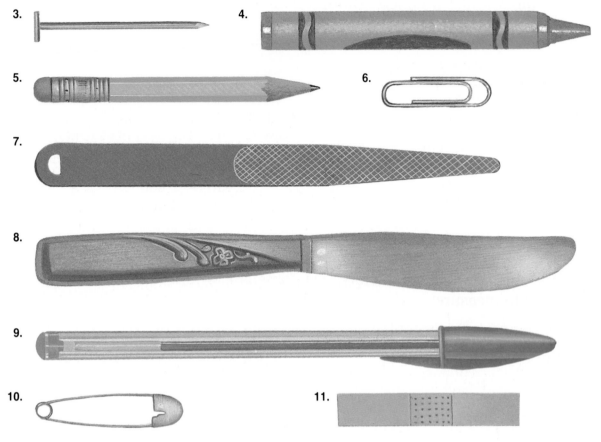

3.

4.

5.

6.

7.

8.

9.

10.

11.

MIXED PRACTICE
Maintaining and Reviewing Skills

Add or subtract.

12. $4.6 + 3.9$ **13.** $6.1 - 5.8$ **14.** $3.7 + 6.5$ **15.** $8.2 - 3.6$ **16.** $7.4 - 3.5$

CHALLENGE

Estimate the length of each object listed below. Then
use a centimeter ruler to find the actual length of each
object. How close were your estimates?

17. a crayon

18. your pencil

19. your thumb

20. your desk

MEASUREMENT

Relating Centimeters, Meters, and Kilometers

Other metric units for measuring length are the **meter (m)** and the **kilometer (km)**.

> 100 centimeters (cm) = 1 meter (m)
> 1 000 meters = 1 kilometer

The width of a doorway is about 1 meter. You can walk a distance of 1 kilometer in about 20 minutes.

2 m = ■ cm	3 km = ■ m
Think: 1 m = 100 cm	Think: 1 km = 1 000 m
2 m = 200 cm	2 km = 2 000 m
	3 km = 3 000 m

PRACTICE

Which unit, centimeters, meters, or kilometers, would you use to measure:

1. the length of your foot?

2. the length of a river?

3. the width of a window?

4. the distance you can walk in one hour?

Copy and complete.

5. 4 m = ■ cm

6. 3 km = ■ m

7. 5 m = ■ cm

8. 9 km = ■ m

9. 6 km = ■ m

10. 10 m = ■ cm

MIXED PRACTICE
Maintaining and Reviewing Skills

Copy and complete.

11. 7 m = ■ cm

12. 4 km = ■ m

13. 2 m = ■ cm

Use a centimeter ruler. Measure the length of each object to the nearest centimeter.

14.

15.

APPLICATION

Using Measurement: Area

Area is the number of square units that cover a surface.

The **square centimeter** is a metric unit of area.

The **square meter** is another metric unit of area.

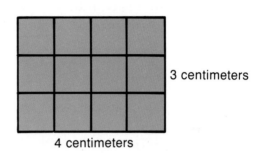

1 centimeter
1 centimeter   1 centimeter
1 centimeter
1 square centimeter

You can count to find the area of this rectangle. The area is 12 square centimeters.

or

You can multiply the length and the width to find the area.

$$4 \quad \times \quad 3 \quad = 12$$

Area: 12 square centimeters

3 centimeters

4 centimeters

Count to find the area of each rectangle.

16.

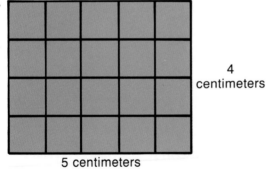

4 centimeters

5 centimeters

Area: ■ square centimeters

17.

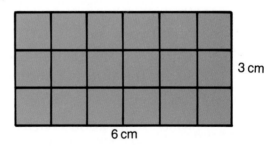

3 cm

6 cm

Area: ■ square centimeters

Multiply to find the area of each rectangle.

18. length: 8 centimeters
width: 5 centimeters

19. length: 15 centimeters
width: 9 centimeters

20. length: 13 meters
width: 7 meters

21. length: 37 meters
width: 6 meters

Use MEASUREMENT to find the area of a rectangle.

EXTRA PRACTICE—page 447

Exploring PLAN, SOLVE, and CHECK

The last three steps of the problem-solving plan show how to find the answer to a problem.

1. READ In 1804, the Lewis and Clark expedition left to explore the northwestern United States. A Native American woman, Sacagawea (Bird Woman), was interpreter and guide for the expedition. Mike first read about Sacagawea in 1986. How many years after the start of the expedition did Mike read about her?

2. KNOW

Facts I Know	What I Need to Find	Key Facts
Sacagawea interpreter and guide expedition started 1804 Mike read about Sacagawea in 1986.	how many years from start of expedition to Mike's reading	expedition started 1804 Mike read about Sacagawea in 1986.

3. PLAN Ask yourself: Which operation should I use? To find the number of years from 1804 to 1986, subtract.

4. SOLVE Carry out the plan.
Write the number sentence: 1986 − 1804 = ■
                                    1986 − 1804 = 182

Mike read about Sacagawea 182 years after the start of the Lewis and Clark expedition.

5. CHECK There are two ways to check this answer.
An estimate of 1986 − 1804 is

$$2000 - 1800 = 200.$$

This is close to 182.
Also use addition to check subtraction.

$$\begin{array}{r} 1986 \\ -1804 \\ \hline 182 \end{array} \qquad \begin{array}{r} 1804 \\ +\ 182 \\ \hline 1986 \end{array}$$

FOCUS | Explore the PLAN, SOLVE, and CHECK steps.

PRACTICE

For each problem, what you need to find is given. The **key facts** are underlined.

For both problems, copy and complete these steps.

3. PLAN Select the operation. Write a PLAN sentence.

4. SOLVE Carry out the plan. Write a number sentence. Write the answer.

5. CHECK Estimate. Check with another operation.

1. After the <u>1912</u> Olympics, a Native American named Jim Thorpe became the number one male athlete in the United States. Native Americans were not granted United States citizenship until <u>1924</u>. How many years before he became a citizen was Jim Thorpe considered America's best athlete?
Find: number of years 1912 was before 1924

2. In the 1970s, there were about <u>47,800 Sioux</u> Native Americans in the United States and about 5,100 in Canada. There were about <u>21,500 Iroquois</u> in the United States and about 21,300 in Canada. About how many Sioux and Iroquois were there in the United States in the 1970s?
Find: total number of Sioux and Iroquois in United States

Class Project

Divide into small groups of students. Make a PLAN and then SOLVE the following problem.

The table at the right shows the Native American population in the United States for three different years. By how much did the population increase or decrease during each period of time? Use history books or an encyclopedia to give a reason for each population change.

Native American Population	
1492	1,115,000
1890	90,000
1950	357,000

Introducing and Relating Grams and Kilograms

The **gram (g)** and the **kilogram (kg)** are metric units used to measure mass.

Light objects are measured using grams.

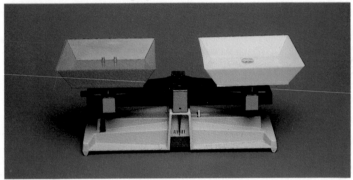

The mass of a dime is about 2 grams.

Heavier objects are measured using kilograms.

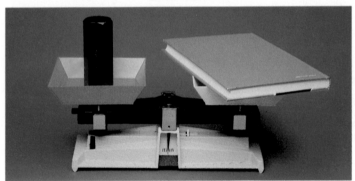

The mass of the book is about 1 kilogram.

$$1\ 000 \text{ grams (g)} = 1 \text{ kilogram (kg)}$$

GUIDED PRACTICE

Copy and complete.

1.   3 000 g = ■ kg
   Think: 1 000 g = 1 kg
           2 000 g = 2 kg
           3 000 g = ■ kg

2.   2 kg = ■ g
   Think: 1 kg = 1 000 g
           2 kg = ■ g

FOCUS | Use MEASUREMENT to measure mass.

PRACTICE

Choose the correct measure.

3.

8 g   8 kg

4.

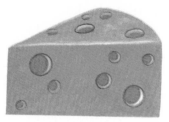

300 g   3 kg

5.

50 g   50 kg

6.

1 g   1 kg

Copy and complete.

7. 5 kg = ▪ g   **8.** 8 kg = ▪ g   **9.** 4 000 g = ▪ kg

10. 6 000 g = ▪ kg   **11.** ▪ g = 3 kg   **12.** ▪ kg = 7 000 g

MIXED PRACTICE
Maintaining and Reviewing Skills

Which unit, centimeters, meters, or kilometers, would you use to measure:

13. the length of your thumb?   **14.** the length of a car?

15. the width of a chair?   **16.** the height of a flagpole?

17. the distance from Washington, D.C., to New York?

CHALLENGE

18. If one dime has a mass of 2 grams, what is the value of 100 grams of dimes?

19. If 20 magazines have a mass of 1 kilogram, how many grams is 1 magazine?

EXTRA PRACTICE—page 447

MEASUREMENT

Telling Time

You use clocks to tell time. They show the hours and minutes of each day. There are 24 hours in one day. There are 60 minutes in 1 hour. Use A.M. to write times between 12 midnight and 12 noon. Use P.M. to write times between 12 noon and 12 midnight.

These clocks show 5:10.

10 minutes after 5 or five ten.

These clocks show 2:40.

20 minutes to 3 or two forty.

PRACTICE

Write the time shown on each clock.

1.

■ minutes after ■

2.

■ minutes after ■

3.

■ minutes to ■

Write the times.

4. 20 minutes after 8

5. five forty-five

6. twenty-two minutes after 10

7. half past seven

MIXED PRACTICE

Maintaining and Reviewing Skills

Add or subtract.

8. $6.3 - 4.8$

9. $7.2 + 8.9$

10. $3.6 + 12.4$

11. $8.1 - 5.6$

APPLICATION

Using Measurement

This table shows 24 hours in Peggy's life.

Time	Activity
7:15 A.M. to 7:45 A.M.	wakes up, brushes her teeth, and gets dressed
7:45 to 8:05	eats breakfast
8:05 to 8:20	leaves home and goes to school
8:20 to 11:40	goes to class
11:40 to 12:30 P.M.	eats lunch
12:30 to 3:00	goes back to classes
3:00 to 3:15	leaves school and goes home
3:15 to 3:30	arrives home and calls friends
3:30 to 5:00	plays with friends
5:00 to 6:00	eats supper
6:00 to 7:35	does her homework
7:35 to 8:15	takes a bath
8:15 to 8:30	goes to bed
8:30	falls asleep

12. How long does it take Peggy to wake up, brush her teeth, and get dressed?

13. How long does it take Peggy to get to school?

14. How long does Peggy play with her friends?

15. How long does it take Peggy to eat her supper?

16. How long does it take Peggy to do her homework?

17. How long does Peggy sleep?

Using Mental Arithmetic

You can count by ones, fives, or tens to find how many minutes there are between two given times.

How many minutes between

18. 1:05 and 1:50?

19. 6:30 and 6:55?

20. 3:10 and 3:40?

21. 7:08 and 7:21?

22. 8:20 and 8:45?

23. 9:42 and 9:51?

Use NUMBER skills and MEASUREMENT to find elapsed time.

LOOKING BACK
Reviewing and Testing Chapter 11

In Chapter 11 you formulated problems about a class talent show. Look at pages 138 and 139.

1. Write a sentence telling how you thought the class could work together to solve the problems of planning and appearing in the show.

You learned something new about centimeters, meters, and kilometers. To review what you learned, study the sample exercises on pages 140 and 142. Then use these skills to measure the length of the object in exercise 2 to the nearest centimeter. Copy and complete exercises 3–5.

2. ▬▬▬▬▬▬▬▬▬▬▬▬▬▬▬▬▬▬▬▬

3. 2 m = ■ cm   4. 5 km = ■ m   5. 8 m = ■ cm

You learned how to use the PLAN, SOLVE, and CHECK steps of the Five-Step PROBLEM SOLVING Plan. To review, look at pages 144 and 145.

6. In 1984, about 24,300 people lived in 24 developments in Somers. North Salem's 4 developments were home to about 6,800 people. About how many more people lived in the developments in Somers than in North Salem?

You learned something new about grams and kilograms. To review, look at page 146. Copy and complete exercises 7–9.

7. 5 kg = ■ g   8. 7 000 g = ■ kg   9. ■ g = 4 kg

You learned about telling time. To review, look at page 148. Write each time for exercises 10 and 11.

10. 15 minutes after 6   11. three forty-five

| FOCUS | Review and test skills learned and practiced. |

150

LOOKING AHEAD

Preparing for New Skills for Chapter 12

In the next chapter, you will focus on

- formulating problems about building a tunnel.
- using metric units to measure capacity.
- using statistics and probability.
- measuring temperature.
- using measurement: volume.
- how math is used in technology.

Learning more about measuring capacity and temperature with metric units will be easier if you brush up on what you already know about these units. First review the examples. Then complete exercises 1–6.

Milliliters (mL) and **liters** (L) are metric units used to measure capacity. One milliliter is about an eyedropper full. It is used to measure small amounts of liquid.

There are 1 000 milliliters in a liter. A liter will fill a large pitcher. Liters are used to measure larger amounts of liquid.

Degrees Celsius (°C) are metric units used to measure temperature. The thermometer on the right is a Celsius thermometer.

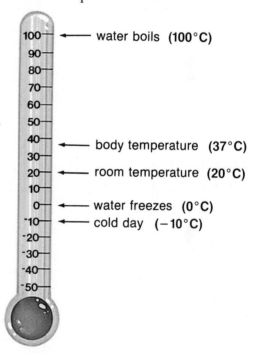

water boils (100°C)

body temperature (37°C)

room temperature (20°C)

water freezes (0°C)

cold day (−10°C)

PRACTICE

Would you measure in milliliters or liters?

1. water in a pool

2. liquid in a teaspoon

3. glass of milk

4. liquid in a large pail

Use the thermometer to answer these questions.

5. What is a normal body temperature?

6. What is a normal room temperature?

Review MEASUREMENT in preparation for learning a new skill.

CHAPTER 12

Metric Measurement

DATA

Simplon Railroad Tunnel

Two parallel tunnels; one railroad track in each tunnel

Length
  12 miles or about 19 kilometers

Inside temperature
  As high as 130°F or about 54°C

Behind tunnel walls
  Boiling and freezing streams

In 1898, two teams of workers started blasting a tunnel through a mountain from opposite sides. Eight years later, when the two teams met in the middle of the mountain, they had formed the Simplon Railroad Tunnel—the longest tunnel in the world.

During those eight years, sixty lives were lost, and the workers met with one problem after another. What caused such problems? Well, if you've ever tried to dig a tunnel through a sand castle, you might be able to make some pretty good guesses.

Look at the picture and the data. What things can go wrong when building a long tunnel?

Could these things have been predicted? Explain.

Estimating and Measuring Capacity

The **milliliter (mL)** and the **liter (L)** are metric units used to measure liquids.

This cube holds 1 milliliter of liquid. The volume of this cube is 1 cubic centimeter.

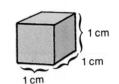

This cube holds 1 liter of liquid. The volume of this cube is 1 000 cubic centimeters.

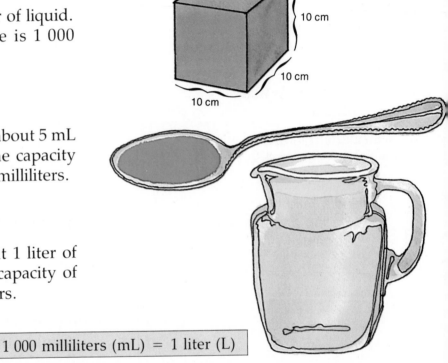

A small spoon holds about 5 mL of liquid. You measure the capacity of small containers using milliliters.

A pitcher holds about 1 liter of liquid. You measure the capacity of large containers using liters.

1 000 milliliters (mL) = 1 liter (L)

GUIDED PRACTICE

Which unit, milliliters or liters, would you use to measure the capacity of:

1. an eyedropper? milliliters

2. a can of paint?

3. a fish tank?

4. a baby bottle?

5. a barrel?

6. a test tube?

PRACTICE

Which unit, milliliters or liters, would you use to measure
the amount of liquid in:

7. a can of motor oil?

8. a glass of orange juice?

9. a pail of water?

10. a thermos?

11. the gas tank of a car?

12. a bowl of punch?

13. a can of soup?

14. a jug of apple cider?

Choose the correct measure.

15.

300 mL   300 L

16.

35 mL   35 L

MIXED PRACTICE

Maintaining and Reviewing Skills

Copy and complete.

17. 1 000 mL = ■ L

18. 5 m = ■ cm

19. 2 km = ■ m

20. 20 m = ■ cm

21. 3 kg = ■ g

22. 6 000 g = ■ kg

CHALLENGE

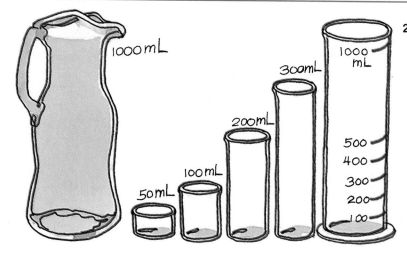

23. The pitcher at the left is used to fill the four containers. The remainder of the liquid is poured into the cylinder at the right. How much water will be poured into the cylinder?

MEASUREMENT
Metric Units of Capacity

Capacity measures how much liquid a container can hold. Look at the different shaped containers.

There are 100 mL of liquid in each container. Notice that this amount of liquid looks very different in different shaped containers.

$$1\ 000 \text{ milliliters (mL)} = 1 \text{ liter (L)}$$

	3 000 mL = ■ L		5 L = ■ mL
Think:	1 000 mL = 1 L	Think:	3 L = 3 000 mL
	2 000 mL = 2 L		4 L = 4 000 mL
	3 000 mL = 3 L		5 L = 5 000 mL

PRACTICE

Copy and complete.

1. 4 000 mL = ■ L
2. 7 000 mL = ■ L
3. 5 000 mL = ■ L

4. 2 L = ■ mL
5. 6 L = ■ mL
6. 3 L = ■ mL

7. 9 000 mL = ■ L
8. 7 L = ■ mL
9. 4 L = ■ mL

MIXED PRACTICE
Maintaining and Reviewing Skills

Copy and complete.

10. 2 000 mL = ■ L
11. 8 L = ■ mL
12. 4 km = ■ m

13. 600 cm = ■ m
14. 7 m = ■ cm
15. 2 000 m = ■ km

FOCUS | Use MEASUREMENT to measure capacity.

APPLICATION

Using Measurement: Volume

The **volume** of a figure is the number of cubic units that will fit inside the figure.

The **cubic centimeter** is a metric unit of volume.

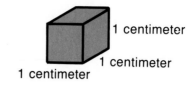

1 cubic centimeter

The **cubic meter** is another metric unit of volume.

You can count to find the volume of this figure. The volume is 24 cubic centimeters.

or

You can multiply the length, the width, and the height to find the volume in cubic centimeters.

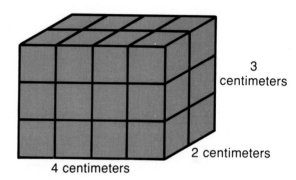

Volume = length × width × height

$$4 \times 2 \times 3 = 24$$

Volume: 24 cubic centimeters

Count to find the volume of each figure.

16.

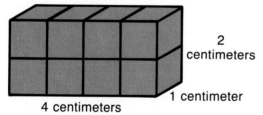

Volume: ■ cubic centimeters

17.

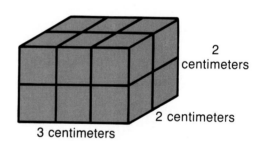

Volume: ■ cubic centimeters

Multiply to find the volume of each figure.

18. length: 6 centimeters
width: 3 centimeters
height: 5 centimeters

19. length: 13 centimeters
width: 7 centimeters
height: 8 centimeters

20. length: 12 meters
width: 6 meters
height: 7 meters

21. length: 18 meters
width: 4 meters
height: 7 meters

Use MEASUREMENT to find the volume of a figure.

EXTRA PRACTICE—page 447

Estimating and Measuring Temperature

The **degree Celsius (°C)** is the metric unit used to measure temperature. Look at this Celsius thermometer.

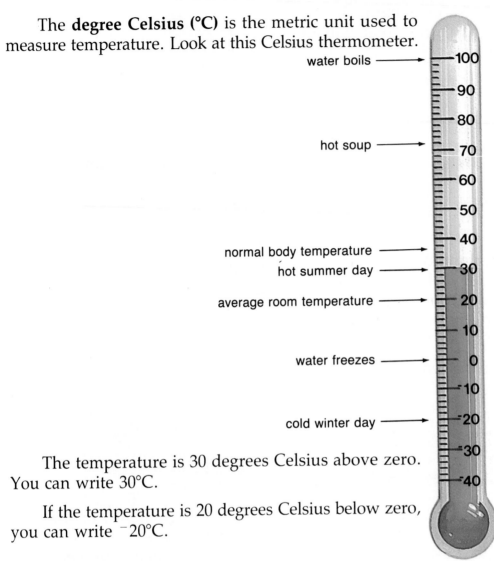

water boils → 100
90
80
hot soup → 70
60
50
40
normal body temperature →
hot summer day → 30
average room temperature → 20
10
water freezes → 0
‑10
cold winter day → ‑20
‑30
‑40

The temperature is 30 degrees Celsius above zero. You can write 30°C.

If the temperature is 20 degrees Celsius below zero, you can write ⁻20°C.

GUIDED PRACTICE

Use the Celsius thermometer above.
What is the temperature for each?

1. water boils 100°C

2. normal body temperature

3. hot summer day

4. water freezes

5. average room temperature

6. cold winter day

7. spring day

8. swimming weather

FOCUS | Use MEASUREMENT to measure temperature.

PRACTICE

Read the temperature in degrees Celsius on each thermometer.

9.    10.    11.    12.

Choose the correct measure.

13. sled-riding weather
    32°C   ⁻10°C

14. a cold drink
    35°C   5°C

15. winter day
    28°C   0°C

16. a hot drink
    16°C   70°C

17. inside a freezer
    32°C   ⁻16°C

18. swimming weather
    32°C   75°C

MIXED PRACTICE

Maintaining and Reviewing Skills

Add or subtract.

19. $13 + 6 =$ ■   20. $25 - 7 =$ ■   21. $75 + 18 =$ ■   22. $48 - 19 =$ ■

CHALLENGE

23. On a hot day, the noon temperature was the same as the morning and evening temperatures together. All three temperatures add up to 80°C. What was the temperature at noon?

MEASUREMENT
Estimating and Measuring Temperature

Each mark on this Celsius thermometer stands for 2 degrees Celsius. This thermometer shows 32°C.

The temperature was 10°C and it rose 12 degrees. The temperature would then be 22°C.

The temperature was 20°C and it fell 35 degrees. The temperature would then be ⁻15°C.

PRACTICE

Copy and complete this table.

	Temperature Was	Rose or Fell	New Temperature
1.	30°C	rose 4 degrees	■
2.	15°C	fell 8 degrees	■
3.	■	fell 12 degrees	⁻12°C
4.	23°C	■	29°C
5.	17°C	rose 6 degrees	■
6.	■	rose 4 degrees	20°C
7.	9°C	■	⁻3°C
8.	12°C	fell 11 degrees	■
9.	■	rose 5 degrees	0°C
10.	13°C	■	8°C

MIXED PRACTICE
Maintaining and Reviewing Skills

Use a Celsius thermometer.
What is the temperature for each?

11. a winter day

12. a summer day

13. a fall day

14. a spring day

FOCUS | Use MEASUREMENT to measure temperature.

APPLICATION
Using Measurement

Choose the best temperature for each.

15. going to the beach	a. 10°C	b. 31°C	c. 18°C
16. oven temperature	a. 20°C	b. 40°C	c. 180°C
17. sweater weather	a. 10°C	b. ⁻15°C	c. 30°C
18. raking leaves	a. 30°C	b. 9°C	c. 0°C
19. fever temperature	a. 40°C	b. 100°C	c. 60°C
20. ice-skating weather	a. 25°C	b. ⁻5°C	c. 15°C
21. water for a bath	a. 43°C	b. 75°C	c. 10°C
22. hot cocoa	a. 29°C	b. 50°C	c. 73°C
23. room temperature	a. 21°C	b. 37°C	c. 50°C
24. building a snowman	a. 32°C	b. 0°C	c. 27°C

Using Mental Arithmetic

The chart below shows the comparison of temperatures on two spring days in New York City.

	6 A.M.	9 A.M.	12 noon	3 P.M.	6 P.M.	9 P.M.
April 2	10°C	17°C	25°C	24°C	20°C	18°C
April 3	7°C	10°C	15°C	16°C	14°C	12°C

25. What was the temperature difference between 9 A.M. and 9 P.M. on April 2?

26. What was the difference in temperature at 3 P.M. on April 2 and April 3?

27. What was the temperature difference between 6 A.M. and 9 P.M. on April 3?

28. What was the temperature difference between 6 A.M. and 9 P.M. on April 2?

29. At which time was the temperature difference between April 2 and April 3 the greatest?

Use MEASUREMENT to measure temperature.
Use MENTAL ARITHMETIC to compare temperatures.

Input and Output

Data that are fed into a computer is called **input**. Input is often typed on a **keyboard** connected to the computer. The information typed on the keyboard appears on a screen that looks something like a television. The computer screen is sometimes called a **monitor**.

A computer can store input, or it can do calculations with input, or it can compare input to other data. What a computer does with data is called **data processing**. Data that has been processed by a computer is called **output**.

After a computer processes data, it can store this information on a **disk** or a **tape**. A computer can also use data already stored on a disk or tape as input. Disks and tapes are used for both input and output.

People can look at output in two ways.

1. The computer can send output to the screen. As long as the computer is on, output on the screen can be read. If the computer is turned off, information that was on the screen is erased.

2. The computer can send output to a printer. A printer prints information onto paper. What is printed on paper can't be erased.

A computer can show output on a screen more quickly than it can print the same output on a printer. Computer users often do most of their work using only the screen. They print output only when they are finished working.

CRITICAL THINKING

1. What is input?

2. What is output?

3. What path does information follow? Start with input.

4. What are the two ways a person can read output?

5. What are the advantages of reading output on a screen?

6. What are the advantages of reading output that has been printed?

FOCUS | Use LOGIC to understand input and output.

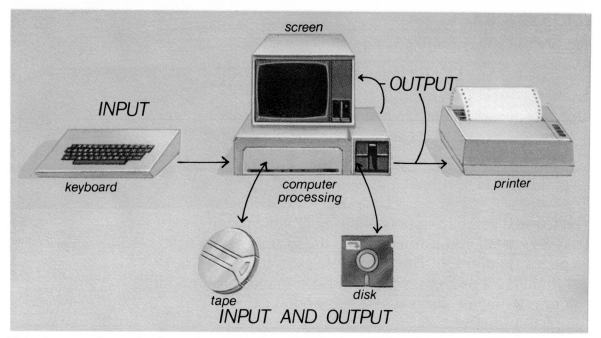

This diagram shows the flow of information through a personal computer. A personal computer has the same basic parts as a large mainframe computer but on a much smaller scale.

A mainframe computer, terminal, and printers can generate great amounts of data in a short period of time.

Reviewing and Testing Chapter 12

In Chapter 12 you formulated problems about building a long tunnel. Look at pages 152 and 153.

1. Write a sentence telling what problems you might have when building a long tunnel.

You learned something new about milliliters and liters. To review what you learned, study the sample exercises on pages 154 and 156. Then use these skills to tell which unit, milliliters or liters, you would use to measure the amount of liquid for exercises 2 and 3. Copy and complete exercises 4–6.

2. a glass of milk

3. a bathtub

4. 3 000 mL = ■ L   5. 9 L = ■ mL   6. 6 000 mL = ■ L

You learned something new about measuring temperature in degrees Celsius. To review, look at pages 158 and 160. Choose the correct measure for exercises 7–9. Find the new temperature, in degrees Celsius, for exercises 10 and 11.

7. a very cold winter day   8. a hot summer day   9. a snowy winter day

   $-10°C$ $32°C$ $75°C$ $32°C$ $28°C$ $0°C$

10. The temperature was 21°C. It rose 8 degrees.

11. The temperature was 6°C. It fell 10 degrees.

You learned about computers and some computer terms. To review, look at pages 162 and 163.

12. Name two ways that a computer can store processed data.

13. What is the term used to describe data that has been processed by a computer?

FOCUS | Review and test skills learned and practiced.

LOOKING AHEAD

Preparing for New Skills for Chapter 13

In the next chapter, you will focus on

- formulating problems about a soccer game.
- multiplying hundreds.
- using patterns and functions.

- multiplying 3-digit numbers by 1-digit numbers.
- estimating products.
- using measurement.

New multiplication skills will be easier to master if you brush up on those multiplication skills you already know. First review Models A and B. Then complete Exercises 1–12.

Model A

Multiply the ones.

```
  T | O
  4 | 3
×   | 3
----------
    | 9
```

Multiply the tens.

```
H | T | O
  | 4 | 3
× |   | 3
-------------
1 | 2 | 9
```

Model B

Multiply the ones. Regroup.

```
  T | O
  1 |
  6 | 8        8
×   | 2      × 2
----------    ----
  | 6         16
```

Multiply the tens.

```
H | T | O
  | 1 |        6T
  | 6 | 8     × 2
× |   | 2     -----
-------------  12T
1 | 3 | 6     + 1T
              -----
               13T
```

PRACTICE

Multiply.

1. 43 × 3	2. 25 × 2	3. 61 × 4	4. 64 × 2	5. 73 × 3	6. 21 × 5
7. 53 × 4	8. 32 × 6	9. 67 × 2	10. 64 × 3	11. 47 × 5	12. 43 × 7

Review NUMBER skills in preparation for learning a new skill.

FOCUS   Formulate several problems using picture cues, text, and data.

13

Multiplication by a 1-Digit Number

DATA

Game		Soccer
Score		
Redbirds	4	
White Stars	3	
Minutes in a game		40
Minutes left to play		5
Players on the field		
Redbirds	11	
White Stars	11	
Players injured		
Redbirds	2	
White Stars	0	
Players waiting to play		
Redbirds	0	
White Stars	2	
Win/loss record to date		
Redbirds	6 wins/	
	5 losses	
White Stars	11 wins/	
	0 losses	

Soccer is a fast-paced, exciting game. As you can see from the picture, these two players are giving it everything they've got. As you can see from the data, seven goals have been scored in all, and some players have been injured. There are only about five minutes left to play. Using this action photograph and the data given, tell several possible ways that this game might end.

First decide what you think is going to happen next to each of the players shown. What problems might each team have? Predict how the game will end. Give your reasons.

Multiplying Hundreds

Roger has 4 coin albums. Each album has 100 coins in it. How many coins does Roger have altogether?

You can add:

$$100 + 100 + 100 + 100 = 400$$

Or, you can multiply:

$$4 \times 100 = 400$$

Roger has 400 coins altogether.

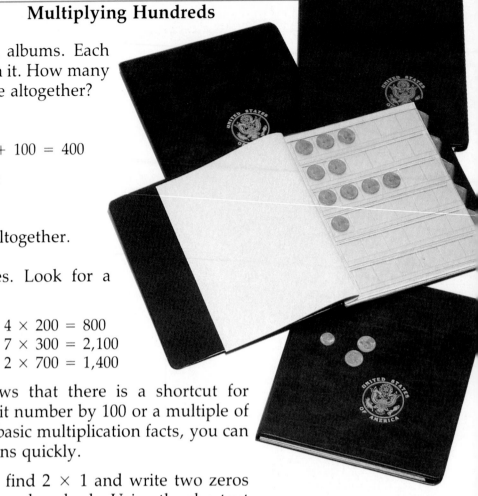

Study these examples. Look for a pattern.

$3 \times 100 = 300$	$4 \times 200 = 800$
$6 \times 100 = 600$	$7 \times 300 = 2,100$
$5 \times 100 = 500$	$2 \times 700 = 1,400$

The pattern shows that there is a shortcut for multiplying a one-digit number by 100 or a multiple of 100. If you know the basic multiplication facts, you can do these multiplications quickly.

To find 2×100, find 2×1 and write two zeros after the product to show hundreds. Using the shortcut you can find 6×500 by multiplying 6×5. The answer is 3,000. How would you find 9×400?

GUIDED PRACTICE

Multiply. Remember to write the correct number of zeros in the product.

1. $\begin{array}{r} 100 \\ \times\ 7 \\ \hline 700 \end{array}$	**2.** $\begin{array}{r} 500 \\ \times\ 3 \\ \hline ■■00 \end{array}$	**3.** $\begin{array}{r} 300 \\ \times\ 6 \\ \hline 1,8■■ \end{array}$	**4.** $\begin{array}{r} 100 \\ \times\ 9 \\ \hline ■00 \end{array}$	**5.** $\begin{array}{r} 600 \\ \times\ 4 \end{array}$	**6.** $\begin{array}{r} 900 \\ \times\ 8 \end{array}$

7. 5×700 **8.** 1×800 **9.** 3×400 **10.** 6×900 **11.** 8×500

FOCUS	Use NUMBER skills to multiply hundreds.

PRACTICE

Find each product. Use the shortcut.

12. 100
    × 8

13. 300
    × 3

14. 700
    × 6

15. 600
    × 9

16. 800
    × 8

17. 900
    × 4

18. 500
    × 8

19. 800
    × 4

20. 500
    × 6

21. 100
    × 5

22. 700
    × 7

23. 700
    × 5

24. 800
    × 6

25. 500
    × 7

26. 600
    × 3

27. 200
    × 4

28. 900
    × 5

29. 400
    × 6

30. 2 × 600

31. 8 × 300

32. 4 × 400

33. 2 × 300

34. 7 × 800

35. 3 × 700

36. 4 × 500

37. 9 × 300

38. 7 × 900

39. 4 × 300

40. Last month Mr. Wong sold 500 yo-yos. This month he sold 4 times that many yo-yos. How many yo-yos did he sell this month?

41. Mrs. Kay ordered 5 boxes of baseball cards. There are 500 baseball cards in each box. How many baseball cards did she order altogether?

MIXED PRACTICE

Maintaining and Reviewing Skills

Add, subtract, or multiply.

42. 300
    × 6

43. 700
    × 4

44. 496
    +328

45. 740
    −369

46. 53
    × 6

47. 2,408
    +3,974

48. 7 × 300

49. 485 − 269

50. 3 × 24

51. 96 − 48

52. 9 × 60

CHALLENGE

Replace each ▌ with the correct number.

53. ▌00
    × 2
    ─────
    600

54. ▌▌0
    × 2
    ─────
    200

55. ▌00
    × 3
    ─────
    2,4▌▌

56. ▌00
    × 7
    ─────
    ▌,6▌▌

57. 600
    × ▌
    ─────
    5,▌▌▌

EXTRA PRACTICE—page 447

MULTIPLICATION
Finding Missing Factors

Study these examples.

$$4 \times \blacksquare = 400 \qquad 3 \times \blacksquare = 1{,}800$$
$$6 \times \blacksquare = 600 \qquad 5 \times \blacksquare = 3{,}500$$
$$\blacksquare \times 100 = 900 \qquad \blacksquare \times 700 = 5{,}600$$

To find the missing factor in each example, you can use division. If you know the basic division facts through $81 \div 9$, you can do these examples easily. To find $4 \times \blacksquare = 400$, find $4 \div 4$ and write two zeros after the quotient to show hundreds. Using the shortcut, you can find $\blacksquare \times 600 = 2{,}400$ by finding $24 \div 6$. How would you find $7 \times \blacksquare = 6{,}300$?

PRACTICE

Find the factor that makes each sentence true.

1. $4 \times \blacksquare = 2{,}800$
2. $6 \times \blacksquare = 3{,}600$
3. $2 \times \blacksquare = 200$

4. $9 \times \blacksquare = 8{,}100$
5. $\blacksquare \times 500 = 4{,}000$
6. $\blacksquare \times 300 = 2{,}100$

7. $7 \times \blacksquare = 6{,}300$
8. $\blacksquare \times 400 = 2{,}000$
9. $8 \times \blacksquare = 2{,}400$

10. $\blacksquare \times 600 = 4{,}200$
11. $1 \times \blacksquare = 600$
12. $6 \times \blacksquare = 5{,}400$

13. $\blacksquare \times 800 = 1{,}600$
14. $4 \times \blacksquare = 1{,}600$
15. $\blacksquare \times 700 = 4{,}900$

16. A gardening store ordered 1,000 tulip bulbs. They received 200 bags of tulip bulbs. How many tulip bulbs were in each bag?

17. A tomato farm ordered 1,600 tomato plants. There are 8 tomato plants in each crate. How many crates of tomato plants did they receive?

MIXED PRACTICE
Maintaining and Reviewing Skills

Find the missing number.

18. $3 \times \blacksquare = 2{,}700$
19. $\blacksquare \times 400 = 2{,}400$
20. $421 + \blacksquare = 710$
21. $805 - \blacksquare = 356$

| FOCUS | Use ALGEBRA and LOGIC to find missing factors. |

170

APPLICATION

Using Patterns and Functions

Find the output for each multiplication function machine.

22.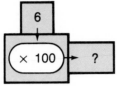

23.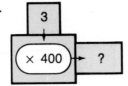

24.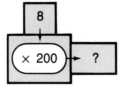

25.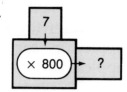

Find the rule for each multiplication function machine.

26.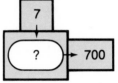

27.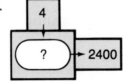

28.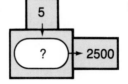

29.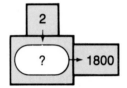

Find the input for each multiplication function machine.

30.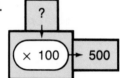

31.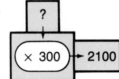

32.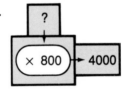

33.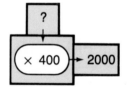

Find the output, rule, or input for each multiplication function machine.

34.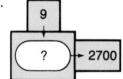

35.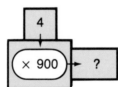

36.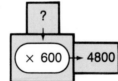

37.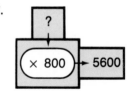

Problem Solving: Using PLAN, SOLVE, and CHECK

Study each group of measures. PLAN by thinking of all of them as either liters or milliliters. SOLVE by writing them in order from least to greatest. CHECK by using the unit of measure you did <u>not</u> use in the PLAN.

38. 3 L, 3 500 mL, 300 mL, 30 L   **39.** 4 000 mL, 400 L, 45 L, 400 mL

Use PATTERNS AND FUNCTIONS to find missing factors and products.
Apply the PLAN, SOLVE, and CHECK steps of the Five-Step PROBLEM SOLVING Plan.

Multiplying 3-Digit Numbers by 1-Digit Numbers

Lili works at Wilkin's Apple Farm. Yesterday she picked and filled 3 crates with apples. She put 132 apples in each crate. How many apples did Lili pick altogether?

To find how many apples Lili picked yesterday, multiply: 3 × 132.

Multiply the ones.

```
  H T O
  1 3 2
×     3
------
      6
```

Multiply the tens.

```
  H T O
  1 3 2
×     3
------
    9 6
```

Multiply the hundreds.

```
  H T O
  1 3 2
×     3
------
  3 9 6
```

Lili picked 396 apples yesterday.

Find 6 × 275. You will need to regroup.

Multiply the ones.
Regroup.

```
Th H T O
      3
    2 7 5      5
  ×     6    × 6
  --------   ----
        0     30
```

Multiply the tens.
Regroup.

```
Th H T O       7T
    4 3       × 6
    2 7 5     ----
  ×     6     42T
  --------   + 3T
      5 0    ----
              45T
```

Multiply the hundreds.

```
Th H T O       2 H
    4 3       × 6
    2 7 5     ----
  ×     6     12 H
  --------   + 4 H
  1 6 5 0    ----
              16 H
```

6 × 275 = 1,650

GUIDED PRACTICE

Multiply. Be sure to regroup when you need to.

1.
```
  321
×   3
-----
  963
```

2.
```
   1
  248
×   2
-----
 ■96
```

3.
```
   2
  172
×   4
-----
 ■88
```

4.
```
  416
×   3
-----
■,■■8
```

5.
```
  561
×   6
```

6.
```
  749
×   5
```

| FOCUS | Use NUMBER skills to multiply 3-digit numbers by 1-digit numbers.

EXTRA PRACTICE—page 447

172

PRACTICE

Multiply.

7. 411×2 8. 342×4 9. 473×4 10. 192×7 11. 547×3 12. 252×2

13. 623×4 14. 175×6 15. 743×5 16. 468×3 17. 639×4 18. 594×8

19. 391×2 20. 425×4 21. 617×3 22. 534×7 23. 745×2 24. 243×3

25. 3×332 26. 5×324 27. 4×869 28. 6×241 29. 2×965

30. 7×417 31. 3×456 32. 8×198 33. 4×372 34. 9×515

35. 9×716 36. 4×312 37. 5×456 38. 3×647 39. 2×817

40. Mr. Cravens has 4 crates of strawberries. There are 175 strawberries in each crate. How many strawberries does he have in all?

41. Ms. Pitkins ordered 8 cases of fruit juice. There are 122 cans of fruit juice in each case. How many cans of fruit juice did she order?

MIXED PRACTICE
Maintaining and Reviewing Skills

Add, subtract, or multiply.

42. 364×5 43. 631×8 44. $493 + 389$ 45. $721 - 58$ 46. $4,643 - 2,964$ 47. $8,106 + 958$

48. 5×96 49. $372 + 829$ 50. $9,803 - 2,658$ 51. 7×85

CHALLENGE

52. Joanne is thinking of a 3-digit number and a 1-digit number. The product of the numbers is 856. What could the two numbers be?

EXTRA PRACTICE—page 447

MULTIPLICATION
Multiplying 3-Digit Numbers by 1-Digit Numbers

Sometimes you multiply a 3-digit number by a 1-digit number without regrouping. Sometimes you need to regroup.

Without regrouping	Without regrouping	With regrouping	With regrouping
		$2\,3$	$1\,2$
213	123	159	147
$\times\ \ \ 3$	$\times\ \ \ 2$	$\times\ \ \ 4$	$\times\ \ \ 3$
639	246	636	441

Often you estimate first to find a reasonable answer. Here is one way to estimate.

Write.	Estimate.	Find the exact product.
		$3\,1$
194 $\longrightarrow$	200	194
$\times\ \ \ 4$	$\times\ \ \ 4$	$\times\ \ \ 4$
	800	776

The product is close to 800. The answer is reasonable.

PRACTICE

Estimate. Then find the exact product.

1. 317	**2.** 605	**3.** 294	**4.** 193	**5.** 290	**6.** 204
$\times\ \ 2$	$\times\ \ 4$	$\times\ \ 6$	$\times\ \ 7$	$\times\ \ 4$	$\times\ \ 9$

7. 4×308 8. 7×151 9. 8×191 10. 6×542 11. 5×639

MIXED PRACTICE
Maintaining and Reviewing Skills

Estimate. Then find the exact answer.

12. 473	**13.** 547	**14.** 841	**15.** 72	**16.** 529	**17.** 67
$\times\ \ 2$	$\times\ \ 5$	$+368$	$\times\ \ 3$	-387	$\times\ \ 6$

18. 6×43 19. $46 + 75$ 20. $91 - 37$ 21. 5×91 22. $165 + 341$

FOCUS | Use NUMBER skills to multiply 3-digit numbers by 1-digit numbers.

APPLICATION
Using Measurement

One pair of scissors has a mass of 115 grams. What is the mass of 7 pairs of the same scissors?

Write: 7 x 115 = ■
Solve: 7 x 115 = 805

Seven pairs of scissors have a mass of 805 grams.

How heavy would 7 items of the same size be?

23. Copy and complete the table.

Item	1 ITEM Mass in Grams	7 ITEMS Your Estimate in Grams	7 ITEMS Actual Mass in Grams
Small book	420		
Tissue box	365		
Stapler	695		

Exploring With a Calculator

Follow these steps to help you find the largest possible product using 4 different digits.

24. Copy the product table.

25. Choose any 3 different digits from the circle.

26. Write them as a 3-digit number in the first column.

27. Choose another digit. Write it in the second column.

28. Use a calculator to find the product. Write the product in the last column.

PRODUCT TABLE		
3-Digit	1-Digit	Product

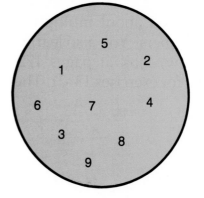

Use MEASUREMENT and NUMBER skills to multiply 3-digit numbers by 1-digit numbers.
Use a CALCULATOR to multiply 3-digit numbers by 1-digit numbers.

175

LOOKING BACK
Reviewing and Testing Chapter 13

In Chapter 13 you formulated problems about a soccer game. Look at pages 166 and 167.

1. Write a sentence telling how you predicted the outcome of the game.

You learned about multiplying hundreds by 1-digit numbers. To review what you learned, study the sample exercises on page 168. Then use this skill to find each product for exercises 2–12.

2. 100
   × 6

3. 100
   × 3

4. 300
   × 2

5. 500
   × 8

6. 900
   × 9

7. 9 × 100

8. 2 × 200

9. 3 × 400

10. 6 × 700

11. Ralph has 5 bags of pennies. Each bag holds 100 pennies. How many pennies does Ralph have altogether?

12. Sherry packed 5 crates of aluminum cans. Each crate holds 200 cans. How many cans did Sherry pack in all?

You learned about multiplying 3-digit numbers by 1-digit numbers. You also learned more about estimating. To review, look at pages 172 and 174. Estimate each product for exercises 13–21. Then find each exact product.

13. 123
    × 3

14. 413
    × 2

15. 312
    × 4

16. 592
    × 5

17. 688
    × 4

18. 3 × 516

19. 8 × 490

20. 3 × 725

21. 9 × 897

FOCUS | Review and test skills learned and practiced.

LOOKING AHEAD
Preparing for New Skills for Chapter 14

In the next chapter, you will focus on

- formulating problems about a trapeze act.
- dividing 3-digit numbers by 1-digit numbers.
- finding averages.
- using measurement.
- checking division.
- using patterns and functions.
- how math is used in music.

New division skills will be easier to learn if you brush up on the division skills you already have. First, review the basic division facts shown on page 454 of the Data Bank. Then, study Model A. Do exercises 1–24.

Model A

Estimate the tens digit.

$6\overline{)88}$

$6\overline{)8}$ is about 1.
Use 1 as the tens digit.

Multiply and subtract.

```
    T | O
    1 |
6 ) 8 | 8
  - 6 |
    2 |
```

Bring down the ones. Estimate the ones digit.

```
    T | O
    1 |
6 ) 8 | 8
  - 6 | ↓
    2 | 8
```

$6\overline{)28}$ is about 4.
Use 4 as the ones digit.

Multiply and subtract. Write the remainder.

```
    T | O
    1 | 4 R4
6 ) 8 | 8
  - 6 |
    2 | 8
  - 2 | 4
      | 4
```

PRACTICE

Divide.

1. $2\overline{)29}$	2. $4\overline{)56}$	3. $4\overline{)75}$	4. $3\overline{)34}$	5. $85 \div 8$	6. $54 \div 3$
7. $5\overline{)37}$	8. $3\overline{)20}$	9. $8\overline{)69}$	10. $7\overline{)51}$	11. $34 \div 6$	12. $55 \div 9$
13. $7\overline{)85}$	14. $3\overline{)19}$	15. $6\overline{)72}$	16. $4\overline{)29}$	17. $85 \div 2$	18. $67 \div 8$
19. $5\overline{)46}$	20. $9\overline{)61}$	21. $3\overline{)75}$	22. $6\overline{)27}$	23. $43 \div 3$	24. $84 \div 5$

Review NUMBER skills in preparation for learning a new skill.

FOCUS | Formulate problems using picture cues, text, and data.

14

Division by a 1-Digit Number

DATA

Scene   Trapeze act in circus

Trapeze artists   Rico
                                 Tania

Years with circus
    Rico   25
    Tania   5

Years on trapeze
    Rico   20
    Tania   1

Falls into net today
    Rico   0
    Tania   1

Age
    Rico   40
    Tania   22

Stage fright (per week)
    Rico   1
    Tania   6

The circus is an enchanting place for the audience. It demands skill and courage from the circus artists. As you can see from the picture, trapeze artists have to work with precision. The data shows you that Tania is quite new at the trapeze. Tania fell into the net a few minutes before this picture was taken. Rico is very experienced and steady. Using the photograph and the data, tell several ways the two artists might continue the performance.

First think about ways Tania and Rico might finish the performance. What might Tania worry about? What are Rico's concerns? Picture them at the very end of the performance. How might they look and feel? Give your reasons.

Think about the audience. Most of them do not know the data. They just see the performance. What might they know about Tania? How would they know? Explain.

Dividing 3-Digit Numbers by 1-Digit Numbers

Mr. Green receives 621 basketballs for his 4 sporting goods stores. If he sends the same number of basketballs to each store, how many basketballs will each store receive? How many will be left?

Use these steps to divide 621 by 4.

Estimate the hundreds digit.

$$4\overline{)621}$$

$4\overline{)6}$ is about 1.
Use 1 as the hundreds digit.

Multiply and subtract.

	H	T	O
	1		
4$\overline{)}$	6	2	1
	−4		
	2		

Estimate the tens digit. Multiply and subtract.

	H	T	O
	1	5	
4$\overline{)}$	6	2	1
	−4		
	2	2	
	−2	0	
		2	

$4\overline{)22}$ is about 5.
Use 5 as the tens digit.

Estimate the ones digit. Multiply and subtract. Write the remainder.

	H	T	O	
	1	5	5	R1
4$\overline{)}$	6	2	1	
	−4			
	2	2		
	−2	0		
		2	1	
	−	2	0	
			1	

$4\overline{)21}$ is about 5.
Use 5 as the ones digit.

Mr. Green will send 155 basketballs to each store. One basketball will be left over.

Use these steps to divide 240 by 5.

Estimate the hundreds digit.

H	T	O
5$\overline{)}$2	4	0

Since 5 is greater than 2, there is no hundreds digit.

Estimate the tens digit.

H	T	O
	4	
5$\overline{)}$2	4	0

$5\overline{)24}$ is about 4.
Use 4 as the tens digit.

Multiply and subtract.

	H	T	O
		4	
5$\overline{)}$	2	4	0
	−2	0	
		4	

Estimate the ones digit. Multiply and subtract.

	H	T	O
		4	8
5$\overline{)}$	2	4	0
	−2	0	
		4	0
	−	4	0
			0

$5\overline{)40}$ is 8. Use 8 as the ones digit.

FOCUS | Use NUMBER skills to divide 3-digit numbers by 1-digit numbers.

GUIDED PRACTICE

Divide.

1. $\begin{array}{r} 256\,R1 \\ 3\overline{)769} \\ -6 \\ \hline 16 \\ -15 \\ \hline 19 \\ -18 \\ \hline 1 \end{array}$

2. $\begin{array}{r} 8\overline{)488} \\ -48 \\ \hline \blacksquare \\ -8 \\ \hline 0 \end{array}$

3. $\begin{array}{r} 2\overline{)328} \\ -2 \\ \hline 12 \\ -\blacksquare\blacksquare \\ \hline \blacksquare \\ -8 \\ \hline 0 \end{array}$

4. $\begin{array}{r} 5\overline{)711} \\ -\blacksquare \\ \hline 21 \\ -\blacksquare\blacksquare \\ \hline 11 \\ -\blacksquare\blacksquare \\ \hline 1 \end{array}$

5. $\begin{array}{r} 9\overline{)138} \\ -9 \\ \hline \blacksquare\blacksquare \\ -45 \\ \hline \blacksquare \end{array}$

PRACTICE

Divide.

6. $5\overline{)565}$ 7. $6\overline{)426}$ 8. $3\overline{)518}$ 9. $8\overline{)472}$ 10. $2\overline{)325}$

11. $2\overline{)375}$ 12. $4\overline{)306}$ 13. $6\overline{)294}$ 14. $3\overline{)478}$ 15. $7\overline{)847}$

16. $5\overline{)145}$ 17. $8\overline{)524}$ 18. $9\overline{)489}$ 19. $3\overline{)369}$ 20. $2\overline{)982}$

21. $5\overline{)680}$ 22. $4\overline{)873}$ 23. $6\overline{)750}$ 24. $2\overline{)859}$ 25. $5\overline{)788}$

26. $3\overline{)647}$ 27. $4\overline{)329}$ 28. $6\overline{)897}$ 29. $4\overline{)330}$ 30. $7\overline{)320}$

31. $162 \div 3$ 32. $244 \div 4$ 33. $783 \div 9$ 34. $712 \div 7$

35. Loni has 235 books to pack in 5 boxes. If she packs the same number of books in each box, how many books will each box contain?

36. Joe is shipping 128 pairs of sneakers to 4 stores. Each store will get the same amount. How many pairs of sneakers will each store receive?

MIXED PRACTICE
Maintaining and Reviewing Skills

Multiply or divide.

37. $639 \div 4$ 38. $428 \div 6$ 39. 5×717 40. $89 \div 3$

41. 4×300 42. 8×408 43. $74 \div 2$ 44. $68 \div 4$

DIVISION
Finding Averages

Jason and his family went on a car trip. The first day they traveled 212 miles. The second day they traveled 256 miles. The third day they traveled 267 miles. What was the average number of miles the family traveled each day?

To find the average, add the numbers and divide the sum by the number of addends.

$$\begin{array}{r} 212 \\ 256 \\ +267 \\ \hline 735 \end{array}$$
There are 3 addends, so the divisor is 3.
$$\begin{array}{r} 245 \\ 3\overline{)735} \end{array}$$

The family traveled an average of 245 miles per day.

PRACTICE

Find the average for each group of numbers.

1. 54   31   35   62   28
2. 253   314   102
3. 386   124   284   102
4. 130   365   234   123
5. 204   114   213   164   300
6. 645   243
7. 264   312   423
8. 27   16   33   45   52   61
9. 15   22   25   30
10. 82   87   95
11. 134   176   207   189   249
12. 56   49   45   50

MIXED PRACTICE
Maintaining and Reviewing Skills

Add, subtract, multiply, or divide.

13. 724 + 368 + 409
14. 636 ÷ 6
15. 4 × 268
16. 7,815 − 3,496
17. 895 ÷ 9
18. 6 × 500
19. 25,916 + 4,914
20. 465 ÷ 4
21. 7 × 506
22. 324 + 516 + 186
23. 3,584 − 1,286
24. 926 ÷ 7

FOCUS   Use NUMBER skills to find averages.

182

APPLICATION

Using Measurement

Mr. Garth went on a 5-day hike. In all he hiked 125 miles. If Mr. Garth hiked the same number of miles each day, how many miles a day did he hike?

To find the average number of miles hiked each day, divide:

125 ÷ 5 = 25.

Mr. Garth hiked 25 miles a day.

25. The chart below shows how many days and miles Mr. Garth has walked on different hiking trips. Find the average number of miles per day he hiked during each trip.

Days	Miles Hiked	Average Miles per Day
4	88	■
5	115	■
6	126	■
7	105	■
8	144	■
9	126	■

Problem Solving: Using PLAN, SOLVE, and CHECK

Use the table to answer the questions. Remember to PLAN, SOLVE, and CHECK.

26. On the average, who is taller, a 9-year-old boy or girl?

27. For which other years is the answer the same as for problem 26?

TYPICAL HEIGHT IN CENTIMETERS					
Age	Boys	Girls	Age	Boys	Girls
2	86	86	11	143	144
3	94	94	12	149	151
4	102	101	13	156	157
5	109	106	14	163	160
6	116	114	15	169	161
7	121	120	16	173	162
8	127	126	17	176	163
9	132	132	18	176	163
10	137	138			

28. What is the average height for boys in the age range of 8–10 years?

29. What is the average height for girls in the age range of 8–10 years?

Use NUMBER skills to find averages.
Apply the PLAN, SOLVE, and CHECK steps of the Five-Step PROBLEM SOLVING Plan.

Dividing 3-Digit Numbers by 1-Digit Numbers

One weekend during the summer 450 people were white-water rafting on the Gauley River. Each raft held 9 people. How many rafts were on the river?

Here is a way to solve the problem.

Estimate the hundreds digit.

$9 \overline{)450}$

Since 9 is greater than 4, there is no hundreds digit.

Estimate the tens digit. Multiply and subtract.

H	T	O
	5	

$9 \overline{)4\,5\,0}$
$-4\,5$
0

$9 \overline{)45}$ is 5. Use 5 as the tens digit.

Bring down the ones. Estimate the ones digit. Multiply and subtract.

H	T	O
	5	0

$9 \overline{)4\,5\,0}$
$-4\,5\,\downarrow$
$0\,0$
-0
0

$9 \overline{)0}$ is 0. Use 0 as the ones digit.

There were 50 rafts on the river.

Here is another example.

Estimate the hundreds digit.

$4 \overline{)807}$

$4 \overline{)8}$ is 2. Use 2 as the hundreds digit.

Multiply and subtract.

H	T	O
2		

$4 \overline{)8\,0\,7}$
-8
0

Bring down the tens. Estimate the tens digit. Multiply and subtract.

H	T	O
2	0	

$4 \overline{)8\,0\,7}$
$-8\,\downarrow$
$0\,0$
-0
0

$4 \overline{)0}$ is 0. Use 0 as the tens digit.

Bring down the ones. Estimate the ones digit. Multiply and subtract.

H	T	O
2	0	1 R3

$4 \overline{)8\,0\,7}$
-8
$0\,0$
$-0\,\downarrow$
$0\,7$
-4
3

$4 \overline{)7}$ is about 1. Use 1 as the ones digit. Write the remainder.

FOCUS | Use NUMBER skills to divide 3-digit numbers by 1-digit numbers.

GUIDED PRACTICE

Divide.

40	58	2□2	2□4 R□	□2□ R□
1. 6)240	2. 7)406	3. 3)606	4. 2)509	5. 5)614
−24↓	− ■■↓	−6↓	−4↓	− ■↓
00	56	0	10	■■
− 0	− ■■	−0↓	−10↓	− ■■↓
0	■	■	9	■■
		−■	−■	− ■■↓
		0	■	■

PRACTICE

Divide.

6. 6)702   7. 4)406   8. 3)609   9. 7)490   10. 8)404

11. 2)320   12. 9)506   13. 4)340   14. 5)407   15. 4)502

16. 100 ÷ 5   17. 208 ÷ 5   18. 303 ÷ 3   19. 402 ÷ 4   20. 650 ÷ 5

21. A shipment of 120 life jackets was sent to the raft store. Six jackets were packed in each carton. How many cartons were there?

22. A shipment of 100 paddles arrived at the raft store. There were 4 paddles in each box. How many boxes of paddles were there?

MIXED PRACTICE
Maintaining and Reviewing Skills

Add, subtract, multiply, or divide.

23. 365 ÷ 5   24. 739 ÷ 4   25. 458 − 297   26. 71 ÷ 3

27. 4 × 86   28. 397 + 238   29. 6,721 − 349   30. 6 × 245

31. 4,309 + 2,996   32. 3 × 640   33. 94 ÷ 7   34. 6,941 − 856

CHALLENGE

35. One rafting company carried an average of 90 people a day for 7 days. If there are 6 people in each raft, how many rafts were used during this time?

EXTRA PRACTICE—page 448

DIVISION
Checking Division With Multiplication

Multiplication and division are related operations. You can use multiplication to check a division problem.

$$\begin{array}{r} 403 \longleftarrow \text{Quotient} \\ 2\overline{)806} \\ \uparrow \quad \uparrow \\ \end{array}$$
Divisor Dividend

$$\begin{array}{r} 403 \longleftarrow \text{Quotient} \\ \times \quad 2 \longleftarrow \text{Divisor} \\ \hline 806 \longleftarrow \text{Dividend} \end{array}$$

When you multiply the quotient by the divisor, the product should be the same as the dividend.

When you have a remainder, this is how to check the problem.

$$\begin{array}{r} 120\,\text{R}2 \\ 5\overline{)602} \\ -5 \\ \hline 10 \\ -10 \\ \hline 2 \\ -0 \\ \hline 2 \end{array}$$

$$\begin{array}{r} 120 \\ \times \quad 5 \\ \hline 600 \\ + \quad 2 \\ \hline 602 \end{array}$$

Multiply the quotient by the divisor.

Add the remainder.

The answer should equal the dividend.

PRACTICE

Divide. Check by multiplying.

1. $6\overline{)360}$　　2. $9\overline{)830}$　　3. $3\overline{)307}$　　4. $5\overline{)530}$　　5. $8\overline{)805}$

6. $4\overline{)502}$　　7. $4\overline{)440}$　　8. $3\overline{)270}$　　9. $7\overline{)380}$　　10. $2\overline{)530}$

11. $180 \div 3$　　12. $910 \div 9$　　13. $810 \div 4$　　14. $640 \div 8$　　15. $350 \div 3$

MIXED PRACTICE
Maintaining and Reviewing Skills

Multiply or divide. Check each answer.

16. $7\overline{)910}$　　17. $6\overline{)550}$　　18. 8×246　　19. $3\overline{)76}$　　20. 4×37

21. $808 \div 8$　　22. 6×304　　23. $94 \div 6$　　24. $41 \div 7$　　25. 5×98

| FOCUS | Use NUMBER skills to check division of 3-digit numbers by 1-digit numbers. |

186

APPLICATION

Using Patterns and Functions

You can use repeated subtraction to solve a division problem. Find $400 \div 100$.

$$
\begin{array}{r}
400 \\
-100 \\
\hline
300 \\
-100 \\
\hline
200 \\
-100 \\
\hline
100 \\
-100 \\
\hline
0
\end{array}
$$

a. Start with 400.

b. Keep subtracting 100 until you reach 0.

c. You have subtracted 100 four times. So, $400 \div 100 = 4$.

Use repeated subtraction to find the answers to these exercises.

26. $700 \div 100$ **27.** $450 \div 50$ **28.** $200 \div 25$ **29.** $392 \div 49$

30. $266 \div 38$ **31.** $582 \div 97$ **32.** $252 \div 36$ **33.** $800 \div 100$

34. $387 \div 43$ **35.** $360 \div 72$ **36.** $504 \div 84$ **37.** $728 \div 91$

Solving Problems

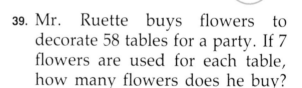

38. The main dining room seats 220 people. If 4 people are seated at each table, how many tables are needed?

39. Mr. Ruette buys flowers to decorate 58 tables for a party. If 7 flowers are used for each table, how many flowers does he buy?

40. One dining room is reserved for 130 people. Six people will sit at each table. How many tables are needed?

41. A dining room is set up for 160 people. Two tables are set for 8 people each. All of the other tables are set for 4 people. How many tables are set for 4 people?

42. Write a word problem that you can solve by dividing 604 by 2. Solve the problem.

Use PATTERNS AND FUNCTIONS to relate subtraction to division.
Use NUMBER skills to solve problems.

Talking Drum Rhythms

Some people use rhythm to send messages by drums. The best known talking drums are the slit drum of Central Africa and the hour-glass drum of West Africa.

This is how they work. Drummers memorize a long list of sentences. Each sentence has a certain rhythm and contains different pitches—high tones and low tones. Some syllables are stressed more than others.

In $\frac{3}{4}$ time signature a dotted half note 𝅗𝅥. gets 3 beats, a half note 𝅗𝅥 gets 2 beats, a quarter note ♩ gets one beat, and an eighth note ♪ gets $\frac{1}{2}$ beat.

Say the sentence below.

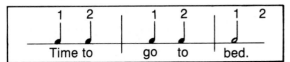

The first syllable in each measure is stressed. Each measure has two syllables, except the last. The voice could go up and down for high tones and low tones.

The hour-glass drum has a skin drumhead at each end, with cords strung between them. The drummer beats the drum while holding it under his arm. When he wants high tones he squeezes the drum, making the drumheads tighter. He uses rhythm, pitch, and stress to send drum messages.

Here are two drum messages written in music notation. Notice the $\frac{2}{4}$ time signature. It means two beats per measure, and a quarter note gets one beat.

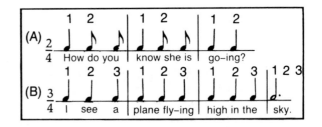

CRITICAL THINKING

1. Look at message A. How many beats are in each measure? Tap the beats, 1-2, 1-2, as you say the message. Tap the message as though on a drum.

2. Look at message B. How many beats are in each measure? Name two ways to know the answer. How many measures does it have?

FOCUS | Use NUMBER skills to understand and analyze talking drum rhythms.

African drums are used mainly for entertainment. Specially constructed drums are sometimes played at ceremonial occasions to honor a figure of authority. People in distant villages send messages by beating drums.

LOOKING BACK
Reviewing and Testing Chapter 14

In Chapter 14 you formulated problems about a trapeze act. Look at pages 178 and 179.

1. Write a sentence telling what could happen to an inexperienced trapeze artist.

You learned about dividing 3-digit numbers by 1-digit numbers and about finding averages. To review, look at pages 180 and 182. Then divide for exercises 2–11. Find the average for each group of numbers for exercises 12–14.

2. $8\overline{)968}$ 3. $7\overline{)943}$ 4. $4\overline{)647}$ 5. $5\overline{)717}$ 6. $6\overline{)744}$

7. $9\overline{)846}$ 8. $5\overline{)463}$ 9. $8\overline{)489}$ 10. $7\overline{)319}$ 11. $8\overline{)352}$

12. 243 645   13. 130 206 534   14. 284 102 386 124

You learned more about checking division with multiplication. To review, look at pages 184 and 186. Divide and check for exercises 15–24.

15. $7\overline{)840}$ 16. $2\overline{)460}$ 17. $4\overline{)503}$ 18. $3\overline{)608}$ 19. $5\overline{)607}$

20. $4\overline{)200}$ 21. $5\overline{)650}$ 22. $6\overline{)504}$ 23. $7\overline{)409}$ 24. $9\overline{)304}$

You learned about talking drum rhythms. To review, look at pages 188 and 189. Use $\frac{3}{4}$ time.

25. In $\frac{3}{4}$ time, how many beats does a half note equal?

26. In $\frac{3}{4}$ time, how many beats does an eighth note equal?

FOCUS Review and test skills learned and practiced.

Preparing for New Skills for Chapter 15

In the next chapter, you will focus on

- formulating problems about building birdhouses.
- classifying triangles.
- using measurement.

- using a problem-solving strategy.
- comparing and measuring angles.
- relating angles to clock hands.

Learning more about angles and triangles will be easier if you brush up on what you already know about them. First review the examples below. Then complete the exercises at the bottom of the page.

When 2 rays meet and share the same endpoint, they form an angle. Look at the angles below. The farther apart the rays are, the larger the angle is. The closer the rays are, the smaller the angle is.

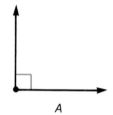

A

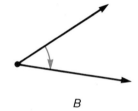

B

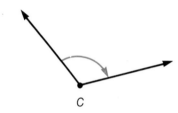

C

This angle forms a square corner.

This angle is smaller than angle *A* or *C*.

This angle is larger than angle *A* or *B*.

A triangle is a figure with 3 sides and 3 angles. In this triangle, angle *A* is a square corner. Angles *B* and *C* are both smaller than angle *A*.

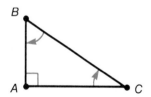

PRACTICE

Is the angle larger or smaller than a square corner?

1.

2.

3.

4.

Review GEOMETRY in preparation for learning a new skill.

FOCUS | Formulate problems using picture cues, text, and data.

Geometry

Birds are everywhere! You can see them in a backyard or on a city street. They fly above rooftops and gather in playgrounds. Outdoor birds are wild, but there are ways of getting to know them.

Birds need places to take shelter and to raise their families. Often, they use holes in trees. But sometimes there aren't many to be found. One way to help your neighborhood birds is to invite them to a birdhouse.

Danny Berger and his mother, Karen, put up a birdhouse in their backyard. Not all the birds used it. What was wrong? Using the data, decide what problems Danny and Mrs. Berger had. What could they do to solve these problems?

Classifying Triangles by Lengths of Sides

All triangles have 3 sides. Sometimes all the sides are the same length. Measure the sides with a ruler.

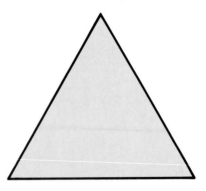

Sometimes 2 sides are the same length. Sometimes 0 sides are the same length. Measure the sides with a ruler.

3 sides the same length

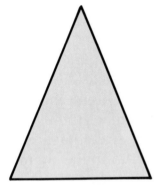

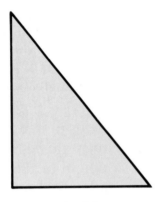

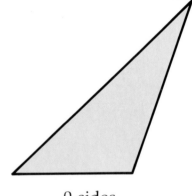

2 sides
the same length

0 sides
the same length

0 sides
the same length

GUIDED PRACTICE

Write how many sides are the same length.

1.

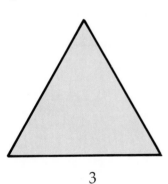

3

2.

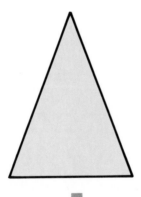

■

3.

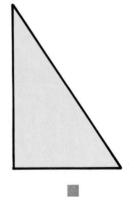

■

FOCUS   Use GEOMETRY to classify triangles by lengths of sides.

PRACTICE

Copy each triangle. Write how many sides are the same length.

4.
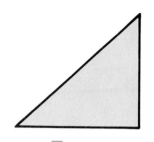
▪

5.

▪

6.
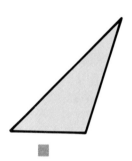
▪

7.
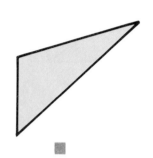
▪

8.
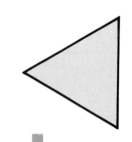
▪

9.

▪

MIXED PRACTICE
Maintaining and Reviewing Skills

Multiply or divide.

10. 400
    × 6

11. 346
    × 3

12. 715
    × 4

13. 269
    × 7

14. 806
    × 5

15. 734 ÷ 5

16. 689 ÷ 7

17. 6 × 351

18. 358 ÷ 3

19. 475 ÷ 8

20. 8 × 432

21. 5 × 743

22. 856 ÷ 9

CHALLENGE

23. How many triangles can you see?

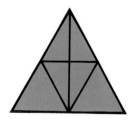

GEOMETRY
Using Triangles in Tiling Patterns

These designs are called **tiling patterns.** The shapes fit together like tiles, with no space between them.

How many triangles fit together to make this rectangle?

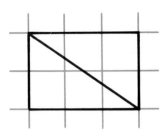

How many triangles fit together to make this rectangle?

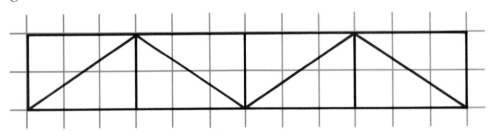

PRACTICE

Copy each tiling pattern and color it in an interesting way.

1. 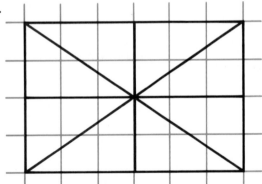   **2.**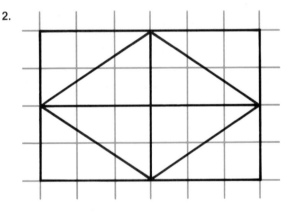

MIXED PRACTICE
Maintaining and Reviewing Skills

Add, subtract, multiply, or divide.

3. 768 ÷ 8   **4.** 495 + 682   **5.** 764 − 389   **6.** 4 × 326

7. 5,638 − 964   **8.** 670 + 3,901   **9.** 7 × 507   **10.** 646 ÷ 5

FOCUS | Use GEOMETRY to complete tiling patterns with triangles.

196

APPLICATION

Using Measurement

11. Copy the table. Then measure the sides of each triangle. Write the letter of each triangle in the correct column.

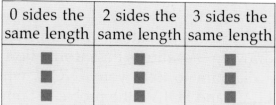

0 sides the same length	2 sides the same length	3 sides the same length
■ ■ ■	■ ■	■ ■ ■

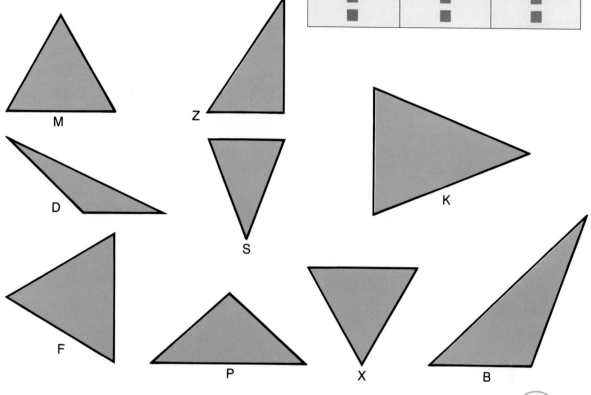

Solving Problems

Write *true* or *false*.

12. The lengths of the sides of a triangle are 5 cm, 5 cm, and 5 cm. It has three sides the same length.

13. The lengths of the sides of a triangle are 8 cm, 4 cm, and 5 cm. It has two sides the same length.

14. The lengths of the sides of a triangle are 4 cm, 4 cm, and 3 cm. It has no sides the same length.

15. The lengths of the sides of a triangle are 6 cm, 9 cm, and 9 cm. It has three sides the same length.

16. The lengths of the sides of a triangle are 5 cm, 8 cm, and 5 cm. It has two sides the same length.

17. Write a problem using the lengths 7 cm, 7 cm, and 7 cm. Then tell if the problem is true or false.

Use MEASUREMENT to classify triangles by lengths of sides and to solve word problems.

Selecting a Strategy: Using a Diagram

Selecting a strategy is part of the PLAN step. Using a diagram is a strategy you can choose. A **diagram** is a drawing that shows the information you are given. Use a diagram to help you KNOW what the problem is. PLAN and SOLVE the problem. Sometimes the diagram is given. Sometimes you need to draw your own.

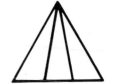

1. READ   How many triangles are there in this figure?

2. KNOW   Ask yourself: What am I being asked to find? What is the total number of triangles? Which **key facts** do I know? The larger triangle is divided into 3 smaller triangles. Two or more smaller triangles can be put together to form a new, larger triangle.

3. PLAN   Select a strategy: try using a diagram. Draw a diagram to help see all of the triangles. Keep redrawing the figure to identify the triangles. Number the triangles as you find them.

4. SOLVE

 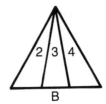 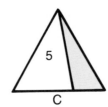 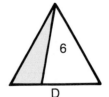

There are 6 triangles in the original figure.

5. CHECK   Look at Diagrams A and B: One very large triangle and 3 smaller ones can be seen easily. The smaller triangles can be put together to form other triangles.

Look at Diagrams C and D: Triangles 2 and 3 form triangle 5, and triangles 3 and 4 form triangle 6. Recount the triangles to find that six is a reasonable answer.

FOCUS   Evaluate information as part of the Five-Step PROBLEM-SOLVING Plan.

PRACTICE

Draw a diagram to help you SOLVE each problem.
CHECK that the answer is reasonable.

1. How many triangles are there in this figure?

2. A square garden measures 10 feet on each side. There are some colorful rocks placed along one side. The first rock is in the corner, and one rock is placed every 2 feet. How many rocks are there? Hint: The answer is not 5 rocks.

3. There are 4 people. Each person will shake every other person's hand once. How many different handshakes will there be? Hint: Mary's shaking John's hand is the same as John's shaking Mary's hand.

4. Five posts are placed in a row. The posts have a rope that goes through a hole in the middle of each post and connects them. Each post is 1 foot wide and is 5 feet from the next post. How much rope is needed?

Use the diagram below. There are 4 people standing in line at a record store. Read each clue. Then answer the questions. The second clue follows from the first clue.

1st	2nd	3rd	4th
?	?	?	?

5. Clue: Charles is in front of Darla and behind Bart. Charles is in third place. In which place is Darla? In which places could Bart be?

6. Clue: Anne is in front of Bart. In which place is Anne? In which place is Bart? In what order are the people, first through fourth?

Class Project

Divide into small groups of students. As a group, draw a figure using triangles and line segments. Then prepare a written description of the figure. Trade descriptions, but not pictures, with another group. Draw each other's figures from the descriptions. How good are the descriptions? How close are the drawings?

GEOMETRY
Comparing Sizes of Angles

Look at the space between each pair of pencils.

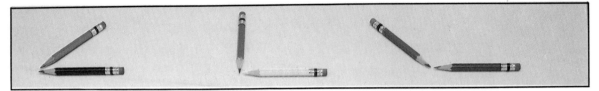

As the pencils move further apart, the space between them gets larger.

When two rays have the same endpoint, it is called an **angle.**

As the rays move further apart, the measure of the angle between them gets larger.

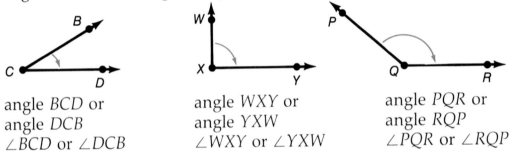

angle *BCD* or
angle *DCB*
∠*BCD* or ∠*DCB*

angle *WXY* or
angle *YXW*
∠*WXY* or ∠*YXW*

angle *PQR* or
angle *RQP*
∠*PQR* or ∠*RQP*

∠*WXY* is a **right angle.** It makes a square corner.
∠*BCD* is smaller than a right angle.
∠*PQR* is larger than a right angle.

GUIDED PRACTICE

Write the names of the angles in order from smallest to largest.

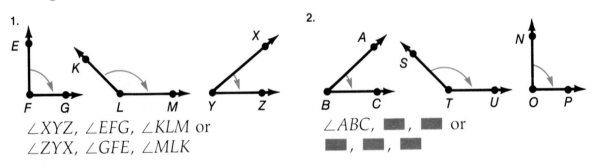

1.
∠*XYZ*, ∠*EFG*, ∠*KLM* or
∠*ZYX*, ∠*GFE*, ∠*MLK*

2.
∠*ABC*, ■, ■ or
■, ■, ■

FOCUS   Use GEOMETRY to compare sizes of angles.

200

PRACTICE

Write the names of the angles in order from smallest
to largest.

3.

4.

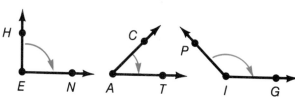

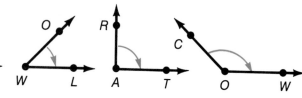

5.

6.

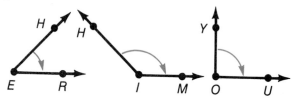

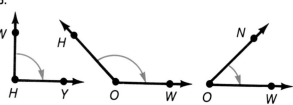

Write *true* or *false*. Remember, a square corner is called
a right angle.

7.

8.

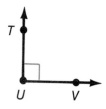

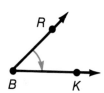

∠*TUV* is a right angle.   ∠*RBK* is a right angle.

9. A square has four right angles.   **10.** A rectangle has no right angles.

MIXED PRACTICE
Maintaining and Reviewing Skills

Multiply or divide.

11. $768 \div 4$ **12.** 7×185 **13.** $247 \div 7$ **14.** $817 \div 9$ **15.** 4×481

16. 6×356 **17.** $529 \div 3$ **18.** $864 \div 5$ **19.** 9×307 **20.** 464×6

CHALLENGE

21. Name ten objects in your classroom that have right
angles.

EXTRA PRACTICE—page 448

GEOMETRY
Making a Simple Protractor

A **protractor** is used to measure angles. To make a protractor, follow these steps.

Step 1: Cut out a large circle from tracing paper and fold it into 4 equal parts.

Step 2: Open the circle and label it like this.

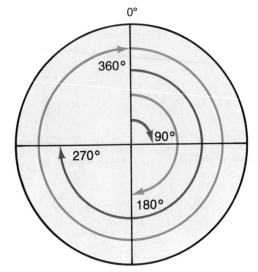

A circle is divided into 360 degrees.
A **right angle** has **90°**.

PRACTICE

Use your protractor. Write how many degrees.

1.

2.

3.

MIXED PRACTICE
Maintaining and Reviewing Skills

Write *true* or *false*. Remember, a square corner is called a right angle.

4.

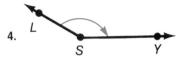

∠LSY is smaller than a right angle.

5.

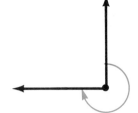

∠GBF is larger than a right angle.

APPLICATION

Using Measurement: Time

Look at the angle formed by the hands of this clock.

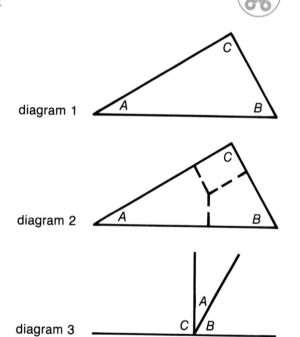

12:15
The angle is **about 90°**.

12:10
The angle is **about 60°**.

12:05
The angle is **about 30°**.

Draw the clock hands for each time. Write **about 90°**, **about 60°**, or **about 30°**.

6. 3:00

7. 3:10

8. 3:05

9. 9:00

10. 8:55

11. 8:50

12. 11:45

13. 6:15

Problem Solving: Using a Diagram

14. <u>Get Ready:</u> Draw any triangle. Label its angles A, B, and C as in diagram 1. Cut out the triangle. Then cut it into three pieces as shown by the dashed lines in diagram 2.

<u>Experiment:</u> Rearrange the three pieces so that A, B, and C fit together as in diagram 3. Now rearrange them again in a different order.

<u>Learn:</u> Do A, B, and C always form a straight line? Try several other triangles. The angles of any triangle always form a straight line or a **straight angle.**

diagram 1

diagram 2

diagram 3

Use MEASUREMENT to relate angles to clock hands.
Use a diagram and apply the Five-Step PROBLEM SOLVING Plan.

LOOKING BACK

Reviewing and Testing Chapter 15

In Chapter 15 you formulated problems about a birdhouse. Look at pages 192 and 193.

1. Write a sentence telling what you would need to know to build a birdhouse.

You learned about classifying triangles by the lengths of their sides. To review, study the sample exercises on page 194. Then use this skill to write how many sides are the same length for exercises 2–4.

2.

3.

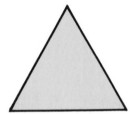

4.

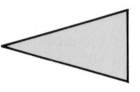

You learned how to use a diagram to help you evaluate information as part of the Five-Step Problem-Solving Plan. To review, look at pages 198 and 199. Draw a diagram to help you solve this problem or to check if the answer is reasonable.

5. Draw a triangle inside a square so that each vertex touches a side of the square. How many triangles can you find?

You learned about comparing and measuring angles. To review, look at pages 200 and 202. Use your protractor to measure the angles in exercises 6–8.

6.

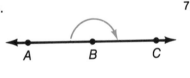

7.

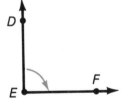

8.

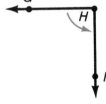

FOCUS Review and test skills learned and practiced.

LOOKING AHEAD
Preparing for New Skills for Chapter 16

In the next chapter, you will focus on

■ formulating problems about a dogsled race.
■ relating solid figures and their patterns.
■ using logic.

■ identifying and drawing circles (diameters and radii).
■ using measurement: time.
■ how math is used in geography.

Learning about solid figures will be easier if you review what you already know about plane figures. First review the examples below.

Then complete the exercises that follow. It may be helpful to refer to the examples as you complete your work.

Look at the figures below. What kind of shape is the shaded area of each one?

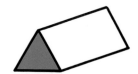

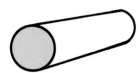

The shaded area is a square.

The shaded area is a circle.

The shaded area is a triangle.

PRACTICE

Look at each figure. What shape is the shaded area?

1.
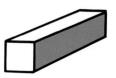

2.
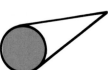

3.

4.

5.

6.

Review GEOMETRY in preparation for learning a new skill.

FOCUS | Formulate problems using picture cues, text, and data.

Geometry

DATA

Arctic Dogsled Race

Temperature	$-40°F$
Length of race	150 miles
Miles left in race	50
Number of sleds at start of race	12
Number of sleds left	3

Names of sled teams
left in race   Sakia
Ukak
Nanuk

Standings so far
First place   Nanuk
Second place   Sakia
Third place   Ukak

Food supply
Nanuk   2-day supply left
Sakia   1-day supply left
Ukak   3-day supply left

Average distance
traveled per day   25 miles

Eskimos are a group of Native Americans who live in the northernmost regions of North America. It gets very cold that far north. There is ice on the ground almost all year round. There are very few roads up there. So, many Eskimos travel in dogsleds. The Eskimos are proud of their dogs and are very kind to them.

Some Eskimos have cross-country dogsled races. The sled drivers try to make sure they bring enough food to last the entire race. If they run out of food, they may have to stop and catch some fish to eat. If the race is long, the teams have to camp out overnight.

Look at the picture and the data. Imagine what a dogsled race is like. Think of some problems a dogsled team might have. Predict how this race will end. Give your reasons.

Building Solid Geometric Figures

Here are some solid geometric figures.

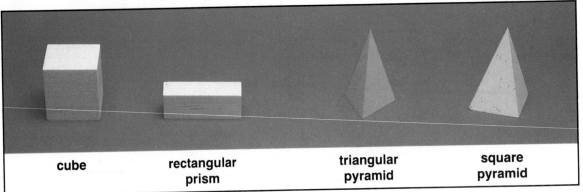

| cube | rectangular prism | triangular pyramid | square pyramid |

You can build solid figures with patterns.

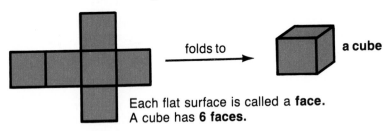

folds to → a cube

Each flat surface is called a **face**.
A cube has **6 faces**.

GUIDED PRACTICE

Look at each solid figure and the pattern it was folded from. Name the solid figure.

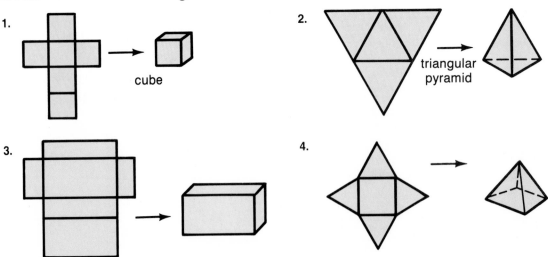

1. → cube

2. → triangular pyramid

3. →

4. →

| **FOCUS** | Use GEOMETRY to see relationships between solid figures and their patterns. |

PRACTICE

Name the solid figure each folded pattern forms.

5.

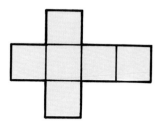

6.

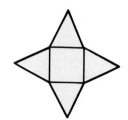

7.

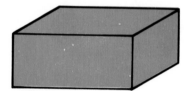

8.

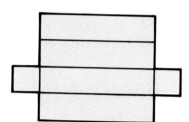

Write the number of faces.

9.

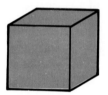

10.

MIXED PRACTICE

Maintaining and Reviewing Skills

Name each figure.

11.

12.

13.

14.

CHALLENGE

15. Here are six views of the same cube. Which letter is opposite which? Make a cube to help you.

EXTRA PRACTICE—page 448

GEOMETRY
Determining if Patterns Make Solid Figures

You have seen that some patterns will make solid figures. Others will not.

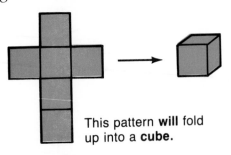

This pattern **will** fold up into a **cube**.

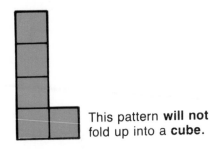

This pattern **will not** fold up into a **cube**.

PRACTICE

Write *yes* or *no*.

 1.
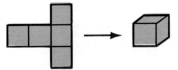

2.
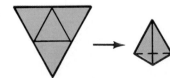

3.
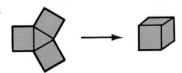

4.

5.
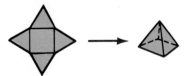

6.

MIXED PRACTICE
Maintaining and Reviewing Skills

Name each solid figure.

 7.
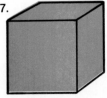

8.

9.

10.
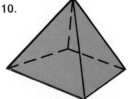

FOCUS   Use GEOMETRY to determine if given patterns will make given solid figures.

Using Logic

You can use logical thinking to complete this sentence about a solid figure.

**If all 6 faces are squares,
then the solid figure is a ■.**

Think: Which solid figures have 6 faces?
Which one has 6 faces that are squares?

If all 6 faces are squares,
then the solid figure is a **cube.**

Use logical thinking to complete each sentence.

11. If all 4 faces are triangles, then the solid figure is a ■.

12. If 4 faces are rectangles and 2 faces are squares, then the solid figure is a ■.

13. If a pyramid has 4 triangular faces, then the fifth face is a ■.

Problem Solving: Using a Diagram

14. <u>Get Ready:</u> On graph paper, draw and then cut out patterns that are made of 6 squares that touch side to side.
<u>Experiment:</u> Fold your patterns to form boxes that have tops.
<u>Examples:</u>

Forms a box with a top.   Forms a box without a top.

<u>Organize:</u> How many patterns could you make that formed boxes with tops? There are some that will form boxes and others that will not. Sort and identify your patterns. Compare them with a friend.

Use LOGIC to draw conclusions about solid geometric figures.
Use a diagram and apply the Five-Step PROBLEM SOLVING Plan.

Finding the Center of a Circle and Drawing Radii

Look at this circle. It has been folded in half twice and then opened up. The dotted lines show where it was folded.

The **center** of the circle is the point where the fold lines cross.

The **radius** of the circle is a line segment from the center to the edge.

How many **radii** (more than one radius) do you see?

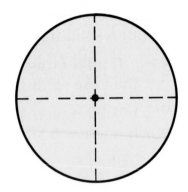

Look at the solid fold lines on this circle. A line segment that passes through the center and goes right across the circle from edge to edge is called a **diameter.**

How many diameters do you see?

What do you notice about the **diameter** and **radius** of a circle?

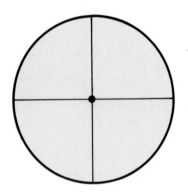

GUIDED PRACTICE

Trace and cut out the circles. Fold them twice. Mark the center and draw the radii.

1.

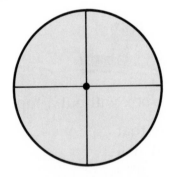

2.

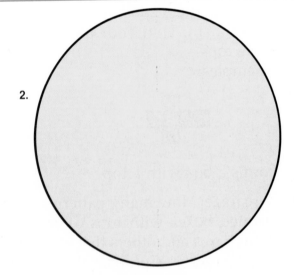

Your circle should look like this.

FOCUS   Use GEOMETRY to find centers, radii, and diameters of circles by folding.

212

PRACTICE

Write how many radii and diameters are shown.

3.

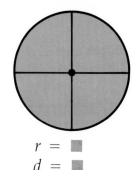

$r = $ ▨
$d = $ ▨

4.

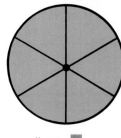

$r = $ ▨
$d = $ ▨

5.

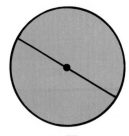

$r = $ ▨
$d = $ ▨

6.

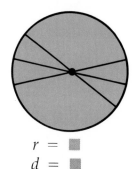

$r = $ ▨
$d = $ ▨

7.

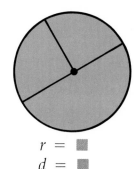

$r = $ ▨
$d = $ ▨

8.

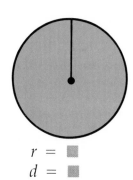

$r = $ ▨
$d = $ ▨

9. The radius of a circle is 4 cm. What is the diameter?

10. The diameter of a circle is 6 cm. How long is the radius?

11. The diameter of a circle is 7 cm. How long is the radius?

12. The radius of a circle is 2.5 cm. What is the diameter?

MIXED PRACTICE
Maintaining and Reviewing Skills

Will these patterns make solid figures? Write *yes* or *no*.

13.

14.

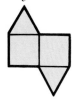

CHALLENGE

15. Trace around a circle and cut it out. Fold it in half twice. Draw the radii. Connect the outer end points of the radii with a ruler. What shape do you get?

GEOMETRY
Drawing Circles

A circle can be drawn if you have the center point and the radius.

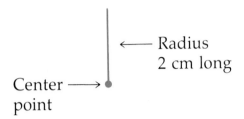

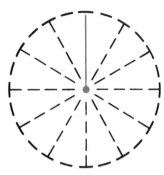

Start at the center point and draw more radii. Use a compass to join the outside points to form a circle.

How would you draw a circle using the center point and the diameter?

PRACTICE

Draw each circle.

1. radius = 3 cm   2. radius = 4 cm   3. radius = 5 cm

4. radius = 2.5 cm   5. radius = 4.5 cm   6. radius = 3.5 cm

7. diameter = 6 cm   8. diameter = 9 cm   9. diameter = 7 cm

10. diameter = 8 cm   11. diameter = 10 cm   12. diameter = 5 cm

13. Are any of the circles above the same size?

14. Which circles are the same size? Why?

MIXED PRACTICE
Maintaining and Reviewing Skills

Copy and complete.

15. radius = 5 cm   16. radius = ■ cm   17. radius = 1.5 cm
    diameter = ■ cm   diameter = 4 cm   diameter = ■ cm

18. radius = ■ cm   19. radius = 3.4 cm   20. radius = ■ cm
    diameter = 12 cm   diameter = ■ cm   diameter = 18 cm

FOCUS   Use GEOMETRY to draw circles using center points, radii, and diameters.

APPLICATION

Using Measurement: Time

This clock was drawn by using the center point and a diameter of 3 cm. The radius is 1.5 cm.

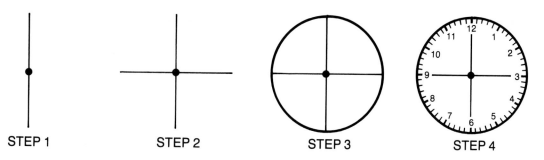

STEP 1   STEP 2   STEP 3   STEP 4

Draw each clock. Then show the time.

21. diameter = 4 cm
    time = 5:00

22. radius = 2.5 cm
    time = 7:30

23. diameter = 3 cm
    time = 9:05

24. radius = 3 cm
    time = 10:03

25. diameter = 5 cm
    time = 6:24

26. radius = 4 cm
    time = 2:47

Solving Problems

27. A circle has a line segment that passes through the center and goes across the circle from edge to edge. Is this line segment called a radius or a diameter?

28. Christina has a large jar that she fills with small rocks she collects. The bottom of the jar has a diameter of 34 cm. What is the radius of the bottom of the jar?

29. Florence has a coat that closes with one large button. The button has a diameter of 8 cm. What is the radius of the button?

30. Michael and Peter shared a pizza pie after school. The pie had a diameter of 30 cm. What was the radius of the pie?

31. Nicole chose a round mirror for her bedroom. The mirror has a radius of 12.5 cm. What is the diameter of the mirror?

32. Ann bought a grapefruit and cut it in half. She measured the radius. It was 6 cm. What was the diameter?

Use GEOMETRY and MEASUREMENT to draw clocks from center points and radii or diameters and show the time.
Use GEOMETRY to solve problems.

215

Scale

Claudius Ptolemy, a Greek scientist of the second century A.D., wrote a book called *Geography* which listed basic rules for how maps should be made. Cartographers, or mapmakers, still use many of his rules today.

Ptolemy knew that most mapmakers at that time did not bother about how big or small things were on their maps, so maps were very inaccurate.

When maps are drawn so that big and little things are kept in their proper size relationship, the map is said to be *drawn to scale*. On a map showing a 5-mile road and a 10-mile road, the drawing of the 10-mile road will be twice as long as that of the 5-mile road.

Scale is shown on maps in numbers or with a small ruler called a graphic scale. The numbers compare map distance with real distance by using a fraction or ratio. A map scale of 1:100 (1/100) means that 1 inch on the map represents 100 miles of actual distance. The graphic scale for such a map would look like this:

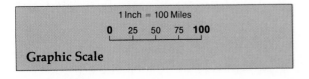

1 Inch = 100 Miles

0   25   50   75   **100**

Graphic Scale

Maps can be large or small scale. Large scale means that there are many details. A scale of 1:10 is large scale. Small scale uses very few details. A scale of 1:1,000,000 is small scale.

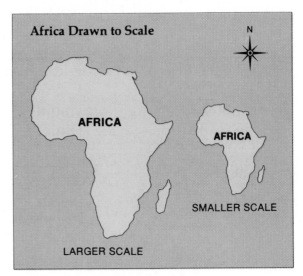

Africa Drawn to Scale

N

AFRICA

AFRICA

SMALLER SCALE

LARGER SCALE

CRITICAL THINKING

1. Look at the two maps on page 217. How are they similar? How are they different?

2. Which mapmakers did not care about scale? How can you tell?

3. What places in the world are missing from the two maps? Why do you think this happened?

4. Compare the oceans on the maps. How do they differ?

FOCUS   Use NUMBER skills to understand and analyze maps.

Ptolemy's second century map shows his interpretation of a round world on a flat surface. The size of the earth is underestimated and Europe and Asia are shown as over half the world's size.

This is a ninth century T-O map named for its T-form of the major waterways and the O as the outer edge of ocean surrounding the world.

In Chapter 16 you formulated problems about a dogsled race. Look at pages 206 and 207.

1. Write a sentence telling how you would train a dog to enter a dogsled race.

You learned something new about building solid figures from patterns. To review what you learned, study the sample exercise on page 208. Then use this new skill to name the solid figure formed by each folded pattern for exercises 2–3.

2.

3.

You learned about circles and drawing circles. To review, look at pages 212 and 214. Write how many radii and diameters are shown in the circles in exercises 4–6. Draw each circle for exercises 7–9.

4. 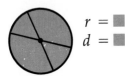 $r = \blacksquare$
$d = \blacksquare$

5. 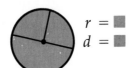 $r = \blacksquare$
$d = \blacksquare$

6. 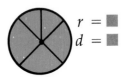 $r = \blacksquare$
$d = \blacksquare$

7. radius = 5 cm

8. radius = 6.5 cm

9. diameter = 9 cm

10. The diameter of a circle is 20 cm. What is the radius?

11. The radius of a circle is 12 cm. What is the diameter?

Copy and complete.

12. radius = 7 cm
diameter = $\blacksquare\blacksquare$ cm

13. radius = $\blacksquare\blacksquare$ cm
diameter = 36 cm

You learned about maps that are drawn to scale. Look at pages 216 and 217 to review how and why mapmakers use scales.

14. Why are maps drawn to scale?

FOCUS | Review and test skills learned and practiced.

LOOKING AHEAD

Preparing for New Skills for Chapter 17

In the next chapter, you will focus on

- formulating problems about recycling.
- relating fractions and decimals (hundredths).
- understanding place value through hundredths.
- using measurement.
- comparing and ordering decimals through hundredths.
- using algebra.

Learning about fractions and decimals as hundredths will be easier if you brush up on what you already know about fractions and decimals as tenths. First review the examples below. Then complete the exercises that follow. Refer to the examples as you work.

Look at the rectangle. It is divided into 10 equal parts. Each part equals one tenth of the whole. Six parts are shaded. You can describe the shaded part using words, a fraction, or a decimal.

$$\text{six tenths} = \frac{6}{10} = 0.6$$

A number line can be used to show fractions and decimals that are the same.

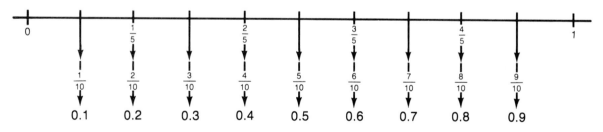

PRACTICE

Use the number line to complete.

1. $\frac{2}{5} = \frac{4}{10} = $ ■

2. $\frac{4}{5} = $ ■ $= 0.8$

3. ■ $= \frac{2}{10} = 0.2$

4. $\frac{3}{10} = $ ■

5. $\frac{9}{10} = $ ■

6. ■ $= 0.5$

7. ■ $= 0.1$

8. $\frac{7}{10} = $ ■

Review NUMBER skills in preparation for learning a new skill.

QUARTERLY REVIEW/TEST

Write the letter of the correct answer.

How much of each shape is shaded?

1.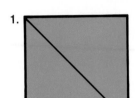

A. $\frac{2}{2}$

B. $\frac{3}{4}$

C. $\frac{0}{2}$

D. $\frac{0}{6}$

2.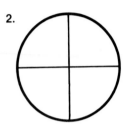

E. $\frac{4}{4}$

F. $\frac{2}{6}$

G. $\frac{0}{4}$

H. $\frac{5}{5}$

3.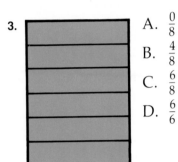

A. $\frac{0}{8}$

B. $\frac{4}{8}$

C. $\frac{6}{8}$

D. $\frac{6}{6}$

What is the equivalent fraction?

4. $\frac{2}{4}$ E. $\frac{1}{2}$ F. $\frac{4}{4}$ 5. $\frac{2}{3}$ A. $\frac{1}{2}$ B. $\frac{0}{3}$ 6. $\frac{1}{4}$ E. $\frac{1}{2}$ F. $\frac{3}{12}$

G. $\frac{0}{4}$ H. $\frac{2}{6}$ C. $\frac{4}{6}$ D. $\frac{1}{3}$ G. $\frac{3}{8}$ H. $\frac{2}{2}$

What is the equivalent decimal?

7. $\frac{3}{10}$ A. 0.3   B. 3.0   8. $\frac{5}{10}$ E. 1.0   F. 5.5   9. $\frac{1}{5}$ A. 1.0   B. 5.0

C. 3.3   D. 0.33   G. 0.5   H. 5.0   C. 0.1   D. 0.2

Add or subtract.

10. 4.7   E. 5.0   F. 5.9   11. 12.5   A. 47.1   B. 4.71
    +1.2   G. 9.5   H. 0.59   +34.6   C. 0.471   D. 471

12. 9.6   E. 0.23   F. 23   13. 15.4   A. 27   B. 0.27
    −7.3   G. 2.3   H. 2.9   −12.7   C. 2.1   D. 2.7

What unit is used to measure

14. the mass of a car?

E. cm   F. kg   G. m   H. g

15. the length of a rug?

A. cm   B. kg   C. m   D. g

16. the weight of a small book?

E. cm   F. kg   G. m   H. g

17. the amount of water in a pool?

A. mL   B. kg   C. L   D. g

FOCUS   Review concepts and skills taught in Chapters 9 through 16.

Multiply.

18.
$$\begin{array}{r} 300 \\ \times\ 4 \end{array}$$
E. 120   F. 1,200
G. 1,600   H. 12

19.
$$\begin{array}{r} 700 \\ \times\ 8 \end{array}$$
A. 5,600   B. 56
C. 4,800   D. 560

20.
$$\begin{array}{r} 500 \\ \times\ 9 \end{array}$$
E. 45   F. 5,400
G. 450   H. 4,500

21.
$$\begin{array}{r} 900 \\ \times\ 6 \end{array}$$
A. 5,400   B. 54
C. 540   D. 4,500

22.
$$\begin{array}{r} 231 \\ \times\ 3 \end{array}$$
E. 963   F. 793
G. 693   H. 903

23.
$$\begin{array}{r} 248 \\ \times\ 4 \end{array}$$
A. 992   B. 882
C. 725   D. 929

Divide.

24. $5\overline{)340}$ E. 68   F. 96
G. 690   H. 35

25. $7\overline{)673}$ A. 96   B. 86
C. 68   D. 96 R1

26. $4\overline{)274}$ E. 57   F. 86 R2
G. 68 R2   H. 68

27. $3\overline{)639}$ A. 213   B. 213 R1
C. 312   D. 312 R2

How many sides are the same length?

28.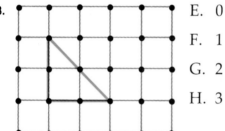
E. 0
F. 1
G. 2
H. 3

29.
A. 0
B. 1
C. 2
D. 3

What is the name of the angle?

30.
E. ∠ABC   F. ∠CAB
G. ∠BCA   H. ∠BAC

31.
A. ∠EDF   B. ∠EFD
C. ∠DEF   D. ∠DFE

How many faces does each solid figure have?

32.
E. 4   F. 5
G. 6   H. 8

33.
A. 4   B. 5
C. 6   D. 8

17

Decimals

DATA

Job
   Recycling bottles and cans

Town   Middletown

Number of blocks
   in neighborhood   5

Number of houses
   per block   10

Average number of bottles
   and cans per house   20

Number of kids
   collecting   3

Bottles and cans collected
   so far
      Alice   50
      Theresa   40
      Sidney   25

Amount recycling center
   pays for each item   4¢

Distance to recycling
   center   2 miles

Have you ever wondered what happens to old newspapers or old bottles and cans? Many times they are just thrown away. But sometimes people save them. These people know that the paper the news is printed on and old bottles and cans can be used again. Reusing something instead of throwing it away is called **recycling.**

Recycling helps keep our streets clean. It also helps to conserve our natural resources. Children can even earn some spending money by helping in a recycling drive. They collect old newspapers or old bottles and cans and take them to a recycling center. They get paid for each item they bring in.

Look at the data. What items are the people recycling? How much money do you think each person will earn? What problems might these people face? What are some other things that might be recycled? Think of all the advantages of recycling things. Discuss your answers.

Hundredths

Kira has a piece of graph paper divided into 100 squares of the same size. She colors in one square or **one-hundredth** of the whole piece of graph paper.

You can describe the colored part using words, a fraction, or a decimal.

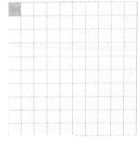

one - hundredth

$$\frac{1}{100} = 0.01$$

↑

decimal point

John has two pieces of graph paper. Each piece is divided into 100 squares of the same size. He colors in one whole piece and 28 squares of the second piece. John colors in **one and twenty-eight hundredths.**

one and twenty-eight hundredths

$$1\frac{28}{100} = 1.28$$

↑

decimal point

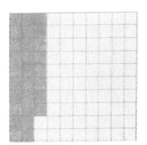

You can use a place-value chart to show ones, tenths, and hundredths.

GUIDED PRACTICE

Write a fraction and a decimal to tell how much is colored.

1.

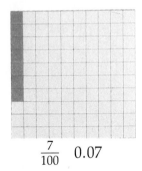

$\frac{7}{100}$ 0.07

2.

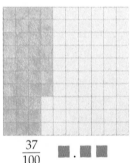

$\frac{37}{100}$ ■.■■

3.

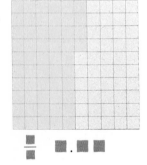

$\frac{\blacksquare}{\blacksquare}$ ■.■■

FOCUS   Use NUMBER skills to relate fractions and decimals.

PRACTICE

Write as a fraction and as a decimal.

4. 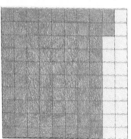   5. 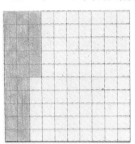   6. 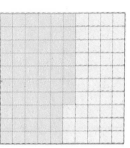   7.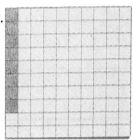

Write as a decimal.

8. $\frac{18}{100}$ **9.** $2\frac{73}{100}$ **10.** $\frac{4}{100}$ **11.** $\frac{68}{100}$ **12.** $1\frac{21}{100}$ **13.** $\frac{9}{100}$

14. $3\frac{2}{100}$ **15.** $\frac{43}{100}$ **16.** $\frac{99}{100}$ **17.** $1\frac{51}{100}$ **18.** $2\frac{14}{100}$ **19.** $\frac{62}{100}$

Write the number in the tenths place.

20. 1.38   **21.** 0.52   **22.** 1.93   **23.** 2.61   **24.** 0.49

Write the number in the hundredths place.

25. 1.72   **26.** 2.18   **27.** 0.49   **28.** 1.26   **29.** 0.64

30. What fraction can be written as 0.67?

31. What fraction can be written as 0.03?

MIXED PRACTICE
Maintaining and Reviewing Skills

Write as a decimal.

32. $\frac{42}{100}$ **33.** $\frac{84}{100}$ **34.** $\frac{7}{100}$ **35.** $1\frac{19}{100}$ **36.** $\frac{4}{10}$ **37.** $1\frac{3}{10}$

38. $\frac{1}{10}$ **39.** $6\frac{9}{10}$ **40.** $\frac{7}{10}$ **41.** $2\frac{2}{10}$ **42.** $1\frac{4}{10}$ **43.** $7\frac{5}{10}$

CHALLENGE

44. I am a decimal. The number in my ones place is zero. The number in my tenths place is three times the number of eyes on a cat. The number in my hundredths place is two times the number of legs on a horse. What decimal am I?

EXTRA PRACTICE—page 449

PLACE VALUE
Hundredths

Look at these decimal squares and place-value charts. They show you how to write decimals.

0.07   0 ones 0 tenths 7 hundredths

 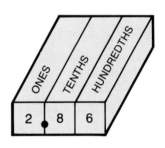

0.41   0 ones 4 tenths 1 hundredth

 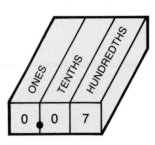 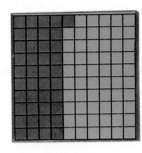 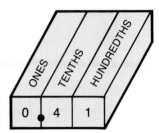

2.86   2 ones 8 tenths 6 hundredths

PRACTICE

Write the missing numbers.

1. 0.39 = ■ ones ■ tenths ■ hundredths

2. ■.55 = 2 ones ■ tenths ■ hundredths

3. 38.27 = ■ tens ■ ones ■ tenths ■ hundredths

4. 596.02 = ■ hundreds ■ tens ■ ones ■ tenths ■ hundredths

Write which place the 8 is in.

5. 0.28   6. 1.83   7. 8.64   8. 0.98   9. 1.78

MIXED PRACTICE
Maintaining and Reviewing Skills

Write which place the 5 is in.

10. 0.35   11. 15.3   12. 1,564   13. 57,361   14. 85,306

FOCUS | Use NUMBER skills to study place value of decimals.

226

APPLICATION
Using Measurement

 $\frac{1}{100}$ of a dollar

$0.01

 $\frac{5}{100}$ of a dollar

$0.05

 $\frac{10}{100}$ of a dollar

$0.10

 $\frac{25}{100}$ of a dollar

$0.25

Copy and complete.

	Whole Dollars	Parts of a Dollar	Dollars and Cents
	3	$\frac{8}{100}$	$3.08
15.	5	$\frac{39}{100}$	▬
16.	▬	▬	$1.75
17.	4	$\frac{12}{100}$	▬
18.	0	$\frac{50}{100}$	▬
19.	▬	▬	$13.98

Using Estimation and Mental Arithmetic

About how much does each toy cost? Round to the nearest dollar. Round up when the cents are 50 or more. Round down when the cents are 49 or less.

20.

$8.98

21.

$9.50

22.

$7.65

23.

$9.40

24.

$10.47

Use MEASUREMENT to relate fractions, decimals, and money.
Use ESTIMATION and MENTAL ARITHMETIC to find approximate prices.

Comparing and Ordering Through Hundredths

Mike's model canoe is 7.73 cm long. His model sailboat is 7.76 cm long. Which model is longer?

Compare the decimals. Look at each place. Look at the ones place first.

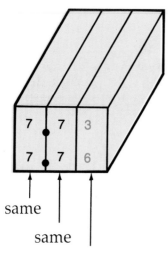

Remember:
< means **is less than**
> means **is greater than**

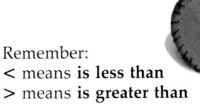

same

same

6 > 3   so   7.76 > 7.73

Check by looking at the number line. Numbers to the right are greater: 7.76 is to the right of 7.73.

7.73   7.76

The model sailboat is longer.

GUIDED PRACTICE

Write > or <. Compare the ones, the tenths, and the hundredths. Check by looking at the number line.

1. 7.71 < 7.75   2. 7.73 > 7.72   3. 7.78 > 7.74   4. 7.70 < 7.80

5. 7.72 ● 7.71   6. 7.70 ● 7.76   7. 7.79 ● 7.78   8. 7.75 ● 7.71

9. 7.80 ● 7.72   10. 7.75 ● 7.79   11. 7.70 ● 7.71   12. 7.77 ● 7.80

FOCUS   Use NUMBER skills to compare and order through hundredths.

PRACTICE

Write >, <, or =.

13. 1.26 ● 1.25   14. 0.17 ● 0.71   15. 2.35 ● 2.35   16. 7.29 ● 7.09

17. 3.57 ● 3.47   18. 1.56 ● 1.56   19. 0.79 ● 0.70   20. 4.60 ● 4.62

21. 6.29 ● 5.29   22. 2.91 ● 2.90   23. 1.06 ● 1.09   24. 0.22 ● 0.20

25. 3.64 ● 3.64   26. 7.19 ● 7.09   27. 0.45 ● 0.54   28. 5.76 ● 5.79

29. 0.68 ● 0.65   30. 9.04 ● 9.40   31. 6.75 ● 6.75   32. 4.92 ● 4.29

Write the greatest decimal.

33. 3.75, 3.73, 3.78, 3.70   34. 0.39, 0.34, 0.36, 0.32

35. 1.53, 1.58, 1.55, 1.50   36. 4.03, 4.06, 4.15, 4.12

Write in order from shortest to longest.

37. Julia has three model cars. Their lengths are 7.15 cm, 7.60 cm and 7.23 cm.

38. Karl has four model planes. Their lengths are 15.45 cm, 14.21 cm, 15.72 cm and 15.13 cm.

MIXED PRACTICE
Maintaining and Reviewing Skills

Write >, <, or =.

39. 7.46 ● 7.64   40. 8.21 ● 7.21   41. 0.65 ● 0.68   42. 0.4 ● 0.7

43. 3.2 ● 3.2   44. 19.1 ● 18.9   45. 497 ● 479   46. 5,126 ● 5,162

Write in order from least to greatest.

47. 8.43   9.34   8.37   9.45   48. 8.1   7.4   7.1   7.6

CHALLENGE

49. These decimals are written in order from greatest to least. Find the missing digits.

4.71, 4.7■, 4.60, 4.■2, 4.49, 4.■0, ■.39, 3.75

DECIMALS

Comparing Tenths and Hundredths

The length of a roller skate is 0.3 m. The length of an ice skate is 0.30 m. Which skate is longer?

Look at these decimal squares. They show that 0.3 = 0.30.

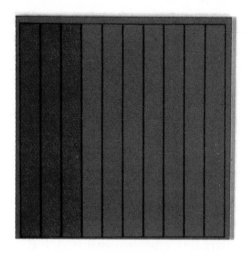

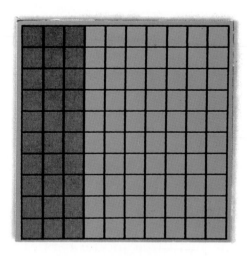

0.3	0.30
three tenths	thirty hundredths

The skates are the same length.

PRACTICE

Solve.

1. A baseball bat is 0.73 m long. A ski pole is 0.79 m long. Which is shorter?

2. A golf shoe is 0.19 m long. A sneaker is 0.2 m long. Which is longer?

3. A tennis racket is 0.7 m long. A baseball bat is 0.70 m long. Which is longer?

4. Write a word problem for these lengths: 0.81 m, 0.89 m. Then write the answer.

MIXED PRACTICE
Maintaining and Reviewing Skills

Write >, <, or =.

5. 2.56 ● 2.76   6. 3.4 ● 3.40   7. 842 ● 729   8. 356 ● 360

FOCUS | Use NUMBER skills to compare tenths and hundredths.

APPLICATION
Using Algebra: Inequalities

2.4

2.36 2.37 2.38 2.39 2.40 2.41 2.42 2.43 2.44 2.45 2.46

Is 2.38 > 2.41 true or false?

Look at the number line. Numbers to the right are greater: 2.41 is greater than 2.38.

2.38 > 2.41 is false.

Write *true* or *false*.

9. 2.43 > 2.41   **10.** 2.39 < 2.4   **11.** 2.4 > 2.40   **12.** 2.45 > 2.46

13. 2.36 > 2.4   **14.** 2.42 > 2.37   **15.** 2.38 < 2.46   **16.** 2.36 = 2.46

17. 2.4 > 2.41   **18.** 2.40 = 2.4   **19.** 2.37 > 2.45   **20.** 2.44 < 2.45

21. 2.42 < 2.46   **22.** 2.36 < 2.46   **23.** 2.39 = 2.4   **24.** 2.39 > 2.36

Solving Problems

Solve.

25. Sarah has three pieces of graph paper. Each piece is divided into 100 squares of the same size. She colors in two whole pieces and 73 squares of the third piece. Write a mixed number and a decimal to tell how much Sarah colored.

26. Moe has a photo album with two pages left. Each page is divided into 100 spaces of the same size. Moe fills one page and 55 spaces of the second page with pictures. Write a mixed number and a decimal to tell how many pages Moe filled.

27. A red crayon is 9.20 cm long. A yellow crayon is 8.92 cm long. Which crayon is shorter?

28. The front door key is 5.30 cm long. The side door key is 5.03 cm long. Which key is longer?

Use ALGEBRA to identify correct and incorrect inequalities.
Use NUMBER skills to solve problems.

LOOKING BACK

Reviewing and Testing Chapter 17

In Chapter 17 you formulated problems about recycling. Look at pages 222 and 223.

1. Write a sentence telling how you might start a recycling drive.

You learned about naming hundredths as decimals. To review what you learned, study the sample exercises on pages 224 and 226. Then use these skills to write a decimal for exercises 2–7. Copy and complete exercises 8 and 9.

2. $\frac{42}{100}$
3. $\frac{6}{100}$
4. $1\frac{15}{100}$
5. $4\frac{6}{100}$
6. $9\frac{63}{100}$
7. $8\frac{1}{100}$

8. $0.52 =$ ◼ ones ◼ tenths ◼ hundredths

9. $4.07 =$ ◼ ones ◼ tenths ◼ hundredths

You learned about rounding amounts of money mentally in order to estimate. To review, look at page 227. Round each amount to the nearest dollar for exercises 10–15.

10. $2.15
11. $4.75
12. $6.50
13. $8.40
14. $3.50
15. $6.98

You learned about comparing and ordering decimals. To review, look at pages 228 and 230. Write >, <, or = for exercises 16–19. Solve each problem for exercises 20 and 21.

16. 3.58 ● 3.48
17. 0.23 ● 0.32
18. 8.26 ● 8.26
19. 4.07 ● 4.09

20. A cat is 0.36 m long. A dog is 0.4 m long. Which is longer?

21. The brown dog stands 0.8 m tall. The white dog stands 0.80 m tall. Which is taller?

FOCUS | Review and test skills learned and practiced.

Preparing for New Skills for Chapter 18

> **In the next chapter, you will focus on**
>
> - formulating problems about a pet store.
> - writing decimals as words and numbers.
> - using patterns and functions.
> - rounding to the nearest dollar and ten dollars.
> - using measurement: money.
> - how math is used in technology.

Learning about writing whole numbers and hundredths as decimals will be easier if you brush up on what you already know about writing whole numbers and tenths as decimals. First review the example below. Then complete the exercises that follow. You may find it helpful to refer to the example as you work.

How much is colored yellow?

$2\frac{6}{10}$ are colored yellow.

$2\frac{6}{10}$ can be written as 2.6.

 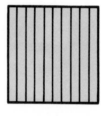 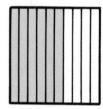

2 squares $\qquad$ $\frac{6}{10}$ of a square

$$\underset{\text{mixed number}}{2\frac{6}{10}} = \underset{\text{decimal}}{2.6}$$

Ones	Tenths
2	6

decimal point

Read $2\frac{6}{10}$ and 2.6 as "two and six-tenths."

PRACTICE

Write the decimal.

1.

Ones	Tenths
6	3

2.

Ones	Tenths
5	2

3.

Ones	Tenths
9	3

4. $4\frac{5}{10}$ **5.** $7\frac{3}{10}$ **6.** $1\frac{7}{10}$ **7.** $8\frac{6}{10}$ **8.** $2\frac{1}{10}$ **9.** $12\frac{9}{10}$

Review NUMBER skills in preparation for learning a new skill.

CHAPTER

18

Decimals and Money

DATA

Rent for store
$600 per month

Working hours for store

Monday–Wednesday, Friday
9:30 A.M. – 7:00 P.M.

Thursday
9:30 A.M. – 9:30 P.M.

Saturday
9:00 A.M. – 8:00 P.M.

Profit during last 5 years

Years 1, 2, 3, 5   Profits up

Year 4   Profits down

Neighborhood
More families moving in

Dave and Paula Yearwood's dream might finally come true. Their savings could buy them this pet store. Then they would have the chance to work together as a family—something they have wanted to do for years.

There was a lot to consider before any decision could be made. Is this a good business to be in? Will they be able to make enough money? The data gives some information that might help them decide.

Think about the Yearwoods and the pet store. How should they go about making their decision? What do they need to know? How can they find this out? What problems might they face? Predict the choice they will make and tell why you do or do not think it's the right one.

Writing as Words and Numbers

Joanna is buying fruit. She wants a bunch of grapes that has a weight of seventy-five hundredths of a kilogram. What does she write on her shopping list next to *grapes*?

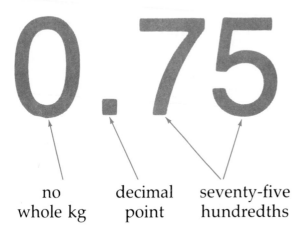

no whole kg	decimal point	seventy-five hundredths

Joanna writes 0.75 kg next to *grapes*.

A bag of oranges is labeled 1.63 kg. How does Joanna read this?

Joanna reads **1.63 kg** as **"one and sixty-three hundredths kilograms."**

GUIDED PRACTICE

Write each decimal. Put in a zero and a decimal point if there are no whole ones. Put in a decimal point in place of *and*.

1. two and forty-seven hundredths 2.47

2. thirty-nine hundredths 0.■ ■

3. four and twenty-three hundredths 4.■ ■

4. eighty-eight hundredths ■.■ ■

5. six and nineteen hundredths ■.■ ■

FOCUS	Use NUMBER skills to write decimals as words and numbers.

PRACTICE

Write each decimal.

6. fifty-four hundredths

7. eleven hundredths

8. fifty hundredths

9. sixty-one hundredths

10. five and twenty-nine hundredths

11. ninety-two and thirty-six hundredths

12. one hundred thirteen and seven hundredths

Write in words.

13. 0.64   14. 2.71   15. 8.02   16. 0.22   17. 5.52

18. 16.95   19. 24.13   20. 10.91   21. 11.77   22. 31.43

23. A box of strawberries is labeled 2.15 kg.

24. A bag of apples is labeled 0.33 kg.

25. A bunch of bananas is labeled 1.08 kg.

26. A watermelon is labeled 3.11 kg.

MIXED PRACTICE

Maintaining and Reviewing Skills

Write each number.

27. thirty-six hundredths

28. five hundredths

29. seven tenths

30. sixty-one hundredths

31. seven and forty-seven hundredths

32. two hundred eleven and one tenth

33. fifty-six

34. eighty-seven

CHALLENGE

35. Rearrange these words to make the decimal closest to 500.

twenty, one, four, ninety, hundredths, five, and, hundred

DECIMALS

Review Writing as Words and Numbers

Decimals can be written as words or numbers.

1.62 = one and sixty-two hundredths

8.45 = eight and forty-five hundredths

12.07 = twelve and seven hundredths

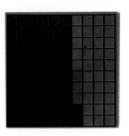

Read decimals as they are written in words.

PRACTICE

Write *true* or *false*.

1. 0.87 = eighty-seven hundredths

2. 3.4 = four and three tenths

3. 1.09 = one and nine tenths

4. 2.11 = two and eleven hundredths

5. 6.6 = six and six hundredths

6. 0.04 = four hundredths

Write the missing words.

7. 12.41 = twelve and forty-one ■

8. 57.9 = fifty-seven and nine ■

9. 123.64 = one hundred twenty-three and ■

10. 298.2 = two ■ ninety-eight and ■

MIXED PRACTICE

Maintaining and Reviewing Skills

Write each decimal.

11. thirty-two and fifty-three hundredths = ■

12. two hundred thirteen and seven hundredths = ■

13. seventy-nine and 4 tenths = ■

14. three hundred forty-one and nine tenths = ■

FOCUS | Use NUMBER skills to review writing decimals as words and numbers.

238

APPLICATION
Using Patterns and Functions

In the left column are decimals written as numbers. In the right column are decimals written as words. If you add 0.01 to each decimal on the left you will get a decimal on the right.

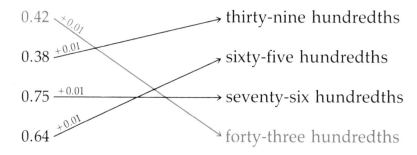

0.42 — thirty-nine hundredths
0.38 — sixty-five hundredths
0.75 — seventy-six hundredths
0.64 — forty-three hundredths

15. Write the decimals below in two columns. Put the numbers on the left and the words on the right. Add 0.01 to each decimal on the left and draw an arrow to the sum on the right. Write the rule on the arrow.

    0.21, 0.15, 0.54, sixteen hundredths, fifty-five hundredths, twenty-two hundredths

Solving Problems

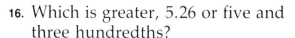
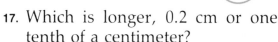

16. Which is greater, 5.26 or five and three hundredths?

17. Which is longer, 0.2 cm or one tenth of a centimeter?

18. Which is lighter, 1.8 kg or one and seven tenths kilograms?

19. Which is more, 1.24 mL or one and twenty-five hundredths milliliters?

20. Which is shorter, 0.83 m or eighty-one hundredths of a meter?

21. Which is heavier, 2.6 kg or two and four tenths kilograms?

22. Write a problem using 2.46 mL and two and thirty-six hundredths milliliters. Then solve.

23. Write a problem using two and six tenths kilograms and 2.5 kg. Then solve.

Use PATTERNS AND FUNCTIONS to relate decimal words and numbers.
Use NUMBER skills to solve problems.

Rounding to the Nearest Dollar

Jennifer made a list of all the money she earned from her summer jobs.

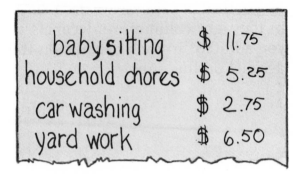

She wanted to get a quick idea of how much money she earned for each job. She used a number line to round each amount to the nearest dollar.

babysitting	$11.75	rounds up to	⟶ $12.00
household chores	$ 5.25	rounds down to	⟶ $ 5.00
car washing	$ 2.75	rounds up to	⟶ $ 3.00
yard work	$ 6.50	rounds up to	⟶ $ 7.00

- $2.75 is closer to $3 than to $2
- $5.25 is closer to $5 than to $6
- $6.50 is exactly between $6 and $7
- $6.50 rounds up to $7

GUIDED PRACTICE

Round to the nearest dollar.

1. $2.65 → $3

2. $7.18 → $7

3. $9.91

4. $27.28

5. $56.51

6. $0.95

7. $3.75

8. $49.50

9. $12.12

10. $20.49

11. $99.50

12. $6.25

13. $19.90

14. $5.05

15. $13.80

16. $1.49

17. $7.51

18. $9.85

FOCUS Use NUMBER skills to round to the nearest dollar.

PRACTICE

Round to the nearest dollar.

19. $11.01   **20.** $19.48   **21.** $2.98   **22.** $19.95   **23.** $6.14

24. $45.68   **25.** $215.50   **26.** $288.88   **27.** 57.17   **28.** $36.37

29. $17.50   **30.** $33.40   **31.** $99.95   **32.** $42.19   **33.** $59.99

Are these amounts rounded correctly? Write *yes* or *no*.

34. $19.50 ⟶ $20.00   **35.** $4.50 ⟶ $4.00

36. $25.55 ⟶ $25.00   **37.** $11.90 ⟶ $12.00

38. $111.11 ⟶ $112.00   **39.** $13.89 ⟶ $14.00

40. $1.98 ⟶ $2.00   **41.** $103.49 ⟶ $104.00

42. $12.48 ⟶ $12.00   **43.** $234.50 ⟶ $235.00

MIXED PRACTICE
Maintaining and Reviewing Skills

Round to the nearest dollar.

44. $9.47   **45.** $15.61   **46.** $34.52   **47.** $43.34   **48.** $71.75

Round to the nearest hundred.

49. 342   **50.** 635   **51.** 871   **52.** 429   **53.** 919

CHALLENGE

54. Jennifer has $26.25. She wants to buy the following items:

school supplies	$ 7.25
shoes	$11.98
book bag	$ 5.50

Estimate her expenses. Do you think she will have enough money?

    Add the actual amounts. Exactly how much money will be left?

MONEY
Rounding to the Nearest Ten Dollars

You know how to round amounts of money to the nearest dollar. Now you will round dollar amounts to the nearest ten dollars.

Round $78.29 to the nearest ten dollars.

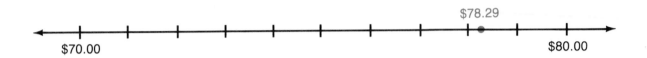

$78.29 is between $70.00 and $80.00
$78.29 is closer to $80.00
$78.29 rounds up to $80.00

When rounding to the nearest ten dollars, if the digit in the ones place is 5 or more, round up. If the digit in the ones place is less than 5, round down.

PRACTICE

Round to the nearest ten dollars.

1. $11.86
2. $23.84
3. $19.49
4. $46.58
5. $33.60

6. $87.20
7. $74.50
8. $65.00
9. $81.97
10. $13.60

11. $55.23
12. $26.00
13. $41.95
14. $63.92
15. $89.05

16. $96.79
17. $131.56
18. $112.00
19. $78.45
20. $146.25

MIXED PRACTICE
Maintaining and Reviewing Skills

Round to the nearest ten dollars.

21. $64.91
22. $27.31
23. $18.45
24. $79.01
25. $115.10

Round to the nearest dollar.

26. $6.47
27. $12.39
28. $35.71
29. $7.64
30. $136.84

FOCUS | Use NUMBER skills to round to the nearest ten dollars.

APPLICATION
Using Measurement: Money

The Rodriguez family is going camping for two weeks. They need to buy several things before they go. About how much do they spend, rounded to the nearest $10?

31. Copy the chart. Round each actual price to the nearest $10. Then add the rounded prices.

Item	Actual Price	Rounded to Nearest $10
Tent	$59.98	$60
4 sleeping bags	$62.00	■
Folding table	$18.50	■
4 folding chairs	$24.00	■
Food	$86.84	■
		■ Total

Solving Problems

32. The gas for the car cost $28.13. The fee for the camp site was $73.50. What was the total cost to the nearest $10?

33. The family went to the beach for a day. They spent $3.20 on juice and $7.65 on food. What was the total cost to the nearest $1?

34. Each person bought a book to take on vacation. The prices were $5.49, $4.25, $3.50, and $6.98. What was the total cost to the nearest $1?

35. Mrs. Lee bought new bathing suits for the children. Maria's suit cost $17.98. Juan's suit cost $14.98. What was the total cost to the nearest $10?

36. The Lee family bought new sweatshirts. Maria's and Juan's sweatshirts each cost $7.98. Mr. and Mrs. Lee's sweatshirts each cost $12. What was the total cost to the nearest $10?

37. The family went to a museum. They spent $9.60 to get into the museum and $12.75 on souvenirs. They had lunch at the museum for $8.27. What was the total cost of the trip to the museum to the nearest $1?

Use MEASUREMENT and NUMBER skills to solve problems and find totals to the nearest $1 and nearest $10.

243

Flowcharts

A flowchart is a chart that shows the steps in a process. A flowchart uses different-shaped boxes to show the different kinds of steps in a process.

Circles show the beginning and end of the process.

Rectangles show the steps in the process.

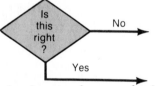

Diamonds show where a decision has to be made.

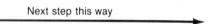

Next step this way

These different kinds of steps are connected with arrows.

Flowcharts give a rough plan to show how to do something. Drawing a flowchart is helpful in deciding how to solve many kinds of problems.

Here is a flowchart that shows the process of getting ready for school.

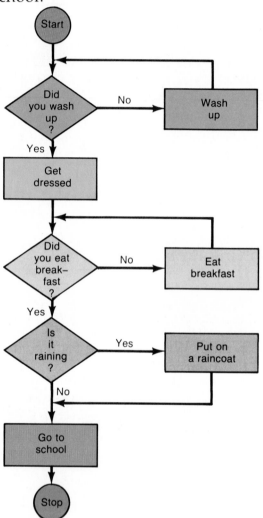

CRITICAL THINKING

Washing up, getting dressed, and eating breakfast are all processes. Pick one and draw a flowchart for it.

FOCUS | Use LOGIC to understand flowcharts.

Flowcharts can be used to show how information flows in a computer.

LOOKING BACK
Reviewing and Testing Chapter 18

In Chapter 18 you formulated problems about a pet store. Look at pages 234 and 235.

1. Write a sentence telling what things you would want to know when buying a pet store.

You learned about writing decimals as words and numbers. To review what you learned, study the sample exercise on page 236. Then use this skill to write a decimal for exercises 2–6.

2. twenty-three hundredths

3. ninety hundredths

4. six and eleven hundredths

5. fifty-seven and two hundredths

6. forty-nine and seventy-five hundredths

You learned about rounding amounts of money. To review, look at pages 240 and 242. Round to the nearest dollar for exercises 7–10. Round to the nearest ten dollars for exercises 11–14.

7. $5.13

8. $8.55

9. $16.50

10. $87.38

11. $11.63

12. $45.75

13. $79.13

14. $34.98

You learned about flowcharts and how different shaped boxes show different kinds of steps in a process. To review, look at pages 244 and 245.

15. What shape is used to show the beginning and end of a process?

16. What shape is used to show where a decision has been made?

17. What shape is used to show the steps in the process?

FOCUS | Review and test skills learned and practiced.

Preparing for New Skills for Chapter 19

In the next chapter, you will focus on

- formulating problems about a circus.
- adding decimals and money.

- using measurement.
- using a problem-solving strategy.
- subtracting decimals and money.

Learning more about addition and subtraction with decimals will be easier if you review what you have already learned. Review Models A and B. Then complete the exercises.

Model A

Line up the decimal points.	Add the tenths. Regroup.	Add the ones. Regroup.	Add the tens. Put the decimal point in the sum.

T	O	Ts
2	3.	6
+1	9.	7

T	O	Ts
	1	
2	3.	6
+1	9.	7
		3

6Ts
+7Ts
13Ts

T	O	Ts
1	1	
2	3.	6
+1	9.	7
	3	3

1
3
+9
13

T	O	Ts
1	1	
2	3.	6
+1	9.	7
4	3.	3

1T
2T
+1T
4T

Model B

Line up the decimal points.	Regroup. Subtract the tenths.	Regroup. Subtract the ones.	Subtract the tens. Put in the decimal point.

T	O	Ts
5	4.	6
−3	6.	7

T	O	Ts
	3	16
5	4.	6
−3	6.	7
		9

T	O	Ts
	13	
4	3	16
5	4.	6
−3	6.	7
	7	9

T	O	Ts
	13	
4	3	16
5	4.	6
−3	6.	7
1	7.	9

Regroup 4 ones 6 tenths as 3 ones 16 tenths.

Regroup 5 tens 3 ones as 4 tens 13 ones.

PRACTICE

Add. Use Model A.

Subtract. Use Model B.

1. 34.4
    +12.7

2. 43.7
    +24.6

3. 27.6
    +12.5

4. 65.4
    −36.7

5. 35.2
    −21.4

6. 46.8
    −27.9

Review NUMBER skills in preparation for learning a new skill.

Formulate problems using picture cues, text, and data.

CHAPTER 19

Addition and Subtraction of Decimals

DATA

Circus schedule

New York	Sept. 3–10
Cleveland	Sept. 13–20
Chicago	Sept. 22–29
Denver	Oct. 3–11
San Diego	Oct. 16–23

Mileage

New York to Cleveland
482 miles

Cleveland to Chicago
341 miles

Chicago to Denver
867 miles

Denver to San Diego
1,241 miles

Personnel

Acrobats	25
Clowns	23
Jugglers	11
Elephants	20
Horses	14
Bears	5
Lions	9
Trainers	13
Musicians	12
Ringmaster	1

Everyone loves the circus. We laugh at the clown. We gasp when the tightrope walker almost loses his balance. We cheer when the lion tamer puts her head into the mouth of a ferocious lion.

But what happens when the show is over and the audience has gone home? What happens when the circus has to move on to the next city to perform? Everything from the biggest elephant to the smallest fleck of glitter has to be packed up and transported.

What a job! What problems! How would *you* move a circus?

Make a list of all the things you would have to do. Then, suggest ways to accomplish these tasks.

Adding Hundredths

Sometimes you need to regroup hundredths.
Add: 2.38 + 1.29

  +

Add the hundredths. Regroup.

```
  O | Ts | Hs
     |    | 1
  2  | 3  | 8
+ 1  | 2  | 9
     |    | 7
```

Add the tenths.

```
  O | Ts | Hs
     | 1  |
  2  | 3  | 8
+ 1  | 2  | 9
     | 6  | 7
```

Add the ones. Write the decimal point in the answer.

```
  O | Ts | Hs
     | 1  |
  2  | 3  | 8
+ 1  | 2  | 9
  3  | 6  | 7
```

Sometimes you need to write zeros before you add.
Add: 2.4 + 3.75

Write 2.4 as 2.40.

```
  2.40
+ 3.75
```

Add.

```
   1
  2.40
+ 3.75
  6.15
```

GUIDED PRACTICE

Add.

1.
```
  4.16
+ 3.82
  7.98
```

2.
```
   1 1
  0.87
+ 0.56
  ■.43
```

3.
```
  5.26
+ 2.3
```

4.
```
  7.54
+ 1.97
```

5.
```
  1.3
+ 5.81
```

6.
```
  8.47
+ 0.65
```

7.
```
  2.83
+ 2.47
```

8.
```
  8
+ 2.38
```

9.
```
  4.8
+ 2.45
```

10.
```
  1.96
+ 3.46
```

11.
```
  4.37
+ 2.8
```

12.
```
  6.07
+ 3.96
```

13. 4.35 + 6.28

14. 3.6 + 5.87

15. 6.01 + 8.6

16. 4.91 + 5

FOCUS | Use NUMBER skills to add decimals.

PRACTICE

Add.

17. 4.67
    +3.59

18. 2.75
    +5.75

19. 5.8
    +3.64

20. 6.29
    +1.09

21. 7.37
    +2.25

22. 8.93
    +3.2

23. 4.31
    +3.56

24. 6.28
    +3.71

25. 1.67
    +3.24

26. 5.23
    +2.39

27. 6.5
    +8.49

28. 7
    +4.28

29. 10.31
    + 2.67

30. 15.5
    + 5.43

31. 22.05
    + 7.51

32. 31.63
    + 4.8

33. 11.25
    + 5.85

34. 25.77
    + 7.68

35. $2.17 + 5.29$

36. $7.3 + 5.48$

37. $6.15 + 8.2$

38. $2.42 + 9$

39. $5.85 + 6.52$

40. $6.58 + 8.5$

41. $2.69 + 3.87$

42. $6.2 + 4.07$

43. $7.09 + 6.07$

44. $6.41 + 6.9$

45. $3.6 + 4.84$

46. $10.46 + 2.7$

47. Greg rode his bike 3.4 kilometers to the movies. He then rode 4.21 kilometers to see his friend. How many kilometers did Greg ride?

48. Erica's bike trip to the store was 5.46 kilometers. She took the short cut home and rode 4.89 kilometers. How many kilometers did Erica ride?

MIXED PRACTICE
Maintaining and Reviewing Skills

Add or subtract.

49. 6.34
    +2.93

50. 8.7
    +4.29

51. 7.2
    −3.8

52. 4
    +9.6

53. 19.4
    − 6.7

54. 7.6
    +5

CHALLENGE

Add.

55. 4.13
    3.28
    +0.36

56. 2.69
    5.9
    +3.17

57. 7.83
    8.73
    +9.2

58. 10.6
    5.79
    + 6

59. 2.65
    6.93
    +2.85

60. 5.14
    6.07
    +3.96

EXTRA PRACTICE—page 449

ADDITION OF DECIMALS
Adding Money

Chang bought a boat model for $4.15. He also bought some paints and glue for $2.36. How much money did Chang spend?

To find how much money Chang spent altogether, add: $4.15 + $2.36.

Adding money is like adding whole numbers. Remember to write the dollar sign and the cent point in the answer.

$$\begin{array}{r} \overset{1}{} \\ \$4.15 \\ + 2.36 \\ \hline \$6.51 \end{array}$$

Chang spent $6.51 altogether.

Helen's Hobby Shop

DATE

Item	Price
model boat	$4.15
paint and glue	2.36

PRACTICE

Add.

1. $3.56
   + 3.41

2. $6.72
   + 0.89

3. $7.24
   + 1.87

4. $0.46
   + 0.38

5. $4.59
   + 7.90

6. $6.24
   + 3.99

7. $5.64
   + 4.03

8. $3.78
   + 1.55

9. $5.76
   + 4.22

10. $18.75
    + 2.38

11. $17.15
    + 2.98

12. $14.39
    + 3.91

13. $9.17 + $1.86

14. $2.12 + $4.86

15. $7.36 + $3.75

16. $5.82 + $3.48

17. $1.98 + $4.30

18. $8.14 + $4.69

19. $5.64 + $2.68

20. $6.83 + $6.29

MIXED PRACTICE
Maintaining and Reviewing Skills

Add or subtract.

21. $10.76
    + 3.49

22. $12.46
    + 4.96

23. 4.82
    + 4.9

24. 12.8
    − 3.9

25. 9.4
    + 11.37

26. 34.6
    − 19.7

FOCUS   Use NUMBER skills to add money.

252

APPLICATION

Using Measurement

This table shows distances between towns in kilometers that the Fisher family traveled on their vacation.

Start From	Destination	Kilometers Traveled
Gomer	Blauvelt	25.64
Blauvelt	Kobelt	16.47
Kobelt	Stormville	19.85
Stormville	Danville	38.4
Danville	Katonah	21.96
Katonah	Arbery	18
Arbery	Stanhope	15.08

To find the total distance the Fishers traveled from Gomer to Blauvelt to Kobelt, use the table and add.

$$\overset{1\ 1}{}$$

Gomer to Blauvelt ⟶ 25.64 km
Blauvelt to Kobelt ⟶ + 16.47 km
Gomer to Blauvelt to Kobelt ⟶ 42.11 km

Use the table to find the total distances the Fishers traveled between the towns listed below.

27. Kobelt to Stormville to Danville

28. Katonah to Arbery to Stanhope

29. Stormville to Danville to Katonah

30. Danville to Katonah to Arbery to Stanhope

31. Gomer to Blauvelt to Kobelt to Stormville

Exploring With a Calculator

32. Can you find the two numbers that are in the wrong boxes in this addition square?

Use your calculator to add across and down to correct the addition square.

3.84	15.09	10.59
6.75	13.8	28.89
18.93	20.55	39.48

Use NUMBER skills and MEASUREMENT to add decimals.
Use a CALCULATOR to add decimals.

PROBLEM SOLVING
Selecting a Strategy: Finding a Pattern

Finding a pattern is a strategy you can use when you PLAN and SOLVE a problem. Finding a rule helps you find a pattern. A rule tells you how the items in a pattern relate to each other.

1. READ What is the next number in this number pattern? 10, 30, 50, 70, 90, ▪

2. KNOW Ask yourself: What do I need to find? What is the rule for the number pattern? How are the numbers related to each other from left to right? What number comes after 90 in this number pattern? What **key facts** do I need? The numbers become greater from left to right.

3. PLAN Select a strategy: try finding a pattern. Find out which operation is used. Find the rule that shows how the numbers are related to each other. Addition or multiplication can be used to produce greater numbers.

4. SOLVE The second number is 20 more than the first number. The third number is 20 more than the second number. The same rule works for the next numbers. Rule: Add 20.

$$10 + 20 = 30 \qquad 30 + 20 = 50$$
$$50 + 20 = 70 \qquad 70 + 20 = 90$$

Find the next number: $90 + 20 = 110$.
The next number in the pattern is 110.

5. CHECK Adding 20 to each given number gives a sum equal to the next number to the right. It seems reasonable that adding 20 to 90 gives 110, or the next number in the pattern.

FOCUS Evaluate information as part of the Five-Step PROBLEM-SOLVING Plan.

254

Write the letter of the rule that describes each pattern.

1. 220, 200, 180, 160, 140
   A. Add 20.
   C. Multiply by 20.
   B. Subtract 20.
   D. Divide by 20.

2. 1, 3, 9, 27, 81
   A. Add 3.
   C. Multiply by 3.
   B. Add 6.
   D. Divide by 3.

3. 625, 125, 25, 5, 1
   A. Subtract 500.
   C. Multiply by 5.
   B. Add 100.
   D. Divide by 5.

4. 5, 11, 23, 47, 95
   A. Add 6.
   C. Multiply by 2 and then subtract 1.
   B. Add 12.
   D. Multiply by 2 and then add 1.

Write the rule. Then copy and complete the pattern.

5. 3, 18, 33, 48, ■, ■

6. 370, 330, 290, 250, ■, ■

7. 512, 256, 128, 64, ■, ■

8. 5, 20, 80, ■, ■, 5,120

9. 17, 19, ■, 23, ■, 27

10. 3, 15, ■, ■, 1,875, 9,375

11. 425, 410, 395, ■, 365, ■

12. 3, 9, 21, 45, ■, ■

Class Project

Divide into small groups of students. On a piece of paper, write a list of five number patterns that have an "Add" rule and five that have a "Multiply" rule. Put at least four numbers in each pattern. On another piece of paper, list the rules that go with each pattern. Trade lists of patterns with another group. Each group will need to write the other's rules and write the next number in each pattern.

Subtracting Hundredths

Sometimes you need to regroup before subtracting.
Subtract: 3.64 − 1.38

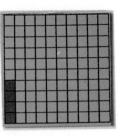

Subtract the ones. Write
the decimal point in
the answer.

**Regroup. Subtract
the hundredths.**

O	Ts	Hs
	5	14
3.	6̸	4̸
−1.	3	8
		6

**Subtract the
tenths.**

O	Ts	Hs
	5	14
3.	6̸	4̸
−1.	3	8
	2	6

O	Ts	Hs
	5	14
3.	6̸	4̸
−1.	3	8
2.	2	6

Sometimes you need to write zeros before you
subtract.

Subtract: 4 − 2.43

Write 4 as 4.00.

```
  4 . 0 0
− 2 . 4 3
```

Subtract.

```
        9
  3   1̸0 10
  4̸ . 0̸ 0̸
− 2 . 4 3
  1 . 5 7
```

GUIDED PRACTICE

Subtract.

1. 5.16
   −3.04
   ■.■2

2. 3.78
   −1.90

3. 7.04
   −3.28

4. 8.41
   −4.36

5. 9.36
   −4.85

6. 4.5
   −2.76

7. 9
   −8.17

8. 6.82
   −0.74

9. 5.9
   −4.36

10. 7.21
   −5.8

11. 6
   −3.46

12. 8.1
   −6.52

| FOCUS | Use NUMBER skills to subtract decimals. |

PRACTICE

Subtract.

13.	4.81 −1.22	14.	1.62 −0.48	15.	5.73 −3.09	16.	7.69 −6.51	17.	6.9 −3.24	18.	4.96 −3.28
19.	9.06 −3.74	20.	2.6 −0.88	21.	4.88 −1.91	22.	5.19 −1.60	23.	5.89 −3	24.	7.44 −0.63
25.	2.71 −1.44	26.	9 −2.16	27.	7.8 −2.51	28.	6 −2.95	29.	2.09 −1.75	30.	9 −0.35

31. $5.17 - 2.69$ 32. $6.1 - 4.24$ 33. $9.64 - 4.13$ 34. $2.12 - 1.5$

35. $6.36 - 0.89$ 36. $6.81 - 2.33$ 37. $5.38 - 1.22$ 38. $4.81 - 3.69$

39. $2.43 - 1.35$ 40. $8 - 7.16$ 41. $4 - 3.15$ 42. $9 - 6.81$

43. Jodi ran the 30-meter dash in 9.63 seconds. Laurie ran the dash in 8.7 seconds. How much faster did Laurie run the 30 meters?

44. Billy swam 100 meters in 50.83 seconds. John swam 100 meters in 51 seconds. How much faster did Billy swim the 100 meters?

MIXED PRACTICE

Maintaining and Reviewing Skills

Add or subtract.

45.	7.43 −3.62	46.	9.46 +3.29	47.	14.63 − 9.81	48.	8 −6.75	49.	16.4 + 4.65	50.	36.42 +17.38

51. $5 - 3.21$ 52. $4.6 + 3.98$ 53. $18.21 + 15$ 54. $14.9 - 6$

CHALLENGE

Find the missing digits.

55.	6.■4 −3.2■ ■.29	56.	■.5■ −2.■6 7.21	57.	9.4■ −■.■8 3.08	58.	7.■3 −■.6■ 2.06	59.	■.6■ −5.■1 3.09

EXTRA PRACTICE—page 449

SUBTRACTION OF DECIMALS
Subtracting Money

Kira had $8. She bought a kite for $3.75. How much money does she have left?

To find how much money Kira has left, subtract: $8 − $3.75.

Subtracting money is like subtracting whole numbers. Remember to write zeros if you need to and to write the dollar sign and cent point in the answer.

Write $8 as $8.00. Then subtract.

$ 3.75

```
        9
    7  1̶0̶ 10
 $8̶ . 0̶ 0̶
 − 3 . 7 5
 $4 . 2 5
```

Kira has $4.25 left.

PRACTICE

Subtract.

1. $5.63 −1.22	2. $4.87 −3.29	3. $7.53 −0.64	4. $2.48 −1.88	5. $8.16 −5.42	6. $3.98 −3.49
7. $5.75 −2.97	8. $8.06 −4.37	9. $4.96 −3.66	10. $7.00 −0.56	11. $6.92 −4.35	12. $11.56 − 9.47

13. $9.52 − $8.29   14. $2.16 − $0.44   15. $6.43 − $1.02   16. $5.43 − $2

MIXED PRACTICE
Maintaining and Reviewing Skills

Add or subtract.

17. $3.46 −2.97	18. $4.29 −1.98	19. $3.56 +2.47	20. $16.50 − 0.75	21. $13.46 +29.50	22. $47.35 +34.68

23. $8.69 − $6.77   24. $17 + $21.89   25. $14 − $6.85   26. $11.50 + $14

FOCUS | Use NUMBER skills to subtract money.

APPLICATION

Using Measurement

This bar graph shows how many centimeters (cm) of rainfall different cities got during March.

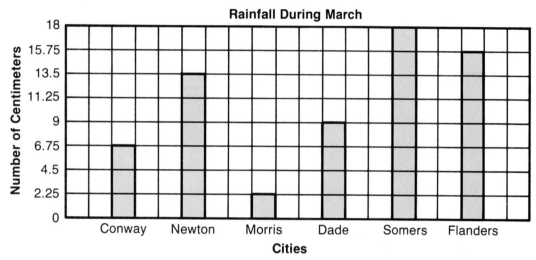

Rainfall During March

Use this bar graph to answer these questions.

27. How many centimeters of rain did Newton and Dade get altogether?

28. How many more centimeters of rain did Flanders get than Morris?

29. Somers usually gets 23.43 cm of rain during March. How much less rain did they get this March?

30. How much rain did Conway, Dade, and Newton get altogether?

31. How much more rain did Dade get than Morris?

Exploring With a Calculator

32. Pretend that you have $20. Use your calculator and use *subtraction only* to find out how much money you would have left if you bought all of the following things.

> a box of crayons for $2.59
> a package of colored paper for $1.20
> a pair of scissors for $3.75

Use NUMBER skills and MEASUREMENT to subtract decimals.
Use a CALCULATOR to subtract decimals.

LOOKING BACK
Reviewing and Testing Chapter 19

In Chapter 19 you formulated problems about a circus. Look at pages 248 and 249.

1. Write a sentence telling about the problems you might encounter if you owned a circus.

You learned about adding decimals and amounts of money. To review what you learned, study the sample exercises on pages 250 and 252. Then use these skills to find each sum for exercises 2–10.

2. 5.37
    +2.41

3. 3.85
    +1.29

4. 6.13
    +1.9

5. $4.62
    +4.38

6. $2.98
    +0.17

7. 3.09 + 2.56

8. 7 + 1.53

9. $5.15 + $2.35

10. $16.08 + $0.93

You learned how to find and continue a pattern to help you evaluate information as part of the Five-Step PROBLEM–SOLVING Plan. To review, look at pages 254 and 255. For exercises 11–14, write the rule. Then copy and complete the pattern.

11. 4, 30, 56, 82, ■, ■

12. 7, 21, 63, ■, ■, 1,701

13. 425, 400, ■, ■, 325, ■

14. 816, 408, ■, ■, 51

You learned about subtracting decimals and amounts of money. To review, look at pages 256 and 258. Find each difference for exercises 15–23.

15. 6.58
    −3.41

16. 3.02
    −1.56

17. 8.3
    −5.17

18. $9.25
    −4.72

19. $5.30
    −0.89

20. 4.13 − 1.82

21. 7 − 1.87

22. $6.09 − $3.99

23. $8 − $6.89

FOCUS | Review and test skills learned and practiced.

LOOKING AHEAD
Preparing for New Skills for Chapter 20

In the next chapter, you will focus on

- formulating problems about a tornado.
- multiplying amounts of money by 1-digit numbers.
- using statistics and probability.
- multiplying 4-digit numbers by 1-digit numbers.
- using measurement.
- how math is used in science.

New multiplication skills will be easier to learn if you brush up on multiplication skills you already know. Review the basic multiplication facts shown on page 454 of the Data Bank. Then, study Models A and B and complete exercises 1–12.

Model A

Multiply the ones.

```
  H T O
  3 2 4
×     2
──────
      8
```

Multiply the tens.

```
  H T O
  3 2 4
×     2
──────
    4 8
```

Multiply the hundreds.

```
  H T O
  3 2 4
×     2
──────
  6 4 8
```

Model B

Multiply the ones. Regroup.

```
    1
  H T O
  2 6 5          5
×     3        × 3
──────        ────
      5         15
```

Multiply the tens. Regroup.

```
  1 1
  H T O          6T
  2 6 5         × 3
×     3        ────
──────          18T
    9 5        + 1T
              ────
                19T
```

Multiply the hundreds.

```
  1 1
  H T O          2H
  2 6 5         × 3
×     3        ────
──────           6H
  7 9 5        + 1H
              ────
                7H
```

PRACTICE

Multiply.

1. $\begin{array}{r} 423 \\ \times\ \ 2 \\ \hline \end{array}$
2. $\begin{array}{r} 312 \\ \times\ \ 3 \\ \hline \end{array}$
3. $\begin{array}{r} 543 \\ \times\ \ 2 \\ \hline \end{array}$
4. $\begin{array}{r} 210 \\ \times\ \ 6 \\ \hline \end{array}$
5. $\begin{array}{r} 643 \\ \times\ \ 2 \\ \hline \end{array}$
6. $\begin{array}{r} 432 \\ \times\ \ 3 \\ \hline \end{array}$

7. $\begin{array}{r} 423 \\ \times\ \ 4 \\ \hline \end{array}$
8. $\begin{array}{r} 253 \\ \times\ \ 5 \\ \hline \end{array}$
9. $\begin{array}{r} 342 \\ \times\ \ 9 \\ \hline \end{array}$
10. $\begin{array}{r} 256 \\ \times\ \ 8 \\ \hline \end{array}$
11. $\begin{array}{r} 475 \\ \times\ \ 7 \\ \hline \end{array}$
12. $\begin{array}{r} 675 \\ \times\ \ 2 \\ \hline \end{array}$

Review NUMBER skills in preparation for learning a new skill.

FOCUS   Formulate problems using picture cues, text, and data.

20

Multiplication by a 1-Digit Number

DATA

Weather pattern
  Tornado

Occur most often
  Location
    United States' Midwest
      and states that border
      the Gulf of Mexico
  Time of year
    Spring or early summer
  Type of weather
    Hot, humid days

Speed
  About 20 miles per hour

Distance traveled
  About 20 miles

Width of path
  About 500 yards

A tornado is a powerful twisting windstorm that can cause destruction in its path. This is how a tornado develops. A thundercloud becomes very dark. A twisting funnel forms at the bottom of the cloud. Heavy rain, hail, and lightning start. A hissing noise can be heard as the funnel hits the ground. The hissing becomes a loud roar when it begins to move along the ground. The high winds blow down everything in the tornado's path.

Using the data and the text given, tell what you would see and what you would do if the National Weather Service issued a tornado warning on your radio. Pick a place where you might be living. Describe the weather before the tornado. Pretend that your neighborhood is 10 miles away from the tornado at the time of the warning.

Multiplying With Money

Marta, Rico, and Becca went to a concert at the Hollywood Bowl. Each ticket cost $9.32. How much did they pay for the 3 tickets?

To find how much they paid for the 3 tickets, multiply: 3 × $9.32.

Multiplying with money is like multiplying whole numbers.

Multiply the ones.

Th	H	T	O
	9	3	2
×			3
			6

Multiply the tens.

Th	H	T	O
	9	3	2
×			3
		9	6

Multiply the hundreds.

Th	H	T	O
	9	3	2
×			3
2	7	9	6

Write the product as dollars and cents. The 3 tickets cost $27.96.

Sally and David bought discount tickets for the same concert. Each ticket cost $8.45. How much did they pay for the 2 tickets?

Multiply the ones.
Regroup.

Th	H	T	O
		1	
	8	4	5
×			2
			0

Multiply the tens.

Th	H	T	O
		1	
	8	4	5
×			2
		9	0

Multiply the hundreds.

Th	H	T	O
		1	
	8	4	5
×			2
1	6	9	0

The 2 tickets cost $16.90.

GUIDED PRACTICE

Multiply. Remember to write the dollar sign and cent point in your answers.

1. $2.21
    × 4
    ———
    $8.84

2. ²⁴
    $6.47
    × 6
    ———
    $38.82

3. $9.83
    × 5
    ———

4. $8.86
    × 4
    ———

5. $6.32
    × 9
    ———

FOCUS | Use NUMBER skills to multiply 3-digit money amounts by 1-digit numbers with and without regrouping.

PRACTICE

Multiply. Write the product as dollars and cents.

6. $0.05
   × 7

7. $0.02
   × 8

8. $0.28
   × 4

9. $0.16
   × 6

10. $0.91
    × 6

11. $1.43
    × 5

12. $3.55
    × 6

13. $7.99
    × 7

14. $7.66
    × 4

15. $4.00
    × 6

16. $0.14
    × 4

17. $0.65
    × 3

18. $0.66
    × 9

19. $1.26
    × 6

20. $3.35
    × 4

21. $2.24
    × 9

22. $3.56
    × 4

23. $4.26
    × 8

24. $6.65
    × 7

25. $5.32
    × 9

26. 4 × $4.44

27. 2 × $5.44

28. 3 × $6.12

29. 4 × $7.05

30. Jerry sold 4 tickets to his class play. Each ticket cost $4.25. How much money did Jerry receive for the 4 tickets?

31. Marge and her friends bought 7 concert programs. Each program cost $1.59. How much did they pay for the 7 programs altogether?

MIXED PRACTICE

Add, subtract, or multiply.

32. $3.46
    × 5

33. $7.06
    × 3

34. $9.21
    − 6.43

35. $4.64
    + 3.89

36. $0.64
    × 7

37. 6 × $5.81

38. $8.46 − $0.78

39. $6.31 + $7.29

40. $7.04 − $3.96

CHALLENGE

Find the missing numbers.

41. $8.■4
    × 6
    ─────
    $50.■4

42. $■.43
    × 8
    ─────
    $7■.44

43. $7.■2
    × 4
    ─────
    $28.■8

44. $■.05
    × 3
    ─────
    $18.1■

MULTIPLICATION

Estimating Products

Gina is paid $8.45 a month for delivering newspapers. About how much money does she earn in 6 months?

To find out **about** how much money Gina earns, **estimate** the product.

Write.   Estimate.

$8.45   Round to the → $8.00
× 6   nearest dollar.   ×   6
                          $48.00

Gina earns about $48.00 in 6 months.

PRACTICE

Estimate by rounding to the nearest dollar.

1. $1.48	2. $3.64	3. $4.99	4. $6.50	5. $4.19
× 7	× 9	× 5	× 8	× 8

6. $3.27	7. $7.44	8. $5.10	9. $2.54	10. $4.12
× 5	× 2	× 8	× 4	× 6

11. 4 × $2.08 12. 6 × $3.21 13. 5 × $5.27 14. 7 × $4.23

15. 9 × $6.44 16. 8 × $2.95 17. 3 × $6.99 18. 8 × $2.28

19. John is going to receive $2.52 an hour for cleaning Mr. Brown's garage. If he works for 6 hours, about how much money will he make?

20. Lynn works 8 hours a week in her grandfather's store. She is paid $4.36 an hour. About how much does she make a week?

MIXED PRACTICE

Estimate by rounding to the nearest dollar.

21. 6 × $3.06   22. $4.75 + $3.21   23. $8.29 − $4.96   24. $7.34 + $7.86

FOCUS | Use NUMBER skills to estimate products.

266

APPLICATION

Using Measurement

Mark wanted to buy 3 shirts. They cost $9.95 each. The shirts are going on sale for $7.95 each. How much will Mark save by buying the shirts on sale?

To find out how much the shirts cost at the regular price, multiply: 3 × $9.95.

$$\begin{array}{r} \$9.95 \\ \times\quad 3 \\ \hline \$29.85 \end{array}$$

To find out how much the shirts cost on sale, multiply: 3 × $7.95.

$$\begin{array}{r} \$7.95 \\ \times\quad 3 \\ \hline \$23.85 \end{array}$$

To see how much is saved, subtract the sale price from the regular price.

$$\begin{array}{r} \$29.85 \\ -\$23.85 \\ \hline \$\ 6.00 \end{array}$$

Find the total savings for these items.

	Number of Items	Regular Price For One	Sale Price For One	Total Savings
25.	4 blouses	$8.78	$5.95	■
26.	3 belts	$4.85	$2.98	■
27.	5 shirts	$9.35	$7.78	■

Exploring With a Calculator

This multiplication exercise can be written two ways.

$$(3 \times 124) + (3 \times 573) \quad \text{or} \quad 3 \times (124 + 573)$$

It is usually easier and faster to solve the exercise when it is written the second way.

First add the numbers in parentheses. $124 + 573 = 697$
Then multiply the sum by the factor. $3 \times 697 = 2{,}091$

Try both ways on a calculator. See which way is easier for you. Then use the calculator to solve the following.

28. $(2 \times 425) + (2 \times 213)$ **29.** $(5 \times 345) + (5 \times 254)$ **30.** $(3 \times 243) + (3 \times 354)$

Use NUMBER skills and MEASUREMENT to solve problems involving money.
Use a CALCULATOR to explore computations.

Multiplying 4-Digit Numbers by 1-Digit Numbers

Ms. Lopez travels to Chicago 3 times a year. Each round trip is 1,231 miles. How many miles does Ms. Lopez travel in all?

To find how many miles in all, multiply: 3 × 1,231.

Multiply the ones.	Multiply the tens.	Multiply the hundreds.	Multiply the thousands.

Th	H	T	O
1	2	3	1
×			3
			3

Th	H	T	O
1	2	3	1
×			3
		9	3

Th	H	T	O
1	2	3	1
×			3
	6	9	3

Th	H	T	O
1	2	3	1
×			3
3	6	9	3

Ms. Lopez travels 3,693 miles in all.

Last year Ms. Lopez made 4 trips to San Francisco. Each round trip was 2,343 miles. How many miles did Ms. Lopez travel in all?

Multiply the ones. Regroup.	Multiply the tens. Regroup.	Multiply the hundreds. Regroup.	Multiply the thousands.

Th	H	T	O
			1
2	3	4	3
×			4
			2

Th	H	T	O
		1	1
2	3	4	3
×			4
		7	2

Th	H	T	O
	1	1	1
2	3	4	3
×			4
	3	7	2

Th	H	T	O
	1	1	1
2	3	4	3
×			4
9	3	7	2

Ms. Lopez traveled 9,372 miles in all.

GUIDED PRACTICE

Multiply.

1. 2,341
    ×   2
    —————
    4,682

2. 3 32
    3,675
    ×   5
    —————
    18,375

3. 2,132
    ×   3

4. 4,325
    ×   4

5. 6,325
    ×   7

6. 4,374
    ×   5

7. 2,978
    ×   2

8. 5,473
    ×   8

9. 7,813
    ×   6

10. 3,462
    ×   9

FOCUS | Use NUMBER skills to multiply 4-digit numbers by 1-digit numbers with and without regrouping.

PRACTICE

Multiply.

11.	1,324 × 2	12.	3,156 × 3	13.	5,673 × 6	14.	4,206 × 5	15.	2,851 × 7
16.	3,765 × 2	17.	6,487 × 5	18.	3,509 × 3	19.	4,521 × 4	20.	7,243 × 2
21.	4,763 × 7	22.	2,978 × 4	23.	3,754 × 8	24.	6,452 × 3	25.	1,423 × 9
26.	2,435 × 6	27.	1,645 × 9	28.	7,324 × 3	29.	3,287 × 7	30.	8,345 × 2

31. Ms. Russo is a pilot. She has flown from coast to coast 2 times. Each trip was 6,684 miles round trip. How many miles did Ms. Russo fly in all?

32. Louis likes to ride trains. He has traveled 1,256 miles by train for each of the last 5 years. How many miles has Louis traveled in all?

MIXED PRACTICE
Maintaining and Reviewing Skills

Add, subtract, multiply, or divide.

33.	4,325 × 3	34.	7,041 × 6	35.	49,361 + 24,868	36.	75,091 − 64,896	37.	3.45 + 7.68

38. 764 ÷ 5   39. 8 × 672   40. 64,801 − 2,943   41. 8,642 + 19,006

42. 7 × 309   43. 656 ÷ 8   44. 4.96 − 3.89   45. 7.4 + 6.29

CHALLENGE

46. Mr. Jacobson sailed 1,236 miles during each of the first 3 years he had his boat. He sailed 1,572 miles during each of the next 3 years. How many miles did Mr. Jacobson sail in all?

EXTRA PRACTICE—page 450

MULTIPLICATION
Estimating Products

Mr. Gregory owns a dairy farm. He sells 1,265 dozen eggs a week. To the nearest hundred, about how many dozen eggs does Mr. Gregory sell in 5 weeks?

To find about how many in all, estimate the product.

$$\begin{array}{r} 1{,}265 \\ \times \quad 5 \\ \hline \end{array}$$
Rounded to the nearest hundred $\longrightarrow$

Estimate.
$$\begin{array}{r} 1{,}300 \\ \times \quad 5 \\ \hline 6{,}500 \end{array}$$

Mr. Gregory sells about 6,500 dozen eggs in 5 weeks.

PRACTICE

Round to the nearest hundred and then estimate the product.

1. $\begin{array}{r} 4{,}175 \\ \times \quad 2 \\ \hline \end{array}$
2. $\begin{array}{r} 3{,}768 \\ \times \quad 5 \\ \hline \end{array}$
3. $\begin{array}{r} 7{,}224 \\ \times \quad 7 \\ \hline \end{array}$
4. $\begin{array}{r} 9{,}214 \\ \times \quad 3 \\ \hline \end{array}$
5. $\begin{array}{r} 4{,}756 \\ \times \quad 6 \\ \hline \end{array}$

6. $\begin{array}{r} 2{,}758 \\ \times \quad 9 \\ \hline \end{array}$
7. $\begin{array}{r} 3{,}218 \\ \times \quad 7 \\ \hline \end{array}$
8. $\begin{array}{r} 9{,}245 \\ \times \quad 2 \\ \hline \end{array}$
9. $\begin{array}{r} 4{,}287 \\ \times \quad 3 \\ \hline \end{array}$
10. $\begin{array}{r} 6{,}234 \\ \times \quad 5 \\ \hline \end{array}$

11. Mr. Gregory sells 2,345 gallons of milk a week. Round to the nearest hundred and then estimate how many gallons of milk he sells in 4 weeks.

12. Mr. Gregory's brother makes and sells cheese. He sells 1,978 pounds of cheese a month. Round to the nearest hundred and then estimate how many pounds of cheese he sells in 3 months.

MIXED PRACTICE
Maintaining and Reviewing Skills

Add, subtract, or multiply.

13. $\begin{array}{r} 3{,}516 \\ \times \quad 4 \\ \hline \end{array}$
14. $\begin{array}{r} 7{,}673 \\ \times \quad 3 \\ \hline \end{array}$
15. $\begin{array}{r} 49{,}617 \\ -28{,}964 \\ \hline \end{array}$
16. $\begin{array}{r} 38{,}464 \\ +29{,}968 \\ \hline \end{array}$
17. $\begin{array}{r} 75{,}018 \\ -\ 9{,}864 \\ \hline \end{array}$

FOCUS | Use NUMBER skills to estimate products.

APPLICATION

Using Measurement

There are 1,760 yards in a mile. How many feet are in a mile?

Think: 1 yard = 3 feet
      1 mile = 3 × 1,760 feet

$$\begin{array}{r} 1{,}760 \\ \times \quad\quad 3 \\ \hline 5{,}280 \end{array}$$

There are 5,280 feet in a mile.

Use multiplication to complete the following table.

	Miles	Yards	Feet
18.	2	3,520	■
19.	3	5,280	■
20.	4	■	21,120
21.	5	■	■

Exploring With a Calculator

Try this with a calculator.

Multiply: 2 × 9   2 × 99   2 × 999   2 × 9,999
Products: 18   198   1,998   19,998

What pattern do you see? What do you think 2 × 99,999 will be? Try it on your calculator and see if you are right.

Use your calculator to find the first 4 products in each row. Look for the pattern and guess the last product. Use your calculator to see if you were right.

22. 3 × 9   3 × 99   3 × 999   3 × 9,999   3 × 99,999

23. 4 × 4   4 × 44   4 × 444   4 × 4,444   4 × 44,444

24. 5 × 8   5 × 88   5 × 888   5 × 8,888   5 × 88,888

25. 7 × 6   7 × 66   7 × 666   7 × 6,666   7 × 66,666

26. 8 × 3   8 × 33   8 × 333   8 × 3,333   8 × 33,333

27. 9 × 9   9 × 99   9 × 999   9 × 9,999   9 × 99,999

Use MEASUREMENT and a CALCULATOR to multiply 4-digit numbers by 1-digit numbers.

Orbit

The Earth, though it seems to stand still, is actually traveling through outer space. It follows a path around the sun called a solar orbit. It moves at the rate of 66,600 miles an hour. The length of time it takes for the Earth to make one complete orbit around the sun is one year.

Each of the nine planets of our solar system has its own orbit. And each planet takes a different amount of time to circle the sun. This means that the length of a year is different for each planet.

Planets that are closest to the sun have the shortest years. This is because the closer a planet is to the sun, the shorter its orbit.

Mercury, the planet nearest the sun, orbits the sun in only 88 Earth days. Pluto, the planet farthest from the sun, takes about 248 Earth *years* to make a complete trip around the sun.

The chart shows how far from the sun each planet is. It also shows how long it takes each planet to orbit the sun in Earth days or years.

CRITICAL THINKING

1. The Earth travels 66,600 miles each hour. How many miles does it travel in one day? Use a calculator.
   a. 2,775 miles
   b. 1,598,400 miles
   c. 159,840 miles

2. Is the length of a year the same on every planet? Why?

3. One astronaut goes to Mercury and another goes to Mars for 5 Earth years. Which astronaut makes more complete trips around the sun in that time?

4. If you could live on Jupiter for 24 Earth years, how many birthdays would you have celebrated in Jupiter years? If you could live on Pluto for 248 Earth years, how many birthdays would you have celebrated in Pluto years?

Name of Planet	Distance From the Sun (in Millions of Miles)	Length of Orbit
Mercury	36	88 days
Venus	67	225 days
Earth	93	365 days
Mars	142	687 days
Jupiter	483	12 years
Saturn	886	29 years
Uranus	1,782	84 years
Neptune	2,792	165 years
Pluto	3,664	248 years

FOCUS | Use NUMBER skills and LOGIC to relate orbits to the lengths of years.

Jupiter

Mercury

Earth

Saturn

In Chapter 20 you formulated problems about tornados. Look at pages 262 and 263.

1. Write a sentence telling what you would see and hear if you sighted a tornado.

You learned about multiplying amounts of money by 1-digit numbers. You also learned more about estimating. To review what you learned, study the sample exercises on page 264 and 266. Then use these skills to estimate each product for exercises 2–10. Then find each exact product.

2. $2.31 × 3	3. $5.34 × 2	4. $1.14 × 4	5. $6.39 × 2	6. $8.90 × 5

7. 6 × $3.33   8. 3 × $5.62   9. 8 × $4.50   10. 9 × $7.25

You learned about multiplying 4-digit numbers by 1-digit numbers. You also learned something new about estimating. To review, look at pages 268 and 270. Estimate each product to the nearest hundred for exercises 11–20. Then find each exact product.

11. 4,123 × 2	12. 2,312 × 3	13. 4,516 × 4	14. 1,123 × 5	15. 3,670 × 4
16. 5,287 × 2	17. 7,915 × 6	18. 8,492 × 8	19. 1,837 × 6	20. 7,281 × 8

You learned about the orbit of the planets in our solar system. To review, look at pages 272 and 273. Then answer the questions below.

21. Which planet has the shortest orbit?

22. Which planets are closer to the sun than the earth?

FOCUS | Review and test skills learned and practiced.

LOOKING AHEAD
Preparing for New Skills for Chapter 21

In the next chapter, you will focus on
- **formulating problems about a flower garden.**
- **dividing amounts of money.**
- **using logic.**
- **dividing 4-digit numbers by 1-digit numbers.**
- **using measurement.**

New division skills will be easier to learn if you brush up on division skills you already know. First, review the basic division facts shown on page 454 of the Data Bank. Then, study Model A and complete exercises 1–18.

Model A

Estimate the hundreds digit.

$3\overline{)734}$

$3\overline{)7}$ is about 2. Use 2 as the hundreds digit.

Multiply and subtract.

	H	T	O
2			
3)	7	3	4
−6			
1			

Estimate the tens digit. Multiply and subtract.

	H	T	O
2	4		
3)	7	3	4
−6	↓		
1	3		
−1	2		
	1		

Estimate the ones digit. Multiply and subtract.

	H	T	O	
2	4	4		R2
3)	7	3	4	
−6				
1	3			
−1	2			
	1	4		
	−1	2		
		2		

PRACTICE

Divide.

1. $3\overline{)654}$ 2. $4\overline{)624}$ 3. $2\overline{)673}$ 4. $6\overline{)781}$ 5. $8\overline{)942}$ 6. $5\overline{)734}$

7. $4\overline{)354}$ 8. $2\overline{)187}$ 9. $5\overline{)475}$ 10. $8\overline{)766}$ 11. $3\overline{)276}$ 12. $6\overline{)346}$

13. $4\overline{)634}$ 14. $5\overline{)327}$ 15. $2\overline{)716}$ 16. $8\overline{)792}$ 17. $6\overline{)489}$ 18. $3\overline{)227}$

Review NUMBER skills in preparation for learning a new skill.

FOCUS Formulate problems using picture cues, text, and data.

CHAPTER **21**

Division

DATA

Gardener	Mrs. Williams
Light in garden	Full sun

Type of flower

China aster
Blooms   Summer
Sunlight   Full sun

Primrose
Blooms   Winter, spring
Sunlight   Shade

Balsam
Blooms   Summer
Sunlight   Filtered sun

Cornflower
Blooms   Spring
Sunlight   Full sun

Cosmos
Blooms   Summer
Sunlight   Full sun

To see a variety of colorful flowers, go to a public garden. Walk through an open field to see wildflowers in bloom. You can also enjoy flowers by growing them from seed. Planting a small flower garden will bring bursts of color to your home. It will also make working outdoors rewarding fun.

Mrs. Williams has decided to start her own flower garden. She has a small patch of ground near her house where she will plant the garden. But before she buys flower seeds, she must do some thinking. She would like the flowers to bloom at the same time. She also knows that her garden will get full sun during the day, not part sun or shade.

Using the picture and the data, think about what Mrs. Williams needs to do to plant her garden. What problems will she face? What decisions must she make? Predict how Mrs. Williams will plan her garden. Give your reasons.

Dividing Money

A store is having a sale on school supplies. The price for 2 lunch boxes is $7.98. Each lunch box costs the same. How much is one lunch box?

Divide amounts of money the same way as you divide whole numbers. To divide $7.98 by 2, write $2\overline{)798}$.

Estimate the hundreds digit.

$2\overline{)798}$

$2\overline{)7}$ is about 3. Use 3 as the hundreds digit.

Multiply and subtract.

H	T	O
3		

$2\overline{)7\,9\,8}$
-6
$\ \ 1$

Estimate the tens digit. Multiply and subtract.

H	T	O
3	9	

$2\overline{)7\,9\,8}$
$-6\downarrow$
$\ \ 1\,9$
$-1\,8$
$\ \ \ \ 1$

Estimate the ones digit. Multiply and subtract.

H	T	O
3	9	9

$2\overline{)7\,9\,8}$
-6
$\ \ 1\,9\downarrow$
$-1\,8\downarrow$
$\ \ \ \ 1\,8$
$\ -1\,8$
$\ \ \ \ \ \ 0$

Write the dollar sign and cent point in the quotient.

$$\frac{399}{2\overline{)798}} \rightarrow \frac{\$3.99}{2\overline{)\$7.98}}$$

The price of one lunch box is $3.99.

To divide $2.36 by 4, write $4\overline{)236}$.

Estimate the hundreds digit.

$4\overline{)236}$

Since 4 is greater than 2, there is no hundreds digit.

Estimate the tens digit.

$4\overline{)236}$

$4\overline{)23}$ is about 5. Use 5 as the tens digit.

Multiply and subtract.

H	T	O
	5	

$4\overline{)2\,3\,6}$
$-2\,0$
$\ \ \ \ 3$

Estimate the ones digit. Multiply and subtract.

H	T	O
	5	9

$4\overline{)2\,3\,6}$
$-2\,0\downarrow$
$\ \ \ \ 3\,6$
$\ -3\,6$
$\ \ \ \ \ \ 0$

Write the dollar sign and cent point in the quotient.

$$59 \rightarrow \$0.59$$

FOCUS | Use NUMBER skills to divide amounts of money.

GUIDED PRACTICE

Divide.

$$
\begin{array}{r} \$1.52 \\ 3\overline{)\$4.56} \\ -3 \\ \hline 1\,5 \\ -1\,5 \\ \hline 06 \\ -6 \\ \hline 0 \end{array}
\qquad
\begin{array}{r} \$0.67 \\ 4\overline{)\$2.68} \\ -2\,4 \\ \hline 2\blacksquare \\ -\blacksquare\blacksquare \\ \hline 0 \end{array}
$$

1. 3)$4.56   2. 4)$2.68   3. 5)$6.95   4. 8)$3.60   5. 6)$8.04

$$
\begin{array}{r} \$1.\blacksquare9 \\ 5\overline{)\$6.95} \\ -5 \\ \hline 1\,9 \\ -1\,5 \\ \hline 45 \\ -\blacksquare\blacksquare \\ \hline 0 \end{array}
\qquad
\begin{array}{r} \$0.\blacksquare5 \\ 8\overline{)\$3.60} \\ -3\,2 \\ \hline \blacksquare\blacksquare \\ -\blacksquare\blacksquare \\ \hline 0 \end{array}
\qquad
\begin{array}{r} \$\blacksquare.\blacksquare\blacksquare \\ 6\overline{)\$8.04} \\ -\blacksquare \\ \hline 2\blacksquare \\ -\blacksquare\blacksquare \\ \hline 2\blacksquare \\ -\blacksquare\blacksquare \\ \hline 0 \end{array}
$$

PRACTICE

Divide.

6. 4)$6.84   7. 7)$4.90   8. 3)$1.26   9. 6)$8.58   10. 5)$3.95

11. 2)$5.50   12. 8)$3.60   13. 7)$8.61   14. 4)$3.96   15. 3)$5.34

16. 6)$2.64   17. 4)$6.12   18. 2)$1.24   19. 7)$6.51   20. 5)$7.95

21. $9.84 ÷ 6   22. $4.44 ÷ 2   23. $6.86 ÷ 7

MIXED PRACTICE
Maintaining and Reviewing Skills

Multiply or divide.

24. $7.62 ÷ 6   25. 5 × $3.29   26. 584 ÷ 4

27. 7 × $1.58   28. 929 ÷ 3   29. 6 × 4,132

CHALLENGE

30. Which offer is the better buy?

DIVISION

Dividing Money

Remember to divide amounts of money the same way you divide whole numbers. Write the dollar sign and cent point in the quotient.

Look at these examples.

```
      $0.86              $2.37
 5) $4.30           4) $9.48
   -4 0               -8
     30                1 4
    -30               -1 2
      0                 28
                       -28
                         0
```

PRACTICE

Divide.

1. 2) $4.36   2. 4) $3.12   3. 3) $5.19   4. 5) $1.95   5. 8) $8.16

6. 7) $5.25   7. 3) $7.02   8. 6) $3.00   9. 2) $9.50   10. 9) $7.47

11. 4) $4.16   12. 8) $6.96   13. 5) $7.25   14. 7) $4.83   15. 6) $9.24

16. $3.45 ÷ 5   17. $4.77 ÷ 3   18. $4.06 ÷ 2   19. $3.66 ÷ 6   20. $9.84 ÷ 8

MIXED PRACTICE

Maintaining and Reviewing Skills

Add, subtract, multiply, or divide.

21. 4) $7.68   22. 7) $4.34   23. 8 × $2.43   24. $4.85 + $4.36

25. 3 × 2,807   26. 4,948 − 2,689   27. 3) 842   28. 7,860 + 4,949

29. 639 ÷ 5   30. 5 × 649   31. 864 + 396   32. 45,106 − 3,968

33. 7 × 506   34. 9) 461   35. 34,309 + 28,964   36. 4 × 3,064

FOCUS   Use NUMBER skills to divide amounts of money.

APPLICATION

Using Logic

Use logic and number skills to think about this statement.

If 3 pages for a photo album cost $3.00, then 1 page costs $1.00.

Think: $3.00 ÷ 3 = $1.00

37. Copy and complete the table.

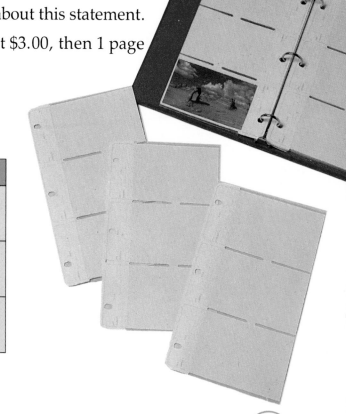

If	Then
8 album pages cost $6.96	1 album page costs _____.
4 rolls of film cost $9.40	1 roll costs _____.
5 prints cost $4.75	1 print costs _____.

Problem Solving: Finding a Pattern

For each exercise use division to find the price of 1 item. Write a pattern that shows the following from left to right:

Price for 4, Price for 3, Price for 2, Price for 1. Then write the subtraction rule that describes the pattern from left to right.

Example: 4 for $2.00
Pattern: $2.00, $1.50, $1.00, $0.50
Rule: Subtract $0.50.

38. 4 for $9.60   **39.** 4 for $6.00   **40.** 4 for $6.60

41. 4 for $.96   **42.** 4 for $3.40   **43.** 4 for $2.16

Use LOGIC to complete statements.
Find a pattern and apply the Five-Step PROBLEM SOLVING Plan.

Dividing 4-Digit Numbers by 1-Digit Numbers

In one day an airline carried 1,242 people to the New York area on 9 flights. If each flight carried the same number of people, how many were on each flight?

Divide 1,242 by 9.

Estimate the hundreds digit.

$9\overline{)1,242}$

$9\overline{)12}$ is about 1.

Multiply and subtract.

Th	H	T	O
	1		
9)1	2	4	2
−	9		
	3		

Estimate the tens digit. Multiply and subtract.

Th	H	T	O
	1	3	
9)1	2	4	2
−	9	↓	
	3	4	
−	2	7	
		7	

Estimate the ones digit. Multiply and subtract.

Th	H	T	O
	1	3	8
9)1	2	4	2
−	9		
	3	4	
−	2	7	↓
		7	2
−		7	2
			0

There were 138 people on each flight.

Divide 7,826 by 3.

Estimate the thousands digit. Multiply and subtract.

Th	H	T	O
2			
3)7	8	2	6
−6			
1			

Estimate the hundreds digit. Multiply and subtract.

Th	H	T	O
2	6		
3)7	8	2	6
−6	↓		
1	8		
−1	8		
	0		

Estimate the tens digit. Multiply and subtract.

Th	H	T	O
2	6	0	
3)7	8	2	6
−6			
1	8		
−1	8	↓	
	0	2	
−		0	
		2	

Estimate the ones digit. Multiply and subtract.

Th	H	T	O	
2	6	0	8	R2
3)7	8	2	6	
−6				
1	8			
−1	8			
	0	2		
−		0	↓	
		2	6	
−		2	4	
			2	

FOCUS | Use NUMBER skills to divide 4-digit numbers by 1-digit numbers.

GUIDED PRACTICE

Divide.

$$\begin{array}{r} 2{,}834 \\ 1.\ 3\overline{)8{,}502} \\ -6 \\ \hline 25 \\ -24 \\ \hline 10 \\ -9 \\ \hline 12 \\ -12 \\ \hline 0 \end{array}$$

$$\begin{array}{r} 219\ \text{R6} \\ 2.\ 7\overline{)1{,}539} \\ -14 \\ \hline 1▮ \\ -7 \\ \hline 6▮ \\ -63 \\ \hline ▮ \end{array}$$

$$\begin{array}{r} 1{,}▮47\ \text{R1} \\ 3.\ 4\overline{)5{,}389} \\ -4 \\ \hline ▮3 \\ -12 \\ \hline ▮▮ \\ -16 \\ \hline 29 \\ -28 \\ \hline ▮ \end{array}$$

$$\begin{array}{r} 7▮6 \\ 4.\ 8\overline{)5{,}648} \\ -▮▮ \\ \hline 04 \\ -0 \\ \hline 48 \\ -▮▮ \\ \hline ▮ \end{array}$$

$$\begin{array}{r} 1{,}▮8▮ \\ 5.\ 5\overline{)6{,}930} \\ -▮ \\ \hline 19 \\ -15 \\ \hline ▮▮ \\ -40 \\ \hline 3▮ \\ -30 \\ \hline ▮ \end{array}$$

PRACTICE

Divide.

6. $5\overline{)5{,}377}$ 7. $3\overline{)2{,}960}$ 8. $2\overline{)8{,}276}$ 9. $6\overline{)2{,}375}$ 10. $4\overline{)3{,}128}$

11. $7\overline{)6{,}065}$ 12. $3\overline{)5{,}150}$ 13. $5\overline{)7{,}515}$ 14. $4\overline{)4{,}574}$ 15. $8\overline{)7{,}960}$

16. $9{,}318 \div 2$ 17. $7{,}269 \div 9$ 18. $5{,}999 \div 7$ 19. $7{,}515 \div 6$

20. There are 1,168 passengers on 8 flights. Find the average number of passengers on each flight.

21. A pilot flies a total of 2,100 miles on 4 flights. Find the average number of miles for each flight.

MIXED PRACTICE
Maintaining and Reviewing Skills

Multiply or divide.

22. $6{,}342 \div 5$ 23. $8{,}106 \div 6$ 24. $4 \times 3{,}948$ 25. $498 \div 7$

26. 5×643 27. $804 \div 9$ 28. $296 \div 2$ 29. 7×964

CHALLENGE

30. A pilot makes 4 round-trip flights between two cities. He travels a total of 1,400 miles. What is the distance between the two cities?

EXTRA PRACTICE—page 450

DIVISION
Dividing 4-Digit Numbers by 1-Digit Numbers

When you are dividing 4-digit numbers by 1-digit numbers, the quotient begins in the thousands or hundreds place. Use estimation to find in which place the quotient begins. Look at the examples.

Th	H	T	O
2	3	0	4

$$4\overline{)9\ 2\ 1\ 6}$$
$$-8$$
$$1\ 2$$
$$-1\ 2$$
$$0\ 1$$
$$0$$
$$1\ 6$$
$$-1\ 6$$
$$0$$

Th	H	T	O	
	1	7	8	R3

$$8\overline{)1\ 4\ 2\ 7}$$
$$-8$$
$$6\ 2$$
$$-5\ 6$$
$$6\ 7$$
$$-6\ 4$$
$$3$$

PRACTICE

Divide.

1. $4\overline{)6,243}$ 2. $3\overline{)2,961}$ 3. $6\overline{)7,482}$ 4. $2\overline{)6,813}$ 5. $5\overline{)4,034}$

6. $3\overline{)9,792}$ 7. $8\overline{)1,695}$ 8. $7\overline{)7,675}$ 9. $5\overline{)4,495}$ 10. $9\overline{)6,360}$

11. $8,756 \div 4$ 12. $7,320 \div 7$ 13. $6,300 \div 6$ 14. $5,254 \div 9$

MIXED PRACTICE
Maintaining and Reviewing Skills

Add, subtract, multiply, or divide.

15. $4,984 \div 6$ 16. $7,941 \div 3$ 17. $6 \times 1,284$ 18. $901 - 648$

19. $5\overline{)396}$ 20. 4×864 21. $72,901 - 36,308$ 22. $649 + 1,749$

23. $3 \times 6,461$ 24. $7\overline{)964}$ 25. $8,204 + 398$ 26. $6,911 - 4,985$

27. $7\overline{)643}$ 28. 9×206 29. $7,900 - 1,864$ 30. $396 + 4,581$

FOCUS Use NUMBER skills to divide 4-digit numbers by 1-digit numbers.

APPLICATION

Using Measurement

1 mm is about the width of a pin.

  10 mm = 1 cm or about the width of your finger
  100 cm = 1 m or about the width of a door
1 000 m = 1 km and is used to measure longer distances

Which metric unit would you choose to measure

31. the length of 8 city blocks?

32. the width of a room?

33. the thickness of paper?

34. the width of a T.V. set?

35. the length of a pencil?

36. the length of a book?

37. the height of a door?

38. the thickness of glass?

39. the length of a shoe?

40. the length of a fingernail?

Copy and complete.

41. 2 cm   = _____ mm

42. 20 mm   = _____ cm

43. 1 000 m = _____ km

44. 2 000 m = _____ km

45. 10 mm   = _____ cm

46. 300 cm = _____ m

47. 100 cm = _____ m

48. 1 cm   = _____ mm

49. 3 km   = _____ m

50. 1 km   = _____ m

Solving Problems

Below are answers to problems. Can you write your own problem to match the answer? Use metric measurements.

51. A. It took John 40 minutes to walk 2 km.   Q.

52. A. Inger traveled 1 325 km altogether.   Q.

53. A. It will take 12 meters of fabric to make Glenda's two bedspreads.   Q.

Use MEASUREMENT to choose appropriate metric units of measurement.
Use LOGIC to write problems for given answers.

285

Reviewing and Testing Chapter 21

In Chapter 21 you formulated problems about a flower garden. Look at pages 276 and 277.

1. Write a sentence telling which type of flowers you would grow if you wanted them to bloom at different times.

You learned about dividing amounts of money by 1-digit numbers. To review what you learned, study the sample exercises on pages 278 and 280. Then use this skill to divide for exercises 2–11.

2. $2\overline{)\$4.68}$ 3. $3\overline{)\$9.36}$ 4. $5\overline{)\$6.55}$ 5. $8\overline{)\$2.72}$ 6. $9\overline{)\$1.98}$

7. $4\overline{)\$9.36}$ 8. $7\overline{)\$3.71}$ 9. $9\overline{)\$6.21}$ 10. $5\overline{)\$9.15}$ 11. $8\overline{)\$3.92}$

You learned about using logic to find the prices of single items. To review, look at page 281. Find each answer for exercises 12 and 13.

12. If 4 cans of paint cost $9.36, then what is the cost of 1 can?

13. If 6 oranges cost $2.70, then what is the cost of 1 orange?

You learned about dividing 4-digit numbers by 1-digit numbers. To review, look at pages 282 and 284. Divide for exercises 14–25.

14. $2\overline{)8,422}$ 15. $3\overline{)9,639}$ 16. $2\overline{)9,318}$ 17. $4\overline{)2,100}$ 18. $8\overline{)7,960}$

19. $7\overline{)5,998}$ 20. $6\overline{)2,375}$ 21. $2\overline{)6,813}$ 22. $8\overline{)1,695}$ 23. $9\overline{)5,254}$

24. In 5 days, 3,170 people attended the fair. Find the average number of people who attended the fair each day.

25. A salesperson traveled 7,216 miles in 8 trips. Find the average number of miles for each trip.

| FOCUS | Review and test skills learned and practiced. |

LOOKING AHEAD

Preparing for New Skills for Chapter 22

> **In the next chapter, you will focus on**
>
> - formulating problems about buying sneakers.
> - reading line graphs.
> - making predictions from line graphs.
> - using algebra.
>
> - reading circle graphs.
> - drawing conclusions from circle graphs.
> - how math is used in consumer education.

New graph reading skills will be easier to learn if you brush up on graph reading skills you already know. First review the example below. Then complete exercises 1–4.

This graph shows the number of animals that are for sale in a pet store.

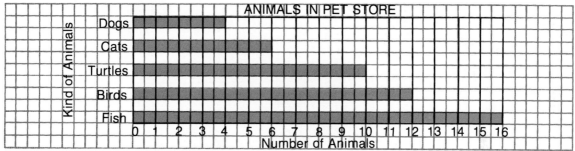

Look at the bar graph. How many birds are there?

Step 1: Find the animal name in the left column.
Step 2: Move your finger to the end of the bar.
Step 3: Follow the line at the end of the bar to the number at the bottom of the graph.

There are 12 birds.

PRACTICE

Use the bar graph to answer these questions.

1. How many cats are there?

2. How many turtles are there?

3. Of which animal are there the most?

4. Of which animal are there the fewest?

Review STATISTICS in preparation for learning a new skill.

FOCUS Formulate problems using picture cues, text, and data.

22

DATA

Event	Sneaker sale
Store	Star Sneakers
Customer	Tracy
Tracy's shoe size	$5\frac{1}{2}$
Spending money	$20
Sale item	Fleet Feet sneakers
Sale price	$13 a pair
Regular price	$18 a pair
Color needed	White
Colors	White Blue
Sizes	4–12 (no half sizes)
Non-sale item	Flying Ace sneakers
Price	$18 a pair
Colors	White Pink
Sizes	4–12 (full and half sizes)

Graphs

Shopping for a new pair of shoes is lots of fun, but it may take time. Sometimes you must go to several stores and try on many pairs of shoes before you find exactly what you want. There are several things you need to know before you make your decision.

As you can see from the picture, Tracy had her eye on a pair of sneakers that are on sale today. The data tells you how much the sneakers cost and what styles are left to buy.

Look at the picture and read the data. Predict whether or not Tracy will buy the sneakers on sale. What problems will she think about? Give reasons for your answer.

Reading Line Graphs

Jason likes to read books. He decided to make a **line graph** to show how many books he read in four months. He made a graph like this.

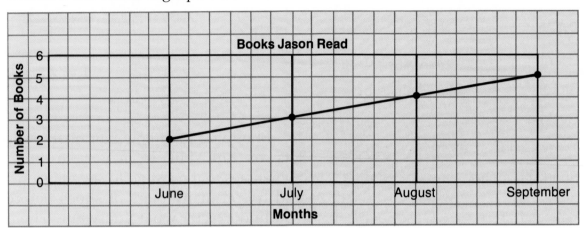

Look at the line graph. How many books did Jason read in June?

Step 1: Find the name of the month along the bottom of the graph.

Step 2: Move your finger up the graph until you come to the dot.

Step 3: Follow the horizontal line the dot is on to the left and read the number of books.

Jason read 2 books in June.

GUIDED PRACTICE

Use the line graph to answer the questions.

1. How many books did Jason read in July?

2. How many books did Jason read in August?

3. In which month did Jason read the most books?

4. In which month did Jason read the fewest books?

5. How many books did Jason read altogether?

6. Did Jason read more books or fewer books as the months went by?

FOCUS Use STATISTICS to read line graphs.

PRACTICE

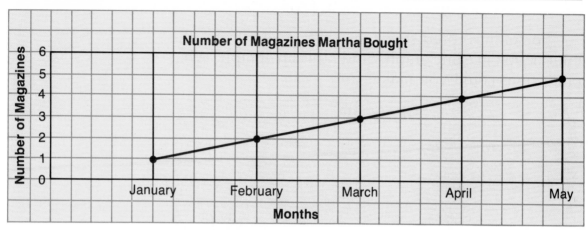

Number of Magazines Martha Bought

Use the line graph to answer the questions.

7. What is the title of the graph?

8. How many months does the line graph show?

9. How many magazines did Martha buy in February?

10. How many magazines did Martha buy in April?

11. In which month did Martha buy the fewest magazines?

12. In which month did Martha buy the most magazines?

13. How many magazines in all did Martha buy in March and April?

14. How many more magazines did Martha buy in May than in March?

15. Did Martha buy more or fewer magazines as the months went by?

16. Do you think Martha will buy more or fewer magazines in June? Why?

MIXED PRACTICE

Maintaining and Reviewing Skills

Multiply or divide.

17. $\$5.76 \div 4$ 18. $6 \times \$1.29$ 19. $9 \times \$3.67$ 20. $\$8.64 \div 9$ 21. $4 \times \$7.08$

CHALLENGE

22. Make a line graph that shows how many things you read in a week. Put the number of things you read along the left side of the graph. Put the days of the week along the bottom of the graph.

EXTRA PRACTICE—page 450

GRAPHS

Making Predictions From Line Graphs

Sometimes predictions can be made from the information in a line graph. Study this line graph. What predictions could you make?

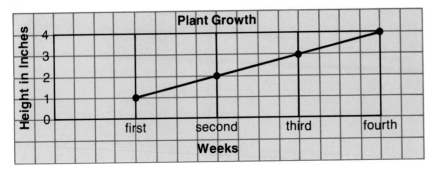

The graph shows that the plants are growing an inch a week. Since they seem to be growing so well, you could make the following prediction.

The plants will probably be healthy.

PRACTICE

This graph shows the number of flowers a plant grew from Monday to Friday.

Write *true* or *false*.

1. The plant is probably healthy.

2. The plant was probably planted correctly.

3. The plant will probably not grow a flower on Saturday.

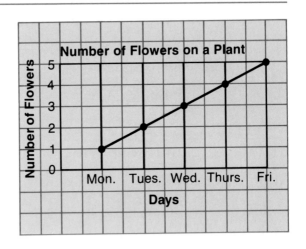

MIXED PRACTICE

Maintaining and Reviewing Skills

Multiply or divide.

4. $603 \div 4$ 5. $339 \div 7$ 6. 8×260 7. 7×100 8. $716 \div 8$

FOCUS   Use STATISTICS AND PROBABILITY to make predictions from line graphs.

APPLICATION

Using Algebra

Look at this graph. The dots on the graph can be located by **ordered pairs** of numbers.

The blue dot is located at the ordered pair (3,4). To locate the blue dot, start at 0. Move 3 spaces to the right. Then go up 4 spaces.

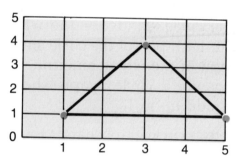

In these ordered pairs, the first number tells how many spaces to the right. The second number tells how many spaces up.

9. What color dot is located at the ordered pair (5,1)?

10. What is the ordered pair for the red dot?

11. What shape do you get when you connect the dots?

Tell what color dot is located at each ordered pair.

12. (2,1)   13. (2,5)

14. (5,5)   15. (5,1)

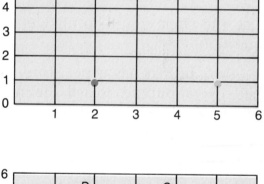

16. What shape do you get when you connect the dots?

Tell the ordered pair for each letter.

17. *A*   18. *B*

19. *C*   20. *D*

21. What shape do you get when you connect the dots?

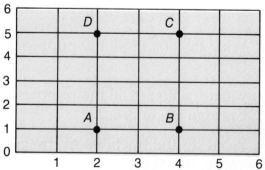

Use ALGEBRA to read ordered pairs on a grid.

Reading Circle Graphs

Betty's pet cat had a litter of kittens. Betty made this **circle graph** to show how the litter of kittens could be divided up by color.

The circle stands for the whole amount. Each part of the circle shows a fraction of the whole amount. The fractions in a circle graph should always add up to 1.

Betty's circle graph stands for the whole litter of kittens. It shows that $\frac{1}{3}$ of the kittens are black, $\frac{1}{3}$ are white, and $\frac{1}{3}$ are black and white.

$$\frac{1}{3} + \frac{1}{3} + \frac{1}{3} = \frac{3}{3} = 1$$

Color of Kittens

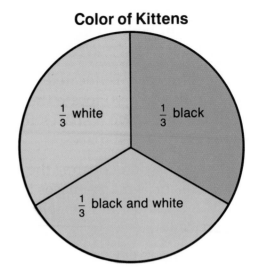

GUIDED PRACTICE

Use the circle graph to answer the questions.

Mr. Brown has a pet store. He has several puppies to sell. He made this circle graph to show how the puppies could be divided up by kind.

1. What fraction of all the puppies are collies? $\frac{2}{4}$ or $\frac{1}{2}$ are collies

2. What fraction of all the puppies are terriers?

3. What fraction of all the puppies are German shepherds?

4. What do the fractions in the circle graph add up to?

Kinds of Puppies

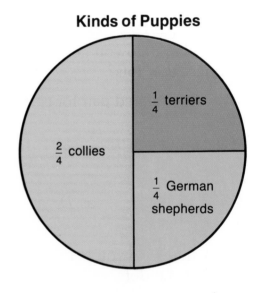

FOCUS | Use STATISTICS to read circle graphs.

PRACTICE

Use the circle graphs to answer the questions.

5. What fraction of all the pets are hamsters?

6. What fraction of all the pets are dogs?

7. What fraction of all the pets are cats?

8. What kind of pet is there the most of?

Pets in Joe's Neighborhood

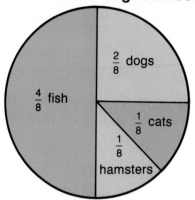

9. What kind of bird is there the most of?

10. What fraction of all the birds are canaries?

11. What fraction of all the birds are finches?

12. What is the total of all the fractions in the circle graph?

Kinds of Birds in Pet Store

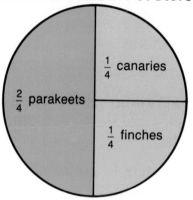

MIXED PRACTICE
Maintaining and Reviewing Skills

Add or subtract.

13.	14.	15.	16.	17.	18.
4.63 + 2.84	7.61 − 3.59	5.78 − 0.59	17.83 + 3.98	26.76 − 13.97	8.04 − 7.96

CHALLENGE

19. Make a circle graph to show how your classmates can be divided up by the color of their hair.

EXTRA PRACTICE—page 450

GRAPHS

Drawing Conclusions From Circle Graphs

Sometimes conclusions can be made from the information in a circle graph. Study this circle graph. What conclusions could you make?

Since $\frac{2}{4}$ of the people like football, it is the favorite sport.

Since more people like football, more people watch it than baseball or basketball.

About as many people like baseball as like basketball.

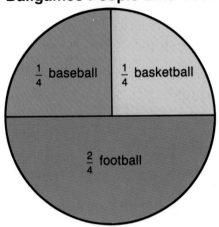

Ballgames People Like Best

PRACTICE

Study this circle graph and answer the questions.

Write *true* or *false*.

1. A sporting goods store would stock more skiing equipment than sleds.

2. More people go ice skating than go sledding.

3. About the same number of people like ice skating as those who like skiing.

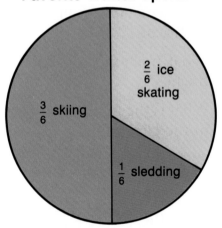

Favorite Winter Sports

MIXED PRACTICE
Maintaining and Reviewing Skills

Add, subtract, multiply, or divide.

4. $7.64 + 9.8$ 5. $7 \times \$2.49$ 6. $4.8 + 3.96$ 7. $7 - 3.92$ 8. $\$7.29 \div 3$

9. $3 \times \$9.04$ 10. $7.96 - 3.4$ 11. $8.2 + 8.04$ 12. $\$6.94 \div 2$ 13. $5 \times \$2.49$

FOCUS | Use STATISTICS AND PROBABILITY to read circle graphs and draw conclusions.

APPLICATION
Using Measurement

A circle graph can be used to show when a person does things during the day and night. Mr. Kim made this circle graph to show when he does things.

Between midnight and 6 A.M., Mr. Kim sleeps.

Between 6 A.M. and noon, Mr. Kim gets up and goes to work.

Between noon and 6 P.M., Mr. Kim eats lunch and goes back to his job.

Between 6 P.M. and midnight, Mr. Kim eats supper, watches TV, and goes to bed.

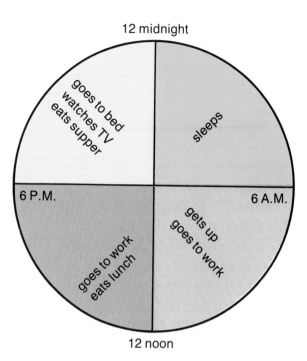

Copy Mr. Kim's circle graph. Then write where each of these activities should go.

14. Mr. Kim gets ready for work.

15. Mr. Kim does his housework.

16. Mr. Kim plays ball with his friends.

17. Mr. Kim walks home from work.

18. Mr. Kim eats breakfast.

19. Mr. Kim gets ready for bed.

Solving Problems

20. Florence's fourth grade class had 20 children in it. Ten children had brown eyes, 5 children had blue eyes, and 5 children had green eyes. Florence made a circle graph to stand for all the children in her class. What fraction of the graph stands for the children with green eyes?

21. The Smith family has 5 people in it. With dinner, Mr. and Mrs. Smith drink water. Their 2 sons drink milk. Their daughter drinks juice. The Smiths made a circle graph to stand for all the people in their family. What fraction of the graph stands for the people who drink milk?

Use MEASUREMENT to record and read events on a circle graph.
Use STATISTICS AND PROBABILITY to solve problems.

Unit Pricing

Which is the better buy? A bag of rice for $3.45 or one for $5.50? The answer seems simple: $3.45 is less than $5.50, so the answer seems to be the $3.45 bag. But, do you know how much rice each bag contains? No. And because you don't know the amount of rice in each bag, you can't tell which bag gives you the most for your money. The $5.50 bag may contain so much more rice than the $3.45 bag that it may actually be a better buy.

When you shop you need to know how much an item costs, and how much of it you are getting for that money. For example, look at the cans of peaches on the opposite page. Notice both the price and weight of the peaches.

When you know the price and the weight, you can figure out the **unit price.** This price tells how much each ounce (or pound, or number) of an item costs. Knowing the unit price of different brands and sizes of the same item helps to compare them to find the best buy.

We can find the unit price by dividing the price of an item by how much of the item there is. When you do this, write the price as a decimal, for example, $0.80 rather than 80¢.

The first can of peaches on the facing page is 8 ounces for $0.80. The unit price is found by dividing $0.80 by 8 ounces. The answer will be in cents per ounce.

$$8 \overline{)\$0.80} \quad \frac{\$0.10}{}$$

These peaches cost $0.10 per ounce.

This can be written as 10¢/oz.

CRITICAL THINKING

1. What is the unit price of the other can of peaches? Which can of peaches is less expensive?

2. Which peanut butter on the shelf is the best buy? Why?

3. What is the unit price of ground meat that is $7.50 for 5 pounds?

4. Which is the best buy?

   a. 5 bunches of carrots for $1.00
   b. 4 bunches of carrots for $0.92
   c. 3 bunches of carrots for $0.54

   Which is the worst buy?

FOCUS | Use NUMBER skills to find unit price.

80¢	$1.20

$1.20	$1.44	$1.68	$1.92

Unit Price	Unit Price
10¢/oz.	4¢/oz.

Unit Price	Unit Price	Unit Price	Unit Price
10¢/oz.	9¢/oz.	7¢/oz.	12¢/oz.

LOOKING BACK
Reviewing and Testing Chapter 22

In Chapter 22 you formulated problems about buying sneakers. Look at pages 288 and 289.

1. Write a sentence telling how you might decide what kind of sneakers to buy.

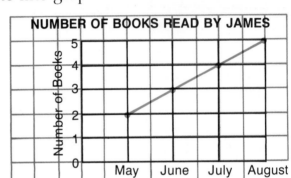

You learned about reading and making predictions from line graphs. To review what you learned, study the sample exercises on pages 290 and 292. Then use these skills to answer the questions about the line graph for exercises 2 and 3.

NUMBER OF BOOKS READ BY JAMES

2. How many more books did James read in August than in May?

3. Do you think James read more or fewer books in April than in May?

You learned about reading and drawing conclusions from circle graphs. To review, look at pages 294 and 296. Answer the questions about the circle graph for exercises 4 and 5.

4. What fraction of the pets are cats?

5. Which type of pet is the favorite?

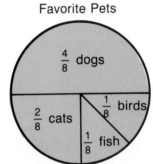

Favorite Pets

$\frac{4}{8}$ dogs

$\frac{1}{8}$ birds

$\frac{2}{8}$ cats

$\frac{1}{8}$ fish

You learned about unit pricing. Look at pages 298 and 299 to review how to determine a best buy.

6. Which is the best buy for oranges?

2 for $.46   4 for $1.00   3 for $.60

| FOCUS | Review and test skills learned and practiced. |

LOOKING AHEAD

Preparing for New Skills for Chapter 23

In the next chapter, you will focus on

- formulating problems about air-traffic controllers.
- writing mixed numbers.
- renaming mixed numbers as fractions.
- using logic.
- using a problem-solving strategy.
- renaming fractions as mixed numbers.
- using measurement.

Learning about writing and renaming improper fractions as mixed numbers will be easier if you brush up on what you already know about fractions that are equivalent to 1 and 0. First review the examples below. Then complete exercises 1–6.

A fraction can be used to tell how much is shaded. Fractions can be used to name one or zero.

Number of shaded parts $\longrightarrow 4$
Total number of equal parts $\longrightarrow 4$
Four fourths are shaded. $\frac{4}{4} = 1$

Number of shaded parts $\longrightarrow 0$
Total number of equal parts $\longrightarrow 4$
Zero fourths are shaded. $\frac{0}{4} = 0$

PRACTICE

Write a fraction that tells how much is shaded. Then write 1 or 0.

1.

2.

3.

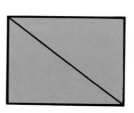

4.

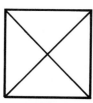

5.

6.

Review NUMBER skills in preparation for learning a new skill.

FOCUS   Formulate problems using picture cues, text, and data.

23

Fractions

DATA

Airport
Gotham International

Time	3:00 P.M.

Runways
No. 1   Closed for repair
No. 2   Open

Jets waiting to land	3

Names of jets waiting
Skywalker
Jetstreamer
Big Red

Fuel supply left
Skywalker	250 gallons
Jetstreamer	750 gallons
Big Red	1,500 gallons

Passengers on board
Skywalker	70
Jetstreamer	50
Big Red	200

Scheduled arrival time
Skywalker	2:15 P.M.
Jetstreamer	3:00 P.M.
Big Red	3:00 P.M.

An airport is a busy, exciting place. Jets fly in and out all the time. Someone must make sure that the jets take off and land safely. That person is the air traffic controller. Air traffic controllers work in control towers just like the one in the picture. They use 2-way radios to talk to the pilots of the jets.

Sometimes many jets may want to land at the same time. When things get backed up, the jets must circle overhead. They wait for the controllers to decide who can land first.

Think about what a busy day at the airport is like; then look at the picture and data. Which jet has the most passengers? Which jet is behind schedule? Why might this jet be late? Which jet can stay in the air the longest if it has to? Think about these things and decide in what order the jets should land.

Writing Mixed Numbers

The lunch special at the Good Food Restaurant is spinach and cheese pie. Each person is served $\frac{1}{4}$ of a pie.

This picture shows how many pieces were left after today's lunch.

There are 7 fourths, or $\frac{7}{4}$, left.

There are 1 whole pie and $\frac{3}{4}$ of another pie left.

There are $1\frac{3}{4}$ pies left.

Read: one and three fourths.

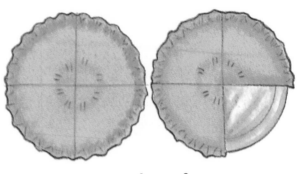

$$1 + \frac{3}{4} = 1\frac{3}{4}$$

$\frac{7}{4}$ and $1\frac{3}{4}$ name the same number.

$\frac{7}{4}$ is an **improper fraction** because the numerator is as great as or greater than the denominator.

$1\frac{3}{4}$ is a **mixed number** because it includes a whole number and a fraction.

GUIDED PRACTICE

How much is shaded? Write a mixed number.

1. 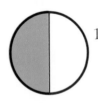 $1\frac{1}{2}$

2.  $1\frac{\blacksquare}{\blacksquare}$

3.

4.

| FOCUS | Use NUMBER skills to write mixed numbers. |

PRACTICE

How much is shaded? Write a mixed number.

5.
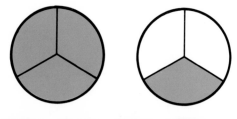

6.
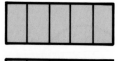
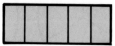
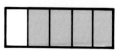

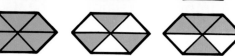

7.
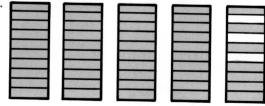

8.

Write a mixed number.

9. $3 + \frac{5}{8}$

10. $6 + \frac{4}{7}$

11. $10 + \frac{1}{10}$

12. $15 + \frac{3}{4}$

13. Carla ate 2 granola bars. Barry ate $\frac{5}{8}$ of a bar. How many granola bars did they eat altogether?

14. Sam broke 3 granola bars into thirds. He kept $\frac{1}{3}$ of a bar and gave the rest to his friends. How many granola bars did he give away?

MIXED PRACTICE

Maintaining and Reviewing Skills

How much is shaded? Write a mixed number or a fraction.

15.

16.

17.

CHALLENGE

18. The Ortez family had spinach and cheese pie for dinner. The children ate $\frac{3}{3}$ of a pie. The parents ate $\frac{4}{6}$ of another pie. Write how much the family ate in all as a fraction and as a mixed number.

FRACTIONS
Renaming Whole and Mixed Numbers as Improper Fractions

An improper fraction can be used to name a whole number.

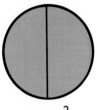 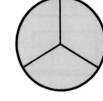  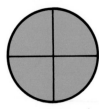 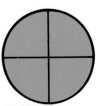

$1 = \frac{2}{2}$ $\qquad$ $2 = \frac{3}{3} + \frac{3}{3} = \frac{6}{3}$ $\qquad$ $2 = \frac{4}{4} + \frac{4}{4} = \frac{8}{4}$

An improper fraction can be used to name a mixed number.

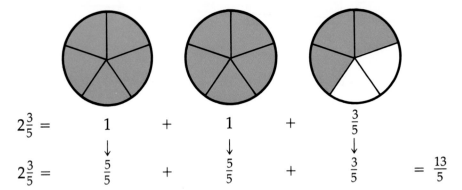

$2\frac{3}{5} =$ $\qquad$ 1 $\qquad + \qquad$ 1 $\qquad + \qquad$ $\frac{3}{5}$

$2\frac{3}{5} =$ $\qquad$ $\frac{5}{5}$ $\qquad + \qquad$ $\frac{5}{5}$ $\qquad + \qquad$ $\frac{3}{5}$ $\qquad = \frac{13}{5}$

PRACTICE

Rename each mixed number as an improper fraction.

1. $2\frac{2}{3} = 1 + 1 + \frac{2}{3} = \frac{\blacksquare}{3} + \frac{\blacksquare}{3} + \frac{2}{3} = \frac{\blacksquare}{3}$

2. $1\frac{1}{2}$ $\qquad$ 3. $2\frac{1}{4}$ $\qquad$ 4. $4\frac{1}{3}$ $\qquad$ 5. $3\frac{2}{5}$ $\qquad$ 6. 5

7. $2\frac{7}{8}$ $\qquad$ 8. $6\frac{1}{6}$ $\qquad$ 9. $5\frac{3}{10}$ $\qquad$ 10. 4 $\qquad$ 11. $10\frac{2}{7}$

MIXED PRACTICE
Maintaining and Reviewing Skills

Write 1 or 0.

12. $\frac{0}{6} = \blacksquare$ $\qquad$ 13. $\frac{9}{9} = \blacksquare$ $\qquad$ 14. $\frac{17}{17} = \blacksquare$ $\qquad$ 15. $\frac{0}{25} = \blacksquare$ $\qquad$ 16. $\frac{11}{11} = \blacksquare$

17. $\frac{0}{42} = \blacksquare$ $\qquad$ 18. $\frac{34}{34} = \blacksquare$ $\qquad$ 19. $\frac{100}{100} = \blacksquare$ $\qquad$ 20. $\frac{0}{50} = \blacksquare$ $\qquad$ 21. $\frac{70}{70} = \blacksquare$

FOCUS | Use NUMBER skills to rename mixed numbers as fractions.

APPLICATION

Using Logic

Number lines can help you to compare fractions and mixed numbers.

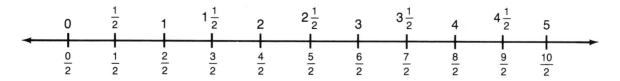

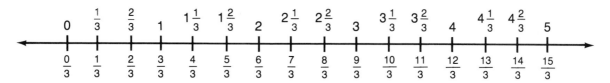

Compare $2\frac{1}{2}$ and $\frac{7}{2}$.

Think: $2\frac{1}{2} = \frac{5}{2}$

$\frac{5}{2} < \frac{7}{2}$, so $2\frac{1}{2} < \frac{7}{2}$

Copy and complete. Write >, <, or =.

22. $\frac{2}{2}$ ● 2

23. $4\frac{1}{2}$ ● $\frac{8}{2}$

24. $2\frac{1}{3}$ ● $\frac{5}{3}$

25. $\frac{11}{3}$ ● $3\frac{2}{3}$

26. $\frac{10}{3}$ ● $4\frac{1}{2}$

27. $\frac{4}{2}$ ● $\frac{6}{3}$

Write in order from least to greatest.

28. $3\frac{1}{2}$, $\frac{3}{2}$, $\frac{10}{2}$

29. $\frac{14}{3}$, $3\frac{1}{3}$, $1\frac{2}{3}$

30. $1\frac{1}{2}$, $2\frac{2}{3}$, $\frac{6}{2}$, $\frac{3}{3}$

Problem Solving: Finding a Pattern

Study each pattern from left to right. Write the rule that describes the pattern (for example: add $\frac{1}{3}$). Then write the number that comes next in the pattern.

31. $\frac{1}{2}$, 1, $1\frac{1}{2}$, 2, $2\frac{1}{2}$

32. $1\frac{1}{3}$, $1\frac{2}{3}$, 2, $2\frac{1}{3}$, $2\frac{2}{3}$

33. 2, $2\frac{1}{4}$, $2\frac{1}{2}$, $2\frac{3}{4}$, 3

34. $3\frac{3}{5}$, $3\frac{4}{5}$, 4, $4\frac{1}{5}$, $4\frac{2}{5}$

35. 4, $4\frac{7}{10}$, $5\frac{2}{5}$, $6\frac{1}{10}$, $6\frac{4}{5}$

36. $\frac{1}{2}$, 2, $3\frac{1}{2}$, 5, $6\frac{1}{2}$

Use LOGIC and NUMBER skills to compare and order fractions and mixed numbers using number lines.
Find a pattern and apply the Five-Step PROBLEM SOLVING Plan.

Selecting a Strategy: Making a List

The five important steps in problem solving are READ, KNOW, PLAN, SOLVE, and CHECK. Making a list is a strategy you can use to PLAN and SOLVE a problem.

1. READ — Use the digits 4, 5, and 6. Each digit can appear only once in a number. How many different three-digit numbers can be formed?

2. KNOW — Ask yourself: What am I being asked to find? How many different three-digit numbers can be made?
What **key facts** do I need?
The three digits are 4, 5, and 6. Each digit can appear only once in a number.

3. PLAN — Select a strategy: try making a list. Start with one digit in the hundreds place. Keep listing until you find all of the possibilities for the tens and ones places. Then go on to using another digit in the hundreds place.

4. SOLVE

Hundreds Place	Tens Place	Ones Place
4	5	6
4	6	5
5	4	6
5	6	4
6	4	5
6	5	4

There are 6 different three-digit numbers.

5. CHECK — The answer is reasonable because the list contains all the possible three-digit numbers that can be formed using the digits 4, 5, and 6.

FOCUS | Evaluate information as part of the Five-Step PROBLEM-SOLVING Plan.

PRACTICE

Make a list to find all of the possible answers to each problem. Problems 1 through 5 ask for arrangements in which all orders must be counted. For example, "34" is different from "43."

1. I am a two-digit number between 31 and 45. I am divisible by 2. What numbers could I be?

2. I am a two-digit number between 52 and 65. I am divisible by 3. What numbers could I be?

3. I am a two-digit number. I am divisible by 2 and by 5. What numbers could I be?

4. Use the digits 7, 8, and 9. Each digit can appear only once in a number. How many three-digit numbers can be formed?

5. Use the digits 1, 2, 3, and 4. Each digit can appear only once in a number. How many four-digit numbers can be formed?

Problems 6 and 7 ask for combinations in which all orders do **not** need to be counted. For example, "1 dime and 3 nickels" is the same as "3 nickels and 1 dime."

6. In how many ways could you give someone 25¢ if you had only dimes and nickels?

7. In how many ways could you give someone 25¢ if you had only nickels and pennies?

Class Project

Lists can be used to organize information that is needed to solve a problem about a long period of time. Divide into small groups of students. Estimate the total cost of notebook paper for all of the students in your class for one entire school year. Make a list of the items you need to think about. Then find your group's estimate. Compare it with the estimates of other groups.

Renaming Improper Fractions as Mixed Numbers

Colored counting rods can be used to show improper fractions, whole numbers, and mixed numbers.

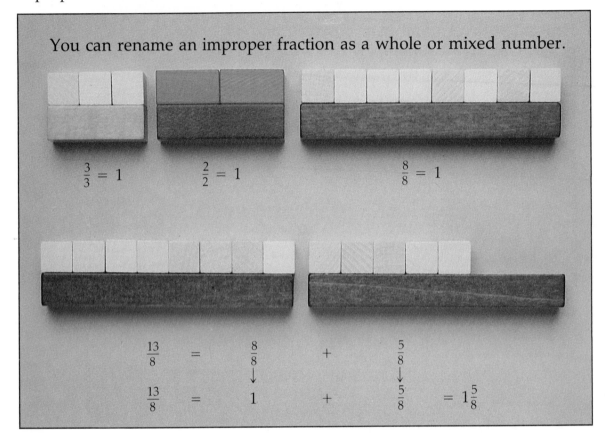

You can rename an improper fraction as a whole or mixed number.

$$\frac{3}{3} = 1 \qquad \frac{2}{2} = 1 \qquad \frac{8}{8} = 1$$

$$\frac{13}{8} = \frac{8}{8} + \frac{5}{8}$$
$$\downarrow \qquad \downarrow$$
$$\frac{13}{8} = 1 + \frac{5}{8} = 1\frac{5}{8}$$

GUIDED PRACTICE

Copy and complete.

1. $\frac{8}{3} = \frac{3}{3} + \frac{3}{3} + \frac{2}{3}$

   $\downarrow \qquad \downarrow \qquad \downarrow$

   $\frac{8}{3} = 1 + \blacksquare + \frac{2}{3} = \blacksquare \frac{\blacksquare}{3}$

2. $\frac{7}{2} = \frac{2}{2} + \frac{2}{2} + \frac{\blacksquare}{\blacksquare} + \frac{1}{2}$

   $\downarrow \qquad \downarrow \qquad \downarrow \qquad \downarrow$

   $\frac{7}{2} = \blacksquare + \blacksquare + \blacksquare + \frac{1}{2} = \blacksquare\frac{\blacksquare}{\blacksquare}$

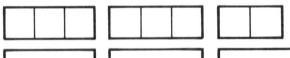

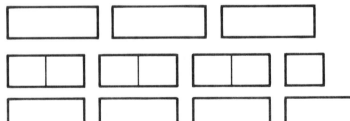

FOCUS Use NUMBER skills to rename fractions as mixed numbers.

PRACTICE

Copy and complete.

3. $\frac{7}{5} = \frac{5}{5} + \frac{2}{5}$

$\frac{7}{5} = \blacksquare + \frac{2}{5} = \blacksquare\frac{\blacksquare}{5}$

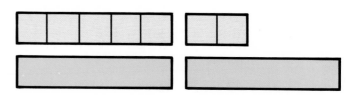

4. $\frac{16}{7} = \frac{7}{7} + \frac{7}{7} + \frac{\blacksquare}{7}$

$\frac{16}{7} = \blacksquare + \blacksquare + \frac{\blacksquare}{7} = \blacksquare\frac{\blacksquare}{7}$

5. $\frac{17}{10} = \frac{10}{10} + \frac{\blacksquare}{10}$

$\frac{17}{10} = \blacksquare + \frac{\blacksquare}{10} = \blacksquare\frac{\blacksquare}{10}$

Rename each improper fraction as a mixed or whole number.

6. $\frac{8}{5}$ **7.** $\frac{23}{7}$ **8.** $\frac{6}{2}$ **9.** $\frac{13}{3}$ **10.** $\frac{17}{6}$

11. $\frac{19}{10}$ **12.** $\frac{41}{8}$ **13.** $\frac{17}{3}$ **14.** $\frac{45}{9}$ **15.** $\frac{13}{4}$

Solve. Write mixed numbers.

16. Mike ran $\frac{8}{8}$ mile in the morning and $\frac{7}{8}$ mile in the afternoon. How far did he run in all?

17. Doris has $\frac{10}{5}$ pounds of clay. Sue has $\frac{2}{5}$ pound more than Doris. How much clay does Sue have?

MIXED PRACTICE

Maintaining and Reviewing Skills

Write each improper fraction as a mixed number.

18. $\frac{21}{8}$ **19.** $\frac{7}{2}$ **20.** $\frac{15}{4}$ **21.** $\frac{16}{3}$ **22.** $\frac{17}{5}$

Copy and complete the equivalent fractions.

23. $\frac{3}{5} = \frac{\blacksquare}{10}$ **24.** $\frac{1}{4} = \frac{\blacksquare}{12}$ **25.** $\frac{2}{3} = \frac{\blacksquare}{6}$ **26.** $\frac{7}{7} = \frac{\blacksquare}{16}$ **27.** $\frac{4}{5} = \frac{\blacksquare}{10}$

CHALLENGE

Write in order from least to greatest.

28. $\frac{9}{3}, \frac{9}{4}, \frac{9}{5}$

29. $\frac{11}{5}, \frac{13}{2}, \frac{12}{7}$

30. $\frac{47}{9}, \frac{41}{10}, \frac{35}{8}$

EXTRA PRACTICE—page 451

FRACTIONS
Dividing to Rename Improper Fractions as Mixed Numbers

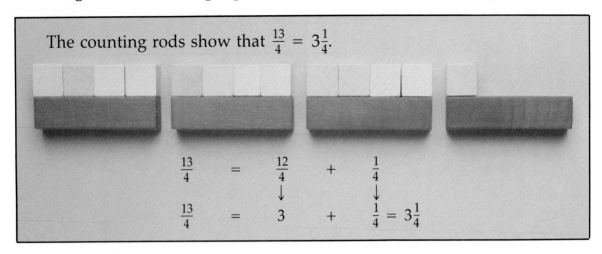

The counting rods show that $\frac{13}{4} = 3\frac{1}{4}$.

$$\frac{13}{4} = \frac{12}{4} + \frac{1}{4}$$

$$\frac{13}{4} = 3 + \frac{1}{4} = 3\frac{1}{4}$$

You can use division to rename an improper fraction as a mixed number.

$\frac{13}{4}$ means $13 \div 4$.

Divide the numerator by the denominator. Then write the remainder as a fraction.

$$\begin{array}{r} 3\,\text{R1 or } 3\frac{1}{4} \\ 4\overline{)13} \\ \underline{12} \\ 1 \end{array}$$

Remainder
Divisor

PRACTICE

Divide. Write the answer as a mixed number.

1. $2\overline{)9}$ 2. $6\overline{)7}$ 3. $5\overline{)23}$ 4. $8\overline{)45}$

5. $2\overline{)11}$ 6. $6\overline{)17}$ 7. $5\overline{)13}$ 8. $4\overline{)19}$

9. $7\overline{)17}$ 10. $3\overline{)23}$ 11. $4\overline{)27}$ 12. $8\overline{)21}$

MIXED PRACTICE
Maintaining and Reviewing Skills

Rename each improper fraction as a mixed number.

13. $\frac{9}{2}$ 14. $\frac{11}{6}$ 15. $\frac{21}{5}$ 16. $\frac{15}{4}$ 17. $\frac{17}{7}$

18. $\frac{25}{8}$ 19. $\frac{23}{4}$ 20. $\frac{22}{3}$ 21. $\frac{17}{2}$ 22. $\frac{53}{6}$

FOCUS | Use NUMBER skills to rename fractions as mixed numbers by using division.

APPLICATION

Using Measurement

Mixed numbers can be used to compare and order customary measures of length.

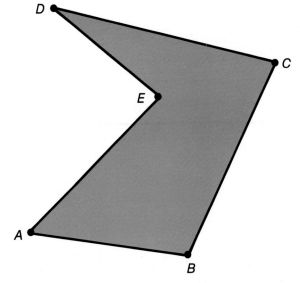

Which line segment is longer, $\overline{AB}$ or $\overline{DE}$?

$\overline{AB}$ is $1\frac{3}{4}$ inches long.

$\overline{DE}$ is $1\frac{1}{2}$ inches long.

$1\frac{1}{2} = 1\frac{2}{4}$, so $1\frac{3}{4} > 1\frac{1}{2}$.

$\overline{AB}$ is longer than $\overline{DE}$.

Which line segment is longer?

23. $\overline{DE}$ or $\overline{BC}$ 24. $\overline{DC}$ or $\overline{DE}$ 25. $\overline{AE}$ or $\overline{DC}$ 26. $\overline{AB}$ or $\overline{DE}$

Name the line segments in order from shortest to longest.

27. $\overline{AB}, \overline{BC}, \overline{DE}$ 28. $\overline{CD}, \overline{AE}, \overline{BC}$ 29. $\overline{AB}, \overline{EA}, \overline{DE}$

Using Mental Arithmetic

Here are two ways to mentally round $2\frac{5}{6}$ to the nearest whole number.

Think:

- $2\frac{5}{6}$ is between 2 and 3.

- $2\frac{3}{6}$ is halfway between 2 and 3.

- $2\frac{5}{6} > 2\frac{3}{6}$, so $2\frac{5}{6}$ is nearer to 3.

Think:

- $\frac{6}{6} = 1$

- $\frac{5}{6}$ is close to $\frac{6}{6}$ or 1.

- So, $2\frac{5}{6}$ is almost $2 + 1$, or 3.

Round each to the nearest whole number.

30. $3\frac{2}{7}$ 31. $1\frac{7}{10}$ 32. $4\frac{2}{3}$ 33. $5\frac{2}{6}$ 34. $8\frac{4}{5}$

35. $\frac{11}{5}$ 36. $\frac{7}{4}$ 37. $\frac{14}{3}$ 38. $\frac{54}{10}$ 39. $\frac{60}{8}$

Use MEASUREMENT to compare and order the lengths of line segments.
Use NUMBER skills and MENTAL ARITHMETIC to round mixed numbers and fractions to the nearest whole number.

LOOKING BACK
Reviewing and Testing Chapter 23

In Chapter 23 you formulated problems about an air controller's job. Look at pages 302 and 303.

1. Write a sentence telling how you decided in what order the jets should land.

You learned about writing mixed numbers and renaming mixed numbers as improper fractions. To review what you learned, study the sample exercises on pages 304 and 306. Then use these skills to write a mixed number for exercises 2–5. For exercises 6–15, rename each mixed number as an improper fraction.

2. $2 + \frac{1}{4}$ 3. $8 + \frac{2}{3}$ 4. $5 + \frac{3}{8}$ 5. $9 + \frac{7}{10}$

6. $1\frac{1}{3}$ 7. $3\frac{2}{5}$ 8. $2\frac{3}{4}$ 9. $7\frac{3}{10}$ 10. $6\frac{5}{8}$

11. $4\frac{2}{7}$ 12. $9\frac{1}{10}$ 13. $5\frac{4}{9}$ 14. $2\frac{5}{12}$ 15. $5\frac{4}{5}$

You learned about making a list as a problem solving strategy. To review, look at pages 308 and 309. Then make a list of all the possible answers to each problem.

16. I am a two-digit number. I am divisible by 2 and by 9. What numbers could I be?

17. In how many ways could you give some change for a dollar if you only have quarters and dimes?

You learned about renaming improper fractions as mixed numbers. To review, look at pages 310 and 312. Rename each improper fraction as a mixed number for exercises 18–27.

18. $\frac{7}{2}$ 19. $\frac{11}{4}$ 20. $\frac{13}{3}$ 21. $\frac{43}{8}$ 22. $\frac{31}{5}$

23. $\frac{23}{6}$ 24. $\frac{63}{10}$ 25. $\frac{22}{9}$ 26. $\frac{97}{10}$ 27. $\frac{31}{12}$

| FOCUS | Review and test skills learned and practiced. |

Preparing for New Skills for Chapter 24

In the next chapter, you will focus on

- formulating problems about brown bears.
- adding fractions and mixed numbers.
- using statistics and probability.
- subtracting fractions and mixed numbers.
- using patterns and functions.
- how math is used in social studies.

Learning more about fractions and mixed numbers will be easier if you review what you already know about fractions. Study Models A and B. Then complete exercises 1–8.

Model A   Add: $\frac{1}{8} + \frac{5}{8}$

Add the numerators.	**Use the same denominator.**	**Simplify. Divide both the numerator and the denominator by the largest whole number you can. (Remainders must be 0.)**
$\frac{1}{8} + \frac{5}{8} = \frac{6}{\blacksquare}$	$\frac{1}{8} + \frac{5}{8} = \frac{6}{8}$	$\frac{6 \div 2}{8 \div 2} = \frac{3}{4}$ ↖Simplest terms

Model B   Subtract: $\frac{11}{12} - \frac{5}{12}$

Subtract the numerators.	**Use the same denominator.**	**Simplify. (If you don't divide by the largest number the first time, you can divide again.)**
$\frac{11}{12} - \frac{5}{12} = \frac{6}{\blacksquare}$	$\frac{11}{12} - \frac{5}{12} = \frac{6}{12}$	$\frac{6 \div 2}{12 \div 2} = \frac{3}{6} = \frac{3 \div 3}{6 \div 3} = \frac{1}{2}$

Divide again.   ↖Simplest terms

PRACTICE

Add. Simplify the answers. Use Model A.

1. $\frac{1}{4} + \frac{1}{4}$ 2. $\frac{3}{8} + \frac{1}{8}$ 3. $\frac{3}{10} + \frac{7}{10}$ 4. $\frac{4}{9} + \frac{2}{9}$

Subtract. Simplify the answers. Use Model B.

5. $\frac{5}{8} - \frac{3}{8}$ 6. $\frac{7}{12} - \frac{1}{12}$ 7. $\frac{9}{10} - \frac{3}{10}$ 8. $\frac{7}{9} - \frac{4}{9}$

Review NUMBER skills in preparation for learning a new skill.

FOCUS   Formulate problems using picture cues, text, and data.

24

Fractions and Mixed Numbers

DATA

Brown bears

Adult weight
> Up to 1,700 pounds

Adult height
> Can measure 10 feet from nose to tail

Fur color
> Ranges from dark brown to almost white

Eyesight   Very poor

Nose and teeth   Very strong

Birth weight $1\frac{1}{2}$ pounds

Dwelling places
> About 1,000 in the 48 mainland U.S.A. states; most others in the Canadian or the Alaskan wilderness

The Zoology Club is studying brown bears, and are they ever big! How big is a big brown bear? Well, it's not as big as an elephant, but it's not too far behind. Brown bears are the largest meat-eating animals on land.

At one time, more than 250,000 of these big creatures roamed throughout North America. Now, most of them live in the wild parts of Canada and Alaska. The few that are left in mainland U.S.A. live in protected areas like Glacier National Park.

Look at the photograph and the data to see what the Zoology Club has already learned about big brown bears. What else might the club members want to learn about these giants? How might they go about studying those things? Think carefully. Then predict what the Zoology Club will do next in its study of big brown bears.

Adding Fractions With Like Denominators

Tony is making a mosaic tile pattern. For each row of 5 tiles, he is using 2 light green tiles, 1 dark green tile, and 2 white tiles. What part of each row is green?

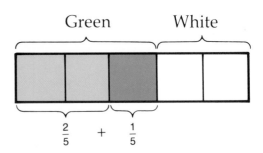

$$\underbrace{}_{\frac{2}{5}} + \underbrace{}_{\frac{1}{5}}$$

Add the fractions.

$$\frac{2}{5} + \frac{1}{5} = \frac{2+1}{5} = \frac{3}{5}$$ ⟵ Add the numerators. 2 + 1 = 3
⟵ Use the same denominator.

So $\frac{3}{5}$ of each row is green.

Karen has two gardens that are the same size. On Monday, she seeded $\frac{3}{4}$ of a garden. On Tuesday, she seeded $\frac{3}{4}$ of another garden. How much of the two gardens did she seed?

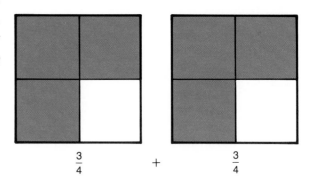

$$\frac{3}{4} \qquad + \qquad \frac{3}{4}$$

Add: $\frac{3}{4} + \frac{3}{4}$

$$\frac{3}{4} + \frac{3}{4} = \frac{3+3}{4} \text{ or } \frac{6}{4}$$

You know that $\frac{4}{4} = 1$.

So $\frac{6}{4} = \frac{4}{4} + \frac{2}{4}$

$$\downarrow \qquad \downarrow$$

$$1 + \frac{1}{2} = 1\frac{1}{2} \leftarrow \textbf{simplest terms}$$

> A mixed number is in simplest terms if the fraction is in simplest terms and names a number less than 1.

Karen seeded $1\frac{1}{2}$ gardens.

GUIDED PRACTICE

Add. Rename in simplest terms.

1.

$$\frac{2}{4} + \frac{1}{4} = \frac{2+1}{4} = \frac{\blacksquare}{\blacksquare}$$

2.

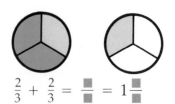

$$\frac{2}{3} + \frac{2}{3} = \frac{\blacksquare}{\blacksquare} = 1\frac{\blacksquare}{\blacksquare}$$

| FOCUS | Use NUMBER skills to add fractions with like denominators. |

318

PRACTICE

Add. Rename in simplest terms.

3. $\frac{2}{8} + \frac{4}{8} = \frac{2+4}{8} = \frac{\blacksquare}{\blacksquare} = \frac{\blacksquare}{\blacksquare}$

4. $\frac{4}{7} + \frac{5}{7} = \frac{4+5}{7} = \frac{\blacksquare}{\blacksquare} = 1\frac{\blacksquare}{\blacksquare}$

5. $\frac{1}{3} + \frac{1}{3}$

6. $\frac{1}{6} + \frac{3}{6}$

7. $\frac{2}{5} + \frac{2}{5}$

8. $\frac{6}{10} + \frac{2}{10}$

9. $\frac{5}{8} + \frac{2}{8}$

10. $\frac{5}{10} + \frac{4}{10}$

11. $\frac{4}{5} + \frac{3}{5}$

12. $\frac{3}{4} + \frac{2}{4}$

13. $\frac{5}{6} + \frac{4}{6}$

14. $\frac{6}{7} + \frac{1}{7}$

15. $\frac{6}{10} + \frac{7}{10}$

16. $\frac{4}{9} + \frac{5}{9}$

17. $\begin{array}{r} \frac{1}{5} \\ + \frac{3}{5} \\ \hline \end{array}$

18. $\begin{array}{r} \frac{7}{8} \\ + \frac{1}{8} \\ \hline \end{array}$

19. $\begin{array}{r} \frac{8}{10} \\ + \frac{7}{10} \\ \hline \end{array}$

20. $\begin{array}{r} \frac{1}{7} \\ \frac{3}{7} \\ + \frac{2}{7} \\ \hline \end{array}$

21. $\begin{array}{r} \frac{2}{9} \\ \frac{7}{9} \\ + \frac{3}{9} \\ \hline \end{array}$

MIXED PRACTICE

Maintaining and Reviewing Skills

Add. Rename in simplest terms.

22. $\frac{3}{4} + \frac{1}{4}$

23. $\frac{5}{8} + \frac{6}{8}$

24. $\frac{2}{6} + \frac{2}{6}$

25. $\frac{3}{10} + \frac{9}{10}$

Write a mixed number.

26. $4 + \frac{3}{5}$

27. $7 + \frac{5}{8}$

28. $6 + \frac{7}{9}$

29. $3 + \frac{1}{3}$

Rename each fraction as a mixed number.

30. $\frac{15}{10}$

31. $\frac{13}{8}$

32. $\frac{17}{3}$

33. $\frac{23}{7}$

34. $\frac{11}{2}$

CHALLENGE

35. Copy the grid. Arrange the fractions below in the grid to form a magic square. The sum of each row, column, and diagonal must be 1. $\frac{1}{6}, \frac{1}{6}, \frac{1}{6}, \frac{2}{6}, \frac{2}{6}, \frac{2}{6}, \frac{3}{6}, \frac{3}{6}, \frac{3}{6}$

FRACTIONS AND MIXED NUMBERS

Adding Mixed Numbers With Like Denominators

Add: $1\frac{3}{4} + 2\frac{3}{4}$

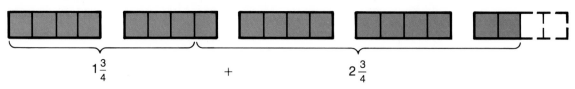

$$\underbrace{\hspace{3cm}}_{1\frac{3}{4}} \quad + \quad \underbrace{\hspace{3cm}}_{2\frac{3}{4}}$$

Add the fractions.	**Add the whole numbers.**	**Rename in simplest terms.**
$\frac{3}{4} + \frac{3}{4} = \frac{6}{4}$	$1 + 2 = 3$	$3\frac{6}{4} = 3 + \frac{4}{4} + \frac{2}{4}$
		$\hspace{2cm}\downarrow \hspace{0.8cm} \downarrow$
		$= 3 + 1 + \frac{1}{2} = 4\frac{1}{2}$

$$\begin{array}{r} 1\frac{3}{4} \\ +2\frac{3}{4} \\ \hline \frac{6}{4} \end{array} \qquad \begin{array}{r} 1\frac{3}{4} \\ +2\frac{3}{4} \\ \hline 3\frac{6}{4} \end{array} \qquad \begin{array}{r} 1\frac{3}{4} \\ +2\frac{3}{4} \\ \hline 3\frac{6}{4} = 4\frac{2}{4} = 4\frac{1}{2} \end{array}$$

PRACTICE

Add. Rename in simplest terms.

1. $\begin{array}{r} 2\frac{2}{5} \\ +3\frac{1}{5} \\ \hline \end{array}$
2. $\begin{array}{r} 4\frac{1}{3} \\ +1\frac{1}{3} \\ \hline \end{array}$
3. $\begin{array}{r} 3\frac{1}{5} \\ +4\frac{3}{5} \\ \hline \end{array}$
4. $\begin{array}{r} 7\frac{1}{2} \\ +2\frac{1}{2} \\ \hline \end{array}$
5. $\begin{array}{r} 3\frac{1}{10} \\ +1\frac{9}{10} \\ \hline \end{array}$

6. $7\frac{5}{12} + 7\frac{11}{12}$ 7. $5\frac{7}{10} + 8\frac{9}{10}$ 8. $9\frac{11}{12} + 8\frac{11}{12}$

MIXED PRACTICE

Maintaining and Reviewing Skills

Add. Rename in simplest terms.

9. $\begin{array}{r} 1\frac{1}{2} \\ +8\frac{1}{2} \\ \hline \end{array}$
10. $\begin{array}{r} 5\frac{1}{6} \\ +2\frac{1}{6} \\ \hline \end{array}$
11. $\begin{array}{r} \frac{1}{12} \\ +\frac{5}{12} \\ \hline \end{array}$
12. $\begin{array}{r} \frac{5}{6} \\ +\frac{5}{6} \\ \hline \end{array}$
13. $\begin{array}{r} \frac{7}{8} \\ +\frac{5}{8} \\ \hline \end{array}$

FOCUS	Use NUMBER skills to add mixed numbers with like denominators.

APPLICATION
Using Statistics and Probability

A two-color counter has one red side and one yellow side.

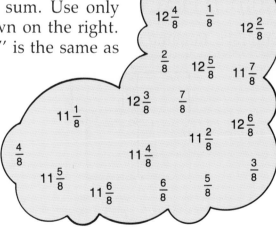

Suppose you toss a two-color counter twice. There are 4 possible outcomes:

RED/RED   RED/YELLOW   YELLOW/RED   YELLOW/YELLOW

The chance, or probability, that you will get *two reds* is 1 out of 4, or $\frac{1}{4}$.

If you toss a two-color counter twice, what is the probability that you will get

14. two yellows?

15. exactly one red?

16. exactly one yellow?

17. at least one red?

18. at least one yellow?

19. two reds or two yellows?

Problem Solving: Making a List

Remember to READ, KNOW, PLAN, SOLVE, and CHECK all problems. See the Five-Step Plan on page 454 in the Data Bank.

List all of the possible different combinations of a mixed number and a fraction that give each sum. Use only the mixed numbers and fractions shown on the right. Remember: The combination "$12\frac{2}{8} + \frac{5}{8}$" is the same as the combination "$\frac{5}{8} + 12\frac{2}{8}$".

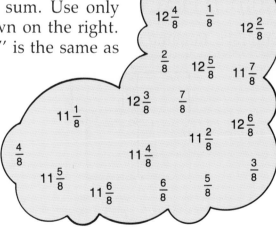

20. The sum is $12\frac{7}{8}$.

21. The sum is $11\frac{5}{8}$.

22. The sum is $12\frac{1}{8}$.

The figures shown:
$12\frac{1}{8}$ $11\frac{3}{8}$
$12\frac{4}{8}$ $\frac{1}{8}$ $12\frac{2}{8}$
$\frac{2}{8}$ $12\frac{5}{8}$ $11\frac{7}{8}$
$12\frac{3}{8}$ $\frac{7}{8}$
$11\frac{1}{8}$ $12\frac{6}{8}$
$11\frac{2}{8}$
$\frac{4}{8}$ $11\frac{4}{8}$
$11\frac{5}{8}$ $\frac{3}{8}$
$11\frac{6}{8}$ $\frac{6}{8}$ $\frac{5}{8}$

Use STATISTICS AND PROBABILITY to write the probability of a single event occurring as a fraction.
Make a list and apply the Five-Step PROBLEM–SOLVING Plan.

FRACTIONS
Subtracting Fractions With Like Denominators

Myra made a mosaic tile pattern. For each row of 5 tiles, she used 2 white tiles and 3 blue tiles. One of the blue tiles fell off. What fractional part of the row are the remaining blue tiles?

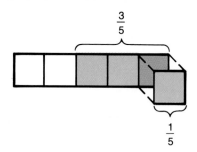

Subtract the fractions.

$$\frac{3}{5} - \frac{1}{5} = \frac{3-1}{5} = \frac{2}{5}$$ ←—— Subtract the numerators. $3 - 1 = 2$
←—— Use the same denominator.

The remaining blue tiles are $\frac{2}{5}$ of the row.

Subtract: $\frac{5}{8} - \frac{3}{8}$

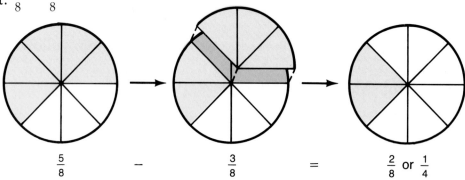

$$\frac{5}{8} \qquad - \qquad \frac{3}{8} \qquad = \qquad \frac{2}{8} \text{ or } \frac{1}{4}$$

GUIDED PRACTICE

Subtract. Rename in simplest terms.

1.

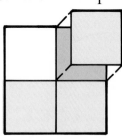

$$\frac{3}{4} - \frac{1}{4} = \frac{3-1}{4} = \frac{\blacksquare}{\blacksquare} = \frac{\blacksquare}{\blacksquare}$$

2.

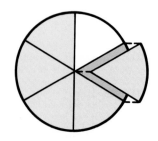

$$\frac{5}{6} - \frac{1}{6} = \frac{\blacksquare}{\blacksquare} = \frac{\blacksquare}{\blacksquare}$$

3. $\frac{6}{7} - \frac{4}{7} = \frac{6-4}{7} = \frac{\blacksquare}{\blacksquare}$

4. $\frac{2}{3} - \frac{1}{3}$

5. $\frac{7}{8} - \frac{1}{8}$

| FOCUS | Use NUMBER skills to subtract fractions with like denominators. |

322

PRACTICE

Subtract. Rename in simplest terms.

6. $\dfrac{3}{10} - \dfrac{1}{10} = \dfrac{3-1}{10} = \dfrac{\blacksquare}{\blacksquare} = \dfrac{\blacksquare}{\blacksquare}$

7. $\dfrac{7}{8} - \dfrac{3}{8} = \dfrac{\blacksquare}{\blacksquare} = \dfrac{\blacksquare}{\blacksquare}$

8. $\dfrac{4}{5} - \dfrac{1}{5} = \dfrac{4-1}{5} = \dfrac{\blacksquare}{\blacksquare}$

9. $\dfrac{7}{9} - \dfrac{4}{9} = \dfrac{7-4}{9} = \dfrac{\blacksquare}{\blacksquare} = \dfrac{\blacksquare}{\blacksquare}$

10. $\dfrac{5}{7} - \dfrac{3}{7}$

11. $\dfrac{8}{9} - \dfrac{2}{9}$

12. $\dfrac{3}{8} - \dfrac{1}{8}$

13. $\dfrac{9}{10} - \dfrac{7}{10}$

14. $\dfrac{7}{12} - \dfrac{1}{12}$

15. $\dfrac{7}{8} - \dfrac{5}{8}$

16. $\dfrac{5}{12} - \dfrac{1}{12}$

17. $\dfrac{7}{10} - \dfrac{3}{10}$

18. $\begin{array}{r} \dfrac{7}{12} \\ -\dfrac{5}{12} \\ \hline \end{array}$

19. $\begin{array}{r} \dfrac{9}{10} \\ -\dfrac{1}{10} \\ \hline \end{array}$

20. $\begin{array}{r} \dfrac{11}{12} \\ -\dfrac{7}{12} \\ \hline \end{array}$

21. $\begin{array}{r} \dfrac{5}{8} \\ -\dfrac{0}{8} \\ \hline \end{array}$

22. $\begin{array}{r} \dfrac{7}{9} \\ -\dfrac{7}{9} \\ \hline \end{array}$

23. Ellen used $\dfrac{3}{8}$ of a pack of paper for an art project. What fractional part of the paper did Ellen not use?

24. Myra has a sheet of paper to divide into fourths. She will use $\dfrac{3}{4}$ of the paper on the bulletin board. What fractional part will not be used?

MIXED PRACTICE
Maintaining and Reviewing Skills

Add or subtract. Rename in simplest terms.

25. $\dfrac{6}{7} - \dfrac{4}{7}$

26. $\dfrac{5}{6} - \dfrac{1}{6}$

27. $\dfrac{3}{8} + \dfrac{3}{8}$

28. $\dfrac{9}{10} - \dfrac{4}{10}$

29. $\dfrac{4}{9} + \dfrac{2}{9}$

30. $\dfrac{11}{12} - \dfrac{4}{12}$

31. $\dfrac{4}{15} + \dfrac{2}{15}$

32. $\dfrac{8}{9} - \dfrac{4}{9}$

CHALLENGE

33. On Saturday, Steve practiced his song for the talent show $\dfrac{1}{4}$ hour in the morning and $\dfrac{2}{4}$ hour in the afternoon. On Sunday, he practiced $\dfrac{1}{8}$ hour in the morning and $\dfrac{1}{8}$ hour in the afternoon. How much more time did Steve practice on Saturday?

FRACTIONS AND MIXED NUMBERS

Subtracting Mixed Numbers With Like Denominators

Subtract: $3\frac{3}{4} - 1\frac{1}{4}$

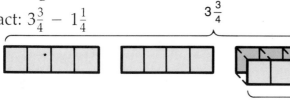

$3\frac{3}{4}$

$1\frac{1}{4}$

Subtract the fractions.	**Subtract the whole numbers.**	**Rename in simplest terms.**
$\frac{3}{4} - \frac{1}{4} = \frac{2}{4}$	$3 - 1 = 2$	$\frac{2}{4} = \frac{2 \div 2}{4 \div 2} = \frac{1}{2}$
		$2\frac{2}{4} = 2\frac{1}{2}$

$$3\frac{3}{4}$$
$$-1\frac{1}{4}$$
$$\overline{\frac{2}{4}}$$

$$3\frac{3}{4}$$
$$-1\frac{1}{4}$$
$$\overline{2\frac{2}{4}}$$

$$3\frac{3}{4}$$
$$-1\frac{1}{4}$$
$$\overline{2\frac{2}{4} = 2\frac{1}{2}}$$

PRACTICE

Subtract. Rename in simplest terms.

1. $9\frac{4}{5}$
   $-6\frac{2}{5}$

2. $8\frac{2}{3}$
   $-3\frac{1}{3}$

3. $6\frac{3}{8}$
   $-2\frac{1}{8}$

4. $8\frac{5}{6}$
   $-1\frac{1}{6}$

5. $5\frac{7}{12}$
   $-2\frac{5}{12}$

6. $9\frac{7}{10} - 5\frac{3}{10}$

7. $16\frac{5}{6} - 9\frac{1}{6}$

8. $15\frac{11}{12} - 7\frac{7}{12}$

MIXED PRACTICE
Maintaining and Reviewing Skills

Add or subtract. Rename in simplest terms.

9. $7\frac{9}{10}$
   $-3\frac{4}{10}$

10. $13\frac{7}{8}$
    $-4\frac{1}{8}$

11. $7\frac{3}{5}$
    $+2\frac{1}{5}$

12. $\frac{7}{12}$
    $-\frac{3}{12}$

13. $\frac{3}{10}$
    $+\frac{3}{10}$

FOCUS | Use NUMBER skills to subtract mixed numbers with like denominators.

APPLICATION

Using Patterns and Functions

Look at the number pattern. $7\frac{6}{8}, 6\frac{5}{8}, 5\frac{4}{8},$ ■, ■, ■

To find the rule and to complete the pattern, think:

$7\frac{6}{8} - 6\frac{5}{8} = 1\frac{1}{8}$ and $6\frac{5}{8} - 5\frac{4}{8} = 1\frac{1}{8}.$

So the rule must be, **Subtract $1\frac{1}{8}$.**

$5\frac{4}{8} - 1\frac{1}{8} = 4\frac{3}{8}$ $4\frac{3}{8} - 1\frac{1}{8} = 3\frac{2}{8}$ $3\frac{2}{8} - 1\frac{1}{8} = 2\frac{1}{8}$

The last three numbers in the pattern must be:

$4\frac{3}{8}, 3\frac{2}{8},$ and $2\frac{1}{8}$

Write the rule for each number pattern.
Then copy and complete the pattern.

14. $\frac{11}{12}, \frac{9}{12}, \frac{7}{12},$ ■, ■, ■

15. $\frac{30}{10}, \frac{25}{10}, \frac{20}{10},$ ■, ■, ■

16. $10\frac{8}{9}, 9\frac{7}{9}, 8\frac{6}{9},$ ■, ■, ■

17. $7\frac{15}{20}, 7\frac{12}{20}, 7\frac{9}{20},$ ■, ■, ■

18. $18\frac{6}{8}, 16\frac{5}{8}, 14\frac{4}{8},$ ■, ■, ■

19. $20\frac{10}{12}, 17\frac{8}{12}, 14\frac{6}{12},$ ■, ■, ■

20. $15\frac{9}{10}, 13\frac{4}{5}, 11\frac{7}{10}, 9\frac{3}{5},$ ■, ■

21. $26\frac{11}{12}, 22\frac{5}{6}, 18\frac{3}{4}, 14\frac{2}{3},$ ■, ■

Solving Problems

Add or subtract to solve each problem.

22. Anna has $6\frac{5}{8}$ feet of lumber. She needs $8\frac{7}{8}$ feet. How much more lumber does she need?

23. Juan has two cats. One weighs $6\frac{3}{4}$ pounds and the other one weighs $10\frac{1}{4}$ pounds. What is the total weight of his two cats?

24. On Saturday, Mike spent $1\frac{7}{8}$ hours building a model plane and $2\frac{3}{8}$ hours playing soccer. How much time did he spend in all on his hobbies?

25. Teresa weighs $72\frac{3}{10}$ pounds. Susan weighs $85\frac{7}{10}$ pounds. Who weighs more? How much more?

Use PATTERNS AND FUNCTIONS to complete number sequences involving subtraction with fractions and mixed numbers.
Use NUMBER skills to solve problems involving addition or subtraction of mixed numbers.

Money

A long time ago, people grew or hunted their own food and made their own clothes, tools, and houses. They traded for other items they needed. They might have traded some seeds for a piece of clothing or a pot for a hoe. This kind of trade is called **barter.** It can be used when only a few different things are being traded.

What would happen if you went into a supermarket and offered the owner a pair of sneakers in exchange for a chicken and six oranges?

The problem with trying to barter today is that there are too many things to trade, and people's needs and wants are different. The store owner might not need a pair of sneakers. Even if he did, he might put a different value on them. For example, he might want the sneakers but think they were worth only a can of tuna fish and two oranges.

Money is useful because everyone agrees on what it is worth, so it can be used to buy anything.

Animal skins, shells, cattle, fish, fishhooks, pots, rings, and salt are some of the many things that have been used as money.

In the 1800s, the Japanese used **tree money.** Metal coins were attached to a metal "trunk." When something was purchased that cost less than the whole tree, coins could be broken off the "branches."

The American colonists in the 1700s used many types of money. One type, the Spanish dollar, was a large metal coin that could be cut into pieces to make change.

Today in the United States, we use coins made of copper, nickel, and zinc and bills made of paper.

CRITICAL THINKING

1. Why do you think cattle were once used as money? Why do you think they are not used in this country today?

2. List some advantages you can see to using money that you could break or cut up to make change. List some disadvantages.

3. Would it make sense to have paper money in denominations of $0.01 and $0.05? Why or why not?

FOCUS | Use NUMBER skills and LOGIC to understand why we need money.

The Japanese coins were broken apart and strung through the holes into units of 100 to 1,000.

The Spanish coin was notched so it could easily be broken to make change.

LOOKING BACK
Reviewing and Testing Chapter 24

In Chapter 24 you formulated problems about brown bears. Look at pages 316 and 317.

1. Write a sentence telling what problems a zoo might have if they had brown bears.

You learned about adding fractions and mixed numbers with like denominators. To review what you learned, study the sample exercises on pages 318 and 320. Then use these skills to find each sum in simplest terms for exercises 2–10.

2. $\dfrac{1}{6}$
$+\dfrac{4}{6}$

3. $\dfrac{2}{10}$
$+\dfrac{6}{10}$

4. $\dfrac{4}{5}$
$+\dfrac{3}{5}$

5. $5\dfrac{1}{3}$
$+3\dfrac{1}{3}$

6. $9\dfrac{1}{12}$
$+4\dfrac{1}{12}$

7. $\dfrac{5}{8} + \dfrac{1}{8}$

8. $\dfrac{4}{6} + \dfrac{5}{6}$

9. $4\dfrac{1}{2} + 5\dfrac{1}{2}$

10. $2\dfrac{5}{6} + 5\dfrac{5}{6}$

You learned about subtracting fractions and mixed numbers with like denominators. To review, look at pages 322 and 324. Find each difference in simplest terms for exercises 11–19.

11. $\dfrac{5}{7}$
$-\dfrac{3}{7}$

12. $\dfrac{7}{8}$
$-\dfrac{5}{8}$

13. $\dfrac{9}{10}$
$-\dfrac{1}{10}$

14. $8\dfrac{4}{5}$
$-5\dfrac{2}{5}$

15. $7\dfrac{3}{8}$
$-1\dfrac{1}{8}$

16. $\dfrac{11}{12} - \dfrac{7}{12}$

17. $\dfrac{7}{10} - \dfrac{3}{10}$

18. $9\dfrac{5}{6} - 2\dfrac{1}{6}$

19. $8\dfrac{9}{10} - 6\dfrac{3}{10}$

You learned about different forms of money and how they were used. To review, look on pages 326 and 327. Then answer the question below.

20. List some things that could be used as money for trading with your friends. Tell why you think they could be used and how you would decide what their individual value is.

| FOCUS | Review and test skills learned and practiced. |

Preparing for New Skills for Chapter 25

In the next chapter, you will focus on

- formulating problems about a frog-jumping contest.
- multiplying 2-digit numbers by 2-digit numbers.
- using measurement: area.
- multiplying 3-digit numbers by 2-digit numbers.
- estimating products.

New multiplication skills will be easier to learn if you brush up on multiplication skills you already know. First, review the basic multiplication facts shown on page 454 of the Data Bank. Then study Models A and B and complete exercises 1–6.

Model A

Multiply the ones.

```
 T | O
2↙
 4 | 7        7
 × | 3       ×3
 ──────      ──
   | 1        21
```

Multiply the tens.

```
 T | O          4
2↙             ×3
 4 | 7          12
 × | 3       →+ 2
 ──────       ──
1 4| 1         14
```

Model B

Multiply the ones.

```
 H | T | O
  2↙
 5 | 4 | 6        6
 × |   | 4       ×4
 ──────────      ──
   |   | 4        24
```

Multiply the tens.

```
 H | T | O          4
 1 | 2↙            ×4
 5 | 4 | 6          16
 × |   | 4       →+ 2
 ──────────       ──
   | 8 | 4          18
```

Multiply the hundreds.

```
 H | T | O          5
 1 | 2 |           ×4
 5 | 4 | 6          20
 × |   | 4       →+ 1
 ──────────       ──
2 1| 8 | 4          21
```

PRACTICE

Multiply. Use Model A.

1.	56 × 3	2.	43 × 5	3.	89 × 2

Multiply. Use Model B.

4.	435 × 3	5.	354 × 6	6.	534 × 4

Review NUMBER skills in preparation for learning a new skill.

Write the letter of the correct answer.

What is the correct decimal for each fraction?

1. $\frac{18}{100}$ A. 0.18   B. 1.8
         C. 18.0   D. 0.01

2. $\frac{38}{100}$ E. 3.8   F. 38.0
         G. 0.38   H. 0.04

3. $\frac{73}{100}$ A. 73.0   B. 7.3
         C. 0.07   D. 0.73

4. $\frac{68}{100}$ E. 0.68   F. 6.8
         G. 68.0   H. 0.06

Which statement is correct?

5. A. 7.85 > 7.81

   B. 6.12 > 6.19

   C. 9.54 < 9.52

   D. 3.76 < 3.75

6. E. 13.87 > 13.89

   F. 15.34 < 15.13

   G. 18.25 > 18.21

   H. 12.06 < 12.03

What is the number?

7. two and fourteen hundredths
   A. 214   B. 2.14
   C. 0.14   D. 0.214

8. four and twenty-four hundredths
   E. 4.24   F. 0.424
   G. 0.24   H. 424

Round to the nearest dollar.

9. $24.35   A. $25.00   B. $25.40
            C. $24.00   D. $24.40

10. $13.75   E. $13.00   F. $14.00
             G. $13.80   H. $13.70

Round to the nearest ten dollars.

11. $47.86   A. $48.00   B. $50.00
             C. $40.00   D. $50.90

12. $32.28   E. $32.00   F. $30.00
             G. $40.00   H. $33.00

Add or subtract.

13. 2.36   A. 37.9   B. 3.79
    +1.43   C. 4.79   D. 379

14. 15.76   E. 778   F. 8.77
    − 7.98   G. 77.8   H. 7.78

FOCUS   Review concepts and skills taught in Chapters 17 through 24.

330

Multiply or divide.

15. $6.45
       × 3

   A. $19.35   **B.** $1.93
   C. $18.35   **D.** $20.35

16. 3,241
       × 3

   E. 8,732   **F.** 9,623
   G. 9,732   **H.** 9,723

17. 3)$6.93

   A. $2.31   **B.** $23.10
   C. $1.31   **D.** $0.231

18. 6)$13.56

   E. $22.60   **F.** $2.26
   G. $3.26   **H.** $2.62

19. 2)8,462

   A. 4,231   **B.** 2,314
   C. 4,321   **D.** 421

20. 3)7,364

   E. 4,254   **F.** 2,454
   G. 2,454 R2   **H.** 3,426

Use the graph to answer the questions.

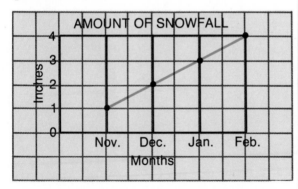

21. How much snow fell in December?

   A. 1 inch   **B.** 2 inches
   C. 3 inches   **D.** 4 inches

22. How much snow fell in November?

   E. 1 inch   **F.** 2 inches
   G. 3 inches   **H.** 4 inches

Use the circle graph to answer the questions.

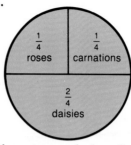

23. What fraction of the flowers are roses?

   A. $\frac{1}{4}$ **B.** $\frac{2}{4}$ **C.** $\frac{3}{4}$ **D.** $\frac{4}{4}$

24. What fraction of the flowers are daisies?

   E. $\frac{1}{4}$ **F.** $\frac{2}{4}$ **G.** $\frac{3}{4}$ **H.** $\frac{4}{4}$

Rename as a mixed number.

25. $\frac{9}{2}$ **A.** $4\frac{1}{2}$ **B.** $3\frac{2}{4}$
        C. $4\frac{2}{4}$ **D.** $4\frac{3}{4}$

26. $\frac{9}{6}$ **E.** $1\frac{2}{3}$ **F.** $2\frac{1}{3}$
        G. $1\frac{1}{2}$ **H.** $1\frac{3}{4}$

27. $\frac{14}{8}$ **A.** $1\frac{2}{4}$ **B.** $1\frac{3}{8}$
        C. $2\frac{3}{4}$ **D.** $1\frac{3}{4}$

Add or subtract.

28. $\frac{3}{4} + \frac{3}{4}$ **E.** $1\frac{1}{2}$ **F.** $1\frac{3}{4}$
              G. $1\frac{1}{4}$ **H.** $2\frac{1}{4}$

29. $\frac{7}{8} - \frac{4}{8}$ **A.** $\frac{3}{8}$ **B.** $\frac{1}{4}$
              C. $\frac{5}{8}$ **D.** $1\frac{3}{8}$

Formulate problems using picture cues, text, and data

CHAPTER 25

Multiplication By a 2-Digit Number

Animals have many ways of moving. Some walk, some trot, some run, and some even hop! A frog hops through the air when it wants to go somewhere.

A frog can travel quite far in just one leap. Some friends who have pet frogs have decided to hold a frog-jumping contest. Each frog begins its jump at a starting line. Each jump is measured carefully. The frog that goes the farthest in a total of 4 jumps is the winner.

Using the data and the picture, think of some problems that the pet owners might have with their frogs during the contest. Predict the outcome of the contest. Give your reasons.

DATA

Event	Frog-jumping contest
Place	Bob's driveway
Scorekeeper	Alison

Frogs	Round	Inches jumped
Nicky	1	5
	2	6
	3	$5\frac{1}{2}$
Inches jumped so far		$16\frac{1}{2}$
Suzy	1	6
	2	$6\frac{1}{2}$
	3	5
Inches jumped so far		$17\frac{1}{2}$
Jasper	1	$5\frac{1}{2}$
	2	6
	3	$6\frac{1}{2}$
Inches jumped so far		18

Multiplying 2-Digit Numbers by 2-Digit Numbers

Carrie collects stickers. She collects 14 bird stickers every week. How many bird stickers does Carrie collect in 12 weeks?

Here is a way to multiply 14 by 12.

Multiply by 2.

T	O
1	4
×1	2
2	8

$$\begin{array}{r} 14 \\ \times 2 \\ \hline 28 \end{array}$$

Multiply by 1 ten.

H	T	O
	1	4
×	1	2
	2	8
1	4	0

$$\begin{array}{r} 14 \\ \times\ 1 \text{ ten} \\ \hline 14 \text{ tens} \\ \text{or } 140 \end{array}$$

Add the products.

H	T	O
	1	4
×	1	2
	2	8
1	4	0
1	6	8

Carrie collects 168 bird stickers in 12 weeks.

Here is a way to multiply 15 by 26. You will need to regroup.

Multiply by 6.

T	O
1	5
×2	6
9	0

$$\begin{array}{r} ^3 \\ 15 \\ \times\ 6 \\ \hline 90 \end{array}$$

Multiply by 2 tens.

H	T	O
	1	5
×	2	6
	9	0
3	0	0

$$\begin{array}{r} ^1 \\ 15 \\ \times\ 2 \text{ tens} \\ \hline 30 \text{ tens} \\ \text{or } 300 \end{array}$$

Add the products.

H	T	O
	1	5
×	2	6
	9	0
3	0	0
3	9	0

GUIDED PRACTICE

Multiply.

1.
$$\begin{array}{r} 22 \\ \times 13 \\ \hline 66 \\ 220 \\ \hline 286 \end{array}$$

2.
$$\begin{array}{r} 54 \\ \times 23 \\ \hline 162 \\ 1\ 080 \\ \hline \blacksquare\ \blacksquare\blacksquare\blacksquare \end{array}$$

3.
$$\begin{array}{r} 67 \\ \times 54 \\ \hline 268 \\ \blacksquare\ \blacksquare\blacksquare\blacksquare \\ \hline \blacksquare\ \blacksquare\blacksquare\blacksquare \end{array}$$

4.
$$\begin{array}{r} 49 \\ \times 32 \\ \hline \blacksquare\blacksquare \\ \blacksquare\ \blacksquare\blacksquare\blacksquare \\ \hline \blacksquare\ \blacksquare\blacksquare\blacksquare \end{array}$$

5.
$$\begin{array}{r} 83 \\ \times 12 \\ \hline \blacksquare\blacksquare\blacksquare \\ \blacksquare\blacksquare\blacksquare \\ \hline \blacksquare\blacksquare\blacksquare \end{array}$$

 FOCUS   Use NUMBER skills to multiply 2-digit numbers by 2-digit numbers.

PRACTICE

Multiply. Regroup when necessary.

6.	27 × 14	7.	32 × 45	8.	29 × 36	9.	41 × 23	10.	18 × 27
11.	62 × 23	12.	48 × 19	13.	50 × 32	14.	76 × 21	15.	84 × 55
16.	77 × 34	17.	91 × 85	18.	63 × 72	19.	88 × 19	20.	52 × 66
21.	94 × 51	22.	38 × 59	23.	15 × 12	24.	92 × 31	25.	73 × 11

26. 83×71 27. 49×39 28. 62×12 29. 19×18

30. 44×63 31. 28×57 32. 71×92 33. 68×23

34. John collects 13 butterfly stickers each week. How many stickers does he collect in 23 weeks?

35. Write a word problem that you could solve by multiplying 24 by 32. Then solve the problem.

MIXED PRACTICE
Maintaining and Reviewing Skills

Add, subtract, multiply, or divide.

36.	42 × 57	37.	75 × 29	38.	725 + 647	39.	49,308 − 4,564	40.	814 × 5

41. $725 \div 8$ 42. 6×406 43. $5,241 + 3,869$ 44. $3,185 \div 6$

CHALLENGE

45. How many minutes are there in one week? Remember, there are 60 minutes in an hour, 24 hours in a day, and 7 days in a week.

MULTIPLICATION
Multiplying 2-Digit Numbers by 2-Digit Numbers

Sometimes you multiply a 2-digit number by a 2-digit number without regrouping. Sometimes you need to regroup.

Without Regrouping

Multiply by 3.	Multiply by 40.	Add the products.
21 ×43 63	21 ×43 63 840	21 ×43 63 840 903

With Regrouping

Multiply by 6.	Multiply by 30.	Add the products.
$\overset{3}{7}5$ ×36 450	$\overset{1}{7}5$ ×36 450 2 250	75 ×36 450 2 250 2,700

PRACTICE

Multiply. Regroup when necessary.

1. 40
×76

2. 86
×87

3. 58
×61

4. 96
×83

5. 97
×92

6. 83
×76

7. 74
×47

8. 38
×84

9. 77
×78

10. 99
×89

11. 52 × 71

12. 18 × 37

13. 94 × 81

14. 74 × 12

15. What is the product of ninety-five multiplied by eighty-four?

16. What is the product of seventy-one multiplied by thirty-eight?

MIXED PRACTICE
Maintaining and Reviewing Skills

Multiply or divide.

17. 13 × 46

18. 59 × 24

19. 6 × 723

20. 3,921 ÷ 7

21. 5 × 2,046

22. 591 ÷ 8

23. 7,042 ÷ 3

24. 7 × 364

25. 8 × 1,974

26. 4,626 ÷ 6

27. 4 × 98

28. 784 ÷ 4

FOCUS | Use NUMBER skills to review multiplying 2-digit numbers by 2-digit numbers.

336

APPLICATION

Using Measurement: Area of a Rectangle

The Grecos put tiles on their kitchen floor. How many square tiles fill the rectangular area?

Use square units to measure the area of a figure.

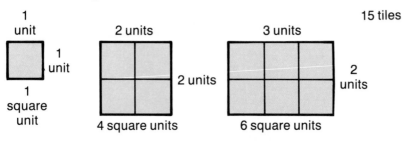

The Grecos could count all the tiles, but a faster way is to multiply. The area of a rectangle equals its length multiplied by its width.

The area of the floor is 180 square units.

Area = Length × Width
    =   15   ×   12
    =   180

Find the areas of these rectangles.

29. 10 units long, 12 units wide

30. 16 units long, 14 units wide

31. 20 units long, 44 units wide

32. 35 units long, 12 units wide

Estimating by Rounding and Mental Arithmetic

A floor is 42 units long and 22 units wide. About how many square units would cover this area?

Remember:	Think:	Round to the nearest ten.	Think:
Area = Length × Width	22 tiles ×42 tiles	20 ×40	2 × 4 = 8 20 × 40 = 800

About 800 square units would cover the floor area.

Estimate the area.

33. 48 × 29   **34.** 37 × 61   **35.** 84 × 38   **36.** 62 × 43

Use MEASUREMENT, ESTIMATION, and MENTAL ARITHMETIC to find areas of rectangles.

Multiplying 3-Digit Numbers by 2-Digit Numbers

Here is a way to multiply 324 by 12.

Multiply by the ones.

Th	H	T	O
	3	2	4
×		1	2
	6	4	8

Multiply by the tens.

Th	H	T	O
	3	2	4
×		1	2
	6	4	8
3	2	4	0

Add.

Th	H	T	O
	3	2	4
×		1	2
	6	4	8
+3	2	4	0
3	8	8	8

$12 \times 324 = 3{,}888$

To multiply 265 by 34, you will need to regroup.

Multiply by the ones.

Th	H	T	O
	2	2	
	2	6	5
×		3	4
1	0	6	0

Multiply by the tens.

Th	H	T	O
	1	1	
	2	6	5
×		3	4
1	0	6	0
7	9	5	0

Add.

Th	H	T	O
	2	6	5
×		3	4
1	0	6	0
+7	9	5	0
9	0	1	0

$34 \times 265 = 9{,}010$

GUIDED PRACTICE

Multiply.

1.
```
    413
  ×  21
    413
 +8 260
  8,673
```

2.
```
    729
  ×  42
  1 458
 +29 160
  ██,███
```

3.
```
    368
  ×  34
  1 472
 +██ ███
  ██,███
```

4.
```
    521
  ×  18
   █ ███
  +█ ███
  █,███
```

5.
```
    820
  ×  43
   █ ███
 +██ ███
  ██,███
```

6.
```
  257
×  32
```

7.
```
  203
×  44
```

8.
```
  428
×  17
```

9.
```
  600
×  23
```

10.
```
  341
×  26
```

11. 34×129

12. 53×207

13. 61×351

14. 42×500

FOCUS   Use NUMBER skills to multiply 3-digit numbers by 2-digit numbers.

PRACTICE

Multiply.

15.	256 × 30	16.	127 × 13	17.	500 × 19	18.	725 × 46	19.	117 × 21
20.	234 × 62	21.	407 × 55	22.	670 × 78	23.	220 × 40	24.	398 × 16
25.	806 × 99	26.	711 × 80	27.	954 × 96	28.	100 × 50	29.	883 × 32
30.	224 × 15	31.	173 × 40	32.	306 × 23	33.	116 × 82	34.	320 × 36

35. 28 × 400   36. 47 × 504   37. 92 × 135   38. 68 × 706

39. 84 × 653   40. 33 × 162   41. 41 × 250   42. 73 × 109

43. Greg delivered 225 cartons to a supermarket's warehouse. Each carton had 24 containers of yogurt. How many containers were delivered in all?

44. A truck was carrying 173 boxes. Each box weighed 28 pounds. What was the total weight of the boxes on the truck?

MIXED PRACTICE
Maintaining and Reviewing Skills

Add, subtract, multiply, or divide.

45.	472 × 35	46.	7,364 + 958	47.	45,381 − 29,645	48.	6,305 × 7	49.	39,462 + 45,079

50. 3,736 ÷ 5   51. 56 × 48   52. 789 + 5,086   53. 9 × 384

CHALLENGE

54. Sylvia delivered 157 dozen eggs. Four dozen eggs were broken. How many eggs were not broken?

MULTIPLICATION
Estimating Products

Sometimes you multiply a 3-digit number by a 2-digit number without regrouping. Sometimes you may need to regroup.

Without regrouping

```
    431
  ×  32
─────────
    862
+12 930
─────────
 13,792
```

With regrouping

```
    795
  ×  47
─────────
  5 565
+31 800
─────────
 37,365
```

Estimating can help you find out if an answer is **reasonable.** Here is one way to estimate.

Write.		Estimate.	Find the exact product.

```
 431    Round to the nearest 100 ⟶    400         431
× 35    Round to the nearest 10  ⟶   × 40        × 38
                                    ──────       ──────
                                    16,000       3 448
                                                +12 930
                                                ──────
                                                16,378
```

The product is close to 16,000.
The answer is reasonable.

PRACTICE

Estimate. Then find the exact product.

1. 919   2. 505   3. 101   4. 650   5. 225
   × 32   × 66   × 23   × 72   × 88

6. 19 × 939   7. 49 × 462   8. 72 × 307   9. 22 × 199   10. 59 × 751

MIXED PRACTICE
Maintaining and Reviewing Skills

Estimate. Then find the exact answer.

11.   627   12.   76   13.   438   14. 3,716   15.   375
     × 32   ×28   +381   −1,146   × 6

APPLICATION

Using Measurement: Area of a Rectangle

The square inch is a customary unit of area.

The square foot and the square yard are other customary units of area.

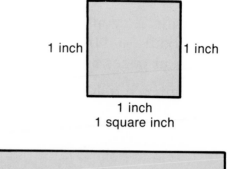

1 square inch

You can multiply the length and the width to find the area of this rectangle.

Area = length × width
   5   ×   2   = 10

Area: 10 square feet

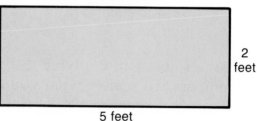

Find the area of each rectangle.

16. length: 7 yards
   width: 4 yards

17. length: 24 inches
   width: 12 inches

18. length: 328 inches
   width: 79 inches

19. length: 38 feet
   width: 29 feet

Exploring With a Calculator

Alex and Joanne want to carpet their home. The length and width of each room are given in the table below. Use your calculator to find the number of square yards of carpeting they need for each room. Then find the cost of carpeting each room.

	20. Living room	21. Bedroom 1	22. Bedroom 2	23. Family room
Length	8 yards	6 yards	4 yards	21 feet
Width	5 yards	4 yards	3 yards	18 feet
Cost per square yard	$21	$13	$12	$18

Use MEASUREMENT to find the area of a rectangle.

LOOKING BACK
Reviewing and Testing Chapter 25

In Chapter 25 you formulated problems about a frog-jumping contest. Look at pages 332 and 333.

1. Write a sentence telling how you predicted the outcome of the contest.

You learned about multiplying 2-digit numbers by 2-digit numbers. To review what you learned, study the sample exercises on page 334. Then use this skill to find each product for exercises 2 to 10.

2. 23 $\times$ 12	3. 48 $\times$ 21	4. 18 $\times$ 19	5. 77 $\times$ 34	6. 92 $\times$ 31

7. 12 $\times$ 62   8. 39 $\times$ 42   9. 28 $\times$ 57   10. 94 $\times$ 51

You learned about estimating products. To review, look at page 337. Estimate each product for exercises 11 to 18.

11. 13 $\times$ 32   12. 37 $\times$ 24   13. 65 $\times$ 31   14. 43 $\times$ 59

15. 47 $\times$ 29   16. 81 $\times$ 36   17. 45 $\times$ 65   18. 71 $\times$ 75

You learned about multiplying 3-digit numbers by 2-digit numbers. You also learned more about estimating. To review, look at pages 338 and 340. Estimate each product for exercises 19 to 27. Then find each exact product.

19. 126 $\times$ 12	20. 118 $\times$ 21	21. 179 $\times$ 34	22. 807 $\times$ 85	23. 535 $\times$ 45

24. 65 $\times$ 109   25. 36 $\times$ 240   26. 28 $\times$ 675   27. 73 $\times$ 785

FOCUS	Review and test skills learned and practiced.

LOOKING AHEAD

Preparing for New Skills for Chapter 26

In the next chapter, you will focus on

- formulating problems about a tourmobile.
- dividing 2-digit numbers by 10 or multiples of 10.
- using algebra.
- dividing 2-digit numbers by 2-digit numbers.
- using measurement.
- how math is used in technology.

New division skills will be easier to learn if you brush up on division skills you already know. First, review the basic division facts shown on page 454 of the Data Bank. Then study Model A and complete exercises 1–12.

Model A

Estimate the tens digit.

$4\overline{)53}$

$4\overline{)5}$ is about 1.
Use 1 as the tens digit.

Multiply and subtract.

T	O
	1	
4$\overline{)}$	5	3
	−4	
	1	

Bring down the ones. Estimate the ones digit.

T	O
	1	3
4$\overline{)}$	5	3
	−4	↓
	1	3

$4\overline{)13}$ is about 3.
Use 3 as the ones digit.

Multiply and subtract. Write the remainder.

T	O
	1	3 R1
4$\overline{)}$	5	3
	−4	↓
	1	3
	−1	2
		1

PRACTICE

Divide.

1. $4\overline{)57}$ 2. $6\overline{)95}$ 3. $3\overline{)76}$ 4. $6\overline{)77}$ 5. $5\overline{)74}$ 6. $8\overline{)91}$

7. $3\overline{)84}$ 8. $6\overline{)78}$ 9. $7\overline{)89}$ 10. $4\overline{)76}$ 11. $8\overline{)97}$ 12. $5\overline{)89}$

Review NUMBER skills in preparation for learning a new skill.

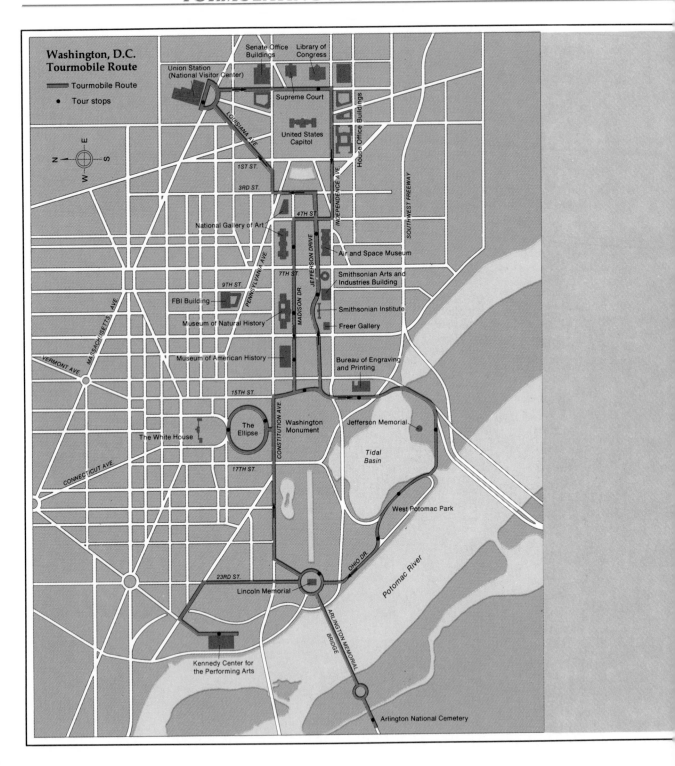

Washington, D.C. Tourmobile Route

▬▬ Tourmobile Route

● Tour stops

Senate Office Buildings

Library of Congress

Union Station (National Visitor Center)

Supreme Court

LOUISIANA AVE.

United States Capitol

House Office Buildings

1ST ST.

3RD ST.

INDEPENDENCE AVE.

SOUTHWEST FREEWAY

4TH ST.

National Gallery of Art

JEFFERSON DRIVE

Air and Space Museum

PENNSYLVANIA AVE.

7TH ST.

Smithsonian Arts and Industries Building

9TH ST.

MADISON DR.

FBI Building

Smithsonian Institute

Museum of Natural History

Freer Gallery

MASSACHUSETTS AVE.

VERMONT AVE.

Museum of American History

Bureau of Engraving and Printing

15TH ST.

CONSTITUTION AVE.

The Ellipse

The White House

Washington Monument

Jefferson Memorial

CONNECTICUT AVE.

Tidal Basin

17TH ST.

West Potomac Park

OHIO DR.

Potomac River

23RD ST.

Lincoln Memorial

ARLINGTON MEMORIAL BRIDGE

Kennedy Center for the Performing Arts

Arlington National Cemetery

26

Division by a 2-Digit Number

DATA

Daily except Christmas

$1\frac{1}{2}$ hours minimum

Board at any of 17 sites

Operates continuously

Adults	$6.50
Children (3–11)	$3.25

Purchase tickets from driver or Tourmobile booths located near tour sites.

Hours

9:00–6:30	June 15– Labor Day
9:30–4:30	Remainder of year

Taking a Tourmobile can be a wonderful way to spend a vacation day. The Tourmobile travels to the most important buildings and monuments in Washington, D.C.

Look at the data and the map at the left. The map shows the route and the stopping places for each site. The data tells you the hours, the cost, where to purchase tickets, and how many places are visited by the Tourmobile.

Which sites on the Tourmobile route might you want to see? Why? Which sites might not interest you? Why? How might you shorten the amount of time you spend on the Tourmobile?

DIVISION
Dividing 2-Digit Numbers by 10 or Multiples of 10

David has a new case for storing cassette tapes. Each row in the case holds 10 tapes. David has 37 tapes. How many rows in the case will be filled? How many tapes will go in the next row? Divide 37 by 10.

Estimate the tens.

$$10\overline{)37}$$

Since 10 > 3, there is no tens digit.

Estimate the ones.

	T	O
		3
10)	3	7

$10\overline{)37}$ is about 3. Use 3 as the ones digit.

Multiply and subtract. Write the remainder.

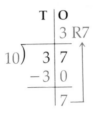

There are 3 rows filled with tapes; 7 tapes are in the next row.

Here is a way to divide 90 by 30.

Estimate the tens.

$$30\overline{)90}$$

Since 30 > 9, there is no tens digit.

Estimate the ones.

	T	O
		3
30)	9	0

$30\overline{)90}$ is 3. Use 3 as the ones digit.

Multiply and subtract.

	T	O
		3
30)	9	0
	−9	0
		0

GUIDED PRACTICE

Divide.

1. $\begin{array}{r} 8 \\ 10\overline{)80} \\ -80 \\ \hline 0 \end{array}$

2. $\begin{array}{r} 2\,R5 \\ 30\overline{)65} \\ -\blacksquare\blacksquare \\ \hline 5 \end{array}$

3. $\begin{array}{r} 1\,R\blacksquare\blacksquare \\ 70\overline{)98} \\ -\blacksquare\blacksquare \\ \hline 28 \end{array}$

4. $\begin{array}{r} \blacksquare\,R7 \\ 80\overline{)87} \\ -80 \\ \hline \blacksquare \end{array}$

5. $\begin{array}{r} \blacksquare \\ 20\overline{)60} \\ -60 \\ \hline \blacksquare \end{array}$

6. $\begin{array}{r} \blacksquare\,R\blacksquare\blacksquare \\ 30\overline{)75} \\ -60 \\ \hline \blacksquare\blacksquare \end{array}$

7. $\begin{array}{r} \blacksquare\,R\blacksquare\blacksquare \\ 50\overline{)96} \\ -50 \\ \hline \blacksquare\blacksquare \end{array}$

8. $\begin{array}{r} \blacksquare \\ 40\overline{)80} \\ -\blacksquare\blacksquare \\ \hline \blacksquare \end{array}$

9. $\begin{array}{r} \blacksquare\,R\blacksquare\blacksquare \\ 60\overline{)73} \\ -\blacksquare\blacksquare \\ \hline \blacksquare\blacksquare \end{array}$

10. $\begin{array}{r} \blacksquare\,R\blacksquare \\ 90\overline{)99} \\ -\blacksquare\blacksquare \\ \hline \blacksquare \end{array}$

FOCUS | Use NUMBER skills to divide 2-digit numbers by 10 or multiples of 10.

PRACTICE

Divide.

11. $10\overline{)89}$ **12.** $60\overline{)92}$ **13.** $30\overline{)60}$ **14.** $20\overline{)79}$ **15.** $50\overline{)83}$

16. $70\overline{)81}$ **17.** $40\overline{)95}$ **18.** $20\overline{)86}$ **19.** $90\overline{)92}$ **20.** $10\overline{)70}$

21. $30\overline{)94}$ **22.** $50\overline{)68}$ **23.** $10\overline{)90}$ **24.** $80\overline{)92}$ **25.** $40\overline{)90}$

26. $76 \div 10$ **27.** $75 \div 60$ **28.** $93 \div 70$ **29.** $98 \div 90$ **30.** $84 \div 30$

31. $93 \div 20$ **32.** $82 \div 10$ **33.** $61 \div 30$ **34.** $75 \div 10$ **35.** $68 \div 40$

36. A carton holds 20 record albums. How many cartons are needed to pack 80 records?

37. An album case holds 10 records. How many cases are needed for 90 records?

MIXED PRACTICE

Maintaining and Reviewing Skills

Multiply or divide.

38. $73 \div 60$ **39.** $59 \div 20$ **40.** 34×18 **41.** $786 \div 4$

42. 7×358 **43.** $458 \div 6$ **44.** $86 \div 4$ **45.** 26×306

46. $826 \div 7$ **47.** $308 \div 8$ **48.** 4×860 **49.** 72×147

50. 64×32 **51.** $97 \div 3$ **52.** $659 \div 5$ **53.** 70×48

54. $316 \div 4$ **55.** 35×461 **56.** 52×39 **57.** $716 \div 8$

CHALLENGE

58. Name a 2-digit number divisible by both 20 and 30.

59. Name two 2-digit numbers divisible by both 20 and 40.

60. Name three 2-digit numbers divisible by both 10 and 30.

DIVISION
Dividing 2-Digit Numbers by 10 or Multiples of 10

When you are dividing a 2-digit number by 10 or multiples of 10, the quotient is in the ones place. Use division facts to help you.

Look at the examples.

$$
\begin{array}{r} 4 \\ 2\overline{)8} \\ -8 \\ \hline 0 \end{array}
\qquad
\begin{array}{r} 4 \\ 20\overline{)80} \\ -80 \\ \hline 0 \end{array}
\qquad
\begin{array}{r} 2\,R1 \\ 3\overline{)7} \\ -6 \\ \hline 1 \end{array}
\qquad
\begin{array}{r} 2\,R10 \\ 30\overline{)70} \\ -60 \\ \hline 10 \end{array}
$$

$$
\begin{array}{r} 5 \\ 1\overline{)5} \\ -5 \\ \hline 0 \end{array}
\qquad
\begin{array}{r} 5 \\ 10\overline{)50} \\ -50 \\ \hline 0 \end{array}
\qquad
\begin{array}{r} 3 \\ 2\overline{)6} \\ -6 \\ \hline 0 \end{array}
\qquad
\begin{array}{r} 3\,R5 \\ 20\overline{)65} \\ -60 \\ \hline 5 \end{array}
$$

PRACTICE

Divide.

1. $10\overline{)62}$
2. $40\overline{)87}$
3. $60\overline{)82}$
4. $20\overline{)98}$
5. $50\overline{)64}$

6. $70\overline{)88}$
7. $30\overline{)76}$
8. $10\overline{)80}$
9. $80\overline{)89}$
10. $20\overline{)79}$

11. $40\overline{)90}$
12. $50\overline{)80}$
13. $30\overline{)60}$
14. $70\overline{)94}$
15. $60\overline{)81}$

16. $80 \div 20$
17. $94 \div 30$
18. $52 \div 40$
19. $70 \div 10$
20. $92 \div 50$

MIXED PRACTICE
Maintaining and Reviewing Skills

Add, subtract, multiply, or divide.

21. $75 \div 20$
22. $96 \div 40$
23. $3,964 + 2,858$
24. 72×38

25. $49,702 - 21,864$
26. 65×251
27. $7,941 - 869$
28. $48,014 + 36,796$

29. $465 \div 7$
30. 3×921
31. 42×65
32. $52,901 - 36,729$

33. 73×48
34. $639 \div 4$
35. $7,281 + 64,396$
36. 34×265

FOCUS | Use NUMBER skills to divide 2-digit numbers by 10 or multiples of 10.

APPLICATION
Using Algebra

There are 80 people seated in a restaurant at 20 tables. Each table has the same number of people. How many people are at each table?

You can write a number sentence for this problem.

$$80 \div 20 = n$$

To solve for n, divide 80 by 20.

$$80 \div 20 = 4 \qquad n = 4$$

There are 4 people at each table.

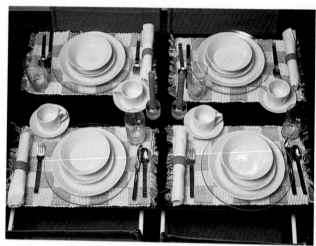

Write and solve a number sentence for each problem.

37. There are 60 plates packed in 10 boxes. How many plates are in each box?

38. There are 50 dinner napkins in bundles of 10 napkins each. How many bundles of napkins are there?

Using Front-End Estimation: Estimating Quotients

To estimate $6\overline{)3,275}$, first find how many digits are in the quotient. Then find the first digit.

$\overset{?\ \blacksquare\blacksquare\blacksquare}{6\overline{)3,275}}$

Since $6 > 3$, the first digit is not in the thousands place.

$\overset{?\blacksquare\blacksquare}{6\overline{)3,275}}$

$6\overline{)32}$ is about 5. The quotient has three digits. The first one is 5.

$\overset{5\blacksquare\blacksquare}{6\overline{)3,275}}$

The quotient is more than 500. It is less than 600. So the estimate is *between 500 and 600.*

Choose the better estimate.

39. $7\overline{)256}$ a. between 300 and 400   b. between 30 and 40

40. $5\overline{)8,149}$ a. between 1,000 and 2,000   b. between 100 and 200

Use ALGEBRA to write and solve number sentences.
Use NUMBER skills to estimate quotients.

Dividing 2-Digit Numbers by 2-Digit Numbers

Lauren has 48 pictures of her classmates that were taken during a class trip. There are 24 students in the class. What is the average number of pictures taken of each student? Divide 48 by 24.

Estimate the tens digit.

```
   T|O
   ─┼──
24)4|8
```

Estimate the ones digit.

```
20  T|O
↑   ─┼──
24) 4|8
```

Multiply and subtract.

```
       T|O
        | 2
        ─┼──
   24)  4|8
      − 4|8
        |─
        |0
```

Since 24 is greater than 4, there is no tens digit.

Round 24 to 20. $2\overline{)4}$ is 2. Try 2 as the ones digit.

2 is the correct ones digit.

The average is 2 pictures of each student.

Divide 92 by 18.

Estimate the tens digit.

```
   T|O
   ─┼──
18)9|2
```

Estimate the ones digit.

```
20  T|O
↑   ─┼──
18) 9|2
```

Multiply and subtract.

```
       T|O
        | 4
        ─┼──
   18)  9|2
      − 7|2
        |──
        2|0
```

Multiply and subtract. Write the remainder.

```
       T|O
        | 5 R2
        ─┼──
   18)  9|2
      − 9|0
        |──
        |2
```

Since 18 is greater than 9, there is no tens digit.

Round 18 to 20. $2\overline{)9}$ is about 4. Try 4 as the ones digit.

20 is greater than 18. 4 is not enough for the ones digit. Try 5.

2 is less than 18. 5 is the correct ones digit.

GUIDED PRACTICE

```
      2 R7            5          4 R▮        ▮R▮▮        ▮R▮▮
1. 37)81       2. 17)85     3. 22)89    4. 27)94    5. 46)62
  −74             −85          −▮▮         −▮▮         −▮▮
    7              ▮            1           13          ▮▮
```

FOCUS Use NUMBER skills to divide 2-digit numbers by 2-digit numbers.

PRACTICE

Divide.

6. $17\overline{)84}$ 7. $27\overline{)53}$ 8. $12\overline{)78}$ 9. $19\overline{)88}$ 10. $34\overline{)81}$

11. $14\overline{)86}$ 12. $22\overline{)91}$ 13. $15\overline{)45}$ 14. $47\overline{)83}$ 15. $29\overline{)98}$

16. $19\overline{)95}$ 17. $43\overline{)90}$ 18. $12\overline{)90}$ 19. $18\overline{)80}$ 20. $11\overline{)97}$

21. $42\overline{)78}$ 22. $16\overline{)60}$ 23. $31\overline{)81}$ 24. $14\overline{)84}$ 25. $46\overline{)94}$

26. $13\overline{)57}$ 27. $23\overline{)92}$ 28. $26\overline{)87}$ 29. $19\overline{)47}$ 30. $21\overline{)62}$

31. $34\overline{)77}$ 32. $23\overline{)84}$ 33. $17\overline{)69}$ 34. $42\overline{)58}$ 35. $27\overline{)96}$

36. During the class trip, 18 students collected a total of 90 leaves for a science project. What is the average number of leaves collected by each child?

37. Ms. Kime brought a bag of 50 apples for the students. There are 24 students. How many apples can each student have if they are evenly divided? How many apples are left?

MIXED PRACTICE
Maintaining and Reviewing Skills

Multiply or divide.

38. $56 \div 13$ 39. $92 \div 31$ 40. 67×34 41. $729 \div 4$

42. 6×487 43. $3,804 \div 9$ 44. $7 \times 4,123$ 45. 34×239

46. $78 \div 20$ 47. $806 \div 5$ 48. 40×760 49. $7,216 \div 4$

50. 36×400 51. 98×30 52. $4 \times 8,010$ 53. 71×587

CHALLENGE

Complete the number sentences.

54. $18 + \blacksquare\blacksquare = 32 \rightarrow 32 \times \blacksquare = 96 \rightarrow 96 \div \blacksquare\blacksquare = 8$

55. $9 + \blacksquare\blacksquare = 24 \rightarrow 24 \times \blacksquare = 96 \rightarrow 96 \div \blacksquare\blacksquare = 2$

DIVISION
Checking Division With Multiplication

Use multiplication to check a division example. Multiply the quotient and the divisor. The product will equal the dividend.

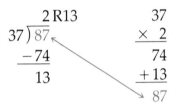

$$
\begin{array}{r} 4 \\ 23\overline{)92} \\ -92 \\ \hline 0 \end{array}
\qquad
\begin{array}{r} 23 \\ \times\ 4 \\ \hline 92 \end{array}
$$

When there is a remainder, follow the same steps, then add the remainder to the product. The sum will equal the dividend.

$$
\begin{array}{r} 2\,\text{R}13 \\ 37\overline{)87} \\ -74 \\ \hline 13 \end{array}
\qquad
\begin{array}{r} 37 \\ \times\ 2 \\ \hline 74 \\ +13 \\ \hline 87 \end{array}
$$

PRACTICE

Divide and check.

1. $27\overline{)93}$ 2. $14\overline{)48}$ 3. $20\overline{)97}$ 4. $18\overline{)90}$ 5. $37\overline{)79}$

6. $46\overline{)98}$ 7. $17\overline{)92}$ 8. $21\overline{)82}$ 9. $12\overline{)50}$ 10. $19\overline{)95}$

11. $31\overline{)58}$ 12. $28\overline{)84}$ 13. $16\overline{)76}$ 14. $28\overline{)98}$ 15. $13\overline{)89}$

MIXED PRACTICE
Maintaining and Reviewing Skills

Multiply or divide.

16. $84 \div 16$ 17. $57 \div 23$ 18. 24×38 19. $69 \div 20$

20. 18×329 21. $438 \div 7$ 22. $4 \times 2,906$ 23. $7,401 \div 4$

24. 35×171 25. $96 \div 40$ 26. $670 \div 5$ 27. 42×396

FOCUS | Use NUMBER skills to divide 2-digit numbers by 2-digit numbers.

352

APPLICATION
Using Measurement

Remember that the formula for finding the area of a rectangle is $A = l \times w$.

You can use this formula to find the width when the area and length are given.

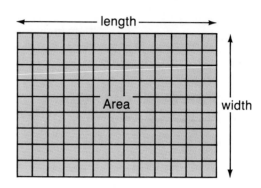

Area ÷ length = width
$A \div l = w$

Use the formula to find the width of a rectangle when the area is 48 square inches and the length is 12 inches.

$$A \div l = w$$
$$48 \div 12 = 4$$

The width of the rectangle is 4 inches.

Use the formula to find the width of the rectangle.

28. A = 81 square in.
l = 27 in.

29. A = 65 square yd
l = 13 yd

30. A = 92 square ft
l = 23 ft

Solving Problems

31. Steve wants to carpet his living room. It is 12 feet long and has an area of 96 square feet. How wide is the living room?

32. Susan wants to tile the kitchen floor. It is 13 feet long and has an area of 91 square feet. What is the width of the kitchen?

33. A roll of wallpaper is 90 feet long. Jerome wants to cut it into strips of 14 feet. How many strips of wallpaper can he get from the roll? How many feet will be left over?

34. The length of a piece of lumber is 88 inches long. Carlos cuts the lumber into 12-inch lengths. How many pieces will he get? How much of the lumber is left?

Use MEASUREMENT and NUMBER skills to find width when the area and length are given and to solve problems.

Computer Graphics

PIXELS ARE SQUARES OF LIGHT

Letters and numbers on a computer screen are made up of tiny squares of light. Each square of light is called a **pixel.**

Pixels on a computer screen can be lit up in different patterns. Pictures can be drawn on a screen by lighting up different patterns of pixels. Pictures drawn with a computer are called **computer graphics.**

A program is a list of instructions a computer follows to do a task. To draw a picture, a computer follows a program that tells it where on the screen to light up pixels. Many computer game programs contain programs for computer graphics. These graphics programs control the way the computer draws the pictures that are part of the game.

A graphics program uses **ordered pairs** of numbers to locate the pixels that are going to be lit up. For example, (2, 1) is an ordered pair. This ordered pair tells the computer to light up the pixel that is 2 spaces to the right and one space up on the computer screen.

This is a computer graphics picture of a man wearing a hat. Each of the squares is a pixel. Each of the pixels can be found by using an ordered pair.

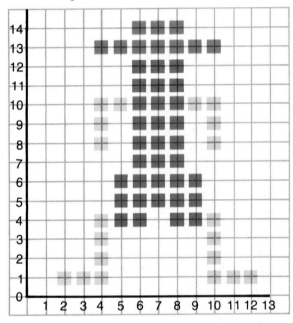

CRITICAL THINKING

1. What are the ordered pairs for the man's feet? For the man's arms?

2. What would the ordered pairs for the man's arms be if they were raised above his head?

FOCUS | Use LOGIC and GEOMETRY to understand computer graphics.

354

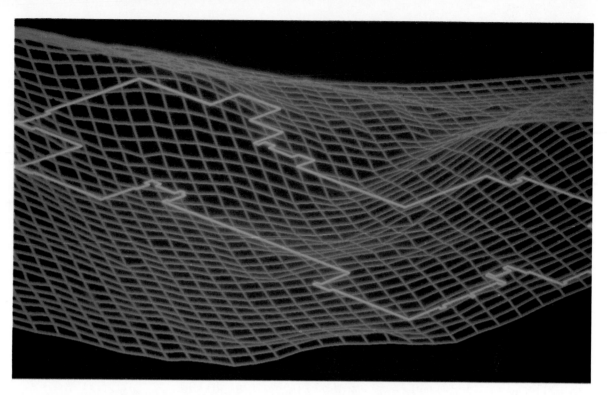

Computer graphics have unique beauty as these architect's plans show.
The plans can be changed on the computer until the architect is satisfied.

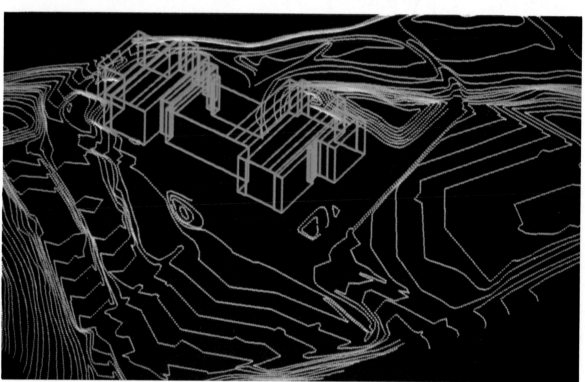

Reviewing and Testing Chapter 26

In Chapter 26 you formulated problems about taking a Tourmobile in Washington, D.C. Look at pages 344 and 345.

1. Write a sentence telling how you would spend $1\frac{1}{2}$ hours on the Tourmobile.

You learned about dividing 2-digit numbers by multiples of 10. To review what you learned, study the sample exercises on pages 346 and 348. Then use this skill to divide for exercises 2–10.

2. $10\overline{)63}$ 3. $20\overline{)60}$ 4. $60\overline{)71}$ 5. $40\overline{)90}$ 6. $50\overline{)98}$

7. $87 \div 10$ 8. $90 \div 30$ 9. $72 \div 20$ 10. $83 \div 40$

You learned about dividing 2-digit numbers by 2-digit numbers. You also learned how to use multiplication to check division. To review, look at pages 350 and 352. Divide and check for exercises 11–19.

11. $32\overline{)98}$ 12. $23\overline{)70}$ 13. $28\overline{)59}$ 14. $18\overline{)90}$ 15. $21\overline{)82}$

16. $84 \div 17$ 17. $98 \div 29$ 18. $58 \div 32$ 19. $78 \div 46$

You learned about computer graphics and how computers are programmed to draw pictures. To review, look at pages 354 and 355. Use the computer graphics picture on page 354 to answer the questions below.

20. What are the ordered pairs for the man's hat?

21. What would be the ordered pairs for the man's head if he didn't have a hat?

FOCUS | Review and test skills learned and practiced.

LOOKING AHEAD
Preparing for New Skills for Chapter 27

In the next chapter, you will focus on

- formulating problems about games.
- dividing 3-digit numbers by 10 or multiples of 10.
- using measurement.
- using a problem-solving strategy.
- dividing 3-digit numbers by 2-digit numbers.

New division skills will be easier to learn if you brush up on the division skills you already know.

First, study Model A. Then, complete exercises 1–18.

Model A

Estimate the tens digit.

$$13\overline{)6\,|\,7}$$

Since 13 is greater than 6, there is no tens digit.

Estimate the ones digit.

$$13\overline{)6\,|\,7}$$

Round 13 to 10. $1\overline{)6}$ is 6. Try 6 as the ones digit.

Multiply and subtract.

$$13\overline{)6\,|\,7} \quad -7\,|\,8$$

6 is too much for the ones digit. Try 5.

Multiply and subtract. Write the remainder.

$$13\overline{)6\,|\,7} \quad -6\,|\,5 \quad |\,2 \qquad 5\,R2$$

5 is the correct ones digit. Since 13 is greater than 2, the remainder is 2.

PRACTICE

Divide.

1. $34\overline{)68}$ 2. $12\overline{)72}$ 3. $42\overline{)84}$ 4. $24\overline{)96}$ 5. $17\overline{)85}$ 6. $31\overline{)93}$

7. $23\overline{)49}$ 8. $32\overline{)97}$ 9. $41\overline{)85}$ 10. $13\overline{)82}$ 11. $26\overline{)88}$ 12. $34\overline{)77}$

13. $42\overline{)75}$ 14. $14\overline{)83}$ 15. $32\overline{)69}$ 16. $27\overline{)91}$ 17. $16\overline{)54}$ 18. $23\overline{)78}$

Review NUMBER skills in preparation for learning a new skill.

FOCUS | Formulate problems using picture cues, text, and data.

CHAPTER

27

Division by a 2-Digit Number

DATA

Number of steps	8

Best times for single dribbles (one dribble per step)

Going up	10 seconds
Going down	6 seconds
Going up and down	18 seconds

Best times for double dribbles (two dribbles per step)

Going up	16 seconds
Going down	10 seconds
Going up and down	28 seconds

"One, two, nothing to do . . . three, four, it's no fun anymore."

Everyone but Jake was away. What could he do with no one around? Ride his bike? Play ball? They weren't much fun to do by himself.

Jake dribbled the ball. "One, two . . ." He dribbled up the steps of his house and then down. Then up a bit faster and down again. Then he tried dribbling twice on each step. "One, two, three, four . . . how many bounces can I score?"

Inventing games when you're all alone isn't easy. Jake is beginning to come up with some good games of his own. All it took was a basketball and a set of stairs!

What other kinds of games do you think Jake has made up? How do you think they are played? What problems did he have to solve? How do you think he might "win" these games?

DIVISION
Dividing 3-Digit Numbers by 10 or Multiples of 10

A bookstore will give 400 stickers to the fourth graders at Madison School for winning first place in the Book Fair. The stickers will be evenly divided among 20 students. How many stickers will each student get?

Could each student get 100 stickers?

$$\frac{?}{20)\,400} \qquad 100 \times 20 = 2,000$$

No; there will be no hundreds digit.

Could each student get at least 10 stickers?

$$\frac{?}{20)\,400} \qquad 10 \times 20 = 200$$

Yes; the first digit will be in the tens place.

Estimate the tens digit.	Multiply and subtract.	Estimate the ones digit.	Multiply and subtract.
$20)\,\overline{400}$ $2)\,\overline{4}$ is 2. Use 2 as the tens digit.	H T O: 2; $20)\,4\,0\,0$; $-4\,0$; 0	H T O: 2; $20)\,4\,0\,0$; $-4\,0\downarrow$; $0\,0$ $2)\,\overline{0}$ is 0. Use 0 as the ones digit.	H T O: 2 0; $20)\,4\,0\,0$; $-4\,0\downarrow$; $0\,0$; $-$; 0; 0

Each student will receive 20 stickers.

You can use what you know to divide 841 by 70.

Estimate the tens digit.	Multiply and subtract.	Estimate the ones digit.	Multiply and subtract. Write the remainder.
$70)\,\overline{841}$ $7)\,\overline{8}$ is about 1. Try 1 as the tens digit.	H T O: 1; $70)\,8\,4\,1$; $-7\,0$; $1\,4$	H T O: 1; $70)\,8\,4\,1$; $-7\,0\downarrow$; $1\,4\,1$ $7)\,\overline{14}$ is 2. Use 2 as the ones digit.	H T O: 1 2 R1; $70)\,8\,4\,1$; $-7\,0\downarrow$; $1\,4\,1$; $-1\,4\,0$; 1

| FOCUS | Use NUMBER skills to divide 3-digit numbers by 10 or multiples of 10. |

360

GUIDED PRACTICE

Divide.

1. $\begin{array}{r} 5\,R10 \\ 50\overline{\smash{)}260} \\ -250 \\ \hline 10 \end{array}$

2. $\begin{array}{r} \blacksquare\,R\blacksquare\blacksquare \\ 40\overline{\smash{)}300} \\ -280 \\ \hline 20 \end{array}$

3. $\begin{array}{r} 1\blacksquare \\ 20\overline{\smash{)}360} \\ -20 \\ \hline 160 \\ -\blacksquare\blacksquare0 \\ \hline 0 \end{array}$

4. $\begin{array}{r} 2\blacksquare\,R\blacksquare \\ 30\overline{\smash{)}755} \\ -\blacksquare\blacksquare \\ \hline 155 \\ -\blacksquare\blacksquare\blacksquare \\ \hline \blacksquare \end{array}$

5. $\begin{array}{r} \blacksquare\,R\blacksquare\blacksquare \\ 60\overline{\smash{)}340} \\ -\blacksquare\blacksquare\blacksquare \\ \hline \blacksquare\blacksquare \end{array}$

PRACTICE

Divide.

6. $30\overline{\smash{)}150}$ 7. $10\overline{\smash{)}140}$ 8. $40\overline{\smash{)}250}$ 9. $90\overline{\smash{)}722}$ 10. $20\overline{\smash{)}420}$

11. $40\overline{\smash{)}170}$ 12. $80\overline{\smash{)}645}$ 13. $30\overline{\smash{)}180}$ 14. $50\overline{\smash{)}500}$ 15. $60\overline{\smash{)}750}$

16. $10\overline{\smash{)}155}$ 17. $90\overline{\smash{)}546}$ 18. $60\overline{\smash{)}362}$ 19. $50\overline{\smash{)}490}$ 20. $40\overline{\smash{)}600}$

21. $287 \div 30$ 22. $805 \div 40$ 23. $332 \div 10$ 24. $245 \div 80$

25. A shipment of 650 books is delivered to the school. Each carton holds 50 books. How many cartons are delivered?

26. A school has 10 boxes of paper. Each one holds 12 packs of paper. All of the paper will be divided evenly among 10 classes. How many packs will each class get?

MIXED PRACTICE
Maintaining and Reviewing Skills

Add, subtract, multiply, or divide.

27. $960 \div 30$ 28. $458 \div 10$ 29. 42×63 30. $42{,}301 + 27{,}829$

31. $6{,}428 - 2{,}597$ 32. $729 \div 6$ 33. 38×264 34. $91 \div 23$

CHALLENGE

35. Susan's brother had a birthday party. To find his age, divide the number of days in a leap year by 50. Add 104 to the remainder. Divide the sum by the number of seconds in a minute. How old is Susan's brother?

DIVISION
Checking Division With Multiplication

When you divide a 3-digit number by 10 or by a multiple of 10, the first number of the quotient will be in the tens or ones place.

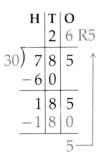

Estimate the tens digit.	**Multiply and subtract.**	**Estimate the ones digit.**	**Multiply and subtract. Write the remainder.**

30) 785

3) 7 is about 2.
Try 2 as the tens digit.

	H	T	O
		2	
30)	7	8	5
	−6	0	
		1	8

	H	T	O
		2	
30)	7	8	5
	−6	0	↓
		1	8	5

3) 18 is 6. Use 6 as the ones digit.

	H	T	O
		2	6 R5
30)	7	8	5
	−6	0	
		1	8	5
		−1	8	0
			5

Use multiplication and addition to check division with a remainder.

$$26 \text{ R}5$$
$$30) \overline{785}$$

$$26$$
$$\times 30$$
$$\overline{780}$$
$$+ \quad 5$$
$$\overline{785}$$

Multiply the quotient by the divisor.

Add the remainder.

The answer is the same as the dividend.

PRACTICE

Divide and check.

1. 10) 463
2. 30) 456
3. 50) 494
4. 20) 680
5. 60) 900

6. 70) 370
7. 40) 299
8. 60) 804
9. 90) 660
10. 20) 396

11. 436 ÷ 10
12. 330 ÷ 20
13. 386 ÷ 40
14. 495 ÷ 60
15. 506 ÷ 30

MIXED PRACTICE
Maintaining and Reviewing Skills

Multiply or divide.

16. 648 ÷ 30
17. 450 ÷ 70
18. 43 × 18
19. 3,961 ÷ 4
20. 21 × 485

FOCUS Use NUMBER skills to divide 3-digit numbers by 10 or multiples of 10.

Using Measurement

21. Erik decided to empty his bank to count the number of coins he had saved. He made stacks of nickels, dimes, and quarters. Use logic and number skills to calculate the total amount of Erik's money.

Exploring With a Calculator

Estimate. Guess if there will be a remainder. Write *yes* or *no*. Then check the answers with a calculator.

22. $30 \overline{)151}$ 23. $50 \overline{)450}$ 24. $20 \overline{)210}$ 25. $50 \overline{)910}$

26. $70 \overline{)770}$ 27. $80 \overline{)644}$ 28. $10 \overline{)170}$ 29. $40 \overline{)370}$

30. $90 \overline{)790}$ 31. $70 \overline{)147}$ 32. $60 \overline{)678}$ 33. $80 \overline{)560}$

Use MEASUREMENT, NUMBER skills, and a CALCULATOR to solve problems.

Selecting a Strategy: Using a Formula

The five important steps in problem solving are READ, KNOW, PLAN, SOLVE, and CHECK. Using a formula is a strategy you can use to PLAN and SOLVE a problem. A formula is an equation that organizes the information you have. It uses letters to stand for numbers. You can use a formula to replace different numbers to solve similar problems.

1. READ Roberto has twice as many marbles as his friend Sam. If Sam has 45 marbles, how many marbles does Roberto have?

2. KNOW Ask yourself: What do I need to find? How many marbles does Roberto have? What **key facts** do I need? Roberto has twice as many, or two times as many, marbles as Sam. Sam has 45 marbles.

3. PLAN Select a strategy: try using a formula.
Think: Let s = Sam's marbles.
        Let r = Roberto's marbles.
        So, r is equal to two times s.
Write a formula.
$$r = 2 \text{ times } s$$
$$r = 2 \times s$$

4. SOLVE Write the formula: $r = 2 \times s$
Replace s with 45: $r = 2 \times 45$
Multiply to find r: $r = 90$
Roberto has 90 marbles.

5. CHECK Twice 50 is 100. Since 45 is a little less than 50, the answer, 90, is reasonable. You can check using addition. Twice 45 means two 45s or 45 + 45. Since 45 + 45 = 90, the answer checks.

FOCUS   Evaluate information as part of the Five-Step PROBLEM-SOLVING Plan.

PRACTICE

In each basketball game, Jo scores 10 more points than Bob. Use the formula: $j = b + 10$. How many points did Jo score if Bob scored

1. 12 points?　　　2. 8 points?　　　3. 19 points?　　　4. 28 points?

5. If Jo scored 32 points, how many did Bob score?

Ronald bowls 5 fewer strikes than Karen. Use the formula: $r = k - 5$. How many strikes did Ronald bowl if Karen bowled

6. 7 strikes?　　　7. 5 strikes?　　　8. 15 strikes?　　　9. 19 strikes?

10. If Ronald had 7 strikes, how many did Karen have?

11. Sam has twice as many baseball cards as Ken. Write a formula that organizes the information.

12. If Ken has 124 cards, how many does Sam have?

13. If Sam has 650 cards, how many does Ken have?

14. Rona plays half as many "Trivia Challenge" games as Alicia. Write a formula that organizes the information.

15. If Alicia played 120 games, how many games did Rona play?

16. If Rona played 35 games, how many games did Alicia play?

Class Project

Divide into small groups of students. Use the information below to find the average height in inches of the students in the group. Compare your results with other groups.

This is the formula for a group of 5 students:

$$H = \frac{a + b + c + d + e}{5}$$

H = average height of the group
$a, b, c, d,$ and e = the heights of the 5 students

Dividing 3-Digit Numbers by 2-Digit Numbers

Divide 384 by 32.

Estimate the tens digit.	Multiply and subtract.	Estimate the ones digit.	Multiply and subtract.

Estimate the tens digit.

30
↑
32) 384

Round 32 to 30.
3) 3 is 1. Try 1 as
the tens digit.

Multiply and subtract.

$$\begin{array}{c|c|c} H & T & O \\ & 1 & \\ \hline 32) & 3 & 8 & 4 \\ & -3 & 2 & \\ \hline & & 6 & \end{array}$$

6 is less than 32.
1 is the correct
tens digit.

Estimate the ones digit.

$$\begin{array}{c|c|c} H & T & O \\ & 1 & \\ \hline 32) & 3 & 8 & 4 \\ & -3 & 2 & ↓ \\ \hline & & 6 & 4 \end{array}$$

3) 6 is 2.
Try 2 as the ones
digit.

Multiply and subtract.

$$\begin{array}{c|c|c} H & T & O \\ & 1 & 2 \\ \hline 32) & 3 & 8 & 4 \\ & -3 & 2 & ↓ \\ \hline & & 6 & 4 \\ & - & 6 & 4 \\ \hline & & & 0 \end{array}$$

Divide 616 by 32.

Estimate the tens digit.

30
↑
32) 616

Round 32 to 30.
3) 6 is 2. Try 2 as
the tens digit.

Multiply and subtract.

$$\begin{array}{c|c|c} H & T & O \\ & 2 & \\ \hline 32) & 6 & 1 & 6 \\ & -6 & 4 & \\ \hline \end{array}$$

64 is greater than
61. 2 is too big for
the tens digit.
Try 1.

Multiply and subtract.

$$\begin{array}{c|c|c} H & T & O \\ & 1 & \\ \hline 32) & 6 & 1 & 6 \\ & -3 & 2 & \\ \hline & 2 & 9 & \end{array}$$

29 is less than 32.
1 is the correct
tens digit.

Estimate the ones digit. Multiply and subtract.

$$\begin{array}{c|c|c} H & T & O \\ & 1 & 9 \ R8 \\ \hline 32) & 6 & 1 & 6 \\ & -3 & 2 & ↓ \\ \hline & 2 & 9 & 6 \\ & -2 & 8 & 8 \\ \hline & & & 8 \end{array}$$

8 is less than 32.
9 is the correct
ones digit.

GUIDED PRACTICE

Divide.

1.
```
      6 R10
28 ) 178
   - 168
      10
```

2.
```
     12
16 ) 192
   - ▮▮
     32
   - ▮▮
      0
```

3.
```
   ▮1
21 ) 231
   - 21
     21
   - ▮▮
      0
```

4.
```
   ▮6 R▮
15 ) 243
   - ▮▮
     9▮
   - 90
     ▮
```

5.
```
   ▮ R▮▮
31 ) 234
   - 217
     ▮▮
```

FOCUS Use NUMBER skills to divide 3-digit numbers by 2-digit numbers.

PRACTICE

Divide.

6. $25\overline{)725}$ 7. $19\overline{)346}$ 8. $55\overline{)495}$ 9. $45\overline{)855}$ 10. $17\overline{)429}$

11. $23\overline{)529}$ 12. $11\overline{)316}$ 13. $26\overline{)628}$ 14. $42\overline{)714}$ 15. $51\overline{)359}$

16. $20\overline{)765}$ 17. $71\overline{)358}$ 18. $31\overline{)657}$ 19. $65\overline{)720}$ 20. $35\overline{)775}$

21. $48\overline{)480}$ 22. $20\overline{)160}$ 23. $75\overline{)850}$ 24. $77\overline{)936}$ 25. $59\overline{)777}$

26. $23\overline{)125}$ 27. $57\overline{)250}$ 28. $43\overline{)258}$ 29. $37\overline{)444}$ 30. $62\overline{)200}$

31. $643 \div 17$ 32. $358 \div 29$ 33. $796 \div 54$ 34. $421 \div 13$ 35. $890 \div 72$

36. $740 \div 74$ 37. $963 \div 82$ 38. $538 \div 64$ 39. $800 \div 59$ 40. $642 \div 39$

41. There are 24 bottles in a case. How many cases can be filled with 360 bottles?

42. At each delivery stop, 15 cases are to be left. How many delivery stops can be made with 180 cases?

MIXED PRACTICE

Maintaining and Reviewing Skills

Multiply or divide.

43. $846 \div 75$ 44. $346 \div 21$ 45. 38×65 46. $765 \div 9$

47. 42×32 48. 56×294 49. $5,638 \div 7$ 50. $678 \div 4$

51. $781 \div 46$ 52. 39×406 53. $7 \times 3,964$ 54. $964 \div 3$

55. $396 \div 4$ 56. $7,834 \div 9$ 57. 56×85 58. 34×186

CHALLENGE

59. Linda had 288 ounces of fruit juice. She poured it into 16-ounce and 32-ounce bottles. She filled five 32-ounce bottles with juice. How many 16-ounce bottles did she fill?

DIVISION

Checking Division With Multiplication

When there is a zero remainder in a division example, it is easy to check the quotient. Just multiply the quotient and the divisor.

$$
\begin{array}{r}
12 \\
18\overline{)216} \\
-18 \\
\hline
36 \\
-36 \\
\hline
0
\end{array}
\qquad
\begin{array}{r}
18 \\
\times 12 \\
\hline
36 \\
+180 \\
\hline
216
\end{array}
$$

When there is a remainder, follow the same steps and add the remainder.

$$
\begin{array}{r}
5\,R13 \\
67\overline{)348} \\
-335 \\
\hline
13
\end{array}
\qquad
\begin{array}{r}
67 \\
\times 5 \\
\hline
335 \\
+\ 13 \\
\hline
348
\end{array}
$$

PRACTICE

Divide and check.

1. $57\overline{)253}$ 2. $36\overline{)580}$ 3. $28\overline{)252}$ 4. $44\overline{)924}$ 5. $12\overline{)512}$

6. $41\overline{)328}$ 7. $63\overline{)823}$ 8. $24\overline{)186}$ 9. $17\overline{)868}$ 10. $62\overline{)682}$

11. $43\overline{)819}$ 12. $75\overline{)450}$ 13. $14\overline{)860}$ 14. $61\overline{)386}$ 15. $49\overline{)896}$

16. $195 \div 39$ 17. $342 \div 18$ 18. $563 \div 56$ 19. $365 \div 45$ 20. $499 \div 17$

MIXED PRACTICE

Maintaining and Reviewing Skills

Divide and check.

21. $46\overline{)396}$ 22. $72\overline{)858}$ 23. $4\overline{)9,328}$ 24. $17\overline{)85}$ 25. $6\overline{)347}$

26. $706 \div 8$ 27. $5,631 \div 9$ 28. $436 \div 3$ 29. $92 \div 24$ 30. $517 \div 7$

FOCUS | Use NUMBER skills to divide 3-digit numbers by 2-digit numbers and to check division with multiplication.

APPLICATION

Using Measurement to Interpret a Remainder

"Thirty days hath September, April, June, and November. . ."

Have you ever wondered why the months of the year have different numbers of days?

Divide the number of days in a year by the number of months in a year.

$$\frac{\text{Number of days}}{\text{Number of months}} = \frac{\text{Number of}}{\text{days in a month}}$$

```
        30 R5
   12 ) 365
       -36
         5
        -0
         5
```

There is a remainder, so the months must have a different number of days.

31. List the months with the number of days in each month. Decide which months have more or less than 30 days.

Make a chart like this one to show the number of days in each month of the year.

Months	Number of Days	More or Less Than 30
Jan.		
Feb.		

Problem Solving: Using a Formula

Remember to READ, KNOW, PLAN, SOLVE, and CHECK all problems. See the Five-Step Plan on page 454 in the Data Bank. Choose the correct formula. Then find each average score.

32. Six students scored 558 points in all.

33. Eleven students scored 814 points in all.

34. Twelve students scored 960 points in all.

FORMULAS
Let A = average
Let T = total score
$A = T \div 12$
$A = T \div 6$
$A = T \div 11$
$A = T \div 2$

Use MEASUREMENT to interpret a remainder.
Use a formula and apply the Five-Step PROBLEM-SOLVING Plan.

LOOKING BACK
Reviewing and Testing Chapter 27

In Chapter 27 you formulated problems about games. Look at pages 358 and 359.

1. Write a sentence telling about a game you might play when you are alone.

You learned about dividing 3-digit numbers by multiples of 10. You also learned to use multiplication to check division. To review what you learned, study the sample exercises on pages 360 and 362. Then use these skills to divide and check for exercises 2–9.

2. $10\overline{)437}$ 3. $10\overline{)507}$ 4. $30\overline{)750}$ 5. $70\overline{)832}$ 6. $20\overline{)195}$

7. $871 \div 10$ 8. $364 \div 60$ 9. $810 \div 50$

You learned about using a formula as a problem solving strategy. To review, look at pages 364 and 365, then solve.

10. Kyung and her friends went bowling. The first game they bowled 80, 94, 97 and 101. To find their average score for the game, use the formula:

$$S = \frac{a + b + c + d}{4}$$

11. Pamela is three years younger than her brother. First write a formula organizing the information. Then solve to find how old Pamela is if her brother is 12.

You learned about dividing 3-digit numbers by 2-digit numbers. You also learned more about checking division. To review, look at pages 366 and 368. Divide and check for exercises 12–20.

12. $53\overline{)385}$ 13. $47\overline{)235}$ 14. $44\overline{)924}$ 15. $17\overline{)956}$ 16. $13\overline{)200}$

17. $226 \div 68$ 18. $589 \div 31$ 19. $650 \div 18$ 20. $760 \div 63$

FOCUS | Review and test skills learned and practiced.

LOOKING AHEAD

Preparing for New Skills for Chapter 28

In the next chapter, you will focus on

- formulating problems about backpacking.
- using customary units to measure length.
- using statistics.
- using customary units to measure weight.
- using patterns and functions.
- how math is used in geography.

Learning more about measuring length and weight with customary units will be easier if you brush up on what you already know about these units. First review the examples. Then complete exercises 1–10.

The **inch** (in.), **foot** (ft), and **yard** (yd) are customary units of length.

The inch is used to measure the length of small things, like books, shoes, and nails.

1 foot = 12 inches   1 yard = 3 feet

A foot and a yard are used to measure the length of longer things like table tops, doors, telephone poles, and floors.

The **ounce** (oz) and the **pound** (lb) are customary units of weight. Ounces are used to measure the weight of small things like a slice of bread or cheese.

There are 16 ounces in a pound. Pounds are used to measure the weight of larger things like cars.

PRACTICE

Is it larger or smaller than a foot?

1. a door   2. an eraser   3. a rug   4. a house   5. a crayon

Would you measure in ounces or pounds?

6. a glass   7. a sock   8. a letter   9. a truck   10. a television

Review MEASUREMENT in preparation for learning a new skill.

FOCUS   Formulate problems using picture cues, text, and data.

28

Customary Measurement

DATA

Activity	Backpacking
Number of hikers	5
Length of hike	10 hours

Food (per hiker)	Weight
2 sandwiches	12 ounces
2 apples	12 ounces
Dried fruit	8 ounces
Water or juice	32 ounces
Total weight	64 ounces
	(4 pounds)

Equipment (per hiker)	Weight
Sweater	12 ounces
Nylon poncho	4 ounces
First-aid kit	8 ounces
Insect spray	8 ounces
Compass	4 ounces
Nylon rope	4 ounces
Total weight	40 ounces
	($2\frac{1}{2}$ pounds)

Backpacking is a popular outdoor activity. The idea of putting some food and equipment into a backpack and starting off on a hike is appealing. But how do you make a backpacking trip a success?

Backpackers first decide where to go. They select food and equipment. No one can enjoy a hike if his or her backpack is too heavy. So all items must be weighed. The best choices are lightweight equipment.

Smart hikers decide beforehand what meals they will want. Then they pack individual portions and unpack only what they need at each meal. Nutritious foods are best, such as sandwiches on whole wheat bread, fresh fruits, and dried fruits.

What can hikers do to make their plan work? What kinds of problems might the hikers face during the trip? Can you think of ways that backpackers can make their trip enjoyable and safe?

Estimating and Measuring Length

The **inch (in.)**, the half inch, and the quarter inch are customary units used to measure length.

1 inch $\frac{1}{2}$ inch $\frac{1}{4}$ inch

Inch rulers are usually marked to show inches, $\frac{1}{2}$ inches, and $\frac{1}{4}$ inches.

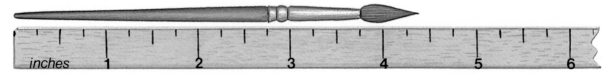

The length of the paint brush is 4 inches to the nearest inch.

$4\frac{1}{2}$ inches to the nearest $\frac{1}{2}$ inch.
$4\frac{1}{4}$ inches to the nearest $\frac{1}{4}$ inch.

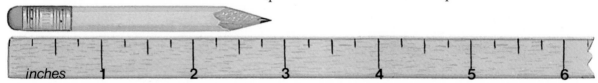

The length of the pencil is 3 in. to the nearest inch.

3 in. to the nearest $\frac{1}{2}$ inch.
$2\frac{3}{4}$ in. to the nearest $\frac{1}{4}$ inch.

GUIDED PRACTICE

Use an inch ruler. Measure the length of each object to the nearest inch.

1. 2 in.

2. ■ in.

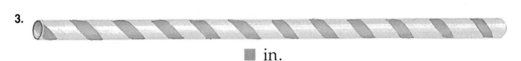

3. ■ in.

FOCUS   Use MEASUREMENT to measure length.

PRACTICE

Use an inch ruler marked to show $\frac{1}{2}$ inches and $\frac{1}{4}$ inches. Measure the length of each object to the nearest inch and $\frac{1}{2}$ inch.

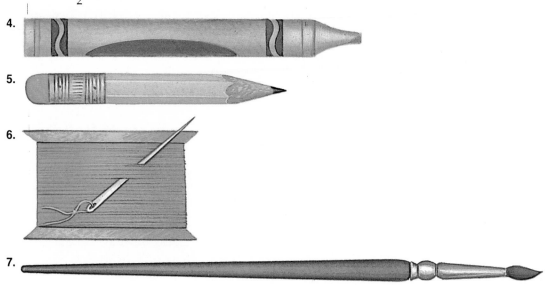

4.

5.

6.

7.

Use an inch ruler. Draw each line segment.

8. 3 in.   **9.** $4\frac{1}{2}$ in.   **10.** $5\frac{1}{4}$ in.   **11.** $2\frac{3}{4}$ in.   **12.** $6\frac{1}{2}$ in.   **13.** $1\frac{3}{4}$ in.

MIXED PRACTICE
Maintaining and Reviewing Skills

Multiply or divide.

14. $769 \div 38$ **15.** 45×56 **16.** $564 \div 40$ **17.** 31×726 **18.** $476 \div 57$

CHALLENGE

19. A snail is at the center of this square spiral. The first "leg" of the spiral is $\frac{1}{4}$ in. long. How far does the snail have to crawl to reach point A if he always follows the spiral?

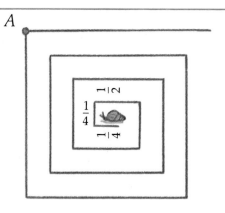

MEASUREMENT

Relating Inches, Feet, Yards, and Miles

Other customary units for measuring length are the **foot (ft)**, the **yard (yd)**, and the **mile (mi).** Study this table.

12 inches (in.) = 1 foot (ft)
3 feet = 1 yard (yd)
36 inches = 1 yard
5,280 feet = 1 mile (mi)
1,760 yards = 1 mile

The distance from your thumb to your elbow is about 1 foot. The length of a baseball bat is about 1 yard. The length of 1 mile is about 1,760 baseball bats laid end-to-end.

5 ft = ■ in.
Think: 1 ft = 12 in.
Multiply: 5 × 12
5 ft = 60 in.

8 yd = ■ ft
Think: 1 yd = 3 ft
Multiply: 8 × 3
8 yd = 24 ft

PRACTICE

Which customary unit, inches, feet, yards, or miles, would you use to measure

1. the length of a car?

2. the width of a lake?

3. the distance from Ohio to New York?

4. the length of a tennis racket?

Copy and complete.

5. 4 ft = ■ in.

6. 5 yd = ■ ft

7. 2 mi = ■ ft

8. 7 yd = ■ ft

9. 1 mi = ■ yd

10. 9 ft = ■ in.

MIXED PRACTICE

Maintaining and Reviewing Skills

Copy and complete.

11. 1 ft = ■ in.

12. 1 mi = ■ ft

13. 1 yd = ■ in.

Use an inch ruler. Draw each line segment.

14. 4 in.   15. $3\frac{1}{4}$ in.   16. $5\frac{1}{2}$ in.   17. $2\frac{3}{4}$ in.   18. $7\frac{1}{4}$ in.   19. 12 in.

FOCUS   Use MEASUREMENT to measure length.

APPLICATION
Using Measurement

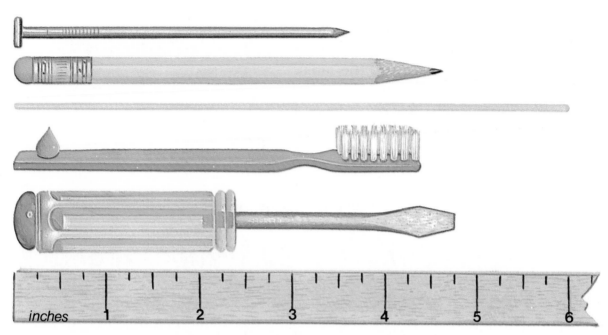

Find the longest object. The piece of spaghetti is the longest object.

20. Name the objects in order from longest to shortest.

21. Name the objects whose lengths are between the length of the spaghetti and the length of the toothbrush.

22. How many objects are longer than the toothbrush?

23. How many objects are shorter than the pencil?

Solving Problems

24. Find the area of the figure. First, divide into rectangles. Then find the area of each rectangle and add to find the total area.

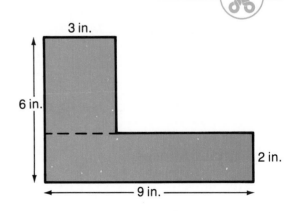

Use MEASUREMENT to measure length and area.

EXTRA PRACTICE—page 452

Estimating and Measuring Weight

The **ounce (oz)**, the **pound (lb)**, and the **ton (t)** are customary units used to measure weight. They are related to each other. Look at the table.

> 16 ounces (oz) = 1 pound (lb)
> 2,000 pounds = 1 ton (t)

Light objects are weighed using ounces.

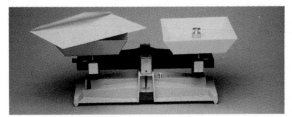

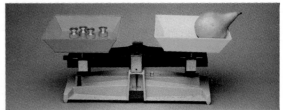

The letter weighs 1 ounce.   The pear weighs 4 ounces.

Heavier objects are weighed using pounds.

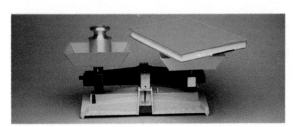

The book weighs 2 pounds.   The boy weighs 75 pounds.

Very heavy objects are weighed using tons.
A small car weighs about 1 ton.
An elephant weighs about 4 tons.

GUIDED PRACTICE

What unit would you use to measure and report the weight of

1. an apple? ounces

2. a dog?

3. an airplane?

4. a pencil?

PRACTICE

What unit would you use to measure and report the weight of

5. a slice of bread?

6. a friend?

7. a hamburger?

8. a cat?

9. a hippopotamus?

10. a goldfish?

11. a nickel?

12. a bus?

Choose the correct measure.

13.

3 oz   3 lb

14.

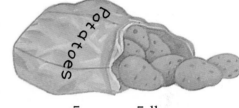

5 oz   5 lb

15.

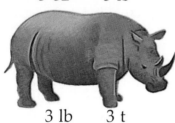

3 lb   3 t

16.

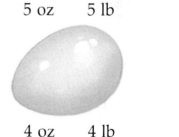

4 oz   4 lb

MIXED PRACTICE

Maintaining and Reviewing Skills

What unit would you use to measure and report

17. the weight of a parakeet?

18. the weight of a truck?

19. the length of your thumb?

20. the height of a bridge?

21. the height of a cat?

22. the width of a building?

23. the distance from Dallas, Texas to Chicago, Illinois?

CHALLENGE

24. One grapefruit and four apples weigh as much as two grapefruits and one apple. One grapefruit weighs as much as ■ apples.

MEASUREMENT
Relating Ounces, Pounds, and Tons

Customary units for measuring weight are the ounce, the pound, and the ton. Study this table.

> 16 ounces (oz) = 1 pound (lb)
> 2,000 pounds = 1 ton (t)

2 lb 2 oz = ■ oz
Think: 1 lb = 16 oz
   Multiply: 2 × 16
      2 lb = 32 oz
2 lb 2 oz = 32 oz + 2 oz = 34 oz

3 t = ■ lb
Think: 1 t = 2,000 lb
   Multiply: 3 × 2,000
      3 t = 6,000 lb

PRACTICE

Copy and complete.

1. 5 lb = ■ oz

2. 2 lb 5 oz = ■ oz

3. 6 lb 1 oz = ■ oz

4. $\frac{1}{2}$ lb = ■ oz

5. 1 lb 9 oz = ■ oz

6. $\frac{1}{2}$ t = ■ lb

7. 3 lb 14 oz = ■ oz

8. $\frac{1}{4}$ lb = ■ oz

9. 4 t = ■ lb

10. 7 lb 3 oz = ■ oz

11. 4 lb 1 oz = ■ oz

12. 9 lb 9 oz = ■ oz

13. Jimmy works in a grocery store. A jar contains 3 lb 6 oz of dry mustard. Jimmy puts the dry mustard into 1 oz bags. How many bags will he fill?

14. A baby chimpanzee weighs $5\frac{1}{2}$ lb. A baby orangutan weighs 6 lb. Who weighs more, the baby chimpanzee or the orangutan? How much more?

MIXED PRACTICE
Maintaining and Reviewing Skills

Copy and complete.

15. 4 lb = ■ oz

16. 1 lb 12 oz = ■ oz

17. 6 t = ■ lb

18. 2 yd = ■ ft

19. 2 mi = ■ yd

20. 3 ft = ■ in.

21. 6 yd = ■ ft

22. 5 ft = ■ in.

23. 1 mi = ■ ft

FOCUS   Use MEASUREMENT to measure weight.

APPLICATION

Using Patterns and Functions

What rule does the function machine use if it changes ounces to pounds?

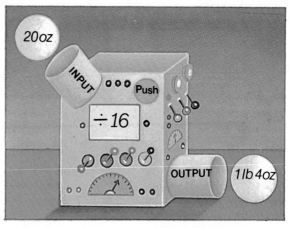

Think: 16 oz = 1 lb
32 oz = 2 lb
48 oz = 3 lb

Since there are 16 ounces in 1 pound, divide by 16 to change ounces to pounds. The rule for the function machine is divide by 16 or ÷ 16.

20 oz = ■ lb ■ oz

$$\begin{array}{r} 1\,\text{R}4 \\ 16\overline{)20} \\ \underline{16} \\ 4 \end{array}$$

20 oz = 1 lb 4 oz

80 oz = ■ lb ■ oz

$$\begin{array}{r} 5\,\text{R}0 \\ 16\overline{)80} \\ \underline{80} \\ 0 \end{array}$$

80 oz = 5 lb 0 oz

Copy and complete.

24. 64 oz = ■ lb

25. 36 oz = ■ lb ■ oz

26. 160 oz = ■ lb

27. 100 oz = ■ lb ■ oz

28. 49 oz = ■ lb ■ oz

29. 171 oz = ■ lb ■ oz

Using Mental Arithmetic

30. The weight of each pumpkin is rounded to the nearest pound to make pricing easier.

8 oz = $\frac{1}{2}$ lb This means that if a weight is 8 oz or more, you should round up. If a weight is less than 8 oz, round down.

Round these weights to the nearest pound.

Weight	8 lb 4 oz	12 lb 12 oz	6 lb 5 oz	7 lb 8 oz	6 lb $7\frac{1}{2}$ oz

Use PATTERNS AND FUNCTIONS to relate ounces, pounds, and tons.
Use MENTAL ARITHMETIC to round weights.

Latitude and Longitude

There is a way to locate places on the earth that uses numbers to identify locations.

Two sets of lines are drawn around the globe. These are called **lines of latitude** and **lines of longitude.**

Lines (meridians) of longitude run north and south, passing through the North and South Poles. A globe has 360 degrees (360°), so there are 360 lines of longitude.

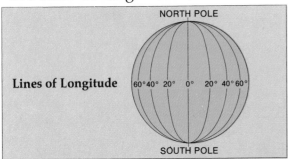

Lines of Longitude   60° 40° 20° 0° 20° 40° 60°

It took a long time to decide where to place 0° longitude, the Prime Meridian. Ptolemy, a second century scientist, drew it through the Fortunate Islands. Today it is drawn through Greenwich, England. The map opposite shows some of the other places 0° was put. Degrees of longitude are counted east of Greenwich to 180° and west of Greenwich to 180°.

Latitude lines (parallels) are measured in distances from the equator—the imaginary line around the middle of the earth. The equator is counted as 0° latitude. The North Pole is 90° north. The South Pole is 90° south.

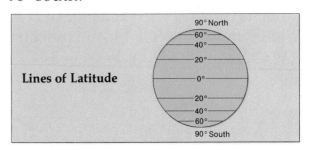

Lines of Latitude

Degrees of latitude and longitude are divided into smaller units that make locating a particular place even more exact.

CRITICAL THINKING

1. What is the latitude for Peking, China; Guadalajara, Mexico; Luxor, Egypt; and Lima, Peru?

2. What is the longitude for Honolulu, Hawaii; Manaus, Brazil; Addis Ababa, Ethiopia; and Greenwich, England?

3. How many different places have been used as 0° longitude?

4. What reason can you think of for having only one place be 0° longitude?

FOCUS Use NUMBER skills and GEOMETRY to understand degrees of latitude and longitude.

Locating Cities Using Longitude and Latitude

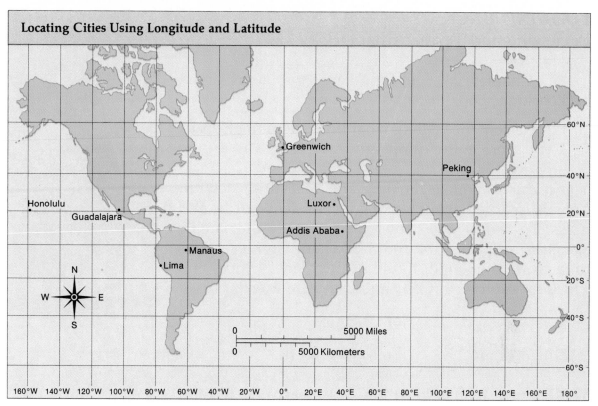

- Greenwich
- Peking
- Honolulu
- Guadalajara
- Luxor
- Addis Ababa
- Manaus
- Lima

60°N
40°N
20°N
0°
20°S
40°S
60°S

160°W 140°W 120°W 100°W 80°W 60°W 40°W 20°W 0° 20°E 40°E 60°E 80°E 100°E 120°E 140°E 160°E 180°

N W E S

0   5000 Miles

0   5000 Kilometers

Locations of the Prime Meridian

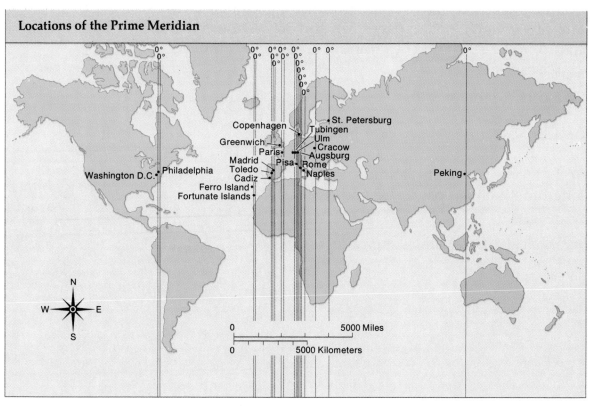

0° 0° 0° 0° 0° 0° 0° 0°

- Copenhagen
- St. Petersburg
- Tubingen
- Ulm
- Greenwich
- Cracow
- Paris
- Augsburg
- Madrid
- Pisa
- Rome
- Toledo
- Naples
- Washington D.C.
- Philadelphia
- Cadiz
- Ferro Island
- Fortunate Islands
- Peking

N W E S

0   5000 Miles

0   5000 Kilometers

383

LOOKING BACK
Reviewing and Testing Chapter 28

In Chapter 28 you formulated problems about backpacking. Look at pages 372 and 373.

1. Write a sentence telling what things you might pack if you were going camping.

You learned about estimating and measuring length. You also learned about relating inches, feet, yards, and miles. To review what you learned, study the sample exercises on pages 374 and 376. Then use these skills to measure the length to the nearest inch, $\frac{1}{2}$ inch, and $\frac{1}{4}$ inch for exercise 2. Copy and complete exercises 3–5.

2. •────────────────•

3. 3 ft = ■ in.   4. 6 yd = ■ ft   5. 2 mi = ■ ft

You learned about estimating and measuring weight. You also learned about relating ounces, pounds, and tons. To review, look at pages 378 and 380. Choose the correct measure in exercises 6 and 7. Copy and complete exercises 8–10.

6. a cat   9 oz or 9 lb   7. a car   2 lb or 2 t

8. 4 lb = ■ oz   9. 1 lb 6 oz = ■ oz   10. 5 t = ■ lb

You learned about latitude and longitude. Look at pages 382 and 383 to review.

11. What latitude and longitude is Oslo, Norway?

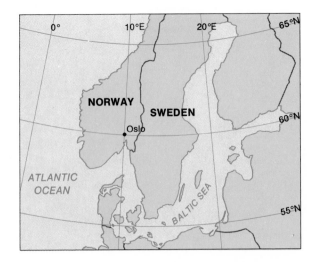

FOCUS | Review and test skills learned and practiced.

LOOKING AHEAD

Preparing for New Skills for Chapter 29

In the next chapter, you will focus on

- formulating problems about starting a business.
- using customary units to measure capacity.
- using statistics and probability.
- measuring temperature.
- using measurement: volume

Learning more about measuring capacity and temperature with customary units will be easier if you brush up on what you already know about these units. First review the examples. Then complete exercises 1–6.

Cups (c), **pints** (pt), **quarts** (qt), and **gallons** (gal) are customary units used to measure capacity.

2 cups = 1 pint

2 pints = 1 quart

4 quarts = 1 gallon

Degrees Fahrenheit (°F) are customary units used to measure temperature. The thermometer on the right is a Fahrenheit thermometer.

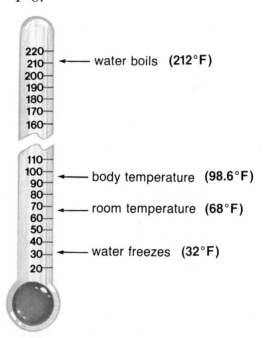

water boils (212°F)

body temperature (98.6°F)

room temperature (68°F)

water freezes (32°F)

PRACTICE

Would you measure in cups, pints, quarts, or gallons?

1. water in a thermos

2. water in a glass

3. water in an aquarium

4. water in a tea kettle

Use the thermometer to answer these questions.

5. What is a normal body temperature?

6. At what temperature does water freeze?

Review MEASUREMENT in preparation for learning a new skill.

FOCUS | Formulate problems using picture cues, text, and data.

29

Customary Measurement

Every neighborhood has many kinds of businesses on which people depend for goods and services. Stores vary greatly in what they offer the public.

Central City's main street is Fifth Street. Most shoppers can get through their shopping lists by going from one end of Fifth Street to the other.

Two of Central City's residents, Martha Choi and Tanya Chase, want to go into business together. They have a number of valuable skills, shown in the data. What possibilities are open to Martha and Tanya? What decisions must they make? Do they face any problems? How can they be successful on Fifth Street?

DATA

Martha's skills
    Photography
    Poster making
    Bookkeeping

Tanya's skills
    Clothing design
    Sewing
    Selling
    Breadmaking

Fifth Street stores
    Bakery
    Shoe repair
    Supermarket
    Toy store
    Women's and men's clothing

Estimating and Measuring Capacity

Customary units for measuring capacity are the **cup**, **pint (pt)**, **quart (qt)**, and **gallon (gal)**.

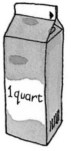

When you measure capacity, you find the amount of liquid a container can hold.

GUIDED PRACTICE

Choose the reasonable answer.

1.

(1 cup)

1 quart

2.

1 pint

1 gallon

3.

1 cup

1 pint

4.

2 quarts

2 gallons

5.

10 pints

10 gallons

6.

1 quart

1 gallon

FOCUS | Use MEASUREMENT to estimate capacity.

PRACTICE
Choose the reasonable answer.

7.
1 qt
1 cup

8.
1 pt
1 gal

9.
1 cup
1 pt

10.
2 pt
2 qt

11.
2 cups
2 pt

12.
50 gal
50 pt

13. A cereal bowl holds about   1 qt   or   1 cup.

14. A teapot holds about   1 qt   or   1 gal.

15. A soup can holds about   1 pt   or   1 cup.

MIXED PRACTICE
Maintaining and Reviewing Skills

Multiply.

16. $\begin{array}{r} 64 \\ \times 23 \\ \hline \end{array}$

17. $\begin{array}{r} 352 \\ \times 35 \\ \hline \end{array}$

18. $\begin{array}{r} 76 \\ \times 84 \\ \hline \end{array}$

19. $\begin{array}{r} 875 \\ \times 9 \\ \hline \end{array}$

20. $\begin{array}{r} 762 \\ \times 78 \\ \hline \end{array}$

21. 58×406

22. 39×39

23. $7 \times 3{,}810$

24. 61×47

CHALLENGE

There are 8 fluid ounces (fl oz) in a cup.
How many fluid ounces are there in

25. 1 pint?

26. 1 quart?

27. 1 gallon?

28. 30 gallons?

MEASUREMENT
Relating Cups, Pints, Quarts, and Gallons

The customary units for measuring capacity are cup, pint, quart, and gallon.

Study the table.

2 cups	= 1 pint (pt)
2 pints	= 1 quart (qt)
4 quarts	= 1 gallon (gal)

Capacity is the amount of liquid a container can hold. Different shaped containers can have the same capacity.

PRACTICE

Copy and complete.

1. 4 cups = ■ pt

2. 6 pt = ■ qt

3. 3 gal = ■ qt

4. 2 qt = ■ cups

5. 2 gal = ■ pt

6. 14 pt = ■ qt

Ring the greater amount.

7. 3 pt   or   2 qt

8. 5 qt   or   12 pt

9. 10 gal   or   32 qt

MIXED PRACTICE
Maintaining and Reviewing Skills

Copy and complete.

10. 8 qt = ■ gal

11. 12 cups = ■ pt

12. 3 ft = ■ in.

13. 3 mi = ■ yd

14. 2 t = ■ lb

15. 2 lb 6 oz = ■ oz

FOCUS | Use MEASUREMENT to relate cups, pints, quarts, and gallons.

APPLICATION
Using Measurement: Volume

The cubic inch is a customary unit of volume.

The cubic foot and the cubic yard are other customary units of volume.

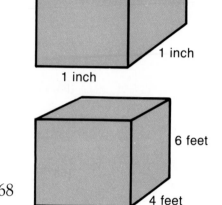

You can multiply the length, the width, and the height to find the volume of a figure.

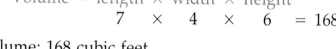

Volume = length × width × height

7 × 4 × 6 = 168

Volume: 168 cubic feet

Find the volume of each figure.

16.

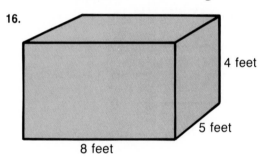

Volume: ■ cubic feet

17.

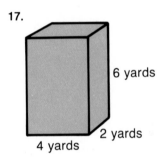

Volume ■ cubic yards

18. length: 9 feet
    width: 4 feet
    height: 8 feet

19. length: 12 inches
    width: 6 inches
    height: 3 inches

20. length: 36 inches
    width: 12 inches
    height: 14 inches

21. length: 8 yards
    width: 7 yards
    height: 4 yards

22. Explain how you would make a model to show the size of 1 cubic foot.

23. Explain how you would make a model to show the size of 1 cubic yard.

Use MEASUREMENT to find the volume of a figure.

Estimating and Measuring Temperature

The **degree Fahrenheit (°F)** is the customary unit used to measure temperature. Look at the Fahrenheit thermometer below.

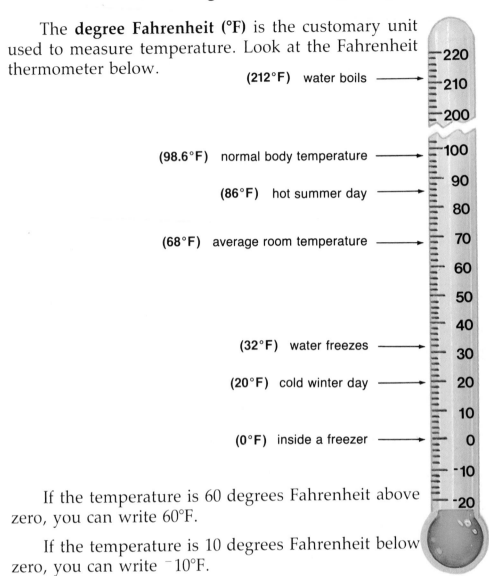

(212°F) water boils ⟶

(98.6°F) normal body temperature ⟶

(86°F) hot summer day ⟶

(68°F) average room temperature ⟶

(32°F) water freezes ⟶

(20°F) cold winter day ⟶

(0°F) inside a freezer ⟶

If the temperature is 60 degrees Fahrenheit above zero, you can write 60°F.

If the temperature is 10 degrees Fahrenheit below zero, you can write ⁻10°F.

GUIDED PRACTICE

Use the Fahrenheit thermometer above.
What is the temperature for each?

1. water boils 212°F

2. water freezes

3. normal body temperature

4. cold winter day

5. average room temperature

6. hot summer day

Read the temperature in degrees Fahrenheit on each thermometer.

7.

8.

9.

10.

Choose the correct temperature.

11. water for a bath

    32°F   95°F

12. a cold drink

    35°F   72°F

13. spring day

    68°F   20°F

14. skiing weather

    26°F   45°F

15. hot soup

    65°F   125°F

16. swimming weather

    40°F   90°F

MIXED PRACTICE

Maintaining and Reviewing Skills

Copy and complete.

17. 2 ft = ■ in.   18. 9 ft = ■ yd   19. 36 in. = ■ ft   20. 5,280 ft = ■ mi

CHALLENGE

21. The temperature was 65°F at 10 A.M. By noon it had risen 10 degrees. It rose 5 more degrees by 2 P.M. Then it fell 6 degrees by 5 P.M. What was the temperature at 5 P.M.?

MEASUREMENT
Estimating and Measuring Temperature

Each mark on this Fahrenheit thermometer stands for 2 degrees Fahrenheit. This thermometer shows 54°F.

If the temperature was 35°F and it rose 13 degrees, the temperature would then be 48°F.

If the temperature was 84°F and it fell 9 degrees, the temperature would then be 75°F.

PRACTICE

Copy and complete this table.

	Temperature Was	Rose or Fell	New Temperature
1.	62°F	rose 7 degrees	■
2.	21°F	fell 11 degrees	■
3.	■	rose 15 degrees	75°F
4.	78°F	fell 19 degrees	■
5.	36°F	■	42°F
6.	■	fell 10 degrees	88°F
7.	⁻6°F	rose 8 degrees	■
8.	85°F	rose 9 degrees	■
9.	67°F	■	52°F
10.	9°F	fell 9 degrees	■

MIXED PRACTICE
Maintaining and Reviewing Skills

Use a Fahrenheit thermometer. What is the temperature for each?

11. water boils

12. normal body temperature

13. average room temperature

14. water freezes

FOCUS | Use MEASUREMENT to measure temperature.

APPLICATION

Using Measurement

This line graph shows the average daily temperatures of Chicago, Illinois during a week in January.

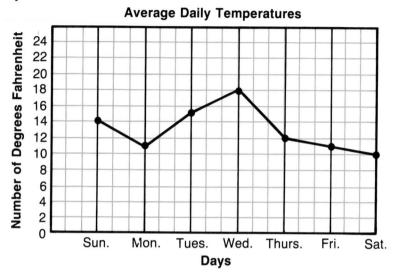

Average Daily Temperatures

Use the line graph to answer these questions.

15. Which day had the highest average daily temperature?

16. Which day had the lowest average daily temperature?

17. On which two days was the average daily temperature the same?

18. On which days was the average daily temperature above 12°F?

19. What was the average temperature for the week?

Using Mental Arithmetic

You can round temperatures to the nearest ten degrees. Round each temperature in this table to the nearest ten degrees.

	City	High Temperature	Low Temperature
20.	New York	47°F	39°F
21.	Dallas	84°F	73°F
22.	Cleveland	43°F	36°F
23.	Miami	85°F	72°F

Use MEASUREMENT to measure temperature.
Use MENTAL ARITHMETIC to round to the nearest ten.

LOOKING BACK

Reviewing and Testing Chapter 29

In Chapter 29 you formulated problems about starting a new business. Look at pages 386 and 387.

1. Write a sentence telling how you think the two women could be successful on 5th Street.

You learned about estimating and measuring capacity. You also learned about relating cups, pints, quarts, and gallons. To review what you learned, study the sample exercises on pages 388 and 390. Then use these skills to choose the reasonable answer for exercises 2 and 3. Copy and complete exercises 4–6.

2. a bottle of juice 1 cup or 1 qt

3. A swimming pool 90 pt or 90 gal

4. 6 cups = ■ pt

5. 8 pt = ■ qt

6. 4 gal = ■ qt

You learned about estimating and measuring temperature in degrees Fahrenheit. Look at pages 392 and 394. Then choose the correct measure for exercises 7 and 8. Find the answers for exercises 9 and 10.

7. hot summer day 85°F or 58°F

8. cold winter day 60°F or 20°F

9. The temperature was 45°F. It rose 12 degrees. What is the new temperature?

10. The temperature was 13°F. It fell 10 degrees. What is the new temperature?

You learned about rounding temperatures. To review, look at page 395. Round each temperature to the nearest ten degrees for exercises 11–15.

11. 24°F   12. 58°F   13. 45°F   14. 79°F   15. 62°F

| FOCUS | Review and test skills learned and practiced. |

LOOKING AHEAD

Preparing for New Skills for Chapter 30

In the next chapter, you will focus on

- formulating problems about saving whooping cranes.
- recognizing similar figures and congruent figures (slides, flips, or turns).
- using measurement.
- finding and continuing patterns.
- using Venn diagrams.
- how math is used in art.

Learning more about shapes and how they are alike and different will be easier if you review some of the things you already know about shapes. First review the example below. Then complete exercises 1–3.

A figure is **symmetric** when it can be folded to make two matching parts. The line along the fold is the **line of symmetry.**

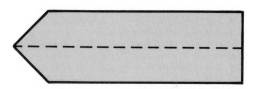

When this figure is folded along the dotted horizontal line, the two parts fit exactly over each other. The line along the fold is a line of symmetry.

When this figure is folded along the dotted vertical line, the parts do not match. The vertical line is not a line of symmetry.

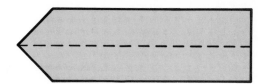

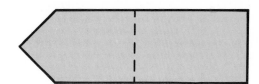

PRACTICE

Is the dotted line a line of symmetry? Write *yes* or *no*.

1.

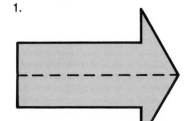

2.

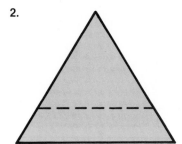

3.

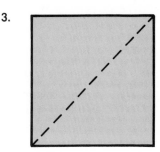

Review GEOMETRY in preparation for learning a new skill.

Formulate problems using picture cues, text, and data.

CHAPTER 30

Geometry and Logic

DATA

Number of whooping cranes
counted on wintering ground

Before government action

1870–1900	Less than 150
1912	80–100
1940	27
1946	20

After government action

1952	28
1958	32
1961	38
1965	44
1969	50
1977	70

Whooping cranes have lived on the continent of North America for over 500,000 years. When the land was unsettled and filled with grassy plains, whooping cranes could be found in great numbers. But, as the land was cleared and drained, the number of whooping cranes grew smaller. Many of the remaining birds died in their journeys from Canada to wintering grounds farther south.

Look at the picture of this Texas wildlife refuge. Over forty years ago, the United States government set aside this land as wintering ground for the whooping crane. In 1952, the government also made it illegal to shoot these birds.

Look at the data. How do you think these government actions have affected the whooping crane?

Understanding Similarity and Congruence

Mrs. Taylor showed her class two triangles. She asked the class if the triangles were the same size and shape. She showed the class 2 more triangles and asked the same questions.

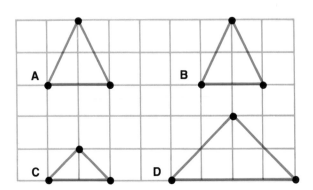

Triangles A and B have the same size and shape. They are called **congruent.**

Triangles C and D have the same shape, but all the sides of triangle D are twice as long as the sides of triangle C. They are called **similar triangles.** If triangles are congruent, they are also similar.

GUIDED PRACTICE

Tell whether these figures are the same size and shape (congruent and similar) or just the same shape (similar).

1.
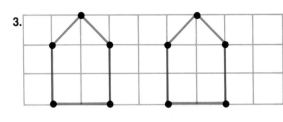
similar

2.
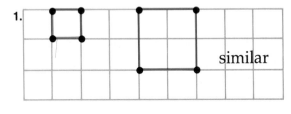
congruent and similar

3.
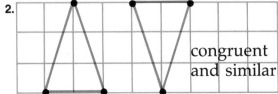

4.
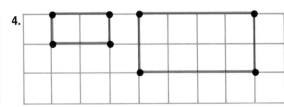

5.
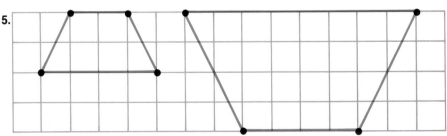

PRACTICE

Copy each figure onto graph paper. Then draw a figure congruent to it.

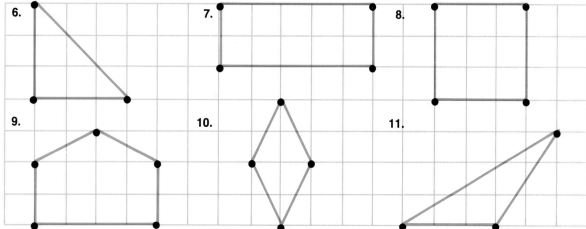

Name the figures that are similar in each row.

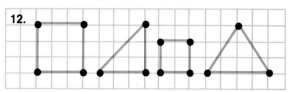

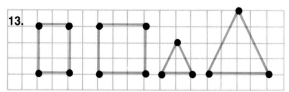

14. Ray's classroom is in the shape of a square. Pat's classroom is exactly the same size and shape. Are the classrooms congruent?

15. The classroom door is in the shape of a rectangle. The windows are the same shape but smaller. Are the door and windows similar or congruent?

MIXED PRACTICE
Maintaining and Reviewing Skills

Tell how many sides and vertices each of these polygons has.

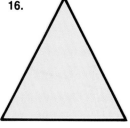

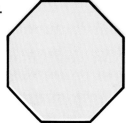

GEOMETRY

Slides, Turns, and Flips

You can move a figure without changing its size or shape. The moves are called **slides, turns,** and **flips.**

Slide—slide the figure to the side, up, or down.

Turn—turn the figure around.

Flip—flip the figure over.

PRACTICE

Tell how each figure has been moved. Write *slide, turn,* or *flip.*

1. Q Q

2. P P

3. M M

4. (shaded figures)

5. (shaded bars)

6. (shaded figures)

MIXED PRACTICE

Maintaining and Reviewing Skills

Name each line, line segment, or ray.

7. A ———— B

8. S ———— T

9. D ———— E

10. O ———— P

APPLICATION

Using Measurement

The distance around the outside of a figure is called the **perimeter.**

You can add the lengths of all the sides of a rectangle to find the perimeter.

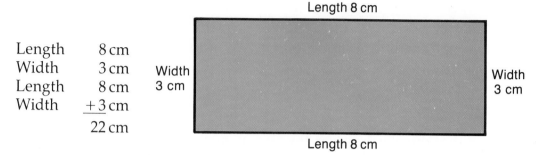

Length	8 cm
Width	3 cm
Length	8 cm
Width	+3 cm
	22 cm

You can also use a formula to find the perimeter of the rectangle.

$$P = 2\,l + 2\,w$$
Perimeter = (2 × length) + (2 × width)
$$P = (2 × 8) + (2 × 3)$$
$$P = 16 + 6$$
$$P = 22 \text{ cm}$$

Use the formula to find the perimeter of these rectangles. They are all similar.

11. $l = 2$ cm
$w = 1$ cm

12. $l = 4$ cm
$w = 2$ cm

13. $l = 8$ cm
$w = 4$ cm

14. $l = 16$ cm
$w = 8$ cm

Solving Problems

A tangram is a puzzle made by cutting a square into 7 pieces. The pieces can be arranged to form many different pictures.

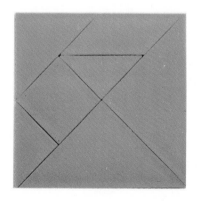

15. Copy the tangram. Then cut the pieces. See what pictures you can make. All of the pieces must be used, and they can not overlap.

Use GEOMETRY and MEASUREMENT to find the perimeter of a rectangle. Use GEOMETRY and LOGIC to solve a tangram puzzle.

LOGIC
Patterns

Mr. Thompson showed his class this picture. He asked the class to find a pattern.

The pattern is one large green frog and then two small yellow frogs.

GUIDED PRACTICE

Look at the objects. Look at the order, size, and color. Write the pattern.

1. one large blue plate, one small pink plate

2. two large red hats, one small ▪ ▪

3. two small yellow gloves, ▪ ▪ ▪ ▪

4. ▪ ▪ ▪ ▪ , ▪ ▪ ▪ ▪

FOCUS | Use LOGIC to find patterns.

404

PRACTICE

Write the pattern. Then draw the next three objects.

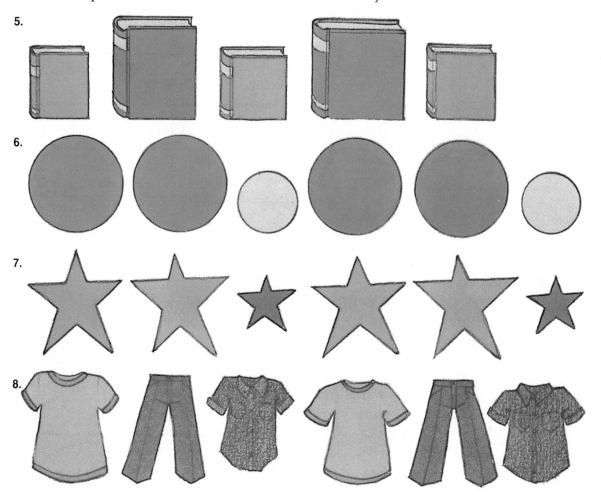

5.

6.

7.

8.

MIXED PRACTICE
Maintaining and Reviewing Skills

Use the formula, $P = 2l + 2w$, to find the perimeter of these rectangles.

9. $l = 3$ cm
$w = 2$ cm

10. $l = 5$ cm
$w = 1$ cm

11. $l = 6$ cm
$w = 4$ cm

12. $l = 11$ cm
$w = 9$ cm

CHALLENGE

13. Make up your own pattern using animal pets. Draw the pattern and write what it is.

LOGIC
Using Venn Diagrams

Look at this picture. What pattern can you see?

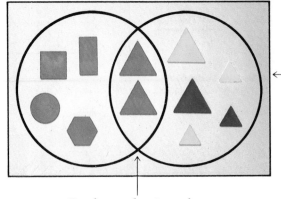

Left: red shapes ⟶

⟵ Right: triangles

Both: red triangles

Suppose you have two groups of shapes. One group is made up of red shapes. The other group is made up of triangles. You can use a **Venn diagram** to see how many of the shapes have similar characteristics.

PRACTICE

Look for a pattern. Write what is in the left circle, what is in the right circle, and what is in both.

1.
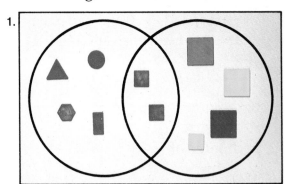

2.
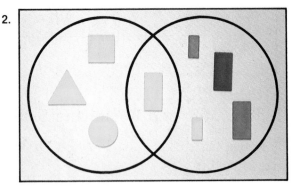

MIXED PRACTICE
Maintaining and Reviewing Skills

3. If there are large red shapes in the right circle and squares in the left circle, what will be in both?

4. If there are small blue shapes in the left circle and hexagons in the right circle, what will be in both?

FOCUS | Use LOGIC to label Venn diagrams.

APPLICATION

Using Patterns and Functions

Look at this pattern. Think of size, shape, and color.

The pattern is large red square, small blue triangle, large blue triangle.

Write each pattern. Then draw and color the next three shapes.

5.

6.

7.

Problem Solving: Using a Formula

8. Find the perimeter of this large red rectangle. Find the length in centimeters. Then find the width in centimeters.

Next use the formula: $P = 2l + 2w$

Multiply the length by two. Multiply the width by two. Add the products together. Remember to write centimeters.

Use PATTERNS AND FUNCTIONS to extend patterns.
Use a formula to solve a problem.

Rectangles

Look at the painting "Open No. 11" by the artist Robert Motherwell. What shapes do you see? Like most paintings, this one is a rectangle. Unlike most paintings, the whole picture is about rectangles! Why did Motherwell paint rectangles? He said that he happened to stand two canvases together. He liked the look of a small rectangle set off by a larger one. What do you think of when you look at Motherwell's painting? Name some rectangles you see around you. Do you see rectangles inside rectangles?

Look at Grant Wood's painting "Midnight Ride of Paul Revere." Here are houses that people lived in more than 200 years ago. What was the shape of the rooms in these houses? How can you tell? What was the shape of the furniture that fit into these rooms?

Find some rectangles in Grant Wood's painting. Do you see shapes that you know are rectangles in real life but that are not actually painted as rectangles? An artist must know how to use mathematics to make you think you are looking at a rectangle when you really aren't.

CRITICAL THINKING

1. Use your centimeter ruler to draw two rectangles. Make one 8 cm long and 4 cm wide. Make the other 4 cm long and 2 cm wide.
   a. Label the sides. Write *width* on the shorter sides of each rectangle. Write *length* on the longer sides.
   b. Write the perimeter of each rectangle in centimeters.
   c. Write the area of each rectangle in square centimeters.
   d. How many small rectangles can fit into the large rectangle? Draw them in your large rectangle. How many times larger is the area of the large rectangle than the area of the small rectangle?

2. Look at the gray rectangle and the rectangle directly under it in "Open No. 11." Both have the same length. Which has a larger area? How can you prove your answer?

3. Think about different peoples you have studied. In what shapes did they build their homes? Can you imagine why they used those shapes?

FOCUS | Use GEOMETRY to recognize and analyze rectangles in art and architecture.

Flat, brick-like areas of color give a feeling of strength to Robert Motherwell's "Open No. 11."

In "Midnight Ride of Paul Revere," Grant Wood creates an historical scene based on the landscape of his home state of Iowa.

LOOKING BACK
Reviewing and Testing Chapter 30

In Chapter 30 you formulated problems about saving the whooping crane. Look at pages 398 and 399.

1. Write a sentence telling how you think government actions have affected the whooping crane.

You learned about similarity and congruence. To review what you learned, study the sample exercises on pages 400 and 402. Then use these skills to tell whether the two figures are congruent or similar for exercises 2 and 3. If they are congruent, tell how the first figure was moved. Write *slide*, *turn*, or *flip*.

2.
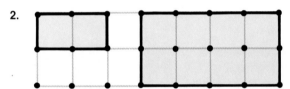

3.
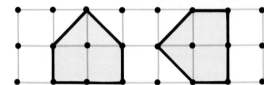

You learned to recognize patterns based on order, size, and color. To review, look at page 404. Write the pattern for exercise 4.

4.

You learned about rectangles in art and architecture. To review, look at pages 408 and 409. Then complete exercise 5.

5. Use your centimeter ruler to draw two rectangles. Make one rectangle 6 cm long and 5 cm wide. Make the other rectangle 4 cm long and 2 cm wide. Write the perimeter of the smaller rectangle in centimeters. Write the area of the larger rectangle in square centimeters.

| FOCUS | Review and test skills learned and practiced. |

LOOKING AHEAD

Preparing for New Skills for Chapter 31

In the next chapter, you will focus on

- **formulating problems about archaeology.**
- **writing and solving open sentences.**
- **using patterns.**
- **using a problem-solving strategy.**
- **identifying a line segment on a grid.**
- **using algebra.**

Learning how to graph ordered pairs of numbers to find points on a grid will be easier if you review what you already know about ordered pairs. First study the example below. Then complete the exercises.

The dots on a grid can be located by ordered pairs of numbers.

The blue dot is located at ordered pair (1,2).

The first number in an ordered pair tells how many spaces to move to the right from 0. The second number tells how many spaces to move up. The yellow dot is at ordered pair (4,1). The red dot is at ordered pair (3,3). What shape do you get when you connect the dots?

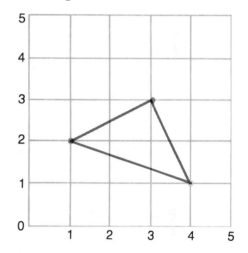

PRACTICE

Use the grid to answer the questions.

Tell the color of the dot located at each ordered pair:

1. (1,1) 2. (1,4) 3. (4,1) 4. (4,4)

5. What shape do you make when you connect the dots in this order: red → yellow → black → blue → red?

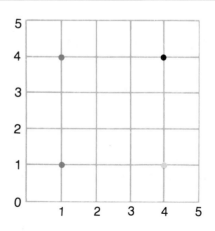

Review ALGEBRA in preparation for learning a new skill.

FOCUS | Formulate problems using picture cues, text, and data.

Algebra

DATA

Height of heads
  10 to 40 feet above ground

Weight
  Up to 50 tons each

Number of statues
  Over 600

Distance moved
  Up to 10 miles from
    quarry where they were
    made

Position of heads
  On hillsides facing the
    ocean

Archaeology is the study of people, customs, and life in ancient times. By digging and searching for clues, archaeologists try to learn what life was like very long ago.

Sometimes clues aren't enough. Take the statues in the photo, for example. About 600 of them were discovered on Easter Island in the South Pacific. Some of the stone heads even have "bodies" buried under 30 feet of ground. Archaeologists know the statues were made miles away on the same island. But the rest is a mystery.

Look at the data to see what archaeologists already know about the statues. What else might an archaeologist want to learn about them? Why do you think Easter Island has remained a mystery? Think carefully. Then predict problems archaeologists might have when exploring the past.

Writing Open Sentences

Mrs. David's class played a game. The class named a number and then Mrs. David named another number. The class had to find the rule that Mrs. David used to name her number. Then they had to write an open sentence to show the rule. An **open sentence** is a number sentence that is neither true nor false until you make it a closed sentence. The class drew this table.

Class number △	1	3	5	10	20	22
Mrs. David's number □	2	6	10	20	40	44

Here is one way to find the rule. Each of Mrs. David's numbers is two times the number given by the class. The rule is, multiply the class number by 2 to get Mrs. David's number. A short way of saying this is: The rule is, Multiply by 2.

To write the open sentence,

Let △ = class number and
Let □ = Mrs. David's number

The open sentence is, $2 \times \triangle = \square$.

GUIDED PRACTICE

Find the rule. Then write an open sentence.

1.

△	1	6	3	5	2
⊗	5	10	7	9	6

Rule: Add 4
Open sentence: $\triangle + 4 = \otimes$

2.

△	4	5	6	7	8
⊖	1	2	3	4	5

3.

⊕	2	4	6	8	10
*	1	2	3	4	5

FOCUS | Use ALGEBRA to write open sentences.

PRACTICE

Find the rule and write an open sentence.

4.

□	5	6	7	8	9	10
△	0	1	2	3	4	5

5.

*	1	2	3	4	5	6
□	3	6	9	12	15	18

6.

⊖	3	6	9	12	15	18
△	1	2	3	4	5	6

7.

△	1	2	3	5	6	10
⊖	5	10	15	25	30	50

8.

☆	1	2	3	4	5	6
□	2	3	4	5	6	7

9.

▽	4	9	11	17	23	35
□	9	14	16	22	28	40

MIXED PRACTICE
Maintaining and Reviewing Skills

Find the missing numbers.

10. $6 + \blacksquare = 7$ **11.** $3 \times \blacksquare = 12$ **12.** $24 \div \blacksquare = 4$ **13.** $15 - \blacksquare = 8$

14. $63 \div \blacksquare = 9$ **15.** $11 \times \blacksquare = 33$ **16.** $17 + \blacksquare = 21$ **17.** $26 + \blacksquare = 31$

18. $18 - \blacksquare = 11$ **19.** $4 \times \blacksquare = 20$ **20.** $56 \div \blacksquare = 7$ **21.** $10 \times \blacksquare = 60$

22. $14 + \blacksquare = 22$ **23.** $70 \div \blacksquare = 10$ **24.** $30 - \blacksquare = 20$ **25.** $7 \times \blacksquare = 77$

26. $\blacksquare + 16 = 20$ **27.** $\blacksquare \times 5 = 45$ **28.** $\blacksquare \div 8 = 8$ **29.** $\blacksquare - 4 = 11$

CHALLENGE

30. The open sentence is, $\square + 7 = \triangle$. Write the rule and make a table.

ALGEBRA
Solving Open Sentences

Mr. Johns drew the table below on the chalkboard. His class had to find the rule and write the open sentence that Mr. Johns used to make the table. Then the class had to find the missing number.

△	2	7	5	8	3	1	9	12
□	7	12	10	13	8	6	14	?

The rule is, Add 5.
The open sentence is, $\triangle + 5 = \square$.

To find the missing number, substitute the number given in the open sentence.

$\triangle + 5 = \square$ Since $\triangle = 12$,
write $12 + 5 = 17$

The missing number is 17.

PRACTICE

Copy the table. Find the rule, write an open sentence, and find the missing numbers.

1.

▽	3	6	5	2	1
⊖	6	9	8	5	?

2.

□	8	7	5	9	10
◇	3	2	0	4	?

MIXED PRACTICE
Maintaining and Reviewing Skills

Find the missing numbers.

3. $6 \times \blacksquare = 18$ 4. $\blacksquare \div 3 = 9$ 5. $13 - \blacksquare = 7$ 6. $9 + \blacksquare = 15$

7. $\blacksquare \times 5 = 50$ 8. $42 \div \blacksquare = 7$ 9. $\blacksquare - 6 = 6$ 10. $\blacksquare + 8 = 17$

11. $12 \times \blacksquare = 36$ 12. $19 - \blacksquare = 10$ 13. $81 \div \blacksquare = 9$ 14. $13 + \blacksquare = 16$

| FOCUS | Use ALGEBRA to write and solve open sentences. |

416

APPLICATION
Using Patterns

Even numbers end in 0, 2, 4, 6, or 8. Odd numbers end in 1, 3, 5, 7, or 9.

The rule for this table is, Add 4.

15. Notice that each △ number in the table is an even number. The number being added, 4, is an even number.

△	4	8	16	22	30
□	8	12	20	26	34

Even number + Even number = __?__ number

The rule for this table is, Add 5.

16. Notice that each △ number in the table is an odd number. The number being added, 5, is an odd number. Complete the table.

△	3	7	15	29	41
□	8	■	■	■	■

Odd number + Odd number = __?__ number

The rule for this table is, Subtract 6.

17. Notice that each △ number in the table is an odd number. The number being subtracted, 6, is an even number. Complete the table.

△	9	13	25	31	47
□	3	■	■	■	■

Odd number − Even number = __?__ number

18. Copy the table below. To complete the table, make each △ number an even number. Then make up a rule to subtract an odd number. Complete the table.

△	6	■	■	■	■	■	■
□	■	■	■	■	■	■	■

Even number − Odd number = __?__ number

Use PATTERNS to find a rule.

Selecting a Strategy: Using Guess and Test

Guess and test is a strategy used to PLAN and SOLVE a problem. Each time you guess an answer and then test it, you learn something new. You learn how close you are getting to the correct answer.

1. READ   In this computation, A and B stand for different digits. What are they?

$$\begin{array}{r} 5A \\ + \ A \\ \hline BB \end{array}$$

2. KNOW   Ask yourself: What do I need to find? What digits for A and B will make the computation correct?
What **key facts** do I need?
A and B are different digits. Each letter A stands for the same digit. Each letter B stands for the same digit.

3. PLAN   Select a strategy: try using guess and test. Guess numbers for A and B and then test to see if they work. SOLVE and CHECK until you find the correct digits for A and B.

Think of

$$\begin{array}{r} 5A \\ + \ A \\ \hline BB \end{array} \quad \text{as} \quad \begin{array}{r} 5\square \\ + \ \square \\ \hline \bigcirc\bigcirc \end{array}$$

4. SOLVE   Guess: A = 2 and B = 4.

$$\begin{array}{r} 5\boxed{2} \\ + \ \boxed{2} \\ \hline \textcircled{4}\textcircled{4} \end{array}$$

SOLVE and CHECK again.

5. CHECK   This test shows that 52 + 2 = 44, which is not true. We know that 52 + 2 = 54, but BB cannot be 54 because the digits are not the same.

4. SOLVE   Guess: A = 8 and B = 6.

$$\begin{array}{r} 5\boxed{8} \\ + \ \boxed{8} \\ \hline \textcircled{6}\textcircled{6} \end{array}$$

5. CHECK   This test shows that 5A + A = BB, or 58 + 8 = 66. Since both As are the same digit and both Bs are the same digit, it is reasonable that A = 8 and B = 6.

FOCUS   Evaluate information as part of the Five-Step PROBLEM-SOLVING Plan.

In each example below, there is one digit, A, that is missing. Within each example, A always stands for the same digit. Guess and test to find A.

1.　　1A
　　+ A
　　────
　　　22

2.　　18
　　+ A
　　────
　　A0

3.　　A4
　　− 1A
　　────
　　1A

4.　　8A
　　− A9
　　────
　　35

In each example below, there are two digits, A and B, that are missing. Within each example, A always stands for the same digit and B always stands for the same digit. Guess and test to find A and B.

5.　　AB
　　+ AB
　　────
　　2B

6.　　6A
　　+ B
　　────
　　A6

7.　　A7
　　+ A6
　　────
　　BB

8.　　AB
　　+ 9
　　────
　　B2

9.　　8A
　　− A3
　　────
　　AB

10.　　A4
　　− 1A
　　────
　　BA

11.　　A6
　　− B
　　────
　　6A

12.　　A1
　　− B
　　────
　　BA

Guess and test to solve each problem.

13. The sum of two numbers is 15. Their difference is 3. What are the numbers?

14. The sum of two numbers is 11. Their product is 30. What are the numbers?

15. The product of two numbers is 32. Their difference is 4. What are the numbers?

16. Two numbers each read the same backward and forward. Their sum is 165. What are the numbers?

Class Project

Divide into small groups of students. Write five "Mystery Examples" that involve addition or subtraction. Example: A3 − 3A = B (Answer: A = 4 and B = 9) Trade your examples (without answers) with those of another group. Each group will guess and test to solve each other's mystery examples.

Identifying Line Segments on a Grid

The points on the grid are located by ordered pairs of numbers. The first number in an ordered pair tells how many units to the right. The second number tells how many units up. Point *A* is located on the graph at the ordered pair (1,2). Point *B* is located on the graph at the ordered pair (2,3).

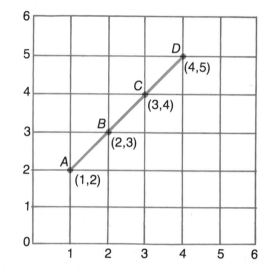

When all the points on this grid are connected, they form a straight line segment. To find the next point on the line segment, look for a pattern.

To help you see the pattern, arrange the ordered pairs in a table. What patterns do the numbers make? What would be the next ordered pair?

Locate it on the grid with your finger.

Points	Ordered Pairs
A	(1,2)
B	(2,3)
C	(3,4)
D	(4,5)
E	(■,■)

GUIDED PRACTICE

1. Use graph paper or draw a grid like the one above. Locate each ordered pair in the table at the right on your grid. Put a point on your grid where each ordered pair is located. Connect the points to make a line segment. Look for the pattern. Find two more ordered pairs to extend the line.

Points	Ordered Pairs
A	(1,2)
B	(2,2)
C	(3,2)
D	(4,2)
E	(■,■)
F	(■,■)

FOCUS | Use ALGEBRA to identify a line segment on a grid.

PRACTICE

Study the grid and then answer the questions.

What ordered pairs identify the following points on the grid?

2. A (■, ■)   3. B (■, ■)

4. C (■, ■)   5. D (■, ■)

6. What is formed when the points are connected?

7. What patterns do the numbers in the ordered pairs make?

8. What ordered pairs would come next to extend the line segment?

9. Use graph paper or draw a grid like the one above. Locate the ordered pairs in the table at the right on your grid. Connect the points. Then add 2 more points to extend the line segment.

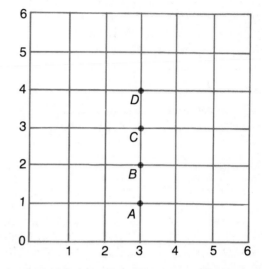

Points	Ordered Pairs
A	(1,5)
B	(2,4)
C	(3,3)

MIXED PRACTICE

Maintaining and Reviewing Skills

Find the missing numbers.

10. 1, 3, ■, 7, ■, 11, 13, ■, ■, 19

11. 2, 5, 8, ■, 14, ■, ■, 23, ■, 29

12. 3, 6, ■, ■, 15, 18, ■, ■, 27, ■

13. 5, 9, 13, ■, 21, 25, ■, ■, 37, 41

CHALLENGE

14. Use graph paper or draw a grid. Locate ordered pairs and connect them by line segments so they form the first initial of your first or last name.

ALGEBRA
Identifying Line Segments on a Grid

The table shows the ordered pairs for 4 points on the grid. Look for the patterns. The first number in each pair is one more than the number above it. The second number is one less than the number above it. The ordered pair for Point *E* will be (4,2). Complete the table and copy the grid. Then locate Points *E, F,* and *G* on the grid and connect the points.

Points	Ordered Pairs
A	(0,6)
B	(1,5)
C	(2,4)
D	(3,3)
E	(4,2)
F	(■,■)
G	(■,■)

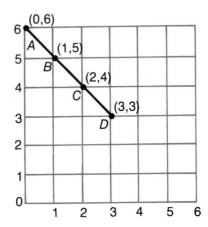

PRACTICE

Complete each table. Then draw a grid for each set of ordered pairs. Connect the points to form a line segment.

1.

(4,0)
(4,1)
(4,2)
(4,3)
(■,■)
(■,■)

2.

(0,0)
(1,1)
(2,2)
(3,3)
(■,■)
(■,■)

3.

(0,2)
(1,2)
(2,2)
(3,2)
(■,■)
(■,■)

MIXED PRACTICE
Maintaining and Reviewing Skills

Add or subtract.

4. 39,406 + 57,897   **5.** 72,615 − 34,907   **6.** 46,364 + 7,896   **7.** 38,640 − 4,864

FOCUS	Use ALGEBRA to identify a line segment on a grid.

APPLICATION

Using Algebra

Some maps are like grids. Places can be located using ordered pairs.

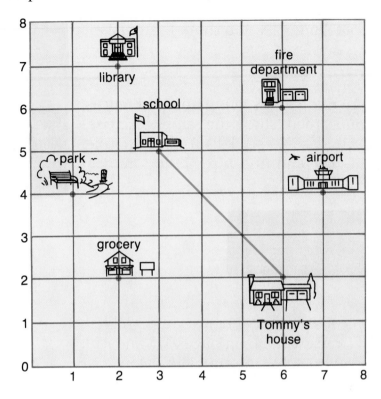

The school is located at (3,5). The library is located at (2,7). If you draw a line segment from Tommy's house to the school, you pass through points (4,4) and (5,3).

Use the map above to answer these questions.

8. What ordered pair gives the location of the grocery store?

9. What ordered pair gives the location of the fire department?

10. What ordered pair gives the location of the airport?

11. What ordered pair gives the location of the park?

12. Lay the edge of a ruler on Point (2,2) and Point (6,2). Using these as endpoints, what other points does the edge of the ruler pass through?

13. Lay the edge of a ruler on Point (6,2) and Point (6,6). Using these as endpoints, what other points does the edge of the ruler pass through?

Use ALGEBRA to locate points on a map.

LOOKING BACK

Reviewing and Testing Chapter 31

In Chapter 31 you formulated problems about archaeological finds. Look at pages 412 and 413.

1. Write a sentence telling why you think Easter Island has a remaining mystery.

You learned about writing and solving open sentences. To review what you learned, study the sample exercises on pages 414 and 416. Use these skills to find the rule, write an open sentence, and find the missing number for exercise 2.

2.

*	4	2	6	10	1	9	7
△	8	6	10	14	5	?	11

You learned how to use guess and test as a problem solving strategy. To review, look on pages 418 and 419. Then use the strategy to solve the problem below.

3. The product of two numbers is 144. Their sum is 24. What are the numbers?

You learned about identifying line segments on a grid. To review, look at pages 420 and 422. For exercises 4–6, complete each table. Then use graph paper to draw a grid for each set of ordered pairs. Connect the points to form line segments.

4.

(3,0)
(3,1)
(3,2)
(■,■)
(■,■)

5.

(1,3)
(2,3)
(3,3)
(■,■)
(■,■)

6.

(1,3)
(2,4)
(3,5)
(■,■)
(■,■)

FOCUS | Review and test skills learned and practiced.

Preparing for New Skills for Chapter 32

In the next chapter, you will focus on

- formulating problems about Quebec City.
- recognizing and comparing place values through hundred thousands.
- using logic and algebra.
- rounding 6-digit numbers to the nearest hundred, thousand, and ten thousand.
- how math is used in consumer education.

Learning more about place value will be easier if you review what you already know about place value. Study the place-value chart and rounding examples below. Then complete exercises 1–10.

Ten Thousands	Thousands	Hundreds	Tens	Ones
2	5	6	8	7
2 ten thousands	5 thousands	6 hundreds	8 tens	7 ones

$$20,000 \ + \ 5,000 \ + \ 600 \ + \ 80 \ + \ 7$$
twenty-five thousand, six hundred eighty-seven $= 25,687$

Round 67,782 to the nearest thousand.

- 67,782 is between 67,000 and 68,000.
- It is closer to 68,000.
- 67,782 rounds up to 68,000.

When a number comes halfway between two thousands it always rounds up. Since 67,500 is halfway between 67,000 and 68,000, it rounds up to 68,000.

PRACTICE

Answer the questions.

1. How many hundreds are in 22,354?   2. How many tens are in 31,624?

3. How many ten thousands are in 87,365?   4. How many thousands are in 12,753?

Round to the nearest thousand.

5. 17,798   6. 34,254   7. 78,683   8. 43,587   9. 61,354   10. 25,828

Review NUMBER skills in preparation for learning a new skill.

FOCUS   Formulate problems using picture cues, text, and data.

32

Using Larger Numbers

DATA

Family members
 Mother
 Father
 Adam, age 14
 Brian, age 10

Time and cost to Quebec City

Plane
 $1\frac{1}{2}$ hours to Montreal, then
  45 minutes more to
  Quebec City
 $129 round trip per person

Train
 10 hours to Quebec City
 $95 round trip per person
 $\frac{1}{2}$ price for Brian

Bus
 12 hours to Quebec City
 $104 round trip per person
 $63 for Brian

Car
 13 hours to Quebec City
 $75 round trip for gas and
  oil
 $20 round trip for tolls

A trip to Europe isn't in the stars for the Alloco family this year; it's just too expensive. So, they're settling on the next best thing—Quebec City, a place in Canada with a real European flavor.

Deciding where to go was easy. But being part of a democratically run family can have its problems. That's why the Allocos have been sitting at their "round table" for a long time. Now that they know where they're going, they can't seem to agree on the best way to get there.

Think about each means of travel shown in the data. What are some arguments for and against each one? How do you think the Allocos will work toward a decision? Predict the choice they will make and tell why.

Writing Numbers to 999,999

Erin reported that the closest distance Mars gets to the sun is about one hundred twenty-eight million, five hundred thousand miles. How can she write this number?

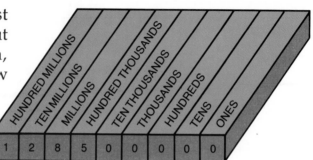

In 128,500,000

the 1 means	1 hundred million	or	100,000,000
the 2 means	2 ten millions	or	20,000,000
the 8 means	8 millions	or	8,000,000
the 5 means	5 hundred thousands	or	+ 500,000

expanded form

128,500,000 standard form

A place-value chart can help you read and write numbers in standard and expanded form.

GUIDED PRACTICE

Write in standard form:

1. 6,000,000 + 10,000 + 5,000 + 800 + 40 + 9   6,015,849

2. 600,000 + 20,000 + 8,000 + 200

3. 200,000,000 + 40,000,000 + 6,000,000 + 300,000 + 1,000 + 500

4. 20,000 + 6,000 + 40 + 7

5. nine hundred fifty million   **6.** nine thousand twenty

7. six million nineteen thousand   **8.** nine hundred thousand

Write the value of the underlined digit.

9. 6<u>3</u>,007,000   **10.** 1<u>25</u>,000   **11.** <u>4</u>58,000,139   **12.** 75,8<u>3</u>2

FOCUS | Use NUMBER skills to find place value.

PRACTICE

Write these numbers in standard form.

13. four hundred twenty million   **14.** three thousand, fifty

15. twenty-eight thousand, thirty   **16.** eighteen thousand, eighty-nine

17. seven hundred six million   **18.** nine hundred thousand, ninety

Write the value of the underlined digit.

19. 789,562,140   **20.** 3,562   **21.** 19,385   **22.** 16,350

23. 216,530,000   **24.** 553,060   **25.** 391,310   **26.** 23,815

27. 186,542   **28.** 797,356   **29.** 68,215,488   **30.** 430,000

MIXED PRACTICE
Maintaining and Reviewing Skills

Divide and check.

31. $17\overline{)323}$ **32.** $25\overline{)350}$ **33.** $11\overline{)792}$ **34.** $51\overline{)663}$

35. $15\overline{)319}$ **36.** $32\overline{)740}$ **37.** $41\overline{)830}$ **38.** $29\overline{)360}$

39. Which items are common to both groups?

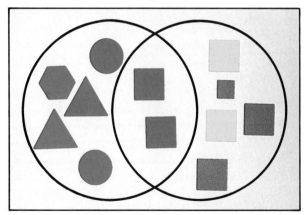

CHALLENGE

40. I am a number whose hundreds and thousands place is 3. My ones place is 2 times the hundreds place. My tens place is 2 less than my hundreds place. Who am I?

PLACE VALUE
Comparing and Ordering Numbers

Sam and Sarah are playing video games. Sam's score is 563,812. Sarah's score is 563,912. They want to see who has the higher score.

Here is one way to compare numbers by comparing digits.

Sam	Sarah	
563,812	563,912	Compare hundred thousands: same
563,812	563,912	Compare ten thousands: same
563,812	563,912	Compare thousands: same
563,812	563,912	Compare hundreds: different

$8 < 9$, so $563,812 < 563,912$. Sarah's score is higher.

PRACTICE

Compare. Write $>$, $<$, or $=$.

1. 856 ● 836
2. 402 ● 402
3. 6,385 ● 6,853
4. 9,952 ● 9,928
5. 63,895 ● 73,985
6. 93,569 ● 93,572
7. 111,616 ● 111,666
8. 756,432 ● 74,381
9. 999,999 ● 999,990

Write the numbers in order from least to greatest.

10. 15   100   1,500   6   24   815   300
11. 38,905   189   6,900   6,756   56,312   256
12. 398,562   399,562   52,160   51,260   561

MIXED PRACTICE
Maintaining and Reviewing Skills

Compare. Write $>$, $<$, or $=$.

13. 346,921 ● 346,912
14. 49.6 ● 49.60
15. 26.45 ● 264.5

Change these improper fractions to mixed numbers.

16. $\frac{4}{3}$
17. $\frac{6}{4}$
18. $\frac{15}{10}$
19. $\frac{25}{2}$

FOCUS | Use NUMBER skills to compare and order numbers.

APPLICATION
Using Logic

Use logic to choose two numbers between 3,656 and 3,890 from this set of numbers.

3,280   3,856   3,776   3,956   3,640

You must find those numbers that are **greater** than 3,656 and **less** than 3,890. First write the numbers in order from least to greatest.

3,280   3,640   3,776   3,856   3,956

Then put 3,656 and 3,890 in their correct places.

$3,656 > 3,640$ and $3,656 < 3,776$

$3,890 > 3,856$ and $3,890 < 3,956$

3,280   3,640   **3,656**   3,776   3,856   **3,890**   3,956

The two numbers between 3,656 and 3,890 are 3,776 and 3,856.

20. Choose two numbers between 89,305 and 96,305 from this set of numbers.

82,352   92,899   99,999   89,966   97,826

Problem Solving: Using Guess and Test

Remember to READ, KNOW, PLAN, SOLVE, and CHECK all problems. See the Five-Step Plan on page 454 in the Data Bank. Use guess and test to think about the missing digits. Write the numbers in order from least to greatest.

21. 9 8 7, ■ ■ 9   9 9 ■, 9 9 9   9 7 ■, 9 9 9

22. 9 9 8, 9 ■ 9 > 9 9 8, 9 8 9 and 9 9 8, 9 ■ 9 < 9 9 ■, 9 9 9

23. 9 7 ■, 9 9 9 < 9 7 9, 9 9 9 and 9 7 ■, 9 9 9 > 9 7 7, 9 9 9

Use LOGIC to compare and order numbers.
Use guess and test and apply the Five-Step PROBLEM SOLVING Plan.

Rounding to the Nearest Ten Thousand

Fairbanks, Alaska, has a population of 22,645. Round 22,645 to the nearest ten thousand:

- 22,645 is between 20,000 and 30,000.
- 22,645 is closer to 20,000.
- 22,645 rounds down to 20,000.

Fairbanks, Alaska, has a population of about 20,000.

When rounding a number to the nearest ten thousand, look at the thousands place. If the digit is 4 or less, round down. If the digit is 5 or more, round up.

Seattle, Washington has a population of 488,474. Round this number to the nearest ten thousand:

- 488,474 is between 480,000 and 490,000.
- 488,474 is closer to 490,000.
- 488,474 rounds up to 490,000.

Seattle, Washington has a population of about 490,000.

GUIDED PRACTICE

Round to the nearest ten thousand.

1.
```
          16,000
10,000        20,000
```

2.
```
              33,285
30,000           40,000
```

3.
```
        65,289
60,000        70,000
```

4.
```
      81,546
80,000           90,000
```

5.
```
    73,721
70,000        80,000
```

6.
```
                    48,250
40,000           50,000
```

| FOCUS | Use NUMBER skills to round numbers to the nearest ten thousand. |

432

PRACTICE

Round to the nearest ten thousand.

7. 56,438   **8.** 29,104   **9.** 331,324   **10.** 115,329

11. 72,155   **12.** 402,350   **13.** 92,138   **14.** 638,277

15. 39,400   **16.** 83,662   **17.** 354,200   **18.** 489,135

19. 79,000   **20.** 85,314   **21.** 364,285   **22.** 140,122

23. 156,080   **24.** 57,346   **25.** 717,399   **26.** 28,146

27. Phoenix, Arizona has a population of 853,266.

28. Denver, Colorado has a population of 504,588.

MIXED PRACTICE
Maintaining and Reviewing Skills

Round to the nearest ten thousand.

29. 72,816   **30.** 635,127   **31.** 86,001   **32.** 344,586

Round to the nearest thousand.

33. 64,796   **34.** 2,739   **35.** 38,571   **36.** 37,164

Round to the nearest hundred.

37. 5,646   **38.** 751   **39.** 28,064   **40.** 7,572

Round to the nearest ten.

41. 846   **42.** 56,271   **43.** 3,955   **44.** 71,394

CHALLENGE

45. Los Angeles, California has a population of 3,096,721. Round this number to the nearest ten thousand.

PLACE VALUE

Rounding to the Nearest Hundred and Nearest Thousand

Round 27,854 to the nearest hundred and to the nearest thousand.

	Nearest Hundred	Nearest Thousand
27,854	27,900	28,000

Round 617,231 to the nearest hundred and to the nearest thousand.

	Nearest Hundred	Nearest Thousand
617,231	617,200	617,000

Look at the digit to the right of the place to which you are rounding. If the digit is 4 or less, round down. If the digit is 5 or more, round up.

PRACTICE

Round to the nearest hundred.

1. 7,651
2. 15,345
3. 68,458
4. 103,296

5. 43,623
6. 8,615
7. 32,298
8. 525,843

9. 5,087
10. 329,327
11. 776,938
12. 428,395

Round to the nearest thousand.

13. 6,688
14. 14,352
15. 29,650
16. 135,286

17. 32,411
18. 26,500
19. 42,990
20. 246,328

21. 9,975
22. 863,128
23. 578,489
24. 930,928

MIXED PRACTICE
Maintaining and Reviewing Skills

Estimate each sum or difference. First round each number to the nearest thousand.

25.	26.	27.	28.	29.
7,846 +3,468	29,058 −13,548	6,531 +15,239	7,488 −5,640	38,960 −4,320

FOCUS | Use NUMBER skills to round numbers to the nearest hundred and nearest thousand.

434

APPLICATION

Using Algebra

Find the value of n.

n rounded to the nearest ten thousand is 50,000.
Is n 57,429 or 49,763?

Round each number to the nearest ten thousand to find n. 57,429 rounded to the nearest ten thousand is 60,000. 49,763 rounded to the nearest ten thousand is 50,000.
$n = 49,763$

Find the value of the letter.

30. d rounded to the nearest ten thousand is 80,000.
Is d 78,275 or 74,999?

31. r rounded to the nearest ten thousand is 20,000.
Is r 24,356 or 14,356?

Exploring With a Calculator

Use your calculator to multiply.

32. 351
    $\times \quad 9$

33. 93
    $\times 15$

What do these two examples have in common? Write sentences to explain your answer.

34. 87
    $\times 21$

35. 81
    $\times 27$

What do these two examples have in common? Write sentences to explain your answer.

Use ALGEBRA to work with rounded numbers. Use a CALCULATOR to multiply numbers and LOGIC to analyze the answers.

Price and Quality

We should consider the cost and the *quality* of items we buy. Quality means how good an item is. Sometimes buying something that costs less does not save money.

Compare the containers of ground meat on page 437. The more expensive meat is actually a better buy because one third of the weight of the cheaper meat is fat, but only one ninth of the more expensive meat is fat. So, you actually pay $1.50 for two thirds of a pound of the cheaper meat while you pay $1.80 for nine tenths of a pound of the more expensive meat. And $1.50 for two thirds of a pound is $2.25 per pound, while $1.80 for nine tenths of a pound is $2.00 per pound.

The meat that seems to be more expensive actually gives you more for your money.

Inexpensive items of poor quality may not last as long as ones of better quality. Ann and Sue went shoe shopping. Ann chose shoes of poor quality for $5.00. Sue chose a better quality pair for $10.00. Soon Ann's shoes wore out because they were not very well made.

She bought another pair of shoes for $9.00. Ann spent a total of $14.00—$5.00 for the first pair of shoes, and $9.00 to replace them.

Sue is still wearing her $10.00 shoes. She spent less in the long run because she spent a little more for something of better quality.

CRITICAL THINKING

1. Compare the packages of ground meat. How can you tell which is the better quality?

2. The bone in the sirloin steak weighs one quarter pound. Which steak gives you more for your money?

3. Is it cheaper to buy the bicycle with the basket and the mirror, or to purchase them separately?

4. What qualities help you judge:
   a. food?
   b. clothes?
   c. toys?

FOCUS | Use NUMBER skills and LOGIC to compare price and quality.

HAMBURGER
$1.50 LB

GROUND SIRLOIN
$1.80 LB

BONELESS STEAK 1¼ LB
$2.25

SIRLOIN STEAK 1¼ LB
$2.00

$130

$110

$30.

LOOKING BACK
Reviewing and Testing Chapter 32

In Chapter 32 you formulated problems about a family trip to Quebec City, Canada. Look at pages 426 and 427.

1. Write a sentence telling how you predicted the kind of transportation the family would choose.

You learned about writing, comparing, and ordering numbers through 999,999. To review what you learned, study the sample exercises on pages 428 and 430. Then use these skills to write each in standard form for exercises 2–5. For exercises 6–8, compare by writing >, <, or =.

2. $400,000 + 50,000 + 6,000 + 100$

3. fifteen thousand, forty-two

4. nine hundred thousand

5. two hundred thousand, six hundred

6. 57,294 ● 47,294

7. 125,613 ● 125,813

8. 41,695 ● 241,695

You learned about rounding numbers to the nearest hundred, thousand, and ten thousand. To review, look at pages 432 and 434. Round each number to the nearest hundred, thousand, and ten thousand for exercises 9–12.

9. 27,814

10. 61,502

11. 387,489

12. 915,367

You learned about comparing price and quality. Look at pages 436 and 437 to review the ways in which you can judge price versus quality.

13. What helps you judge price versus quality when buying meat?

FOCUS | Review and test skills learned and practiced.

LOOKING AHEAD

Preparing For Next Year

This year you focused on

NUMBER SKILLS.	MEASUREMENT.
GEOMETRY.	PATTERNS AND FUNCTIONS.
ALGEBRA.	PROBABILITY AND STATISTICS.
LOGIC.	

It will be easier for you next year if you keep your math skills sharp while you are not at school. Here are a few suggestions for things to do on your vacation that will help you to stay mathematically powerful.

ALGEBRA

If you go bowling, let $\triangle$ stand for the number of pins you knock down. Remember that there are always 10 pins standing at the beginning of each frame. Complete this number sentence for each frame.

$10 -$ pins left standing $= \triangle$.

MEASUREMENT

Plant some bean seeds. These can be grown indoors or outdoors. Measure the plants each week. How much did your plants grow altogether?

NUMBER SKILLS

If you go to the movies, estimate the number of people at the show. Count the number of people in your row. Then multiply by the number of rows in the theater. Use a calculator if you have one. How close was your estimate to the actual number of people in the theater?

GEOMETRY

You see many shapes around you every day. One of these shapes is a circle. Make a list of the circles you see when you are in your kitchen. Can you find any circles outside? Keep a list of them while riding in your car or swimming at the beach or pool.

PATTERNS AND FUNCTIONS

Do you like to play clapping games? If you do, try to play a clapping game with a friend using this code:

1 = Each partner claps own hands.
2 = Partners clap each others' hands.
3 = Each partner crosses arms and claps each others' hands

Try this pattern: 1, 2, 1, 3, 1, 3, 1, 2, 1 Repeat this pattern as long as you can. Make up other patterns and play clapping games with all your friends!

PROBABILITY AND STATISTICS

Summer is a great time to play outside because there are more hours of daylight. Make a chart to record the time you go to bed each night. Do this for a few weeks. Find the average time you go to bed each week. Then make a line graph.

Write the letter of the correct answer.

Multiply.

1. $\begin{array}{r} 15 \\ \times 12 \end{array}$ **A.** 280   **B.** 170   **C.** 180   **D.** 190

2. $\begin{array}{r} 25 \\ \times 15 \end{array}$ **E.** 257   **F.** 375   **G.** 275   **H.** 385

3. $\begin{array}{r} 357 \\ \times 32 \end{array}$ **A.** 11,424   **B.** 12,425   **C.** 11,524   **D.** 12,525

4. $\begin{array}{r} 624 \\ \times 53 \end{array}$ **E.** 34,072   **F.** 34,182   **G.** 33,172   **H.** 33,072

Divide.

7. $10\overline{)70}$ **A.** 8   **B.** 6   **C.** 7   **D.** 3

8. $40\overline{)120}$ **E.** 3   **F.** 4   **G.** 2   **H.** 5

9. $70\overline{)89}$ **A.** 1 R29   **B.** 2 R19   **C.** 1 R19   **D.** 1 R17

10. $14\overline{)84}$ **E.** 5   **F.** 7 R3   **G.** 6   **H.** 6 R1

11. $10\overline{)400}$ **A.** 30   **B.** 40   **C.** 20   **D.** 50

12. $30\overline{)632}$ **E.** 31 R2   **F.** 20 R1   **G.** 21 R2   **H.** 11 R1

13. $23\overline{)164}$ **A.** 7 R3   **B.** 7 R2   **C.** 6 R3   **D.** 8 R3

14. $14\overline{)478}$ **E.** 44 R1   **F.** 54 R2   **G.** 34 R2   **H.** 35 R2

What is the area of the rectangle?

5. length = 15 in.   width = 9 in.
   - **A.** 135 square inches
   - **B.** 235 square inches
   - **C.** 145 square inches
   - **D.** 255 square inches

6. length = 34 cm   width = 25 cm
   - **E.** 750 square centimeters
   - **F.** 860 square centimeters
   - **G.** 950 square centimeters
   - **H.** 850 square centimeters

What unit is used to measure

15. the length of a book?   **A.** in.   **B.** ft   **C.** yd   **D.** mi

16. the length of a rug?   **E.** in.   **F.** ft   **G.** yd   **H.** mi

17. the weight of a truck?   **A.** oz   **B.** lb   **C.** t   **D.** mi

18. the weight of a sandwich?   **E.** oz   **F.** lb   **G.** t   **H.** yd

FOCUS | Review concepts and skills taught in Chapters 25 through 32.

What is the temperature?

19. water boils

    A. 212°F   **B.** 121°F

    C. 312°F   **D.** 100°F

20. water freezes

    E. 0°F   **F.** 32°F

    G. 12°F   **H.** 50°F

21. body temperature

    A. 30°F   **B.** 54°F

    C. 200°F   **D.** 98.6°F

Complete.

22. 6 pints = ▦ cups

    E. 12   **F.** 24   **G.** 18   **H.** 32

23. 16 quarts = ▦ gallons

    A. 8   **B.** 2   **C.** 4   **D.** 6

Which figures are congruent?

24.

    E.   **F.**

    G.   **H.**

What is the perimeter of each rectangle?

25. length = 32 cm   width = 21 cm

    A. 106 cm   **B.** 672 cm

    C. 206 cm   **D.** 572 cm

26. length = 43 m   width = 14 m

    E. 602 m   **F.** 214 m

    G. 114 m   **H.** 432 m

What is the correct open sentence?

27.

△	4	5	6	7	8	9
□	1	2	3	4	5	6

    A. $\triangle + 3 = \square$ **B.** $\triangle - 4 = \square$

    C. $\triangle \times 3 = \square$ **D.** $\triangle - 3 = \square$

28.

✳	2	4	6	8	10
△	6	12	18	24	30

    E. $✳ \div 3 = \triangle$ **F.** $✳ + 3 = \triangle$

    G. $✳ \times 3 = \triangle$ **H.** $✳ \times 2 = \triangle$

What is the value of the *3* in each number?

29. 24,378

    A. 30,000   **B.** 3,000

    C. 300   **D.** 30

30. 352,641

    E. 300,000   **F.** 30,000

    G. 3,000   **H.** 300

Write the letter of the correct answer.

Multiply.

1. 700
    × 6

    A. 1,300 **B.** 4,200
    C. 420 **D.** 2,400

2. 257
    × 15

    E. 3,855 **F.** 2,854
    G. 4,855 **H.** 3,865

3. 532
    × 34

    A. 28,088 **B.** 18,178
    C. 17,088 **D.** 18,088

4. $5.78
    × 9

    E. $5.02 **F.** $42.02
    G. $52.02 **H.** $52.70

What is the area of the rectangle?

5. length = 23 cm   width = 15 cm

   A. 75 square centimeters
   B. 345 square centimeters
   C. 335 square centimeters
   D. 145 square centimeters

What is the perimeter of the rectangle?

6. length = 47 cm   width = 21 cm

   E. 136 cm **F.** 987 cm
   G. 236 cm **H.** 68 cm

Divide.

7. 8)9,785 **A.** 123 R1 **B.** 1,223 R1
   C. 2,123 R2 **D.** 1,223 R4

8. 25)673 **E.** 26 R23 **F.** 126 R1
   G. 25 R23 **H.** 26 R12

9. 32)784 **A.** 27 **B.** 28 R2
   C. 27 R16 **D.** 24 R16

10. 7)$9.59 **E.** $2.37 **F.** $1.47
    G. $10.37 **H.** $1.37

Add or subtract.

11. 43,657
    +12,345

    A. 56,002 **B.** 46,102
    C. 66,012 **D.** 56,112

12. 65,978
    −43,867

    E. 23,111 **F.** 20,121
    G. 22,111 **H.** 34,121

Name the polygon.

13.
    A. triangle
    B. square
    C. circle
    D. octagon

14.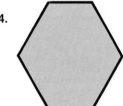
    E. triangle
    F. rectangle
    G. octagon
    H. hexagon

FOCUS | Review concepts and skills taught in Chapters 1 through 32.

What is the correct open sentence?

15.

□	4	5	6	7	8	9
△	2	3	4	5	6	7

A. □ − 2 = △   **B.** □ × 2 = △

C. □ + 2 = △   **D.** □ − 3 = △

16.

✻	3	6	9	12	15	18
□	1	2	3	4	5	6

E. ✻ + 3 = □   **F.** ✻ ÷ 2 = □

G. ✻ − 3 = □   **H.** ✻ ÷ 3 = □

Add or subtract.

17. 32.8
$+15.9$
   A. 48.7   **B.** 58.6
   C. 38.7   **D.** 48.6

18. 78.5
-32.8
   E. 55.6   **F.** 45.9
   G. 45.7   **H.** 35.8

19. $\$25.67$
$-\ 13.75$
   A. $12.95   **B.** $10.29
   C. $11.92   **D.** $11.72

20. $\$65.12$
$+\ 11.32$
   E. $76.44   **F.** $56.35
   G. $76.54   **H.** $86.44

21. $\frac{3}{5} + \frac{4}{5}$
   A. $1\frac{3}{5}$ **B.** $1\frac{2}{5}$
   C. $2\frac{2}{5}$ **D.** $1\frac{1}{5}$

22. $\frac{7}{12} + \frac{8}{12}$
   E. $1\frac{1}{2}$ **F.** $2\frac{3}{4}$
   G. $1\frac{1}{4}$ **H.** $1\frac{1}{12}$

Subtract.

23. $\frac{9}{10} - \frac{8}{10}$
   A. $\frac{3}{10}$ **B.** $\frac{4}{10}$
   C. $\frac{1}{10}$ **D.** $\frac{2}{10}$

24. $\frac{5}{6} - \frac{2}{6}$
   E. $\frac{1}{6}$ **F.** $\frac{1}{2}$
   G. $\frac{2}{3}$ **H.** $\frac{5}{6}$

Rename as a mixed number.

25. $\frac{12}{10}$
   A. $1\frac{1}{5}$ **B.** $2\frac{2}{5}$
   C. $1\frac{2}{5}$ **D.** $1\frac{3}{10}$

26. $\frac{7}{2}$
   E. $2\frac{1}{2}$ **F.** $3\frac{1}{2}$
   G. $1\frac{1}{2}$ **H.** $4\frac{1}{2}$

27. $\frac{16}{5}$
   A. $2\frac{1}{5}$ **B.** $1\frac{2}{5}$
   C. $3\frac{1}{5}$ **D.** $3\frac{2}{5}$

Which figures are similar?

28.

E.   F.

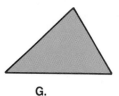

G.   H.

29. What unit is used to measure water in a pool?

   A. cup   **B.** pint

   C. quart   **D.** gallon

EXTRA PRACTICE

Chapter 2 (page 16) Multiply the factors to find each product.

1. $\begin{array}{r} 3 \\ \times 3 \\ \hline \end{array}$
2. $\begin{array}{r} 6 \\ \times 1 \\ \hline \end{array}$
3. $\begin{array}{r} 0 \\ \times 7 \\ \hline \end{array}$
4. $\begin{array}{r} 4 \\ \times 3 \\ \hline \end{array}$
5. $\begin{array}{r} 9 \\ \times 8 \\ \hline \end{array}$
6. $\begin{array}{r} 6 \\ \times 5 \\ \hline \end{array}$

7. $\begin{array}{r} 6 \\ \times 2 \\ \hline \end{array}$
8. $\begin{array}{r} 9 \\ \times 5 \\ \hline \end{array}$
9. $\begin{array}{r} 6 \\ \times 3 \\ \hline \end{array}$
10. $\begin{array}{r} 6 \\ \times 7 \\ \hline \end{array}$
11. $\begin{array}{r} 4 \\ \times 7 \\ \hline \end{array}$
12. $\begin{array}{r} 9 \\ \times 0 \\ \hline \end{array}$

13. 2×5
14. 3×9
15. 3×7
16. 4×9
17. 5×8

18. 4×5
19. 7×7
20. 9×2
21. 8×7
22. 9×9

Chapter 3 (page 36) Find each quotient.

1. $10 \div 2$
2. $30 \div 5$
3. $21 \div 7$
4. $9 \div 3$
5. $24 \div 8$

6. $20 \div 4$
7. $12 \div 6$
8. $18 \div 2$
9. $15 \div 5$
10. $36 \div 9$

11. $2\overline{)12}$
12. $7\overline{)49}$
13. $3\overline{)27}$
14. $6\overline{)42}$
15. $8\overline{)40}$
16. $4\overline{)36}$

17. $4\overline{)28}$
18. $5\overline{)40}$
19. $8\overline{)64}$
20. $3\overline{)18}$
21. $9\overline{)72}$
22. $8\overline{)56}$

Chapter 4 (page 44) Multiply.

1. 3×10
2. 8×10
3. 2×10
4. 7×10
5. 5×10

6. 4×10
7. 3×20
8. 6×10
9. 2×40
10. 9×10

11. $\begin{array}{r} 10 \\ \times 4 \\ \hline \end{array}$
12. $\begin{array}{r} 10 \\ \times 9 \\ \hline \end{array}$
13. $\begin{array}{r} 30 \\ \times 3 \\ \hline \end{array}$
14. $\begin{array}{r} 40 \\ \times 2 \\ \hline \end{array}$
15. $\begin{array}{r} 50 \\ \times 2 \\ \hline \end{array}$
16. $\begin{array}{r} 60 \\ \times 3 \\ \hline \end{array}$

17. $\begin{array}{r} 40 \\ \times 8 \\ \hline \end{array}$
18. $\begin{array}{r} 80 \\ \times 4 \\ \hline \end{array}$
19. $\begin{array}{r} 60 \\ \times 5 \\ \hline \end{array}$
20. $\begin{array}{r} 90 \\ \times 6 \\ \hline \end{array}$
21. $\begin{array}{r} 70 \\ \times 8 \\ \hline \end{array}$
22. $\begin{array}{r} 50 \\ \times 7 \\ \hline \end{array}$

23. $\begin{array}{r} 70 \\ \times 3 \\ \hline \end{array}$
24. $\begin{array}{r} 80 \\ \times 7 \\ \hline \end{array}$
25. $\begin{array}{r} 60 \\ \times 4 \\ \hline \end{array}$
26. $\begin{array}{r} 90 \\ \times 8 \\ \hline \end{array}$
27. $\begin{array}{r} 90 \\ \times 9 \\ \hline \end{array}$
28. $\begin{array}{r} 90 \\ \times 5 \\ \hline \end{array}$

Chapter 5 (page 62) Name each line segment, line, or ray.

1.

2.

3.

4.

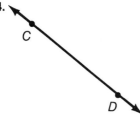

5.

6.

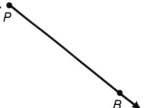

How many line segments form each polygon?

7. triangle   **8.** square   **9.** hexagon   **10.** octagon

Chapter 6 (page 74) Round to the nearest ten.

1. 13,842   **2.** 37,569   **3.** 20,315   **4.** 56,274

Round to the nearest hundred.

5. 18,672   **6.** 43,328   **7.** 64,517   **8.** 89,493

Chapter 7 (page 84) Add.

1.	**2.**	**3.**	**4.**	**5.**	**6.**
234	136	675	264	618	483
+312	+127	+132	+567	+192	+399

7. 613 + 24   **8.** 252 + 39   **9.** 785 + 71   **10.** 367 + 44   **11.** 829 + 71

(page 90) Subtract.

12.	**13.**	**14.**	**15.**	**16.**	**17.**
830	370	610	520	760	950
−124	−155	−339	−189	−692	−877

18. 306 − 153   **19.** 702 − 361   **20.** 407 − 168   **21.** 902 − 639   **22.** 505 − 416

EXTRA PRACTICE

Chapter 8 (page 98) Add.

1.	2.	3.	4.	5.
12,432 +11,234	64,127 +13,832	25,357 +22,497	38,409 +31,742	57,245 +31,899

6.	7.	8.	9.	10.
23,543 + 3,122	47,193 + 2,514	74,983 + 2,286	51,777 + 9,645	80,999 + 9,998

(page 102) Subtract.

11.	12.	13.	14.	15.
56,759 − 24,346	72,487 − 30,176	42,836 − 37,158	91,054 − 63,287	70,853 − 64,999

16.	17.	18.	19.	20.
16,752 − 5,631	36,258 − 4,398	65,604 − 9,358	92,860 − 7,883	75,021 − 7,555

Chapter 9 (page 118) Use these fraction bars to copy and complete the equivalent fractions.

1.
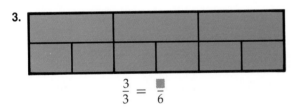
$$\frac{1}{4} = \frac{\blacksquare}{8} \qquad \frac{3}{4} = \frac{\blacksquare}{8}$$

2.
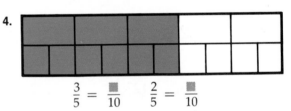
$$\frac{2}{3} = \frac{\blacksquare}{12} \qquad \frac{1}{3} = \frac{\blacksquare}{12}$$

3.
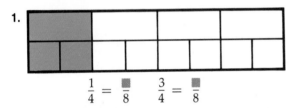
$$\frac{3}{3} = \frac{\blacksquare}{6}$$

4.
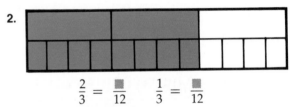
$$\frac{3}{5} = \frac{\blacksquare}{10} \qquad \frac{2}{5} = \frac{\blacksquare}{10}$$

Chapter 10 (page 126) Add.

1.	2.	3.	4.	5.	6.
5.4 +3.4	2.8 +4.6	7.2 +1.9	8.7 +3.8	4.3 +7.7	9.5 +6.9

(page 130) Subtract.

7.	8.	9.	10.	11.	12.
8.5 −3.2	3.8 −2.1	6.9 −1.6	9.6 −4.7	5.2 −2.8	4.1 −1.9

Chapter 11 (page 142) Copy and complete.

1. 2 m = ■ cm
2. 6 m = ■ cm
3. 9 m = ■ cm

4. 4 m = ■ cm
5. 7 m = ■ cm
6. 1 km = ■ m

7. 5 km = ■ m
8. 3 km = ■ m
9. 8 km = ■ m

(page 146) Copy and complete.

10. 3 kg = ■ g
11. 7 kg = ■ g
12. 10 kg = ■ g

13. 4 kg = ■ g
14. 6 kg = ■ g
15. 1 000 g = ■ kg

16. 5 000 g = ■ kg
17. 2 000 g = ■ kg
18. 9 000 g = ■ kg

Chapter 12 (page 156) Copy and complete.

1. 4 L = ■ mL
2. 6 L = ■ mL
3. 8 L = ■ mL

4. 2 L = ■ mL
5. 9 L = ■ mL
6. 1 000 mL = ■ L

7. 5 000 mL = ■ L
8. 3 000 mL = ■ L
9. 7 000 mL = ■ L

10. 3 L = ■ mL
11. 4 000 mL = ■ L
12. 9 L = ■ mL

Chapter 13 (page 168) Multiply.

1. 8×100
2. 4×100
3. 3×500
4. 5×800
5. 7×700

6. $\begin{array}{r} 700 \\ \times\ 4 \\ \hline \end{array}$
7. $\begin{array}{r} 800 \\ \times\ 8 \\ \hline \end{array}$
8. $\begin{array}{r} 900 \\ \times\ 5 \\ \hline \end{array}$
9. $\begin{array}{r} 400 \\ \times\ 7 \\ \hline \end{array}$
10. $\begin{array}{r} 600 \\ \times\ 9 \\ \hline \end{array}$
11. $\begin{array}{r} 300 \\ \times\ 6 \\ \hline \end{array}$

(page 172) Multiply.

12. $\begin{array}{r} 142 \\ \times\ 2 \\ \hline \end{array}$
13. $\begin{array}{r} 321 \\ \times\ 3 \\ \hline \end{array}$
14. $\begin{array}{r} 524 \\ \times\ 4 \\ \hline \end{array}$
15. $\begin{array}{r} 213 \\ \times\ 7 \\ \hline \end{array}$
16. $\begin{array}{r} 655 \\ \times\ 5 \\ \hline \end{array}$
17. $\begin{array}{r} 367 \\ \times\ 6 \\ \hline \end{array}$

18. $\begin{array}{r} 845 \\ \times\ 4 \\ \hline \end{array}$
19. $\begin{array}{r} 913 \\ \times\ 3 \\ \hline \end{array}$
20. $\begin{array}{r} 489 \\ \times\ 6 \\ \hline \end{array}$
21. $\begin{array}{r} 967 \\ \times\ 8 \\ \hline \end{array}$
22. $\begin{array}{r} 529 \\ \times\ 7 \\ \hline \end{array}$
23. $\begin{array}{r} 838 \\ \times\ 9 \\ \hline \end{array}$

EXTRA PRACTICE

Chapter 14 (page 180) Divide.

1. $3\overline{)912}$ 2. $5\overline{)889}$ 3. $7\overline{)945}$ 4. $4\overline{)879}$ 5. $8\overline{)824}$

6. $6\overline{)737}$ 7. $3\overline{)817}$ 8. $9\overline{)952}$ 9. $7\overline{)481}$ 10. $5\overline{)216}$

11. $186 \div 3$ 12. $528 \div 8$ 13. $389 \div 4$ 14. $576 \div 6$ 15. $199 \div 7$

(page 184) Divide.

16. $2\overline{)720}$ 17. $4\overline{)580}$ 18. $7\overline{)730}$ 19. $3\overline{)907}$ 20. $8\overline{)902}$

21. $7\overline{)560}$ 22. $5\overline{)280}$ 23. $6\overline{)307}$ 24. $8\overline{)704}$ 25. $9\overline{)809}$

Chapter 15 (page 200) Write *true* or *false*.

1. $\angle ABC$ is a right angle.

2. 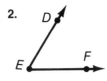 $\angle DEF$ is larger than a right angle.

3. 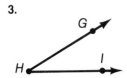 $\angle GHI$ is smaller than a right angle.

4. $\angle JKL$ is smaller than a right angle.

5. A rectangle has four right angles.   6. A square has no right angles.

Chapter 16 (page 208) Write the number of faces.

1. 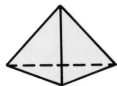   2. 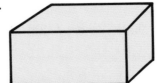   3.

(page 212) Answer the questions.

4. The radius of a circle is 3 cm long. How long is the diameter?

5. The diameter of a circle is 10 cm long. How long is the radius?

6. The diameter of a circle is 12 cm long. How long is the radius?

7. The radius of a circle is 16 cm long. How long is the diameter?

Chapter 17 (page 224) Write as a decimal.

1. $\frac{25}{100}$ 2. $\frac{73}{100}$ 3. $\frac{11}{100}$ 4. $\frac{1}{100}$ 5. $\frac{7}{100}$ 6. $\frac{5}{100}$

7. $1\frac{15}{100}$ 8. $4\frac{64}{100}$ 9. $3\frac{96}{100}$ 10. $2\frac{6}{100}$ 11. $1\frac{8}{100}$ 12. $5\frac{9}{100}$

(page 228) Write >, <, or =.

13. 1.34 ● 1.33   14. 0.52 ● 0.56   15. 6.78 ● 6.78   16. 0.78 ● 0.88

17. 2.07 ● 2.04   18. 4.81 ● 5.21   19. 5.84 ● 5.98   20. 0.66 ● 0.60

Chapter 18 (page 236) Write each decimal.

1. twenty-three hundredths   2. fourteen hundredths

3. ninety hundredths   4. two hundredths

5. sixty-eight and fifty-four hundredths

6. twenty-seven and eight hundredths

7. thirty and forty hundredths

Chapter 19 (page 250) Add.

1.   6.54
   $+3.23$
2.   4.12
   $+7.34$
3.   5.68
   $+4.29$
4.   8.37
   $+8.73$
5.   9.56
   $+7.98$
6.   2.88
   $+7.99$

7. 8.45 + 1.3   8. 3.22 + 9.5   9. 6.84 + 5.6   10. 7.7 + 8.49   11. 4.3 + 9.92

12. 9.4 + 6.78   13. 7.03 + 7.99   14. 4.4 + 9.39   15. 7.55 + 11.4   16. 9.18 + 1.68

(page 256) Subtract.

17.   8.63
    -2.42
18.   2.85
    -1.74
19.   6.71
    -3.81
20.   9.58
    -2.39
21.   7.34
    -5.67
22.   9.17
    -6.39

23. 5.37 − 1.2   24. 4.45 − 2.9   25. 6.18 − 3.8   26. 7.6 − 4.49   27. 5.3 − 1.88

28. 9.8 − 5.91   29. 7.4 − 3.56   30. 5.81 − 4.9   31. 6.2 − 4.37   32. 8.19 − 4.5

EXTRA PRACTICE

Chapter 20 (page 268) Multiply.

1. 3,241
    × 2

2. 3,213
    × 3

3. 4,572
    × 5

4. 6,218
    × 4

5. 5,347
    × 3

6. 1,754
    × 6

7. 2,468
    × 2

8. 6,788
    × 5

9. 8,243
    × 8

10. 1,619
    × 4

11. 9 × 7,355   12. 7 × 1,626   13. 8 × 5,634   14. 9 × 9,827   15. 6 × 9,789

Chapter 21 (page 282) Divide.

1. 2)8,462   2. 3)9,636   3. 7)8,455   4. 2)5,304   5. 6)8,112

6. 4)9,648   7. 3)5,789   8. 5)4,731   9. 3)1,727   10. 8)6,910

11. 2,352 ÷ 6   12. 1,111 ÷ 2   13. 4,062 ÷ 7   14. 3,089 ÷ 5   15. 7,954 ÷ 8

Chapter 22 (page 290) Use the line graph to answer the questions.

1. How many races did Erica enter in January?

2. In which month did she enter the fewest number of races?

3. How many more races did she enter in Feb. than in Dec.?

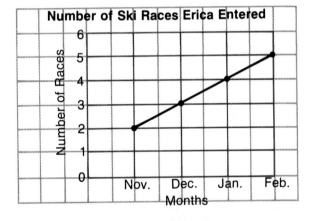

(page 294) Use the circle graph to answer the questions.

4. What fraction of all the puppies are terriers? collies?

5. What is the sum of the fractions in the circle graph?

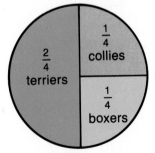

Chapter 23 (page 310) Rename each fraction as a mixed number.

1. $\frac{7}{5}$ 2. $\frac{9}{2}$ 3. $\frac{17}{4}$ 4. $\frac{19}{3}$ 5. $\frac{11}{6}$ 6. $\frac{23}{10}$

7. $\frac{37}{8}$ 8. $\frac{29}{4}$ 9. $\frac{19}{2}$ 10. $\frac{32}{5}$ 11. $\frac{47}{10}$ 12. $\frac{25}{3}$

Chapter 24 (page 318) Add. Rename in simplest terms.

1. $\frac{1}{5} + \frac{1}{5}$ 2. $\frac{3}{4} + \frac{1}{4}$ 3. $\frac{2}{6} + \frac{2}{6}$ 4. $\frac{2}{5} + \frac{4}{5}$ 5. $\frac{3}{10} + \frac{5}{10}$

6. $\frac{1}{8} + \frac{3}{8}$ 7. $\frac{7}{10} + \frac{9}{10}$ 8. $\frac{4}{5} + \frac{4}{5}$ 9. $\frac{1}{6} + \frac{2}{6}$ 10. $\frac{1}{10} + \frac{5}{10}$

(page 322) Subtract. Rename in simplest terms.

11. $\frac{2}{3} - \frac{1}{3}$ 12. $\frac{4}{5} - \frac{3}{5}$ 13. $\frac{5}{8} - \frac{1}{8}$ 14. $\frac{7}{10} - \frac{3}{10}$ 15. $\frac{7}{12} - \frac{5}{12}$

16. $\frac{3}{4} - \frac{1}{4}$ 17. $\frac{9}{10} - \frac{1}{10}$ 18. $\frac{11}{12} - \frac{3}{12}$ 19. $\frac{7}{8} - \frac{3}{8}$ 20. $\frac{9}{10} - \frac{4}{10}$

Chapter 25 (page 338) Multiply.

1. 432×20 2. 123×30 3. 451×50 4. 342×12 5. 536×53

6. 620×37 7. 557×25 8. 186×43 9. 279×64 10. 333×78

11. 82×575 12. 97×801 13. 56×480 14. 87×709 15. 99×903

16. 48×319 17. 75×604 18. 36×475 19. 27×860 20. 84×723

Chapter 26 (page 350) Divide.

1. $15 \overline{)60}$ 2. $31 \overline{)75}$ 3. $22 \overline{)63}$ 4. $18 \overline{)80}$ 5. $56 \overline{)94}$

6. $47 \overline{)79}$ 7. $38 \overline{)76}$ 8. $31 \overline{)81}$ 9. $25 \overline{)63}$ 10. $16 \overline{)64}$

11. $42 \div 11$ 12. $99 \div 29$ 13. $60 \div 41$ 14. $90 \div 34$ 15. $84 \div 12$

16. $75 \div 13$ 17. $94 \div 27$ 18. $62 \div 56$ 19. $84 \div 38$ 20. $79 \div 41$

EXTRA PRACTICE

Chapter 27 (page 360) Divide.

1. $10\overline{)180}$ 2. $10\overline{)240}$ 3. $40\overline{)520}$ 4. $30\overline{)417}$ 5. $20\overline{)400}$

6. $60\overline{)750}$ 7. $20\overline{)958}$ 8. $10\overline{)123}$ 9. $10\overline{)187}$ 10. $20\overline{)160}$

11. $383 \div 50$ 12. $195 \div 40$ 13. $567 \div 80$ 14. $818 \div 90$ 15. $405 \div 70$

(page 366) Divide.

16. $13\overline{)184}$ 17. $18\overline{)427}$ 18. $21\overline{)537}$ 19. $35\overline{)210}$ 20. $67\overline{)820}$

21. $44\overline{)791}$ 22. $59\overline{)817}$ 23. $16\overline{)144}$ 24. $61\overline{)280}$ 25. $44\overline{)220}$

26. $389 \div 76$ 27. $107 \div 12$ 28. $445 \div 82$ 29. $318 \div 53$ 30. $686 \div 99$

Chapter 28 (page 376) Copy and complete.

1. 3 ft = ■ in.   2. 7 ft = ■ in.   3. 10 ft = ■ in.

4. 4 yd = ■ ft   5. 6 yd = ■ ft   6. 9 yd = ■ ft

7. 1 mi = ■ ft   8. 3 mi = ■ ft   9. 2 mi = ■ yd

(page 378) Copy and complete.

10. 3 lb = ■ oz   11. 7 lb = ■ oz   12. 8 lb = ■ oz

13. 9 lb = ■ oz   14. 1 lb 3 oz = ■ oz   15. 4 lb 7 oz = ■ oz

16. 6 lb 10 oz = ■ oz   17. $\frac{1}{2}$ t = ■ lb   18. 5 t = ■ lb

Chapter 29 (page 390) Copy and complete.

1. 6 cups = ■ pt   2. 8 cups = ■ pt   3. 4 pt = ■ qt

4. 10 pt = ■ qt   5. 3 qt = ■ pt   6. 4 qt = ■ pt

7. 3 gal = ■ pt   8. 2 gal = ■ qt   9. 5 gal = ■ qt

Chapter 30 (page 400) Tell whether these figures are similar or both congruent and similar.

1.
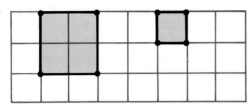

2.
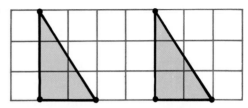

3.
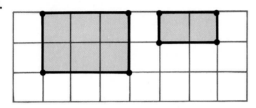

4.
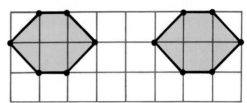

Chapter 31 (page 414) Find the rule and write an open sentence.

1.

○	1	2	3	4	5
△	4	5	6	7	8

2.

*	6	7	8	9	10
□	0	1	2	3	4

3.

□	1	2	3	4	5
▽	4	8	12	16	20

4.

⊕	2	4	6	8	10
⊞	1	2	3	4	5

Chapter 32 (page 428) Write each number in standard form.

1. 30,000 + 2,000 + 50 + 4

2. 10,000 + 1,000 + 800 + 70

3. 800,000,000 + 30,000 + 6,000

4. 400,000 + 9,000 + 600 + 10 + 3

5. six thousand, twenty-three

6. thirty-five million, two hundred

7. nine hundred thousand

8. two hundred thousand, sixteen

Write the value of the underlined digit.

9. 4$\underline{7}$8,050,621

10. 6,13$\underline{5}$

11. $\underline{9}$,128

12. 34,$\underline{6}$52

13. $\underline{1}$7,083

14. 493,$\underline{6}$52,187

15. $\underline{6}$18,794

16. 1$\underline{2}$8,045

DATA BANK

Five-Step Problem-Solving Plan

1. READ   Do I know the meaning of all the words?

2. KNOW   What is the question?
What am I being asked to find?
Which **key facts** do I need to answer the question?

3. PLAN   Which operation should I use?
Which strategy should I choose?

4. SOLVE   Carry out the plan.
Can I write a number sentence?
What is my answer?

5. CHECK   Why is my answer reasonable?
Does it answer the question?

Table of Geometric Shapes

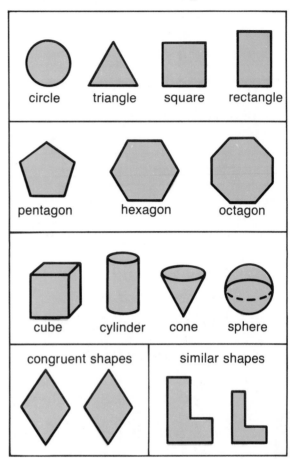

Addition/Subtraction Table

	0	1	2	3	4	5	6	7	8	9
0	0	1	2	3	4	5	6	7	8	9
1	1	2	3	4	5	6	7	8	9	10
2	2	3	4	5	6	7	8	9	10	11
3	3	4	5	6	7	8	9	10	11	12
4	4	5	6	7	8	9	10	11	12	13
5	5	6	7	8	9	10	11	12	13	14
6	6	7	8	9	10	11	12	13	14	15
7	7	8	9	10	11	12	13	14	15	16
8	8	9	10	11	12	13	14	15	16	17
9	9	10	11	12	13	14	15	16	17	18

Multiplication/Division Table

	0	1	2	3	4	5	6	7	8	9
0	0	0	0	0	0	0	0	0	0	0
1	0	1	2	3	4	5	6	7	8	9
2	0	2	4	6	8	10	12	14	16	18
3	0	3	6	9	12	15	18	21	24	27
4	0	4	8	12	16	20	24	28	32	36
5	0	5	10	15	20	25	30	35	40	45
6	0	6	12	18	24	30	36	42	48	54
7	0	7	14	21	28	35	42	49	56	63
8	0	8	16	24	32	40	48	56	64	72
9	0	9	18	27	36	45	54	63	72	81

Table of Measure

Time

1 minute (min)	=	60 seconds (s)
1 hour (h)	=	60 minutes
1 day	=	24 hours
1 week	=	7 days
1 month is about 4 weeks		
1 year	=	365 days / 52 weeks / 12 months
1 leap year	=	366 days
1 decade	=	10 years
1 century	=	100 years

Place-Value Chart

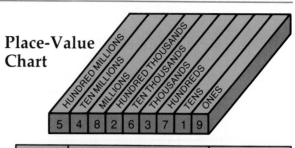

Digit	Place	Value
5	Hundred Millions	500,000,000
4	Ten Millions	40,000,000
8	Millions	8,000,000
2	Hundred Thousands	200,000
6	Ten Thousands	60,000
3	Thousands	3,000
7	Hundreds	700
1	Tens	10
9	Ones	9

Table of Symbols

+	plus
−	minus
×	times; multiplied by
÷	divided by
=	is equal to
≠	is not equal to
>	is greater than
<	is less than
( )	Parentheses mean "do this operation first."
¢	cents
$	dollars
∟	right angle
∠XYZ	angle XYZ
$\overleftrightarrow{AB}$	line AB
$\overline{AB}$	line segment AB
$\overrightarrow{AB}$	ray AB
△	triangle
□	square
▭	rectangle
°	degree
s	second
min	minute
h	hour
y	year

Customary Measure

Length
in. inch
ft foot
yd yard
mi mile

Capacity
c cup
pt pint
qt quart
gal gallon

Weight
oz ounce
lb pound
t ton

Temperature
°F degree Fahrenheit

Metric Measure

Length
mm millimeter
cm centimeter
dm decimeter
m meter
km kilometer

Capacity
mL milliliter
L liter

Mass
mg milligram
g gram
kg kilogram
t ton

Temperature
°C degree Celsius

Table of Metric Measures

Length

1 centimeter (cm) = 10 millimeters (mm)

1 decimeter (dm) = $\begin{cases} 100 \text{ millimeters} \\ 10 \text{ centimeters} \end{cases}$

1 meter (m) = $\begin{cases} 1\ 000 \text{ millimeters}^* \\ 100 \text{ centimeters} \\ 10 \text{ decimeters} \end{cases}$

1 kilometer (km) = 1 000 meters

Area

1 square centimeter (cm^2) = 100 square millimeters (mm^2)

1 square meter (m^2) = $\begin{cases} 100 \text{ square decimeters (dm}^2) \\ 10\ 000 \text{ square centimeters} \end{cases}$

Volume

1 cubic centimeter (cm^3) = 1 000 cubic millimeters (mm^3)

1 cubic decimeter (dm^3) = $\begin{cases} 1\ 000 \text{ cubic centimeters} \\ 1 \text{ Liter (L)} \end{cases}$

1 cubic meter (m^3) = 1 000 000 cubic centimeters

Capacity

1 liter = $\begin{cases} 1\ 000 \text{ milliliters (mL)} \\ 1\ 000 \text{ cubic centimeters} \end{cases}$

Mass

1 gram (g) = 1 000 milligrams (mg)
1 kilogram (kg) = 1 000 grams
1 metric ton (t) = 1 000 kilograms

Temperature

Water freezes at 0 degrees Celsius (0°C).
Water boils at 100 degrees Celsius (100°C).

*According to the United States Metric Association, spaces are used instead of commas in metric measurement.

Table of Customary Measures

Length

1 foot (ft) = 12 inches (in.)

1 yard (yd) = $\begin{cases} \text{3 feet} \\ \text{36 inches} \end{cases}$

1 mile (mi) = $\begin{cases} \text{1,760 yards} \\ \text{5,280 feet} \end{cases}$

Area

1 square foot (ft^2) = 144 square inches (in^2)
1 square yard (yd^2) = 9 square feet
1 acre = 4,840 square yards

Volume

1 cubic foot (ft^3) = 1,728 cubic inches (in^3)
1 cubic yard (yd^3) = 27 cubic feet

Capacity

1 cup (c) = 8 fluid ounces (fl oz)

1 pint (pt) = $\begin{cases} \text{16 fluid ounces} \\ \text{2 cups} \end{cases}$

1 quart (qt) = $\begin{cases} \text{32 fluid ounces} \\ \text{4 cups} \\ \text{2 pints} \end{cases}$

1 gallon (gal) = $\begin{cases} \text{128 fluid ounces} \\ \text{16 cups} \\ \text{8 pints} \\ \text{4 quarts} \end{cases}$

Weight

1 pound (lb) = 16 ounces (oz)
1 ton (t) = 2,000 pounds

Temperature

Water freezes at 32 degrees Fahrenheit (32°F).
Water boils at 212 degrees Fahrenheit (212°F).

addend   Any number to be added.

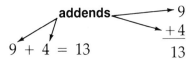
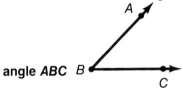

$9 + 4 = 13$

angle   A figure formed by two rays that have the same endpoint.

angle *ABC*

area   The number of square units inside a figure. The area of this figure is six square units.

associative property of addition   The sum of three addends is the same, no matter how they are grouped.
$(3 + 4) + 7 = 3 + (4 + 7)$

associative property of multiplication   The product of three factors is the same, no matter how they are grouped.
$(2 \times 3) \times 6 = 2 \times (3 \times 6)$

average   The sum of a set of numbers divided by the number of addends.

BASIC   The name of a computer language that stands for Beginner's All-Purpose Symbolic Instruction Code.

bug   A mistake in a computer program.

capacity   The amount a container will hold when filled.

circle   A curved figure formed by a set of points that are an equal distance from a center point.

circumference   The distance around a circle.

CLS   (clear screen) A BASIC command used to clear the computer screen.

command   An instruction given to a computer.

common denominator   A common multiple of the denominators of two or more given fractions. A common denominator of $\frac{1}{3}$ and $\frac{3}{4}$ is 12.

commutative property of addition   The order in which two addends are added does not affect the sum.
$5 + 7 = 7 + 5$

commutative property of multiplication   The order in which two factors are multiplied does not affect the product.
$8 \times 3 = 3 \times 8$

composite number   A whole number greater than 1 with more than two different factors.

cone   A solid figure with one circular face and one vertex.

congruent figures Figures with the same size and shape.

cube A rectangular prism with six faces that are all congruent squares.

cylinder A solid figure with two circular bases that are congruent.

decimal A number with place values based on ten. The following are decimals: 5.8   16.07.

degree (°) A unit used to measure angles.

degree Celsius (°C) A unit in the metric system used to measure temperature.

degree Fahrenheit (°F) A unit in the customary system used to measure temperature.

denominator The bottom number in a fraction.

diagonal A line segment that joins two corners of a figure and is not a side or an edge.

diameter A line segment that passes through the center of a circle and joins two points on the circle.

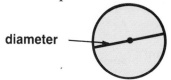

diameter

difference The answer to a subtraction problem.

digit Any of the symbols 0, 1, 2, 3, 4, 5, 6, 7, 8, and 9.

disk A device for storing computer information.

distributive property A property that shows a relationship between addition and multiplication.
$$2 \times (3 + 4) = (2 \times 3) + (2 \times 4)$$

dividend A number that is divided. In $16 \div 2$ or $2\overline{)16}$, the dividend is 16.

divisor A number that divides the dividend. In $16 \div 2$ or $2\overline{)16}$, the divisor is 2.

edge A line segment formed when two faces meet in a solid figure.

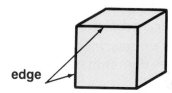

edge

END A BASIC command that tells the computer when the program is finished.

endpoint The point at the end of a segment or a ray.

equation A number sentence that uses an equal sign.

equilateral triangle A triangle with all sides the same length.

equivalent fractions Fractions that name the same number or amount. $\frac{1}{2}$ and $\frac{2}{4}$ are equivalent fractions.

estimate   To find an answer that is close to the actual answer.

even number   A whole number that is a multiple of 2.

expanded form   A way to write numbers that shows the value of each digit.

$$325 = 300 + 20 + 5$$

face   A flat surface of a solid figure.

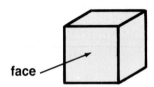

factor   A number that is to be multiplied.

flowchart   A diagram that shows the flow of steps in a process.

fraction   A number that names part of a whole or a group, written with a numerator and a denominator.

$$\frac{3}{4} \begin{array}{l}\leftarrow \text{numerator}\\ \leftarrow \text{denominator}\end{array}$$

graph   A picture used to show information. Examples are bar graph, line graph, circle graph, and pictograph.

graphics   Pictures drawn by a computer.

greater than (>)   A comparison of two numbers where one is larger than the other.

$7 > 5$ "7 is greater than 5"

greatest common factor (GCF)   The greatest number that is a common factor for two or more numbers.

hardware   The physical parts of the computer such as the keyboard, monitor, and cover.

hexagon   A polygon having six sides.

input   Information fed into a computer.

intersecting lines   Lines that cross or meet at one point.

keyboard   A device used for typing information into a computer.

least common multiple (LCM)   The least number (other than zero) that is a common multiple of two or more numbers.

less than (<)   A comparison of two numbers where one is less than the other.

$6 < 7$ "6 is less than 7"

LET   A BASIC command used to give a numerical value to a letter.

line   A line has no endpoints and goes on forever in both directions.

line of symmetry   A line on which a figure is folded so that one part matches exactly on the other part.

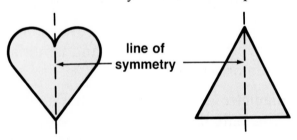

line segment   Part of a line that joins two points.

line segment

mixed number   A number that names a whole number and a fraction.

monitor   A computer screen.

multiple   A number that is the product of a given number and a whole number.

number sentence   An inequality or an equation.

17 > 12   4 + 3 = 7

numerator   The top number in a fraction.

octagon   A polygon having eight sides.

odd number   A whole number that is not divisible by 2. An odd number has 1, 3, 5, 7, or 9 in the ones place.

ordered pair   A pair of numbers that are used to name points on a plane.

ordinal number   A number used to tell order or position, such as *first*, *second*, and *third*.

output   Information processed by a computer.

parallel lines   Two or more lines in the same plane, that are the same distance apart and do not intersect.

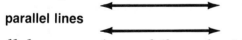

parallel lines

parallelogram   A quadrilateral with opposite sides that are parallel.

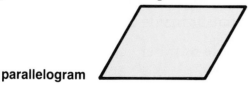

parallelogram

pentagon   A polygon having five sides.

percent (%)   The ratio of a number to 100.

$$\frac{17}{100} = 0.17 = 17\%$$

perimeter   The distance around a figure.

perpendicular lines   Two lines that intersect to form right angles.

pi   A ratio of the circumference of a circle to its diameter. Pi is approximately equal to 3.14.

place value   The value of the place of a digit in a number.

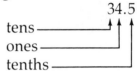

polygon   A closed figure formed by three or more line segments.

prime factor   A prime number that is a factor of a whole number.

prime number   A whole number greater than 1 that has only itself and 1 as factors.

PRINT   A BASIC command that tells the computer to print specific output.

prism   A solid figure with two parallel faces that are polygons.

probability   The chance that a given event will occur.

product   The answer to a multiplication problem.

program   A list of instructions that tells a computer what to do.

pyramid   A solid figure shaped like this:

 or

quadrilateral   A polygon having four sides.

quotient   The answer to a division problem.

radius   A line segment from the center of a circle to a point on it.

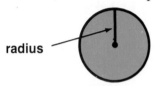

radius

ratio   A comparison of two numbers that can be expressed several ways.

4 to 5   4 : 5 $\frac{4}{5}$

ray   Part of a line with one endpoint which goes on endlessly in one direction.

ray

reciprocals   Two numbers whose product is 1: $\frac{2}{3}$ and $\frac{3}{2}$ are reciprocals, since $\frac{2}{3} \times \frac{3}{2} = \frac{6}{6} = 1$.

rectangle   A quadrilateral with four right angles.

remainder   The number that is left over after a division is completed.

right angle   An angle with a measure of 90°.

RUN   A BASIC command that tells the computer to execute a program.

similar figures   Figures with the same shape that are not necessarily the same size.

simplest terms   A fraction is in simplest terms if 1 is the only number that will divide both the numerator and the denominator.

software   Information that a computer receives and uses. A computer program is software.

sphere   A solid figure with all points the same distance from a center point.

square   A rectangle with four congruent sides.

standard form   The usual or common way to write a number.

sum   The answer to an addition problem.

triangle   A three-sided polygon.

vertex   The point where two rays meet to form an angle.

vertex

volume   The number of cubic units that fit inside a solid figure.

whole number   Any of the numbers 0, 1, 2, 3, 4, 5, and so on.

Art Credits

Tom Leonard: 34, 140-142, 147, 150-151, 158-160, 163, 279, 374-375, 377, 379, 381, 385, 392-394.
Frank Fretz: 154-157, 388-391.
Betsy Day: 172, 240, 252, 300, 304, 347, 404-405.
Dick Sanderson: 98, 216, 344, 382, 383, 384.

Photo Credits

The following abbreviations indicate the position of the photographs on the page: *t*, top; *b*, bottom; *l*, left; *r*, right; *c*, center.

Glyn Cloyd: 8, 18, 19, 126, 130, 226, 230, 238, 250, 256, 299(b), 321, 341, 403, 435, 437(b).
Ken Karp/OPC: 46, 146, 168, 175, 281, 310, 312, 322, 360, 378, 402, 436(t).
Ken Lax: 5, 6, 27, 30, 36, 41, 50, 68, 200, 204, 208, 219, 224, 225, 227, 228, 234, 258, 285, 334, 349.
John Lei/OPC: 20, 21, 44, 406, 407, 429.

2(tl), Ormond Gigli/The Image Bank; 2(br), Group III/Bruce Coleman; 2(tr), Timothy Eagen/Woodfin Camp and Associates; 2(bl), Arthur d'Arazien/The Image Bank; 4, Victoria Beller-Smith; 14, Peter Kaplan/Bruce Coleman; 16, Joe McDonald/Bruce Coleman; 24, Art Resource; 28, Terry McKoy/Taurus Photos; 38, Bill and Jan Moeller/The Image Bank; 42, Jonathan Wright/Bruce Coleman; 48, Gilda Schift/Photo Researchers; 53(t), Erich Hartmann/Magnum Photos; 53(b), David Madison/Bruce Coleman; 56, Horst Shrager/Amwest; 79, Selectman's Meeting Room, Abbot Hall, Marblehead, Massachusetts; 79(inset), The Granger Collection; 82, Katrina Thomas; Photo Researchers; 96, Victoria Beller-Smith; 100, Peter Vadnai/Art Resource; 104, Cara Moore/The Image Bank; 107, Focus on Sports; 112, Everett C. Johnson/Leo de Wys; 124, Jessica Ehlers/Bruce Coleman; 135, McLaughlin Stock Photos; 138, Cary Wolinsky/Stock, Boston; 152, Philip J. Griffith/Magnum Photos; 163, Harvey Lloyd/Peter Arnold; 166, Focus on Sports; 178, Stuart Craig/Bruce Coleman; 182, D.P. Hershkowitz/Bruce Coleman; 183, Kent and Donna Dansen/Photo Researchers; 189(t), Sam Zaslavsky; 189(b), Jacques Jangoux/Peter Arnold; 192, Michael P. Gadomski/Animals, Animals; 206, Rene Burri/Magnum Photos; 217(t), Michael Holford; 217(b), Ann Ronan Pictures; 233, L.L.T. Rhodes/Taurus Photos; 236, Gary Gray/The Image Bank; 245, Apple Computer/PAR; 248, James H. Karales/Peter Arnold; 262, E.R. Degginger/Bruce Coleman; 273, NASA; 276, Clyde H. Smith/Peter Arnold; 280, Schneider/The Stock Market; 288, Victoria Beller-Smith; 299(tl), Murray Alcosser/The Image Bank; 299(tr), S. Raye/FPG; 302, Catherine Ursillo/Photo Researchers; 316, Tom Bledsoe/Photo Researchers; 326(l), Ron Stern/Illustrators Stock Photos; 326(r), Chase Manhattan Bank; 332, Hans Reinhard/Bruce Coleman; 355, Computer Vision/PAR; 356, Van Bucher/Photo Researchers; 358, Joe McNally/Wheeler Pictures; 372, Nicolas DeVore III/Bruce Coleman; 386, Terry McKoy/Taurus Photos; 398, Jeff Foott/Bruce Coleman; 398(inset), Dale and Marion Zimmerman/Bruce Coleman; 408(t), San Francisco Museum of Art; 409(b), Metropolitan Museum of Art, NY; 412, George Holton/Photo Researchers; 426, Ann Hagen Griffith/OPC; 432(l), Cliff Feulner/The Image Bank; 432, Steve McCutcheon.